An Introduction to
Criminal Law

An Introduction to

Criminal Law

Gary Scanlan &
Christopher Ryan

First published in Great Britain 1985 by Financial Training Publications Limited, Avenue House, 131 Holland Park Avenue, London W11 4UT

©Gary P. Scanlan and Christopher L. Ryan, 1985

ISBN: 0 906322 81 2

Typeset by Kerrypress Limited, Luton
Printed by Livesey Limited, Shrewsbury

All rights reserved. No part of this book may be reproduced or transmitted in any form or by any means, electronic or mechanical, including photocopying, recording, or any information storage or retrieval system without prior permission from the publisher.

Contents

Preface	vii
Table of Cases	viii
Table of Statutes	xx
Introduction	1

1 Scenario   11

1.1 Introduction: *actus reus* — 1.2 The external elements of an offence: positive acts — 1.3 Omissions — 1.4 States of affairs as an element in the *actus reus* of an offence — 1.5 Circumstances as an element in the *actus reus* of an offence — 1.6 Absence of an element in the *actus reus* of an offence — 1.7 Consequences as an element in the *actus reus* of an offence — 1.8 The *actus reus* must be caused by the conduct or omission of an individual — 1.9 The issue of causation — 1.10 Summary — 1.11 Questions

2 Mens Rea   33

2.1 Introduction — 2.2 Evil or wicked mind — 2.3 States of mind — 2.4 Negligence — 2.5 Basic and specific intention — 2.6 Intention — 2.7 Recklessness — 2.8 *Mens rea* as to circumstances — 2.9 Coincidence of *actus reus* and *mens rea* — 2.10 Transferred malice — 2.11 Burden of proof — 2.12 Standard or level of proof — 2.13 Proof of *actus reus* — 2.14 Proof of *mens rea* — 2.15 Summary in light of the scenario — 2.16 Questions

3 Strict Liability Offences   71

Scenario — 3.1 The nature of strict liability offences — 3.2 Strict liability offences at common law — 3.3 Strict liability in statutory offences — 3.4 Factors utilised by the courts in determining offences as crimes of strict liability — 3.5 Grave social danger — 3.6 Presumption against the imposition of strict liability — 3.7 Will the imposition of strict liability enhance or assist the enforcement of an offence? — 3.8 The mitigation of strict liability offences — 3.9 The mitigation of statutory strict liability offences: possible common law solutions — 3.10 The justification for the imposition of strict liability — 3.11 Questions

4 Participation in Criminal Offences 97

Scenario — 4.1 Principal participation — 4.2 The principal offender and the innocent agent — 4.3 Secondary participation — 4.4 Presence at the scene of the crime and the inactivity of a secondary party — 4.5 The *mens rea* of a secondary party — 4.6 The need for the commission of an *actus reus* by the principal offender — 4.7 Conviction of secondary party of an offence different from that of the principal offender — 4.8 Liability of principal or secondary party for unforeseen consequences — 4.9 Repentance — 4.10 Victims of crimes as secondary parties — 4.11 Assisting offenders — 4.12 Secondary participation and inchoate offences — 4.13 Summary — 4.14 Participants in a felony — 4.15 Corporate liability — 4.16 Vicarious liability — 4.17 Questions

5 Inchoate Offences 125

5.1 Introduction — 5.2 Liability for *mens rea* alone — 5.3 The scenario — 5.4 Inchoate offences — 5.5 Acts of preparation — 5.6 Attempts — 5.7 Conspiracy — 5.8 Incitement — 5.9 Inchoate inchoate offences — 5.10 Inchoate offences and participation — 5.11 Penalty for inchoate offences

6 Defences 159

6.1 Insanity, insane automatism — 6.2 Non-insane automatism and involuntary conduct — 6.3 Alcohol and drugs — 6.4 Minors — 6.5 Mistake — 6.6 The lawful application of force — 6.7 Defences based upon public policy — 6.8 Coercion — 6.9 Superior orders — 6.10 Necessity — 6.11 The scenario — 6.12 Questions

7 Offences Against the Person 170

7.1 Introduction — 7.2 Non-sexual, non-fatal offences — 7.3 Statutory assaults categorised — 7.4 Sexual/indecent assaults — 7.5 Rape: *actus reus* — 7.6 Homicide

8 Offences Against Property 231

8.1 Introduction — 8.2 Wild foliage — 8.3 Wild animals — 8.4 Property that may be stolen — 8.5 Special forms of proprietary right — 8.6 Theft Act 1968, s. 5(4) — 8.7 Subsequent application of s. 5(1) in special cases of fraud — 8.8 The conduct element in the *actus reus* of theft — 8.9 *Mens rea* — 8.10 Intention permanently to deprive — 8.11 Conditional intent — 8.12 Burglary — 8.13 Dishonesty offences other than theft — 8.14 Handling

Appendix 275

Index 281

Preface

Law is constantly changing despite man's desire for certainty and predictability. The criminal law is no exception. This book seeks to tell the reader the rules and principles of the criminal law as they existed at June 1985. That is the main aim but in doing so it is hoped that the reader will learn something more, in particular that rules change either by way of legislative enactments or because the judges and the courts interpret, adapt or develop them to provide for what they perceive to be the best interests of society. Sometimes this means giving preponderance to the freedoms, liberties, rights and interests of individuals but more often it involves imposing restrictions on the freedom and liberties of every member of society. Sometimes the judiciary acts as a check on the legislature and those branches of the administration (such as the police) which enforce the legal rules but on other occasions the judges are seen to be expansionist to the extent of making the rules of criminal law impinge on our accepted freedoms and in unwarrantedly subjecting individuals to the threat of serious criminal liability and the punishment and stigma that accompany it. Parliamentarians' and judicial perceptions of what is best for society are influenced by a number of political, economic and social factors which are beyond the scope of this book but hopefully the reader will be made more aware of the complexity of the legal system, the changeable nature of the legal rules and the significant role of the judges in creating and maintaining the sort of society in which we live. Whether or not our law is in touch with the social realities of the 20th century is for the reader to decide but hopefully this book points to some of the dangers and limitations of the legal system and the judicial process as evidenced by the current rules and underlying principles of the criminal law.

We are indebted to Alistair MacQueen and Heather Saward of Financial Training Publications Ltd, for encouragement and guidance and to Derek French for copy-editing, needless to say they are not responsible for any of our errors, imperfections or opinions.

Special thanks to Kim Scanlan without whose understanding this book would not have been completed to schedule. Above all we are immensely grateful to our exceptional secretary Marian Hoffmann for her enthusiastic interest, her unstinting patience and her speedy and very efficient typing.

Christopher L. Ryan
Gary P. Scanlan
Faculty of Law
The University of Liverpool

Table of Cases

Abbott v *R* [1977] AC 755, [1976] 3 All ER 140, [1976] 3 WLR 462, 140 JP 567, 120 SJ 538   184
Albert v *Lavin* [1982] AC 546, [1981] 3 All ER 878, [1981] 3 WLR 955, 145 JP 184, 125 SJ 114, 74 Cr App R 150   20, 182
Albert v *Lavin* [1981] 1 All ER 62 8   23, 176, 177
Allen v *Whitehead* [1930] 1 KB 211, [1929] All ER Rep 13, 99 LJ KB 146, 142 LT 141, 94 JP 17, 45 TLR 655, 29 Cox CC 8   122
Allen v *Metropolitan Police Commissioner* [1980] Crim LR 441   179
Alphacell Ltd v *Woodward* [1972] AC 824, [1972] 2 All ER 475, [1972] 2 WLR 1320, 70 LGR 455, 116 SJ 431, [1971] Crim LR 41   81, 82, 83
Anderton v *Burnside*; see *Morris* v *Anderton*
Anderton v *Ryan* [1985] 2 All ER 355, [1985] 2 WLR 969 (HL), [1985] 2 WLR 23   146, 147, 271
Andrews v *Director of Public Prosecutions* [1937] AC 576, [1937] 2 All ER 552, 106 LJ KB 370, 156 LT 464, 101 JP 386, 53 TLR 663, 81 SJ 497, 26 Cr App R 34, 30 Cox CC 576   38, 58
Attorney General's Reference (No. 1 of 1974) [1974] QB 744, [1974] 2 All ER 899, 59 Cr App R 203, [1974] 2 WLR 891, 118 SJ 345, [1974] Crim LR 427   272
Attorney General's Reference (No. 1 of 1975) [1975] QB 733, [1975] 2 All ER 684, [1975] 3 WLR 11, 139 JP 569, 119 SJ 373, 61 Cr App R 118, [1975] Crim LR 449   102, 103–4, 117
Attorney General's Reference (Nos. 1 and 2 of 1979) [1980] QB 180, [1979] 3 All ER 143, [1979] 3 WLR 577, 143 JP 708, 123 SJ 472, 69 Cr App R 266, [1979] Crim LR 585   251, 255
Attorney General's Reference (No. 6 of 1980) [1981] QB 715, [1981] 2 All ER 1057, [1981] 3 WLR 125, 145 JP 429, 125 SJ 426, 73 Cr App R 63   197
Attorney General's Reference (No. 1 of 1983) [1984] 3 All ER 369, [1984] 3 WLR 686, [1985] QB 182   243
Attorney General's Reference (No. 2 of 1983) [1984] AC 456, [1984] 1 All ER 988, [1984] 2 WLR 465, 128 SJ 203, 78 Cr App R 131   180
Attorney General for Northern Ireland v *Gallagher* [1963] AC 349, [1961] 3 All ER 299, [1961] 3 WLR 619, 105 SJ 646, 45 Cr App R 316   169, 172
Attorney General for Northern Ireland's Reference (No. 1 of 1975) [1977] AC 105   180, 181
Atwal v *Massey* [1971] 3 All ER 881, 56, Cr App R 6   273
B v *R* (1958) 44 Cr App R 1, 123 JP 61   173
B & S v *Leathley* [1979] Crim LR 314   253
Bedder v *Director of Public Prosecutions* [1954] 2 All ER 801, [1954] 1 WLR 1119, 98 SJ 556, 38 Cr App R 133   223
Betts v *Stevens* [1910] 1 KB 1, 79 LJ KB 17, 101 LT 564, 73 JP 486, 26 TLR 5, 22 Cox CC 187   77
Blayney v *Knight* [1975] RTR 279, 60 Cr App 269, [1975] Crim LR 237   14
Bloom v *Crowther The Times*, 15 May 1984   268
Bolton (H.L.) (Engineering) Co. Ltd v *T.J. Graham & Sons Ltd* [1957] 1 QB 159, [1956] 3 All ER 624, [1956] 3 WLR 804, 100 SJ 816   119
Bratty v *Attorney-General for Northern Ireland* [1963] AC 386, [1961] 3 All ER 523, [1961] 3 WLR 965, 105 SJ 865, 46 Cr App R 1   65, 162, 163, 164, 165

Table of Cases

Bravery v Bravery [1954] 3 All ER 59, [1954] 1 WLR 1169, 98 SJ 573   196, 197
Brend v Wood (1946) 175 LT 306, 110 JP 317, 62 TLR 462, 90 SJ 381   88
Buckoke v Greater London Council [1971] 1 Ch 655, [1971] 2 All ER 254, [1971] 2 WLR 760, 135 JP 321, 115 SJ 174, [1971] RTR 131   186
C (a minor) v Eisenhower (1984) 78 Cr App R 48, [1984] QB 331   203
Callow v Tillstone (1900) 83 LT 411, 64 JP 823, 19 Cox CC 576   110
Campbell & Cosans v United Kingdom (1982) 4 EHRR 293   199
Carter v Richardson [1974] RTR 314   108
Cassady v Reg Morris (Transport) Ltd [1975] RTR 470, [1975] Crim LR 398   106
Chandler v Director of Public Prosecutions [1964] AC 763, [1962] 3 All ER 142, [1962] 3 WLR 694, 106 SJ 588, 46 Cr App R 347   41
Chan Wing-Siu v The Queen [1985] AC 168, [1984] 3 WLR 677   48, 114
Churchill v Walton [1967] 2 AC 224, [1967] 2 WLR 682, 131 JP 277, 111 SJ 112, [1967] 1 All ER 497, 51 Cr App R 212   151
Cleary v Booth [1893] 1 QB 465, 62 LJ MC 87, 68 LT 349, 57 JP 375, 41 WR 391, 9 TLR 260, 37 SJ 270, 17 Cox CC 611   198
Comer v Bloomfield (1970) 55 Cr App R 305, [1971] RTR 49, [1971] Crim LR 230   135, 136
Commissioner of Police of the Metropolis v Wilson; R v Jenkins [1984] AC 242 [1983] 3 WLR 686, [1983] 3 All ER 448, 77 Cr App R 319   205
Coppen v Moore (No. 2) [1898] 2 QB 306, [1895–9] All ER Rep 926, 67 LJ QB 689, 78 LT 520, 62 JP 453, 46 WR 620, 14 TLR 414, 42 SJ 539, 19 Cox CC 45   121, 123
Coward v Baddeley (1859) 28 LJ EX 260   206
Cundy v Le Cocq (1884) 13 QBD 207, [1881–5] All ER Rep 412, 53 LJ MC 125, 51 LT 265, 48 JP 599, 32 WR 769   76
Cundy v Lindsay (1878) 3 App Cas 459, [1874–80] All ER Rep 1149, 38 LT 573, 42 JP 483, 26 WR 406, 14 Cox CC 93   249
Davey v Lee [1968] 1 QB 366, [1967] 3 WLR 105, 131 JP 327, 111 SJ 212, [1967] 2 All ER 423, 51 Cr App R 303   136
Davidge v Bunnett [1984] Crim LR 297   241
Davies v Director of Public Prosecutions [1954] AC 378, [1954] 1 All ER 507, [1954] 2 WLR 343, 118 JP 222, 98 SJ 161, 38 Cr App R 11   114
Davies v Harvey (1874) LR 9 QB 433, 43 LJ MC 121, 30 LT 629, 38 JP 661, 22 WR 733   78
Director of Public Prosecutions v Camplin [1978] AC 705, [1978] 2 WLR 679, 122 SJ 280, 67 Cr App R 14, [1978] Crim LR 432, [1978] 2 All ER 168   224
Director of Public Prosecutions v Majewski [1977] AC 443, [1976] 2 All ER 142, [1976] 2 WLR 623, 140 JP 315, 120 SJ 299, [1976] Crim LR 374, 62 Cr App R 262   39, 166–7, 168, 170, 171, 172, 181
Director of Public Prosecutions v Merriman [1973] AC 584, [1972] 3 All ER 42, [1972] 3 WLR 545, 135 JP 659, 116 SJ 745, 56 Cr App R 116, [1977] Crim LR 784   113
Director of Public Prosecutions v Morgan [1976] AC 182, [1975] 2 All ER 347, [1975] 2 WLR 913, 139 JP 476, 61 Cr App R 136, 119 SJ 319, [1975] Crim LR 717   39, 57, 111, 171, 174, 175, 176, 177, 192, 211, 213
Director of Public Prosecutions v Newbury [1977] AC 500, [1976] 2 All ER 365, [1976] 2 WLR 918, 140 JP 370, 120 SJ 402, 62 Cr App R 291   228–9
Director of Public Prosecutions v Nock [1978] AC 979, [1978] 2 All ER 654, [1978] 3 WLR 57, 142 JP 414, 122 SJ 417, 67 Cr App R 116   144, 146, 155, 156
Director of Public Prosecutions v Ray [1974] AC 370, [1973] 3 All ER 131, [1973] 3 WLR 359, 136 JP 744, 117 SJ 633, 58 Cr App R 130   258, 259, 260
Director of Public Prosecutions v Rogers [1953] 2 All ER 644, [1953] 1 WLR 1017, 117 JP 424, 97 SJ 541, 37 Cr App R 137   205, 206
Director of Public Prosecutions v Smith [1961] AC 290, [1960] 3 All ER 161, [1960] 3 WLR 546, 124 JP 473, 104 SJ 683, 44 Cr App R 261   42, 67, 203, 218, 219–20, 222
Director of Public Prosecutions v Stonehouse [1978] AC 55, [1977] 2 All ER 909, [1977] 3 WLR 143, 141 JP 473, 121 SJ 491, [1977] Crim LR 544, 65 Cr App R 192   135, 136

Director of Public Prosecutions for Northern Ireland v *Lynch* [1975] AC 653,
[1975] 1 All ER 913, 139 JP 312, [1975] 2 WLR 641, 119 SJ 233, 61 Cr App
R 6, [1975] Crim LR 707   34, 101, 102, 106, 107, 112, 183, 184, 185
Director of Public Prosecutions for Northern Ireland v *Maxwell* [1978] 3 All
ER 1140, [1978] 1 WLR 1350, 143 JP 63, 122 SJ 758, 68 Cr App R 128,
[1978] Crim LR 40   109
Du Cros v *Lambourne* [1907] 1 KB 40, 76 LJ KB 50, 95 LT 782, 70 JP 525,
23 TLR 3, 21 Cox CC 311   106
Eddy v *Niman* (1981) 73 Cr App R 237, [1981] Crim LR 502   246
Edwards v *R* [1973] AC 648, [1973] 1 All ER 152, [1972] 3 WLR 893, 137
JP 119   224
Elliott v *C (a minor)* [1983] 2 All ER 1005, [1983] 1 WLR 939, 147 JP 425,
127 SJ 442, 77 Cr App R 103, [1983] Crim LR 676   56, 57, 58, 59, 212
Fagan v *Metropolitan Police Commissioner* [1969] 1 QB 439, [1968] 3 All ER
442, [1968] 3 WLR 1120, 133 JP 16, 112 SJ 800, 52 Cr App R 700   60, 61, 192, 194, 195
Fairclough v *Whipp* [1951] 2 All ER 834, 115 JP 612, [1951] 2 TLR 909,
95 SJ 699, 35 Cr App R 138   206
Farrell v *Secretary of State for Defence* [1980] 1 All ER 166, [1980] 1 WLR 172,
124 SJ 133, 70 Cr App R 224   179
Ferguson v *Weaving* [1951] 1 KB 814, [1951] 1 All ER 412, 115 JP 142, [1951]
1 TLR 465, 95 SJ 90   123
Gammon (Hong Kong) Ltd v *Attorney-General for Hong Kong* [1984] 2 All ER
503, [1985] AC 1   87, 89, 90
Gardner v *Akeroyd* [1952] 2 QB 743, [1952] 2 All ER 306, 116 JP 460, [1952]
2 TLR 169, 96 SJ 483   123, 142
Garrett v *Arthur Churchill (Glass) Ltd* [1970] 1 QB 92, [1969] 2 All ER 1141,
[1969] 3 WLR 6, 133 JP 509, 113 SJ 381   102
Green v *Burnett* [1955] 1 QB 78, [1954] 3 All ER 273, [1954] 3 WLR 631,
118 JP 536, 98 SJ 771   77
Handyside's case (1746) 2 East PC 652   232
Harding v *Price* [1948] 1 KB 695, [1948] 1 All ER 283, [1948] LJR 1624,
112 JP 189, 64 TLR 111, 92 SJ 112   90–1, 93
Hargreaves v *Diddams* LR 10 QB 582   82
Haughton v *Smith* [1975] AC 476, [1973] 3 All ER 1109, [1974] 3 WLR 1, 138
JP 31, 58 Cr App R 198   137, 143, 144, 145, 156
Herrington v *British Railways Board* [1972] AC 877, [1972] 1 All ER 749,
[1972] 2 WLR 537, 116 SJ 178   51
Hibbert v *McKiernan* [1948] 2 KB 142, [1948] 1 All ER 860, [1948] LJR 1521,
112 JP 284, 64 TLR 256, 92 SJ 259   238
Hill v *Baxter* [1958] 1 QB 277, [1958] 1 All ER 193, [1958] 2 WLR 76, 122 JP
134, 102 SJ 53, 42 Cr App R 51   164
Hills v *Ellis* [1983] QB 685, [1983] 1 All ER 667, [1983] Crim LR 182, 126 SJ 169   77
Howker v *Robinson* [1973] QB 178, [1972] 2 All ER 786, [1972] 3 WLR 234,
136 JP 562, 116 SJ 354   122–3
Hyam v *Director of Public Prosecutions* [1975] AC 55, [1974] 2 All ER 41,
[1974] 2 WLR 607, 138 JP 374, 59 Cr App R 91, 118 SJ 311, [1979] Crim
LR 365   39, 42, 43, 44, 45, 46, 47, 48, 50, 51, 62, 106, 138, 140, 171, 218, 219, 220–1
Jaggard v *Dickinson* [1981] QB 527, [1980] 3 All ER 716, [1981] 2 WLR 118,
124 SJ 847, 72 Cr App R 33, [1980] Crim LR 717   168
James & Son Ltd v *Smee* [1955] 1 QB 78, [1954] 3 All ER 273, [1954] 3 WLR
631, 118 JP 536, 98 SJ 771   77
J.B.H. and J.H. (minors) v *O'Connell* [1981] Crim LR 632   173
Johnson v *Phillips* [1975] 3 All ER 682, [1976] 1 WLR 65, 140 JP 37, 119 SJ
645, [1976] RTR 170, [1975] Crim LR 580   186
Jones v *Brooks* (1968) 52 Cr App R 614, [1968] Crim LR 498, 112 SJ 745   136
Kaitamaki v *R* [1985] AC 147   208, 209, 211
Kamara v *Director of Public Prosecutions* [1974] AC 104, [1973] 2 All ER 1242,
[1973] 3 WLR 198, 137 JP 714, 117 SJ 581, 57 Cr App R 880, [1974] Crim LR 39   149
Keighley v *Bell* (1866) F & F 763   186

Table of Cases xi

King's Norton Metal Co. Ltd v *Edridge Merrett & Co. Ltd* (1897) 14 TLR 98   242
Knuller (Publishing Printing and Promotions) Ltd v *Director of Public Prosecutions*
  [1973] AC 435, [1972] 2 All ER 898, [1972] 3 WLR 143, 136 JP 728, 116 SJ
  545, 56 Cr App R 633   12, 150–1
Lawrence v *Metropolitan Police Commissioner* [1972] AC 626, [1971] 2 All
  ER 1253, [1971] 2 WLR 225, 135 JP 481, 115 SJ 565   246, 262–3, 264
Lee v *Simpson* (1847) 3 CB 871   82
Lennard's Carrying Co. Ltd v *Asiatic Petroleum Co. Ltd* [1915] AC 705   119
Leung Kam-Kwok v *The Queen* (unreported) 19 December 1984, PC   47
Lewis v *Cox* [1984] 3 WLR 875, 128 SJ 596, 148 JP 601, [1984] 3 All ER
  672, [1984] Crim LR 756   77
Lewis v *Dickson* [1976] RTR 431, [1976] Crim LR 442   186
Lim Chin Aik v *R* [1963] AC 160, [1963] 1 All ER 223, [1963] 2WLR 42,
  106 SJ 1028   90, 91
Linnett v *Metropolitan Police Commissioner* [1946] KB 290, [1946] 1 All
  ER 380, 115 LJ KB 513, 174 LT 178, 110 JP 153, 62 TLR 203, 90 SJ 211   123
Lockyer v *Gibb* [1967] 2 QB 243, [1966] 2 All ER 653, [1966] 3 WLR 84,
  130 JP 306, 110 SJ 507, [1966] Crim LR 504   85
Re London and Globe Finance Corporation Ltd [1903] 1 Ch 728, [1900–03]
  All ER Rep 891, 72 LJ Ch 368, 88 LT 194, 51 WR 651, 19 TLR 314   258, 260
Lowe v *Blease* (1975) 119 SJ 695, [1975] Crim LR 513   232
Martin v *State of Alabama* (1944) 31 Ala App 334, 17 So 2d 427   20
Mawji v *R* [1957] AC 526, [1957] 1 All ER 385, [1957] 2 WLR 277 101
  SJ 146, 41 Cr App R 69   153
McC v *Runeckles* [1984] Crim LR 499   172
M'Naghten's case (1843) 10 Cl & F 200, [1843–60] All ER Rep 229,
  4 St Tr NS 847, 1 Town St Tr 314, 1 Car & Kir 130, 8 Scott NR 595   65, 159, 160
Mead's & Belt's case (1823) 1 Lew CC 184   194
Metropolitan Police Commissioner v *Caldwell* [1982] AC 341, [1981] 1 All
  ER 961, [1981] 2 WLR 509, 145 JP 211, 125 SJ 239,
  73 Cr App R 13   39, 51, 52, 53, 57, 192, 212
Metropolitan Police Commissioner v *Charles* [1977] AC 177, [1976] 3 All
  ER 112, [1976] 2 WLR 431, 140 JP 531, 120 SJ 588, 68 Cr App R 334,
  [1977] Crim LR 615   259, 260, 261, 264
Miller v *Minister of Pensions* [1947] 2 All ER 372, [1948] LJR 203, 177
  LT 536, 63 TLR 474, 91 SJ 484   66
Morden v *Porter* (1860) 7 CB (NS) 641   82
Morris v *Anderton* [1984] AC 320, [1983] 3 All ER 288, [1983] 2 WLR
  697, 127 SJ 713, [1983] Crim LR 813   245, 246, 263
Morris v *Tolman* [1923] 1 KB 166, [1922] All ER Rep 182, 92 LJ KB 215,
  128 LT 118, 86 JP 221, 39 TLR 39, 67 SJ 169, 27 Cox CC 345   110–11
Moses v *Winder* [1981] RTR 37, [1980] Crim LR 232   165
Moynes v *Cooper* [1956] 1 QB 439, [1956] 1 All ER 450, [1956] 2 WLR
  562, 120 JP 147, 100 SJ 171, 40 Cr App R 20   243, 264
Mulcahy v *R* (1868) LR 3 HL 306   149
National Coal Board v *Gamble* [1959] 1 QB 11, [1958] 3 All ER 203, [1958]
  3 WLR 434, 122 JP 453, 102 SJ 621, 42 Cr App R 240   101, 102, 107
Oldcastle's case (1419) 1 Hale PC 50, 1 East PC 70   184
Oxford v *Moss* [1976] Crim LR 119   232
Palmer v *R* [1971] AC 814, [1971] 1 All ER 1077, [1971] 2 WLR 831, 115
  SJ 264, 55 Cr App R 223   179–80, 181
Papadimitropoulos v *R* (1957) 98 CLR 249   210
Partington v *Williams* (1975) 62 Cr App R 220, 120 SJ 80   143
Pender v *Smith* [1959] 2 QB 84, [1959] 2 WLR 794, 123 JP 351, 103 SJ 433,
  [1959] 2 All ER 360   147
Pharmaceutical Society of Great Britain v *Logan* [1982] Crim LR 443   80
Pharmaceutical Society of Great Britain, v *Storkwain The Times,* 9 May 1985   80
Powell v *MacRae* [1977] Crim LR 571   237
Proudman v *Dayman* (1941) 67 CLR 536   93

R v *Anderson* [1984] Crim LR 550, 128 SJ 660   148
R v *Anderson & Morris* [1966] 2 QB 110, [1966] 2 All ER 644, [1966] 2 WLR 1195, 130 JP 318, 110 SJ 369, 50 Cr App R 216   114
R v *Andrews Weatherfoil Ltd* [1972] 1 All ER 65, [1972] 1 WLR 118, 115 SJ 888, 56 Cr App R 31   119
R v *Atkinson* (1869) 1 Cox CC 330   20
R v *(Lord) Audley* (1631) Hut 115, 1 Hale PC 629, 3 St Tr 402   214
R v *Ayres* [1984] AC 447, [1984] 2 WLR 257, [1984] 1 All ER 619, 128 SJ 151, 78 Cr App R 232, [1984] Crim LR 353   149, 150
R v *B* [1984] Crim LR 352   154
R v *Bailey* [1983] 2 All ER 503, [1983] 1 WLR 760, 147 JP 558, 127 SJ 425, [1983] Crim LR 533   160, 164, 165, 166, 169, 170
R v *Bainbridge* [1960] 1 QB 129, [1959] 3 All ER 200, [1959] 2 WLR 656, 123 JP 499, 43 Cr App R 194   108
R v *Ball* [1983] 1 WLR 801, 127 SJ 442, [1983] 2 All ER 1089, 77 Cr App R 131, [1983] Crim LR 546   274
R v *Banks* (1873) 12 Cox CC 393   157
R v *Barnard* (1837) 7 C & P 784   258
R v *Barrett* (1980) 72 Cr App R 212, [1980] Crim LR 641, 124 SJ 543   175
R v *Bashir & Manzur* [1969] 3 All ER 692, [1969] 1 WLR 1303, 133 JP 687, 113 SJ 703, 54 Cr App R 1   215
R v *Bateman* (1925) 94 LJ KB 791, [1925] All ER Rep 45, 133 LT 730, 89 JP 162, 41 TLR 557, 69 SJ 622, 28 Cox CC 33, 19 Cr App R 8   37, 227
R v *Bayley & Easterbrook* [1980] Crim LR 503   251
R v *Becerra* (1975) 62 Cr App R 212   115
R v *Beer* (1976) 63 Cr App R 222, [1976] Crim LR 690   47, 69
R v *Belfon* [1976] 3 All ER 46, [1976] 1 WLR 741, 104 JP 523, 120 SJ 329, 63 Cr App R 59, [1976] Crim LR 449   42, 45, 47
R v *Bell* [1984] 3 All ER 842   57
R v *Betts & Ridley* (1930) 144 LT 526, 22 Cr App R 148, 29 Cox CC 259   101
R v *Billinghurst* [1978] Crim LR 553   196
R v *Bird* [1985] 1 WLR 816   179, 180
R v *Birmingham & Gloucester Railway Co.* (1842) 3 QB 233, 3 Ry & Can Cas 148, 2 Gal & Dav 236, 11 LJ MC 134, 6 Jur 804   118
R v *Blaue* [1975] 3 All ER 466, [1975] 1 WLR 1411, 119 SJ 598, 61 Cr App R 271, [1975] Crim LR 648   28
R v *Bloxham* [1983] 1 AC 109, [1982] 1 All ER 582, [1982] 2 WLR 392, 146 JP 201, 126 SJ 154, 74 Cr App R 279   268, 269, 270
R v *Bone* [1968] 2 All ER 644, [1968] 1 WLR 983, 132 JP 420, 112 SJ 480, 52 Cr App R 546   65
R v *Bonsall* [1985] Crim LR 150   149
R v *Bourne* [1939] 1 KB 687   230
R v *Bourne* (1952) 36 Cr App R 125   112, 185
R v *Breckenridge* (1984) 79 Cr App R 244, [1984] Crim LR 174   57, 213
R v *Brindley & Long* [1971] 2 QB 300, [1971] 2 All ER 698, [1971] 2 WLR 895, 135 JP 357, 115 SJ 285, 55 Cr App R 258   116
R v *Brown* (1841) Car & M 314, 4 St Tr NS App A 1369   20
R v *Brown* (1889) 24 QBD 357, 59 LJ MC 47, 61 LT 594, 54 JP 408, 38 WR 95, 15 Cox CC 715   137
R v *Brown* [1970] 1 QB 105, [1969] 3 All ER 198, [1969] 3 WLR 370, 133 JP 592, 113 SJ 639, 53 Cr App R 527   270
R v *Brown* [1972] 2 QB 229, [1972] 2 All ER 1328, [1972] 3 WLR 11, 116 SJ 431, 5 Cr App R 564, [1972] Crim LR 506   224
R v *Brown The Times*, 31 January 1985   254
R v *Bullock* [1955] 1 All ER 15, [1955] 1 WLR 1, 119 JP 65, 99 SJ 29, 38 Cr App R 151   101
R v *Burles* [1970] 2 QB 191, [1970] 1 All ER 642, [1970] 2 WLR 597, 134 JP 258, 114 SJ 86, 54 Cr App R 196   163
R v *Burns* (1984) 79 Cr App R 173   154
R v *Butt* (1884) 51 LT 607, 49 JP 233, 1 TLR 103, 15 Cox CC 564   99

Table of Cases xiii

R v *Button* [1900] 2 QB 597, 69 LJ QB 901, 83 LT 288, 64 JP 600, 48 WR
703, 16 TLR 525, 44 SJ 659, 19 Cox CC 568   135, 136
R v *Byrne* [1960] 2 QB 396   225
R v *Calderwood & Moore* [1983] 10 NIJB   184, 185
R v *Calhaem* (1985) 129 SJ 331   104
R v *Carpenter* (1983) 76 Cr App R 320   205
R v *Cash* [1985] 2 WLR 735   266
R v *Caswell* [1984] Crim LR 111   207
R v *Champ* (1981) 73 Cr App R 367, [1982] Crim LR 108   90
R v *Church* [1966] 1 QB 59, [1965] 2 All ER 72, [1965] 2 WLR 1220, 129
JP 366, 109 SJ 371, 49 Cr App R 206   228
R v *City of Sault Ste Marie* (1978) 85 DLR (3d) 161   94
R v *Clarence* (1888) 22 QBD 23, 58 LJ MC 10, 59 LT 780, 53 JP 149, 37
WR 166, 5 TLR 61, 16 Cox CC 138   195, 204
R v *Clarke* [1949] 2 All ER 448, 33 Cr App R 216   214
R v *Clarke* [1972] 1 All ER 219, 56 Cr App R 225, 116 SJ 56   160
R v *Clarke* [1985] Crim LR 209   124
R v *Clarkson* [1971] 3 All ER 344, [1971] 1 WLR 1402, 135 JP 533, 115
SJ 654, 55 Cr App R 445   101, 104, 106
R v *Codere* (1916) 12 Cr App R 21   161
R v *Cogan & Leak* [1976] QB 217, [1975] 2 All ER 1059, [1975] 3 WLR
316, 139 JP 608, 119 SJ 473, 61 Cr App R 217, [1975] Crim LR 584   100, 111, 214
R v *Collins* (1864) 9 Cox CC 497   137
R v *Collins* [1973] QB 100, [1972] 2 All ER 1105, [1972] 3 WLR 243, 136
JP 605, 116 SJ 432, 56 Cr App R 554   253, 254, 255
R v *Collis-Smith* [1971] Crim LR 716   261
R v *Coney* (1882) 8 QBD 534, 51 LJ MC 66, 46 LT 307, 46 JP 404, 30
WR 678, 15 Cox CC 46   104–5, 196, 198
R v *Cording* [1983] Crim LR 175   272
R v *Corrie* (1918) 83 JP 136   172
R v *Cousins* [1982] QB 526, [1982] 2 All ER 115, [1982] 2 WLR 621, 146
JP 264, 126 SJ 154, 74 Cr App R 363, [1982] Crim LR 444   178
R v *Creamer* [1966] 1 QB 72, [1965] 3 All ER 257, [1965] 3 WLR 583, 129
JP 586, 109 SJ 648, 49 Cr App R 368   114
R v *Cromack* [1978] Crim LR 217   157
R v *Cunningham* [1957] 2 QB 396, [1957] 2 All ER 412, [1957] 3 WLR 76,
121 JP 451, 101 SJ 503, 41 Cr App R 155   48, 49, 50, 53, 62, 202, 212, 218, 219
R v *Cunningham* [1982] AC 566, [1981] 2 All ER 863, [1981] 3 WLR 223,
125 SJ 512, 73 Cr App R 253, [1981] Crim LR 835   44
R v *Dadson* (1850) 3 Car & Kir 148, 2 Den CC 35, T & M 385, 4 New Sess
Cas 431, 20 LJ MC 57, 16 LT OS 514, 14 JP 754, 14 Jur 1051, 4 Cox
CC 358   24, 25, 176
R v *Dalby* [1982] 1 All ER 916, [1982] 1 WLR 425, 146 JP 392, 126 SJ 97, 74 Cr App R 348   229
R v *Davies* [1975] QB 691, [1975] 1 All ER 890, [1975] 2 WLR 586, 139
JP 381, 119 SJ 202, 60 Cr App R 253, [1975] Crim LR 231   224
R v *Davies* [1983] Crim LR 741   172
R v *Davis* [1977] Crim LR 542   111
R v *Dawson* (Nolan & Walmsley) *The Times*, 23 March 1985   203, 205, 228, 229
R v *Deller* (1952) 36 Cr App R 184   24, 25
R v *Devall* [1984] Crim LR 428   248
R v *Dickie* [1984] 1 WLR 1031, 128 SJ 336, 149 JP 1 [1984] 3 All
ER 173, 79 Cr App R 213, [1984] Crim LR 497   162
R v *Donovan* [1934] 2 KB 498, [1934] All ER Rep 207, 103 LJ KB 683,
152 LT 46, 98 JP 409, 50 TLR 566, 78 SJ 601, 25 Cr App R 1, 30 Cox
CC 187   196, 197, 198, 206
R v *Downes* (1983) 77 Cr App R 260, [1983] Crim LR 819, 147 JP 729   232
R v *Dudley and Stephens* (1884) 14 QBD 273, [1881–4] All ER Rep 61, 54
LJ MC 32, 52 LT 107, 49 JP 69, 33 WR 347, 1 TLR 118, 15 Cox CC 624   186

R v *Duffy* [1967] 1 QB 63, [1966] 1 All ER 62, [1966] 2 WLR 229, 130 JP 137, 110 SJ 70, 50 Cr App R 68	25, 182
R v *Duguid* (1906) 75 LJ KB 470, 94 LT 887, 70 JP 294, 22 TLR 506, 50 SJ 465, 21 Cox CC 200	154
R v *Dunnington* [1984] Crim LR 98, [1984] QB 472, [1984] 2 WLR 125, 127 SJ 882, 148 JP 316, 78 Cr App R 171	116
R v *Dyson* [1908] 2 KB 454, [1908–10] All ER Rep 736, 77 LJ KB 813, 99 LT 201, 72 JP 303, 24 TLR 653, 52 SJ 535, 21 Cox CC 669, 1 Cr App R 13	217
R v *Dytham* [1979] QB 722, [1979] 3 All ER 641, [1979] 3 WLR 467, 144 JP 49, 123 SJ 621, 69 Cr App R 387, [1979] Crim LR 666	18, 19
R v *Eagleton* (1855) Dears CC 515	134
R v *Easom* [1971] 2 QB 315, [1971] 2 All ER 945, [1971] 3 WLR 82, 135 JP 477, 115 SJ 485, 55 Cr App R 410, [1971] Crim LR 487	137–8, 251, 255
R v *Edwards* [1975] QB 27, [1974] 3 WLR 285, [1974] 2 All ER 1085, 59 Cr App R 213, [1974] Crim LR 540, 118 SJ 582	65
R v *Esop* (1836) 7 C & P 456	178
R v *Feely* [1973] 1 QB 530, [1973] 1 All ER 341, [1973] 2 WLR 201, 137 JP 157, 117 SJ 54, 57 Cr App R 312	249
R v *Finney* (1874) 12 Cox CC 625	37
R v *Fitzmaurice* [1983] QB 1083, [1983] 1 All ER 189, [1983] 2 WLR 227, 126 SJ 656, [1982] Crim LR 677	156
R v *Fitzpatrick* [1977] NILR 20	184
R v *Flattery* (1877) 2 QBD 410, 46 LJ MC 130, 36 LT 32, 25 WR 398, 13 Cox CC 388	210
R v *Friend* (1820) Russ & Ry 20	17
R v *Ghosh* [1982] QB 1053, [1982] 2 All ER 689, [1982] 3 WLR 110, 146 JP 376, 126 SJ 429, 75 Cr App R 154	249, 258, 274
R v *Gibbins & Proctor* (1918) 82 JP 287, 13 Cr App R 134	17
R v *Gilbert* (1977) 66 Cr App R 237, [1978] Crim LR 216	223
R v *Gilks* [1972] 3 All ER 280, [1972] 1 WLR 1341, 116 SJ 632, 56 Cr App R 734, [1972] Crim LR 585	244
R v *Gill* [1963] 2 All ER 688, [1963] 1 WLR 841, 127 JP 429, 107 SJ 417, 47 Cr App R 166	66, 184
R v *Gilmartin* [1983] QB 953, [1983] 1 All ER 829, [1983] 2 WLR 547, 147 JP 183, 127 SJ 179, 76 Cr App R 238, [1983] Crim LR 330	259
R v *Gittens* [1984] 3 WLR 327, [1984] QB 698, 128 SJ 515, [1984] 3 All ER 252, 79 Cr App R 272, [1984] Crim LR 553	226
R v *Gladstone Williams* (1984) 78 Cr App R 276	23, 176, 177
R v *Graham* [1982] 1 All ER 801, [1982] 1 WLR 294, 146 JP 206, 126 SJ 117, 74 Cr App R 235	183
R v *Grainge* [1984] Crim LR 493	273
R v *Greenhoff* [1979] Crim LR 108	255
R v *Greenstein* [1975] 1 All ER 1, [1975] 1 WLR 1353, 119 SJ 742, 61 Cr App R 296	258
R v *Gregory* (1983) 77 Cr App R 41, [1982] Crim LR 229	256
R v *Griffiths* (1974) 60 Cr App R 14	273
R v *Grundy* [1977] Crim LR 543	115
R v *Gurmit Singh* [1966] 2 QB 53, [1965] 3 All ER 384, [1966] 2 WLR 88, 129 JP 578	129, 130, 131–2
R v *Hall* (1961) 45 Cr App R 366	228
R v *Hall* [1973] QB 126, [1972] 2 All ER 1009, [1972] 3 WLR 381, 136 JP 598, 116 SJ 268, 56 Cr App R 547	241
R v *Hall The Times*, 14 March 1985	273
R v *Halliday* (1889) 61 LT 701, [1886–90] All ER Rep 1028, 54 JP 312, 38 WR 256, 6 TLR 109	204
R v *Hardie* [1984] 3 All ER 848	169
R v *Harling* [1938] 1 All ER 307, 26 Cr App R 127	209
R v *Hensler* (1870) 22 LT 691, 34 JP 533, 19 WR 108, 11 Cox CC 570	26, 261
R v *Hircock* (1978) 67 Cr App R 278, [1979] Crim LR 184	248

Table of Cases

R v Hollinshead [1985] 2 WLR 761, [1985] 1 All ER 850	116, 150
R v Hollis [1971] Crim LR 525	257
R v Hopley (1869) 2 F & F 202	198
R v Howells [1977] QB 614, [1977] 3 All ER 417, [1977] 2 WLR 716, 121 SJ 154, 65 Cr App R 86, [1977] Crim LR 354	84
R v Hudson & Taylor [1971] 2 QB 202, [1981] 2 All ER 244, [1971] 2 WLR 1047, 135 JP 407, 115 SJ 303, 56 Cr App R 1	183, 184, 185
R v Huggins (1730) 2 Str 83, 17 St Tr 309, 2 Ld Raym 1574 1 Barn KB 396, Fitz-G 177	120
R v Humphreys & Turner [1965] 3 All ER 689, 130 JP 45	111
R v Hussey (1924) 89 JP 28, 41 TLR 205, 18 Cr App R 160	180, 182
R v Husseyn (1978) 67 Cr App R 131, [1978] Crim LR 219	251, 255
R v ICR Haulage Co. Ltd [1944] KB 551, [1944] 1 All ER 691, 113 LJ KB 492, 171 LT 180, 108 JP 181, 60 TLR 399, 30 Cr App R 31	119
R v Ilyas (1984) 78 Cr App R 17, (1983) 147 JPN 829	134
R v Instan [1893] 1 QB 450, [1891–94] All ER Rep 1213, 62 LJ MC 86, 68 LT 420, 57 JP 282, 41 WR 368, 9 TLR 248, 37 SJ 251, 17 Cox CC 602	16
R v Irving [1970] Crim LR 642	87
R v Isitt [1978] Crim LR 159, 67 Cr App R 44	164
R v Ismail [1977] Crim LR 557	273
R v James (1837) 3 C & P 131	186
R v Jordan (1956) 40 Cr App R 152	27
R v Jones & Smith [1976] 3 All ER 54, [1976] 1 WLR 672, 120 SJ 299	254
R v Julien [1969] 2 All ER 856, [1969] 1 WLR 839, 133 JP 489, 113 SJ 342, 53 Cr App R 407	180
R v Kanwar [1982] 2 All ER 528, [1982] 1 WLR 845, 146 JP 238, 126 SJ 276, 75 Cr App R 87, [1982] Crim LR 532	269, 270
R v Kelly (unreported) Court of Appeal	114
R v Kemp [1957] 1 QB 399, [1956] 3 All ER 249, [1956] 3 WLR 724, 120 JP 457, 100 SJ 768, 40 Cr App R 121	160, 165
R v Kimber [1983] 3 All ER 316, [1983] 1 WLR 1118, 127 SJ 578, 77 Cr App R 225, [1983] Crim LR 630	23, 175, 176, 177, 213
R v Kopsch (1925) 19 Cr App R 50	161
R v Lambie [1982] AC 449, [1981] 2 All ER 776, [1981] 3 WLR 88, 145 JP 364, 125 SJ 480, 73 Cr App R 294	259
R v Larkin [1943] 1 KB 174, [1943] 1 All ER 217, 112 LJ KB 163, 168 LT 298, 59 TLR 105, 87 SJ 140, 29 Cr App R 18	228
R v Larsonneur (1933) 149 LT 542, 97 JP 206, 77 SJ 486, 24 Cr App R 74, 29 Cox CC 673	20, 21, 72
R v Latimer (1886) 18 QBD 359, [1886–90] All ER Rep 386, 55 LJ MC 135, 54 LT 768, 51 JP 184, 2 TLR 626, 16 Cox CC 70	63, 229
R v Laverty [1970] 3 All ER 432, 134 JP 699, 54 Cr App R 495, [1971] RTR 124	261
R v Lawrence [1982] AC 510, [1981] 1 All ER 974, [1981] 2 WLR 524, 25 SJ 241, 73 Cr App R 1	51, 52, 53, 54, 57, 58, 212
R v Leahy [1985] Crim LR 99	155
R v Lesbini [1914] 3 KB 1116, 84 LJ KB 1102, 112 LT 175, 24 Cox CC 516, 11 Cr App R 7	223
R v Lipman [1970] 1 QB 152, [1969] 3 All ER 410, [1969] 3 WLR 819, 133 JP 712, 113 SJ 670, 53 Cr App R 600	165
R v Lloyd [1967] 1 QB 175, [1966] 1 All ER 107, [1966] 2 WLR 13, 130 JP 118, 109 SJ 955, 50 Cr App R 61	225
R v Lloyd and others [1985] 3 WLR 30	149, 250
R v Lobell [1957] 1 QB 547, [1957] 1 All ER 734, [1957] 1 WLR 524, 121 JP 282, 101 SJ 268, 41 Cr App R 100	65, 181
R v Lomas (1913) 110 LT 239, 78 JP 152, 30 TLR 125, 58 SJ 220, 23 Cox CC 765, 9 Cr App R 220	101
R v McCarthy [1954] 2 QB 105, [1954] 2 All ER 262, [1954] 2 WLR 1044, 98 SJ 356, 38 Cr App R 74	223

R v *McDonnell* [1966] 1 QB 233, [1966] 1 All ER 193, [1965] 3 WLR 1138, 109 SJ
  919, 50 Cr App R 5   154, 155, 156, 157
R v *McDonough* (1962) 106 SJ 961, 47 Cr App R 37   156
R v *McGrowther* (1746) Fost 13, 18 St Tr 391   183
R v *McInnes* [1971] 3 All ER 295, [1971] 1 WLR 1600, 115 SJ 655, 55 Cr
  App R 551   179, 180, 181
R v *Mackie* [1973] Crim LR 438, 57 Cr App R 453   228
R v *McPherson* (1857) Dears & B 197   137
R v *McPherson* [1973] Crim LR 191   246
R v *Mainwaring* (1982) 74 Cr App R 99   242
R v *Malcherek & Steel* [1981] 2 All ER 422, [1981] 1 WLR 690, 125 SJ
  305, 73 Cr App R 173, [1981] Crim LR 401   28, 217
R v *Manley* (1844) 1 Cox CC 104   99
R v *Marriott* [1971] 1 All ER 595, [1971] 1 WLR 187, 135 JP 165, 115 SJ
  11, 55 Cr App R 82   85, 86
R v *Martin* (1881) 8 QBD 54, [1881–5] All ER Rep 699, 51 LJ MC 11, 411
  LT 531, 44 JP 74, 14 Cox 375   204
R v *Mason* (1968) 53 Cr App R 12   206
R v *Meech* [1974] QB 549, [1973] 3 All ER 939, [1973] 3 WLR 507, 138
  JP 6, 117 SJ 713, 58 Cr App R 741   246, 263
R v *Meredith* [1973] Crim LR 253   238, 239–40
R v *Michael* (1840) 9 C & P 356, 2 Mood CC 120   99
R v *Middleton* (1873) LR 2 CCR 38, 42 LJ MC 73, 28 LT 777, 37 JP 629,
  12 Cox CC 417   244
R v *Miller* [1954] 2 QB 282, [1954] 2 All ER 529, [1954] 2 WLR 138, 118
  JP 340, 98 SJ 62, 38 Cr App R 1   203, 214
R v *Miller* [1983] 2 AC 161, [1983] 1 All ER 978, [1983] 2 WLR 539, 127
  SJ 223, 77 Cr App R 17   13, 18, 19, 22, 57, 58, 61, 63, 70
R v *Mills* (1979) 68 Cr App R 327   215
R v *Mitchell* [1983] QB 741, [1983] 2 WLR 938   229
R v *Mohammed Bashir* [1982] Crim LR 687, 77 Cr App R 59   57, 58, 212
R v *Mohan* [1976] QB 1, [1975] 2 All ER 193, [1975] 2 WLR 859, 139 JP
  523, 119 SJ 219, 60 Cr App R 272, [1975] RTR 337, [1975] Crim LR
  283   42, 45, 138, 139, 140, 141
R v *Moloney* [1985] 2 WLR 648   39, 42, 43, 44, 45, 46, 47, 48, 49, 51, 62, 69, 139, 140, 152,
                                                          171, 218, 219, 221, 222, 227, 274
R v *Mowatt* [1968] 1 QB 421, [1967] 3 All ER 47, [1967] 2 WLR 1192, 131
  JP 463, 111 SJ 716, 51 Cr App R 402   202
R v *Moys* [1984] Crim LR 495, 79 Cr App R 72, 128 SJ 548   274
R v *Murtagh & Kennedy* [1955] Crim LR 315   112
R v *Nicklin* [1977] Crim LR 221, [1977] 2 All ER 444, [1977] 1 WLR 403,
  64 Cr App R 205   271
R v *Olugboja* [1982] QB 320, [1981] 1 WLR 585, 73 Cr App R 344   209
R v *Orpin* [1980] 1 WLR 1050, 124 SJ 271, [1980] 2 All ER 321, 70 Cr
  App R 306, [1980] Crim LR 304   39, 52
R v *Page* [1954] 1 QB 170, [1953] 2 All ER 1355, [1953] 3 WLR 895, 97
  SJ 799, 37 Cr App R 189   217
R v *Pagett* (1983) 76 Cr App R 279   229
R v *Patterson* [1962] 2 QB 429, [1962] 2 All ER 340, [1962] 2 WLR 496, 126 JP
  126, 106 SJ 156, 46 Cr App R 106   66
R v *Pearman* [1985] RTR 39, [1984] Crim LR 675   42, 45, 47, 139, 141
R v *Pembliton* (1874) LR 2 CCR 119, [1874–80] All ER Rep 1163, 43 LJ
  MC 91, 30 LT 405, 38 JP 454, 22 WR 553, 12 Cox CC 607   64
R v *Phekoo* [1981] 3 All ER 84, [1981] 1 WLR 1117, 125 SJ 239, 73 Cr
  App R 107, [1981] Crim LR 399   89, 175
R v *Pigg* [1982] 2 All ER 591, [1982] 1 WLR 762, 146 JP 298, 126 SJ 344,
  74 Cr App R 352   142
R v *Pike* [1961] Crim LR 547   227
R v *Pitchley* (1972) 57 Cr App R 30, [1972] Crim LR 705   268, 270

R v *Pitham & Hehl* (1976) 65 Cr App R 45	247
R v *Pittwood* (1902) 19 TLR 37	16, 17, 18
R v *Podola* [1960] 1 QB 325, [1959] 3 All ER 418, [1959] 3 WLR 718, 103 SJ 856, 43 Cr App R 220	163
R v *Pratt* [1984] Crim LR 41	207
R v *Prince* (1875) LR 2 CCR 154, [1874–80] All ER Rep 881, 44 LJ MC 122, 32 LT 700, 39 JP 676, 24 WR 76, 13 Cox CC 138	72, 73, 91, 152, 154
R v *Quick & Paddison* [1973] QB 910, [1973] 3 All ER 347, [1973] 3 WLR 26, 137 JP 763, 117 SJ 371, 57 Cr App R 722, [1973] Crim LR 434	164
R v *R (SM)* (1984) 79 Cr App R 334	56, 57, 58, 214
R v *Raven* [1982] Crim LR 51	224
R v *Reader* (1977) 66 Cr App R 33	273
R v *Reeves* (1839) 9 C & P 25	217
R v *Richards* [1974] QB 776, [1973] 3 All ER 1088, [1973] 3 WLR 888, 138 JP 69, 117 SJ 852, 58 Cr App R 60, [1974] Crim LR 96	113
R v *Rickman* [1982] Crim LR 507	185
R v *Ring* (1892) 17 Cox CC 491	137
R v *Roberts* (1971) 56 Cr App R 95, 115 SJ 405, [1971] 2 All ER 529, [1971] 1 WLR 894	204
R v *Roberts* (1984) 78 Cr App R 41, 148 JP 14	155
R v *Robinson* [1915] 2 KB 342, 84 LJ KB 1149, 113 LT 379, 79 JP 303, 31 TLR 313, 59 SJ 366, 24 Cox CC 726, 11 Cr App R 124	135, 136
R v *Robinson* [1977] Crim LR 173	248
R v *Robinson* [1984] 4 NIJB	177
R v *Rose* (1884) 15 Cox CC 540	182
R v *Russell The Times*, 4 January 1985	257
R v *St. George* (1840) 9 C & P 483	194
R v *Sainthouse* [1980] Crim LR 506	266
R v *Salisbury* (1553) 1 Plow 100	63
R v *Satnam & Kewal* (1984) 78 Cr App R 149	57, 59, 212, 213
R v *Saunders The Times*, 8 February 1985	203
R v *Saunders & Archer* (1576) 2 Plow 473, Fost 371	114, 115
R v *Seers* (1984) 79 Cr App R 261, 149 JP 124, [1983] 2 AC 493	226
R v *Seymour* [1983] 2 AC 493, 2 All ER 1058, [1983] 3 WLR 349, 148 JP 530, 127 SJ 522, 77 Cr App R 215, [1983] Crim LR 742	58, 59, 107, 192, 212, 213, 227, 255, 262
R v *Shannon* (1980) Cr App R 192, 124 SJ 374, [1980] Crim LR 438	180
R v *Sheppard* [1981] AC 394, [1980] 3 All ER 899, [1980] 3 WLR 960, 124 SJ 864, 72 Cr App R 82, [1981] Crim LR 171	77
R v *Shivpuri* [1985] 2 WLR 29	146, 147
R v *Singh* [1973] 1 All ER 122, [1972] 1 WLR 1600, 116 SJ 863, 57 Cr App R 180, [1973] Crim LR 49	183
R v *Skipp* [1975] Crim LR 114	246, 263
R v *Sloggett* [1972] QB 420, [1971] 3 All ER 264, [1971] 3 WLR 628, 135 JP 539, 115 SJ 655, 55 Cr App R 532	267, 268, 270
R v *Smith* [1959] 2 QB 35, [1959] 2 All ER 193,]1959] 2 WLR 623, 123 JP 295, 103 SJ 353, 43 Cr App R 121	27, 28
R v *Smith* [1974] QB 354, [1974] 1 All ER 632, [1974] 2 WLR 20, 138 JP 236, 117 SJ 938, 58 Cr App R 320, [1974] Crim LR 101	178
R v *Smith* [1979] Crim LR 251	17
R v *Smith (David George)* (1985) 82 LS Gaz 198	198
R v *Soanes* [1958] 1 All ER 289, 32 Cr App R 136, 112 JP 193, 92 SJ 155	230
R v *Sockett* (1908) 72 JP 428, 24 LR 893, 52 SJ 729, 1 Cr App R 101	116
R v *Staines* (1974) 60 Cr App R 160, [1975] Crim LR 651	262
R v *Steane* [1947] KB 997, [1947] 1 All ER 813, [1947] LJR 969, 177 LT 122, 111 JP 337, 63 TLR 403, 91 SJ 279, 32 Cr App R 61	41, 42, 46, 68, 106, 171, 183, 184
R v *Stephens* LR 1 QB 702	81
R v *Stephenson* [1979] QB 695, [1979] 2 All ER 1198, [1979] 2 WLR 193, 143 JP 592, 123 SJ 403, 69 Cr App R 213, [1979] Crim LR 590	50, 51

R v Stone & Dobinson [1977] QB 354, [1972] 2 All ER 341, [1977] 2 WLR 169, 121 SJ 83, [1977] Crim LR 166, (1976) 64 Cr App R 186 — 17, 227
R v Storrow & Poole [1983] Crim LR 332 — 232
R v Sullivan [1984] AC 156, [1983] 2 All ER 637, [1983] 2 WLR 123, 127 SJ 460, [1983] Crim LR 257, 148 JP 207, 77 Cr App R 176 — 160, 164
R v Sutton [1977] 3 All ER 476, [1977] 1 WLR 1086, 141 JP 683, 121 SJ 676, 66 Cr App R 21, [1977] Crim LR 569 — 205
R v Taafe [1984] 1 WLR 326, [1984] AC 539 — 24
R v Taylor (1869) LR 1 CCR 194, 38 LJ MC 106, 20 LT 402, 33 JP 358, 17 WR 623, 11 Cox CC 261 — 205
R v Taylor [1979] Crim LR 649 — 257
R v Taylor The Times, 28 December 1983 — 198
R v Tolson (1889) 23 QBD 168, [1886–90] All ER Rep 26, 58 LJ MC 97, 60 LT 899, 54 JP 4, 37 WR 716, 5 TLR 465, 16 Cox CC 629 — 93, 177
R v Tonner & Evans [1984] Crim LR 618, 128 SJ 702 — 150
R v Turner (No. 2) [1971] 2 All ER 441, [1971] 1 WLR 901, 135 JP 419, 115 SJ 405, 55 Cr App R 336, [1971] RTR 396 — 237, 238, 239, 240
R v Twine [1967] Crim LR 710 — 224
R v Tyler & Whatmore [1976] RTR 83 — 98
R v Tyrrell [1894] 1 QB 710, [1891–94] All ER Rep 1215, 63 LJ MC 58, 70 LT 41, 42 WR 225, 10 TLR 167, 38 SJ 130, 17 Cox CC 716 — 115, 153
R v Vantandillo (1815) 4 M & S 73 — 186
R v Venna [1976] QB 421, [1975] 3 All ER 788, [1975] 3 WLR 737, 140 JP 31, 119 SJ 679, 61 Cr App R 310, [1975] Crim LR 701 — 192
R v Vickers [1957] 2 QB 664, [1957] 2 All ER 741, [1957] 3 WLR 326, 121 JP 510, 101 SJ 593, 41 Cr App R 189 — 62, 77, 218, 219
R v Viola [1982] Crim LR 515, [1982] 1 WLR 1138, [1982] 3 All ER 73, 75 Cr App R 125 — 215
R v Waite [1892] 2 QB 600, 61 LJ MC 187, 67 LT 300, 41 WR 80, 8 TLR 782, 36 SJ 745, 17 Cox CC 554 — 173
R v Walker [1984] Crim LR 112 — 232
R v Walkington [1979] 2 All ER 716, [1979] 1 WLR 1169, 123 SJ 704, 68 Cr App R 427, [1979] Crim LR 526 — 253, 254, 255
R v Wallett [1968] 2 QB 13 367, [1968] 2 All ER 296, [1968] 2 WLR 1199, 132 JP 318, 112 SJ 232, 52 Cr App R 271 — 220
R v Wardrope [1960] Crim LR 770 — 168
R v Welsh [1974] RTR 478 — 232
R v White [1910] 2 KB 124, [1908–10] All ER Rep 340, 79 LJ KB 854, 102 LJ 784, 74 JP 318, 26 TLR 466, 54 SJ 523, 22 Cox CC 325, 4 Cr App R 257 — 26
R v Whitefield [1984] Crim LR 97, 79 Cr App R 36 — 115
R v Whitehouse [1977] QB 868, [1977] 3 All ER 737, [1977] 2 WLR 925, 121 SJ 171, 65 Cr App R 33, [1977] Crim LR 689 — 116
R v Whybrow (1951) 95 SJ 745, 35 Cr App R 141 — 138
R v Williams [1893] 1 QB 320, 62 LJ MC 69, 41 WR 332, 9 TLR 198 — 173
R v Williams [1923] 1 KB 340, [1922] All ER Rep 433, 92 LJ KB 230, 87 JP 67, 39 TLR 131, 67 SJ 263, 27 Cox CC 350, 17 Cr App R 56 — 210
R v Williams & Blackwood (1973) 21 WIR 329 — 114
R v Wilson [1955] 1 All ER 744, [1955] 1 WLR 493, 119 JP 216, 99 SJ 321, 39 Cr App R 12 — 194
R v Windle [1952] 2 QB 826, [1952] 2 All ER 1, 116 JP 365, [1952] 1 TLR 1344, 96 SJ 379, 36 Cr App R 85 — 161
R v Winson [1969] 1 QB 371, [1968] 1 All ER 197, [1968] 2 WLR 113, 112 SJ 71 — 122
R v Wood (1830) 4 C & P 381, 1 Mood CC 278 — 203
R v Woodman [1974] QB 754, [1974] 2 All ER 955, [1974] 2 WLR 821, 138 JP 567, 118 SJ 346, 59 Cr App R 200 — 239
R v Woodrow (1846) 15 M & W 404, 16 LJ MC 122, 10 JP 791, 2 New Mag Cas 1, 2 Car H & A 346 — 72
R v Woods (1982) 74 Cr App R 312, [1982] Crim LR 42 — 168

Table of Cases

R v *Woolven* (1984) 77 Cr App R 231, [1983] Crim LR 623	258
R v *Young* [1984] 1 WLR 654, 128 SJ 297, 148 JP 492, 78 Cr App R 288, [1984] 2 All ER 164, [1984] Crim LR 363	86, 166
Rice v *Connolly* [1966] 2 QB 414, [1966] 2 All ER 649, [1966] 3 WLR 17, 130 JP 322, 110 SJ 371	77
Ricketts v *Cox* [1982] Crim LR 184, 74 Cr App R 298	77
Roper v *Taylor's Central Garages (Exeter) Ltd* [1951] 2 TLR 284, 115 JP 445, [1951] WN 383	75
Scott v *Metropolitan Police Commissioner* [1975] AC 819, [1974] 3 All ER 1032, [1974] 3 WLR 741, 139 JP 121, 60 Cr App R 124, 118 SJ 863, [1975] Crim LR 94	149, 150
Searle v *Randolph* [1972] Crim LR 779	86
Shaw v *Directors of Public Prosecutions* [1962] AC 220, [1961] 2 All ER 446, [1961] 2 WLR 897, 125 JP 437, 105 SJ 421, 45 Cr App R 113	12, 150, 151
Sherras v *De Rutzen* [1895] 1 QB 918, [1895–99] All ER Rep 1167, 64 LJ MC 218, 72 LT 839, 59 JP 440, 143 WR 526, 11 TLR 369, 39 SJ 451, 18 Cox CC 157	75, 78, 79, 80, 81, 82, 91, 93
Smedleys Ltd v *Bread* [1974] AC 839, [1974] 2 All ER 21, [1974] 2 WLR 575, 138 JP 439, 118 SJ 363, [1974] Crim LR 309	79–80
Smith v *Baker* [1972] Crim LR 25, [1971] RTR 350	105
Southwark London Borough Council v *Williams* [1971] Ch 734, [1971] 2 All ER 175, [1971] 2 WLR 467, 115 SJ 18	186
Stowager v *John* [1974] RTR 124	78
Sweet v *Parsley* [1970] AC 132, [1969] 1 All ER 347, [1969] 2 WLR 470, 133 JP 188, 113 SJ 86, 53 Cr App R 221	88, 89, 92–3, 95
Tesco Supermarkets Ltd v *Nattrass* [1972] AC 153, [1971] 2 All 127, [1971] 2 WLR 1166, 135 JP 289, 115 SJ 285	119, 120
Thabo-Meli v *R* [1954] 1 All ER 373, [1954] 1 WLR 228, 98 SJ 77	61, 62
Thambiah v *R* [1966] AC 37, [1965] 3 All ER 661, [1966] 2 WLR 81, 109 SJ 832	102
Thornton v *Mitchell* [1940] 1 All ER 339, 104 JP 108, 56 TLR 296, 84 SJ 257	110
Tuck v *Robson* [1970] 1 All ER 1171, [1970] 1 WLR 741, 134 JP 389, 114 SJ 191	106
Vane v *Yiannopoullos* [1965] AC 486, [1964] 3 All ER 820, [1964] 3 WLR 1218, 129 JP 50, 108 SJ 937	122
W (a minor) v *Dolbey* [1983] Crim LR 681	58, 59, 192, 204
Warner v *Metropolitan Police Commissioner* [1969] 2 AC 256, [1968] 2 All ER 356, [1968] 2 WLR 1303, 132 JP 378, 112 SJ 378, 52 Cr App R 373	85, 86, 87, 89, 92, 94
Webley v *Buxton* [1977] QB 481, [1977] 2 All ER 595, [1977] 2 WLR 766, 121 SJ 153, 65 Cr App R 136	147
Wilcox v *Jeffrey* [1951] 1 All ER 464, 115 JP 151, [1951] 1 TLR 706, 95 SJ 157	105
Whitehouse v *Lemon* [1979] AC 617, [1979] 2 WLR 281, 123 SJ 163, [1979] 1 All ER 898, [1979] Crim LR 311, 68 Cr App R 381	43, 45, 73, 91
Willmott v *Atack* [1977] QB 498	77
Winzar v *Chief Constable of Kent The Times*, 28 March 1983	21, 72
Woolmington v *Director of Public Prosecutions* [1935] AC 462, [1935] All ER Rep 1, 104 LJ KB 433, 153 LT 232, 51 TLR 446, 79 SJ 401, 25 Cr App R 72, 30 Cox CC 234	64–5, 93, 162
Worthy v *Gordon Plant (Services) The Times*, 19 March 1985	120
Wrothwell (F.J.H.) Ltd v *Yorkshire Water Authority* [1984] Crim LR 43	81

Table of Statutes

Abortion Act 1967   197, 230
Accessories and Abettors Act 1891   103
  s.8   100, 102, 112, 117
British Nationality Act 1981   217
Child Abduction Act 1984
  s.2   154
  s.11   154
Children and Young Persons Act 1933
  s.50   7, 172
Companies Act 1985   118
Contempt of Court Act 1981   73
Control of Pollution Act 1974
  s.32   81
  s.33   81
Copyright Act 1956   149
Criminal Appeal Act 1968
  s.2(1)   211
  s.12   162
Criminal Attempts Act 1981   128, 133, 137, 142, 143, 144, 146, 147, 156
  s.1(1)   132, 134, 136, 139, 141, 145, 153, 157
  s.1(2)   144, 145, 146, 153
  s.1(3)   141, 144, 145, 146, 153
  s.1(4)   157, 158
  s.1(4)(b)   116
  s.5(1)   155
  s.6   132, 134
  s.6(1)   139
Criminal Damage Act 1971   56, 58
  s.1   168
  s.1(1)   19, 30, 50, 52, 56, 57
  s.1(2)   19, 52, 171
  s.1(2)(b)   39, 40
  s.1(3)   19, 50
  s.3   130
  s.5   168, 178
Criminal Justice Act 1925
  s.47   183
Criminal Justice Act 1967
  s.8   47, 67–8, 131, 167, 170, 212, 220
Criminal Justice Act 1972
  s.36   197
Criminal Justice Act 1982
  s.67   9
Criminal Law Act 1967
  s.1   5, 117
  s.2   5, 6
  s.3(1)   178, 179–82, 186, 215

Criminal Law Act 1967—*continued*
  s.3(2)   23, 179
  s.4(1)   116, 118, 158
  s.5(1)   158
  s.6(3)   147
  s.6(4)   147
Criminal Law Act 1977   100, 102, 128, 147, 150, 153, 154, 156
  s.1   151
  s.1(1)   150, 151, 152, 155
  s.1(2)   152
  s.2(2)   153
  s.3   158
  s.5(1)–(3)   150
  s.5(7)   158
  s.50   10
  s.54   158
Criminal Procedure (Insanity) Act 1964
  ss.1 and 2   162
  s.4   163
  ss.5 and 6   162
Dangerous Drugs Act 1965
  s.5(b)   88
Drugs (Prevention of Misuse) Act 1964
  s.1(1)   85
Explosive Substances Act 1883
  s.4(1)   181
Firearms Act 1968
  s.1   84
  s.1(1)(a)   84
  s.58(2)   84
Food Act 1984
  s.2(1)   79
  s.3   92
  s.3(3)   79
Food and Drugs Act 1955   80
  s.2   92
  s.2(1)   79
  s.3   92
Forfeiture Act 1870   5
Homicide Act 1957   218, 219
  s.1   218
  s.2   65, 112, 224–6
  s.2(1)   226
  s.3   65, 222–4
  s.4   226
Indecency with Children Act 1960   205

Table of Statutes

Infant Life (Preservation) Act 1929 217, 230
  s.1 230
  s.1(2) 217
Infanticide Act 1938 230
Libel Act 1843 73
Licensing Act 1872 10, 76
  s.12 21
  ss.13 and 14 76
  s.16 76
  ss.16(1) and (2) 75
Licensing Act 1902
  s.1 21
Licensing Act 1964 10
  s.59(1) 106
  s.169(1) 123
Magistrates' Court Act 1980 6
  s.24(1) 173
  s.44 100
  s.127 7
Medicines Act 1968
  s.52 80
  s.58(2) 80
Mental Health Act 1983
  ss.47 and 48 163
  s.51 163
Merchandise Marks Act 1887
  s.2(2) 121
Metropolitan Police Act 1839
  s.44 122
Misuse of Drugs Act 1971
  s.5 85, 87
  s.5(2) 92
  s.6 90
  s.28 92
Murder (Abolition of Death Penalty) Act 1965 9
Offences against the Person Act 1861
  s.9 8, 217
  s.18 39, 47, 113, 138, 171, 188, 199, 201–4, 219, 226
  s.20 49, 52, 58, 113, 138, 188, 200–5
  ss.21 and 22 200
  s.23 48, 200, 202
  s.24 200
  ss.26–35 200
  ss.36 and 37 201
  ss.38 and 39 200
  s.40 200, 201
  s.43 201
  s.47 49, 113, 118, 192, 200, 201, 203, 204, 205
  s.51 201
  s.55 72
  s.56 154
  s.57 8, 177
  ss.58 and 59 200, 230
  s.64 20
Official Secrets Act 1911 8
Police Act 1964
  s.51(3) 76, 77

Police and Criminal Evidence Act 1984 6
  s.3 6
  s.24(2) and (3) 6
  s.25 6
  s.25(3) 6
  s.116 6
Powers of Criminal Courts Act 1973
  s.18(2) 158
  s.28 and 29 9
  s.35 9
  s.38 9
Protection from Pollution Act 1977
  s.1(3)(a) 89
Protection of Children Act 1978
  s.1 206
Rivers (Prevention of Pollution) Act 1955
  s.2(1) 81
Road Traffic Act 1930
  s.12(1) 110
Road Traffic Act 1972 14
  s.1 10, 52, 58, 215, 230
  s.2 10, 58, 98
  s.3 37, 110, 165
  s.5(2) 21, 31, 83
  s.5(3) 83
  s.6(1) 103, 108
  s.25 16
  s.40 82, 98
  s.40(5) 83
Road Traffic Regulation Act 1984
  s.87 186
Sexual Offences Act 1956
  s.1(1) 208
  s.1(2) 210
  s.6 115
  s.11 116
  s.12 209
  s.13 208, 209
  s.15 208, 209
  s.15(2) 206
  s.16 208
  s.20 72
  s.44 208
Sexual Offences Act 1961
  s.2(1) 158
Sexual Offences Act 1967
  s.1 4, 208, 209
Sexual Offences (Amendment) Act 1976 14, 57, 211
  s.1 213
  s.1(1) 29, 208, 209
  s.1(2) 168, 175, 178, 187, 211
  s.2(1) 214
  s.4(1) 215
Suicide Act 1961
  s.2 226
Theft Act 1968 232
  s.1 6, 40
  s.1(1) 14, 30, 231, 233, 234
  s.2 98

Theft Act 1968—*continued*
  s.2(1)   249
  s.2(1)(a)   258
  s.2(2)   249
  s.3   247–8
  s.3(1)   15, 245, 247, 249
  s.3(2)   248
  s.4(1)   232, 258
  s.4(2)   232–4
  s.4(2)(a)   233
  s.4(2)(b)   233, 234
  s.4(2)(c)   234
  s.4(3)   234–5
  s.4(4)   235–6
  s.5   236, 264
  s.5(1)   236, 237, 238, 240, 241, 243, 244, 258, 260, 261, 264
  s.5(2)   240
  s.5(3)   240–2
  s.5(4)   242–4, 264
  s.6   250, 251
  s.6(1)   250
  s.6(2)   250, 251
  s.9   127, 253
  s.9(1)(a)   39, 171, 252, 254, 255, 256–7
  s.9(1)(b)   255–7, 257
  s.9(3)   252
  s.10   257
  s.10(1)(a)–(c)   257
  s.12   98
  s.13   232
  s.15   24, 266
  s.15(1)   52, 257–8, 260, 261, 262, 264
  s.15(2)   262
  s.15(3)   258
  s.15(4)   258, 260

Theft Act 1968—*continued*
  s.16(1)   261, 264, 265, 266
  s.16(2)(a)   265
  s.16(2)(b)   264
  s.16(2)(c)   265
  s.22(1)   266, 267–71, 272, 273
  s.24(1)   271
  s.24(2)   272
  s.24(2)(a)   272
  s.24(2)(b)   272, 273
  s.24(3)   271, 272
  s.24(4)   271
  s.25   130, 131, 133, 134
  s.25(1)   130
  s.27(3)   274
  s.34(1)   258
Theft Act 1978   265, 266
  s.1   265
  s.1(1)   266
  s.2   248, 265
  s.2(b)   265
  s.3   265–6
  s.3(1)   266
Trade Description Act 1968
  s.1   80
  s.24   91, 92, 123
  s.24(1)(a)   91
  s.24(1)(b)   92
Trade Union and Labour Relations Act 1974   152
Transport Act 1981
  s.25   103, 108
  Sch.8   103, 108
Trial of Lunatics Act 1883   162
Vehicles (Excise) Act 1971
  s.12(4)   78, 79

STATUTORY INSTRUMENTS

Motor Vehicles (Construction and Use) Regulations 1981 (SI 1017)   82

Introduction

0.1 OUTLINE OF THE BOOK

Student textbooks on criminal law seemingly confuse comprehensiveness with understanding. Students are extolled to consider numerous criminal offences which ultimately lead (presumably by a process of osmosis) to a knowledge of the nature of criminal law.

This book operates on an entirely opposing philosophy. Crimes are discussed in so far as they illustrate the underlying features which are the common constituents of all criminal offences or demonstrate general principles of criminal liability. This is the principle which permeates and determines the structure of the book.

The first six chapters make use of criminal offences to demonstrate (a) the common factors which form their structure (chapters 1–3), (b) the modes of participation in offences (chapter 4), (c) various forms of criminal activity preliminary or prior to a complete offence having been committed (chapter 5) and (d) the nature of defences (chapter 6). Though the last two chapters of the book (chapters 7 and 8) are devoted to a consideration of offences against the person and property respectively, the particular crimes discussed therein have been chosen because of their representative nature and because they confirm in a practical sense the principles discussed in the first six chapters.

A student encouraged to think of criminal law in this way is equipped with a technique which enables him to undertake the analysis of any given offence and place it within a context of general criminal responsibility. The acquisition of this skill and outlook is one of the principal aims of the book. This book does not aim to discuss why persons commit criminal offences or why certain activities are criminal and others are not, or anything about the various theories concerning sentencing persons who have transgressed the criminal law. Those matters form the basis of the study known as criminology rather than a study of fundamental principles of substantive criminal law. Likewise the laws of evidence and criminal procedure are important for a full understanding of the aim and effect of the criminal law but equally they do not form part of the fundamental principles of substantive criminal law. Criminology, evidence, procedure are intermingled with the criminal law and this is shown particularly where the judiciary has a discretion (e.g., in deciding whether or not to accept a plea, or allow a defence to be put to a jury or in deciding on a sentence) and also where the judiciary seeks to alter fundamental principles of criminal law particularly when they refer to public policy; or where they relabel things as matters of evidence rather than substantive law or relabel things as matters of law (for the judge to rule on) rather than matters of fact (for the jury to decide upon).

Throughout the book reference is made to matters of criminal procedure and evidence. A full discussion of those topics is to be found in *A Practical Approach to Criminal Procedure* by Christopher Emmins and *A Practical Approach to Evidence* by Peter Murphy, both published by Financial Training Publications Ltd. Also published by that company is *Cases and Materials on the Theft Acts* by Janet Dine which will be useful for students who want a more detailed knowledge of offences against property than we have been able to provide in a book of this size.

Throughout the book the student is referred to a scenario which illustrates the practical application of the legal principles raised throughout the chapters to a set of factual situations. A student is given the opportunity of considering how the criminal law is developed by the judiciary from such situations, and the problems faced by the courts in determining the modes of participation in crime and the forms of activity which should be regarded as criminal, together with the development of defences. The scenario is subject to constant change within the book, so that the student may see the effect changing factual situations have upon the imposition of criminal liability and consider the policies which determine whether such liability should be imposed in a particular instance.

Criminal law possesses a coherent logical structure but like all human inventions it is plagued with certain anomalies and inconsistencies. This is a product of the judicial process.

0.2 THE JUDICIAL PROCESS

In England and Wales the legal system consists of two separate sets or hierarchies of courts. One set (together with the police, the court officers and the penal institutions) enforce the criminal law on behalf of the State. The other set enforce the civil law between and on behalf of aggrieved individuals in society. Civil law is largely concerned with making one individual pay compensation to another for some wrong done to him under the law of tort (civil wrongs which include such things as liability for negligence, defamation, premises and animals) or compensating for injury arising from a breach of contract or a breach of trust. Otherwise it is concerned with settling disputes as to entitlement or relationships as in dealing with matters of land law, succession or family law. Criminal law, irrespective of what its aim or purpose should be, is punitive.

It punishes any act or omission forbidden by the criminal law. It is easy to point to differences in the aims and procedures of criminal as opposed to civil courts but students sometimes find it difficult initially to appreciate that it is difficult to define what is criminal especially since most acts or omissions which are crimes will also (simultaneously) be civil wrongs known as torts. Generally any act or omission may give rise to two consequences one criminal the other tortious. Your one act or omission may result in your being prosecuted and punished by the State and also in the person you injured bringing an action (i.e., suing you) in the civil courts for compensation called damages. Only in the former will the police and prosecuting authorities be involved and the liberty of the individual be in jeopardy.

Introduction

0.3 SOURCES OF CRIMINAL LAW

Textbooks on the English legal system will tell you that there are various sources of law: custom, the judiciary (common law), the prerogative, legislation and institutions of the European Economic Community. As far as the principles of criminal law dealt with in this book are concerned an appreciation of only two of these creative sources of legal rules is required: common law and legislation. Common law consists of the rules established by the decisions of the judges. These decisions in our system become precedents which are binding on, and therefore must be applied by courts lower in the hierarchy than, the one which made the decision. Legislation consists of statutes or Acts of Parliament and delegated legislation (rules made by bodies other than Parliament but authorised to do so by Parliament). English criminal law is made up of rules contained in statutes, in court precedents (the common law) and in the judicial interpretations of those statutes, which interpretations become the law unless and until Parliament or a higher court alters any such judicial interpretation.

0.4 DEFINING A CRIME

It is difficult to define what is criminal or to distinguish a crime by definition from a tort. Each is a wrong, each is a breach of a legal obligation or rule. Although it is circular the best definition and the best distinguishing feature is that only if the breach of a legal rule (the wrong) has criminal consequences attached to it, will it be a criminal offence. An offence or a crime then is a wrong to society involving the breach of a legal rule which has criminal consequences attached to it (i.e., prosecution by the State in the criminal courts).

Why certain acts or omissions are declared criminal and others are not is also a difficult question as are the questions: what aggravating factors warrant being made the subject of a separate offence and which mitigating factors should be recognised as defences? As with the terminology (see para. 0.5) there is an element of fashion involved in attempts to answer these fundamental issues but the underlying rationale is largely governed by the traditional ethos and ethics of the society, in our case the Judaeo-Christian tradition and the conservatism that accompanies the desire for stability, order and predictability. Morality and notions of blameworthiness based on harm may explain the formulation of the early fundamental crimes (murder, theft, etc.) but do not necessarily fully explain the modern social welfare, moral improvement and traffic offences created by statute. No one philosophy or cause can adequately explain why differing forms of activity are deemed criminal. Morality, economics and politics all play a part. Also there is an interrelationship with the equally complex question: why do people commit crimes? As in defining a crime there are numerous conflicting views and theories in answer to both questions. We cannot go into all these issues in detail nor do we need to so long as the reader is aware of the difficulties and asks himself such questions as whether crime occurs because man is inherently evil or because of his socio-economic condition or because he is diseased or suffering genetic, inherited defects or whether there are other factors or combinations of factors which are responsible? In other words as long as the reader does not study the principles of criminal law in a vacuum but constantly asks himself what is their aim and purpose and whether they achieve those ends. Clearly one of the main aims or functions of the criminal law is the maintenance of order in society but that is not its only function. For example, Lord Simonds in *Shaw* v *DPP* (see para. 5.7.4) dwelt on another function (in his view) when he said its aim is 'to conserve not only the safety and order but also the moral welfare of the State'. Whether or not you agree that that is a legitimate role of the criminal law is another matter but the important point of it is that criminal laws have numerous aims. These laws do maintain public order and the safety and integrity of individuals but also they raise revenue (e.g., the laws punishing those who evade income tax), they regulate business (e.g., they punish the charging of excessive prices and they punish unhygienic practices), they protect employees, they conserve the environment and preserve heritage and they enforce morality.

Today in this country there are literally thousands of offences created by statute which are designed to enforce certain standards in the practice of lawful activities where such activities may result in harm to the public. The rules relating to public hygiene, rules about health and safety at work and rules governing the entry into and conduct of certain businesses or professions are examples. These rules are generally enforceable by way of criminal sanction. Unlike the traditional common law notions of crime these newer statutory offences generally punish omissions as well as positive acts (see para. 1.3) and furthermore they often create offences of strict liability (see chapter 3). This last innovation has produced practical advantages but it means that if a minute prohibited act, omission or event occurs for which you are responsible, you are guilty. Your guilt does not depend as it must in the old common law offences on your state of mind (see chapter 2). You are deemed guilty irrespective of what you intended, thought or believed. Generally the ordinary man or woman in society does not consider persons convicted of these sorts of offences, including traffic violations, 'criminals', that term being popularly reserved to express moral condemnation for the acts of murderers, rapists, thieves and the like and yet those other regulatory or social welfare type offences can cause individuals and society no less suffering and harm. Should not society and the law treat such offenders as blameworthy and reprehensible as the traditional 'criminals'?

Finally, the student should ask in relation to those offences the sole purpose of which is the enforcement of morality, whether or not the type of conduct declared criminal are matters of private morality with which the criminal law should not be concerned at all? If the prohibited conduct does no harm to society or to the participants should that conduct be criminal? Are the criminal offences relating to alcohol, gambling, pornography, bigamy, blasphemy, bestiality, criminal libel, conspiracy to corrupt public morals and conspiracy to outrage public decency outmoded and unreasonable restrictions on our liberty or would individuals and society be at risk if current laws on these matters were abolished? If these laws are essential to our society why are adultery, fornication and seduction not criminal? Occasionally popular demands lead to legislation to withdraw certain conduct from the ambit of the criminal law. One of the best examples is the public debate following the Wolfenden Committee Report 1957 (Cmnd 247) which led to Parliament passing the Sexual Offences Act 1967, s. 1, which declares that homosexual acts between consenting adult males (over the age of 21) in private are no longer a crime.

Introduction

Obviously in this book we cannot and we do not want to deal individually with every crime known to English law. We seek to deal only with the most significant features common to crimes and categories of criminal offences generally. There will be many crimes old and new that we will not discuss (e.g., forgery, bigamy, perjury, incest, kidnapping) and many more that you will not realise even exist. When you do come across any of these offences it is our hope that having read this book you will be able to analyse the constituents of the offence and know its scope. It is the principles common to criminal offences and some understanding of the judicial approach and attitude and the hidden role of morality and public pressure that are important. The particular substantive offences dealt with in detail in the areas of offences against the person (chapter 7) and offences against property (chapter 8) were chosen as the most useful in illustrating those points as well as giving some knowledge of the elements of some specific crimes.

0.5 TERMINOLOGY AND CLASSIFICATION

What is currently vogue in terminology as in fashion changes from time to time. The words 'crime' and 'offence' are synonymous, each has been used in the book but in practice 'crime' is used only in relation to serious offences such as rape or murder, which are called indictable offences (see below). Throughout the book we have chosen to refer to an individual who has been charged with and prosecuted for a criminal offence as the 'accused', the term 'defendant' would serve equally well as it does in other books.

An accused may be tried and found not guilty or acquitted or that person may be found guilty (i.e., convicted) and sentenced. In some instances (see below) a person who has been convicted may appeal either against the severity of the sentence imposed or against the conviction seeking to have it quashed. In these instances we have referred to that person as the appellant or accused.

0.5.1 Felonies and misdemeanours

The terminology for the classification of offences has changed with time but the reader has to be aware of some of the old terms in order to understand the older reported cases. Criminal offences used to be categorised at common law either as felonies or as misdemeanours. Felonies were those crimes which had as their penalty on conviction the forfeiture of land and goods and if Parliament had declared a crime to be a felony without benefit of clergy then the penalty was death as well as forfeiture of property to the State. The Forfeiture Act 1870 abolished forfeiture for felony. A misdemeanour was any offence not amounting to a felony; these were regarded as less serious offences and never incurred the death penalty or forfeiture of property, rather they were punished by fines or imprisonment at the court's discretion. The distinction between the gravity of these two categories of offences and their differing consequences had all but disappeared by the time they were formally abolished by s. 1 of the Criminal Law Act 1967. That Act, by s. 2, put in place of those old categories a new classification — arrestable and non-arrestable offences.

0.5.2 Arrestable and non-arrestable offences

The definition of an arrestable offence first contained in s. 2 of the Criminal Law Act 1967, which concentrated upon the procedural consequences of a crime has been incorporated into and expanded by the Police and Criminal Evidence Act 1984 which will come into force on 1 January 1986. Where an individual has committed an arrestable offence a police officer or a member of the public may arrest him without a warrant. This classification encompasses all offences for which the penalty upon conviction is fixed by law (e.g., the mandatory life sentence in case of murder) or for which a person of 21 years of age or over (not previously convicted) may be sentenced to imprisonment for a term of five years or more (e.g., theft contrary to s. 1 of the Theft Act 1968 has a maximum penalty of ten years' imprisonment and thus is an arrestable offence). In addition s. 24(2) and (3) of the Police and Criminal Evidence Act 1984 declare numerous specific offences to be arrestable offences even though the prescribed penalty on conviction is less than five years' imprisonment. An arrestable offence which is a 'serious arrestable offence' as defined in s. 116 of that Act has enhanced powers of arrest for the police attached to it. The majority of arrestable offences will be indictable offences. In addition s. 25 of the Act gives the police a general power to arrest for any non-arrestable offence no matter how petty provided one of the general arrest conditions specified in s. 25(3) is satisfied (e.g., the name of the relevant person is unknown to, and cannot be readily ascertained by, the constable) and that therefore the service of a summons is impracticable or inappropriate. This new general power of arrest permits arrest without warrant for summary and otherwise non arrestable offences if one of the general arrest conditions are satisified.

0.5.3 Indictable and summary offences

Another classification of criminal offences is by reference to the modes by which offences may be tried. Criminal offences (less serious types) are either tried summarily before a magistrates' court or (the more serious type) are tried on indictment in the Crown Court.

Summary trial, i.e., before magistrates, takes place with regard to offences which are so minor that they must be so tried, or offences for which an accused can elect either to be tried before magistrates or before the Crown Court and has chosen to be tried before the former. (These offences are known as offences triable either way.) A list of such offences is contained in the Magistrates' Court Act 1980; statutes may also specifically provide the offences contained therein must or may be tried summarily. A magistrates' court is comprised of two or more lay magistrates, i.e., individuals who are neither salaried nor in most cases legally qualified. In some cases a magistrates' court may comprise a single stipendiary magistrate (a professional salaried judge who is legally qualified).

Trials on indictment in the Crown Court take place in relation to offences where an accused may elect such a trial (and has so chosen) or where the offence can only be tried in the Crown Court because of its seriousness. Trials on indictment are so named because the trial is commenced by a document known as a bill of indictment which sets out the offence and its particulars with which an accused is charged. A Crown Court trial is before a judge and jury. The trial of an accused is preceded by an initial investigation of the accused's potential criminal liability by magistrates who if convinced that an accused has a case to answer commit him to the Crown Court for trial. This process is known as committal proceedings.

0.6 APPEALS

An accused convicted by a magistrates' court of an offence may appeal by way of a full rehearing of the case to the Crown Court. In this instance the Crown Court consists of lay magistrates and a judge as chairman (usually a circuit judge but with no jury). Any further appeal can only be on a point of law and can be from either the Crown Court following a rehearing as noted above, or from the magistrates' court direct. The appellate court in such instances is the Divisional Court of the Queen's Bench, which comprises two or more High Court judges. There is a final appeal from the Divisional Court to the House of Lords. Such appeals are restricted to instances where a point of law of general public importance is raised and where either court has given leave to appeal.

Where an accused has been convicted of an offence following a trial before the Crown Court (i.e., before judge and jury) he may appeal to the Court of Appeal Criminal Division on a point of law and ultimately to the House of Lords upon the restricted ground that the point of law concerned is of general public importance and leave has been given by either court because it is an issue that should be settled by the House of Lords.

The prosecution may appeal against an accused's acquittal in all cases except where the accused has been acquitted by a jury's verdict — that decision is always final.

0.7 LIMITS ON PROSECUTION

Unlike civil wrongs, in the case of criminal offences there is generally no limitation period. Prosecutions can be brought against an accused at any time, even years after the act or omission giving rise to the allegation of an offence has been committed. Parliament, however, may by statute provide exceptions in specific instances to that general rule (e.g., s. 127 of the Magistrates' Courts Act 1980 provides that all summary prosecutions must be brought within six months of the commission of the offence, again unless a specific statute provides to the contrary).

Certain persons are in effect absolutely immune from prosecution (e.g., the monarch, foreign sovereigns and their emissaries, members of diplomatic staff and persons working for international organisations), others receive a limited immunity (e.g., the administrative and technical staff of an embassy are only immune for acts or omissions done in the course of their duties, visiting armed forces are given a very technical and limited immunity).

Certain children in effect receive immunity from criminal prosecution in the form of a presumption of incapacity to commit crimes. Age can furnish a defence in that the law maintains that no child under 10 years of age can be guilty of an offence (see the Children and Young Persons Act 1933, s. 50 as amended). In relation to a child between the ages of 10 and 14 years there is a rebuttable presumption of incapacity to commit a crime. The prosecution may rebut that presumption by proving not only that the accused child committed the offence but also that he knew what he did was wrong.

All prosecutions are brought on behalf of the Crown which is a synonym for the State and generally they are instituted in the name of the monarch or an officer of the Crown such as the Attorney-General or the Director of Public Prosecutions. In relation to less serious offences the prosecution may be brought in the name of the police or the actual police officer or a representative of a govenment department or local authority or of the private citizen bringing the prosecution. In the latter instances a limitation of sorts arises in that the permission or leave of the Attorney-General or the Director of Public Prosecution or the Home Secretary or some other Minister is sometimes required. Without the necessary approval specified in the particular statute from whichever of those representatives of the Crown the trial cannot proceed and if commenced the proceedings are deemed void. Examples of prosecutions requiring such approval are incest, homosexual offences, theft or unlawful damage to a spouse's property and offences under the Official Secrets Act 1911.

Appeals aside (see above) there is a principle of criminal law that if a competent court finds in favour of an accused and acquits him the prosecution cannot reopen that issue in another trial involving either the same accusation or another necessarily dependent on the issue already adjudged in the accused's favour. This principle against double jeopardy applies equally where a person has been convicted of an offence to prevent him being tried more than once for any one particular act or omission. This principle is based on the doctrine of issue estoppel and the pleas of *autrefois acquit* or *autrefois convict* and prevents endless prosecutions for any one event.

Jurisdiction can be a further limitation to prosecution. In the main English criminal law is concerned with where an offence is committed. If it occurs within the territorial boundaries of England or Wales or on or over the territorial sea of those countries then the offence is triable in either England or Wales irrespective of the nationality of the accused. There are exceptions to this general rule (see chapter 7) in that certain offences (like piracy) are tried here no matter where in the world the offence occurred. British ships and aircraft are considered by the law to be British territory consequently offences committed on board such vessels, no matter where in the world they are, may be tried in England or Wales again irrespective of the accused's nationality. Certain statutes, the best example of which is the Offences against the Person Act 1861, ss. 9 and 57, provide that certain offences (such as murder, manslaughter and bigamy) committed by British citizens abroad may be tried in England and Wales. Finally an individual liable to be tried in England and Wales who flees or escapes to another country may be retrieved by the formal procedure of extradition provided there is an extradition treaty in existence between Britain and the country in which the fugitive has sought refuge.

0.8 EVIDENCE

In criminal prosecutions the law applies the maxims 'He who alleges must prove' and 'The accused is presumed innocent until proven guilty'. To obtain a conviction the prosecution must prove all the constituent elements of the substantive offence in question beyond reasonable doubt. Likewise if a defence is raised the prosecution must disprove it beyond reasonable doubt. In the one or two rare instances where the burden of proof relating to a defence is imposed on the accused then the law specifies that the accused need only prove on a balance of probabilities (the usual civil standard) rather than beyond reasonable doubt.

0.9 PUNISHMENT

There are various theories concerning the purpose of punishment ranging from retribution, through prevention, deterrence and education to rehabilitation. In this country the criminal courts have available to them a number of punishments they may impose following conviction of an individual ranging from deprivation of liberty to absolute and conditional discharges. The death penalty was abolished by the Murder (Abolition of Death Penalty) Act 1965 although it is possible today that a sentence of death could be imposed in limited and exceptional circumstances (e.g., for treason or piracy). Except in the case of murder, for which a mandatory sentence of life imprisonment is automatically imposed, there are no minimum sentences prescribed. Generally the maximum sentence imposable is specified and it is left to the judges' discretion, having considered all the circumstances, what term of imprisonment to impose short of the maximum. Apart from prisons there are remand homes, attendance and detention centres and approved schools. Those accused who are either mentally unfit to plead or found not guilty on grounds of insanity will be detained in a mental institution at Her Majesty's pleasure (until certified safe for release). Where the circumstances warrant it the judge may impose a suspended sentence or give a conditional or an absolute discharge. Where the convicted person may be punished by the imposition of a fine (whether or not in conjunction with a term of imprisonment) generally the maximum fine imposable is prescribed leaving it to the judges' discretion to fix the actual amount which will usually be below the maximum. The Powers of Criminal Courts Act 1973, ss. 28–29, provide complex rules for an extended sentence in the case of a hardened and persistent criminal and the Powers of Criminal Courts Act 1973, ss. 35 and 38 as amended by the Criminal Justice Act 1982, s. 67, permit all criminal courts to award compensation to individuals who have suffered loss as a result of the convicted person's criminal activity.

0.10 STATUTORY AMENDMENT

Many of the statutes contained within the text have been subject to constant amendment, substitution, and repeal (in part or in whole). It would be tedious to note all such changes within the chapters. Where a statutory amendment is crucial to an understanding of the particular offence or the relevant general principles of law, the amendment or amendments have been discussed in the text. Furthermore, where the amendment of a current statute is relevant to its present substantive form, the fact of amendment has been noted. In all other cases, however, we have not generally referred to the statutory amendment.

Thus, amendments to a statute which affected procedural changes relating to matters of evidence, mode of trial or sentence, have been excluded as is the case where the amendment has not affected the substantive elements of the offence. This is also the practice followed where the statute has been used to illustrate a principle of law which has remained unaffected by subsequent statutory amendment, e.g., the consideration of certain aspects of strict liability (see chapter 3) by reference to offences contained in the Licensing Act 1872. Such offences have generally been substantially reproduced in the Licensing Act 1964. Nevertheless, the authorities considering the provisions of the Licensing Act 1872 remain authoritative upon the issue of strict liability.

However, there are two sections used throughout the book which have been subject to important statutory change, to avoid repetition and cross-referencing they are referred to here. Section 1 and s. 2 of the Road Traffic Act 1972 concerned the offences of causing death by dangerous and reckless driving or dangerous and reckless driving simpliciter. It was felt that the ambit of two such serious offences should not contain the element of dangerous which created an unnecessarily wide liability. Consequently s. 50 of the Criminal Law Act 1977 removed the element of dangerous from the definition of these offences which may now only be committed recklessly. The present forms of these offences are noted in the text.

1

Scenario

Four young men, Bruce, Donald, Edward and John, share a flat in the centre of Melchester. They are frequent partygoers. One evening Bruce drives his three companions in his car to the home of Sarah, the girlfriend of Donald. Donald knows that Sarah's parents are out for the evening.

Bruce has driven his friends to various parties in the neighbourhood and though he has not been personally involved the others have frequently got drunk and committed some acts of violence and of vandalism.

In view of such irresponsible behaviour Bruce was unwilling to drive his friends to Sarah's home. Donald told him that if he did not, 'it would be worse for him'. Donald possesses a violent and uncontrollable temper and Bruce fears the consequences of that temper more than what may happen if he drives his friends to Sarah's home.

They arrive at their destination by 7.30 p.m. Sarah is alone; she expected to see only Donald. The situation gets out of hand; she asks the others to leave but they refuse. Bruce, taking a bottle of whisky from the drinks cabinet, goes upstairs and proceeds to drink as much of it as he can.

Edward and John see an opportunity to explore the house; they enter its various parts and, observing a camera, jewellery and silver candlesticks, take them and prepare to leave the house.

Donald also helped himself at the drinks cabinet and has proceeded to get drunk. He makes increasingly hostile but amorous advances towards Sarah. Sarah fearing that to resist could provoke Donald into a spate of violence yields to his demands. They have sexual intercourse.

Sarah's parents then return from the local public house. With them is Alf, the brother of their next-door neighbour, Wilma. They find Sarah heaped in a corner crying and severely distressed. Donald is lying on a couch incapable through drink. Sarah's father, Rex, fearing the worst and in an uncontrollable rage sets upon the unconscious Donald with his fists, his wife Marian shouting encouragement.

Edward and John, seeing the return of Sarah's parents, smash a window in the rear of the house and make their escape. In doing so they accidentally and unintentionally knock over a burning paraffin heater. When some 50 yards from the house they see the flames and realise that they are responsible, nevertheless, afraid of the consequences, they make their escape.

Bruce, still upstairs, is brought to his senses by the smell of smoke and though still drunk he manages to make his way out of the house. He reaches his car and, opening the driver's door, slumps into the seat. He then remains there in a stupor trying to decide whether to drive off and leave his friends. He is still very drunk.

Donald has been badly hurt by Rex's violent attack, he has sustained fractured ribs, jaw and skull. In addition he is bleeding internally. At this stage Rex realising that the house is on fire carries his daughter to safety with the help of his wife. Leaving Sarah, they return to the house and carry Donald to safety, but only after dropping him twice through exhaustion. They place Donald on the pavement but though Rex leaves Donald in the care of Marian she omits either to call for an ambulance or to render the most basic first aid to him. The evening cold plus the injuries sustained send Donald into shock.

Rex's next-door neighbour Wilma having seen the fire and the injured Donald, has telephoned the emergency services and has gone to help. She tried to revive Donald by administering some brandy to him. This only succeeded in choking him and he died as a result.

This scenario considers several criminal offences which will be referred to throughout the first chapter to illustrate the practical application of the general principles discussed there. This format will encourage the acquisition of skills which should enable any student to analyse a given factual situation and determine in such an instance whether any principles of criminal law are applicable. This will encourage a student to think of criminal law as a set of general principles which can be used to analyse a given criminal offence and to consider its application to a given factual situation. In doing so some controversial opinions will be put forward about the reasons for, and nature of, the fundamental principles of English criminal law.

1.1 INTRODUCTION: ACTUS REUS

The foregoing scenario, though unlikely and dramatic is indicative of the kinds of problems that are considered by 'students' of criminal law be they A level, undergraduate, police cadet or officer, lawyer or judge. The questions which must be asked after reviewing the scenario are: Do the facts disclose any possible criminal offences and how many? How are the constituents of a criminal offence determined? Furthermore though criminal offences differ as to the elements by which they are composed; do they nevertheless share a set of common factors and characteristics which demonstrate an underlying uniformity in their structure? Criminal offences viewed in this fashion enable a student to develop a technique which is generally available for the practical analysis of factual or hypothetical situations involving particular crimes.

The elements of a criminal offence may be determined by reference to their sources. Many crimes have been formulated and originated by the judges themselves. These judicial decisions or authorities constitute the common law offences. Examples of such judicial law-making can be seen in the law relating to murder (see paras 7.6 to 7.6.2). For a particularly controversial example see *Shaw* v *DPP* [1962] AC 220 ('conspiracy to corrupt public morals') and *Knuller (Publishing, Printing & Promotions) Ltd* v *DPP* [1973] AC 435 ('conspiracy to outrage public decency') (see para 5.7.4). Their peculiar characteristics can be ascertained by reference to the judicial decisions themselves. These decisions are recorded principally in the law reports. The principal reports are the *Criminal Appeal Reports* (Cr App R), *All England Law Reports* (All ER), *Cox's Criminal*

Cases (Cox CC), the *Weekly Law Reports* (WLR) and the *Law Reports, Queen's Bench Division* (QB).

The second and most important source for criminal offences is statute (Acts of Parliament). These statutes may create entirely new offences or may be codifications of previous common law offences. Most criminal law today is created by Parliament or somebody to whom it has delegated that creative power and is published in statutes (Acts of Parliament) or in the case of delegated lawmaking, in regulations, ordinances or bye-laws. In reality many of these statutory offences are subject to extensive judicial interpretation. In other words once the judiciary have interpreted the words of a statute, it is the meaning they attributed to these words that then becomes the law until a higher court on appeal or Parliament acts to change that interpretation. An examination of the relevant statute and any interpretative case law will determine their particular nature. Reference to these sources will only inform as to the nature and ingredients of an offence. An examination of a number of offences will readily demonstrate that all crimes have in general a shared set of factors in their make-up, which can be applied in the general analysis of all offences.

Almost all of the important or serious offences require before an individual be convicted that he not only brings about the circumstances and consequences of an offence, but that he has done so voluntarily and with a particular state of mind (see chapter 2). The acts or omissions of an individual, together with the relevant circumstances, consequences or states of affairs are known by the Latin term *'actus reus'*. These are the external elements that must be proved. The required state of mind of the individual that must accompany the external elements of an offence is known by a Latin phrase *'mens rea'*. These terms arise from the Latin term, *'Actus non facit reum nisi mens sit rea'*, which can be translated: 'An act does not make a man guilty of a crime, unless his mind be also guilty'. These are the internal elements, that is, the thoughts or beliefs that passed through the mind of the accused at the time of the *actus reus*.

In the case of *R* v *Miller* [1983] 2 AC 161 at p 174 Lord Diplock exhorted criminal lawyers to desist from using bad Latin and considered that it would 'be conducive to clarity of analysis of the ingredients of a crime . . . if we were . . . to think and speak . . . about the conduct of the accused and his state of mind at the time of that conduct, instead of speaking of *actus reus* and *mens rea*'.

Despite this admonition the phrases are short and have enjoyed long usage and for the sake of convenience will be used throughout this book. It should always be remembered that there is no 'magic' in them, they are shorthand for saying that the prosecution must prove with regard to an offence, first that the prescribed or prohibited conduct or events occurred and that the accused was responsible for those events or that conduct (*actus reus*), and secondly it must prove that the accused had a prescribed 'guilty' or 'blameworthy' state of mind at that time (*mens rea*), because of his intention, thought, belief, recklessness or in some cases negligence at that time (see chapter 2).

In this chapter the external elements of certain offences will be examined and their common characteristics discussed together with a consideration of their applicability to the facts contained in the scenario. The offences which will be initially examined are:

(a) The statutory offence of rape. Section 1(1) of the Sexual Offences (Amendment) Act 1976 determines that a man commits rape if:

(i) he has unlawful sexual intercourse with a woman who at the time of intercourse does not consent to it; and
(ii) at the time he knows that she does not consent to the intercourse or he is reckless as to whether she consents to it.

(b) The common law offence of murder as defined by the judges is: 'The unlawful killing of a human being with malice aforethought under the Queen's peace, death following within a year and a day of the infliction of the injury' (3 Co Inst 47).

(c) The statutory offence of theft. The Theft Act 1968, s. 1(1), provides that: 'A person is guilty of theft if he dishonestly appropriates property belonging to another with the intention of permanently depriving the other of it'.

The task of the law student, police officer, lawyer or judge is basically the same: ascertaining and applying the law to the facts of a case to determine whether or not those involved are liable to account to society by trial for a criminal offence.

1.2 THE EXTERNAL ELEMENTS OF AN OFFENCE: POSITIVE ACTS

Most offences have as an element within their *actus reus* the requirement that an individual undertakes a positive act. The *actus reus* may consist entirely of a positive act or omission, but it may in some instances consist of a positive act or omission in conjunction with certain circumstances (e.g., rape). In other instances an *actus reus* may consist of acts or omissions together with circumstances which produce certain specified consequences (e.g., murder).

A positive act is consciously executed conduct, a voluntary willed movement. In the case of *Blayney* v *Knight* (1975) 60 Cr App R 269 the accused during the course of a dispute with the owner of a motor vehicle accidently set it in motion whilst in the driving seat. It was held that the accused was not 'driving' the vehicle for the purposes of any offences within the Road Traffic Act 1972.

This requirement that the actions of an individual are consciously undertaken does not constitute any element of the *mens rea*. It is in fact a more fundamental requirement. This can best be explained when it is claimed by an individual that, though he is responsible for the execution of an act or series of acts, he was not aware that he was so responsible for that conduct. Criminal liability cannot attach in such cases. It has been noted by several authors that voluntariness is an aspect of the *actus reus*, but it is suggested that this is a mistaken view. This is because an individual may bring about the incident of an *actus reus* involuntarily, e.g., while sleep-walking or while insane, but the presence of such matters does not negate the fact that the prohibited act or omission has occurred. Really in such cases the individual is claiming a specific defence known to the law as automatism, i.e., that he is neither aware of nor responsible for his actions. This specific defence is also entirely independent of and unrelated to the general defence that an individual lacks *mens rea*. The different forms of automatism will be considered in chapter 6 on defences. See chapter 2 for a discussion of the concept of *mens rea*. In cases where an individual claims that he lacks *mens rea*, he does not deny that he is aware and responsible for his actions but maintains that he lacks a certain state of mind or attitude to the circumstances and/or consequences which are part of the offence and which his conduct may have brought about.

The type of conduct required for particular offences is easier to establish in some instances than in others. In the crime of rape the only element of conduct required to be proved is the act of sexual intercourse. The other constituents of this crime are the prescribed circumstances in which that conduct must take place. The situation relating to conduct is not so clear in the case of murder. There the required conduct is a killing. Such an act may be brought about by many forms of activity, such as stabbing, shooting, administering poison. The conduct may thus consist of one act or a series of acts each of which is causally connected. In the case of murder the positive conduct consists of an act or series of causally connected acts which cannot be realistically separated from their consequences. If the killing is by way of shooting, it is not the aiming of a loaded gun, nor the pressing of the trigger, which together comprise the forbidden conduct, these actions must be combined with the firing of the bullet and its entry into the victim, but until the consequence of death there is no positive act which can form an element in the *actus reus* of the offence.

In the scenario Donald's act of sexual intercourse is the act which satisfies the conduct element in the *actus reus* of rape. The situation with regard to Rex's beating of Donald is less clear. The beating cannot be separated from the resultant severe injuries. These are causally connected and should be regarded as interrelated. The inflicting of the injuries can be considered as part of the conduct. However, the beating and injuries cannot be regarded as fulfilling the element of killing within the *actus reus* of murder unless they are the cause of the death of Donald. (For a discussion of the issue of causation see later and chapter 7.) The act of killing is only constituted when the consequence of death can be shown to have been the direct result of the beating.

Certain types of conduct require an accompanying mental resolve on the part of the perpetrator before they become complete acts within the definition of a particular offence. In the scenario Edward and John have taken various objects from the house. The offence of theft requires that the action they undertake is the appropriation of property.

Appropriation is conduct which amounts to an 'assumption by a person of the rights of an owner' (see Theft Act 1968 s. 3(1)). Though Edward and John have taken physical possession of the camera, jewellery and candlesticks, that alone could not amount to an appropriation, within the meaning of the term; there must be a mental resolution to treat the property as their own. This mental aspect does not form any element in the *mens rea* of the offence. It is an essential requirement to the act of appropriation. It completes and constitutes conduct which would otherwise be of no legal significance.

1.3 OMISSIONS

The criminal law has always been willing to punish an individual who through his conduct has brought about the *actus reus* of a crime. It was most reluctant however to affix criminal responsibility in cases where an individual's neglect or omission to act had brought about what would otherwise constitute the elements of an offence.

If an individual places an unconscious victim into a bath and turns on the taps and so drowns him, the *actus reus* of murder is established. Yet another, coming across the same victim would be under no obligation either to pull the plug, turn off the taps or seek medical assistance for the unfortunate individual. Such an omission though morally reprehensible will not result in any criminal liability.

The law has in a piecemeal fashion provided exceptions to this principle. The law determines that in certain circumstances an omission to act can form an element in the *actus reus* of an offence. It has done so by imposing in such situations a duty to act, failure to execute that duty constituting an element in the *actus reus*.

1.3.1 Duty to act imposed by statute

Statute may impose a duty upon an individual to act, the failure to execute that duty amounting to an offence. An example is s. 25 of the Road Traffic Act 1972 which provides, *inter alia*, that an individual involved in a road accident where there has been injury to another person or damage to a vehicle not driven by that individual is under a duty to stop and give his name and address to any person reasonably requiring it. There is also imposed a duty to give other information. An individual who fails to provide these particulars when requested to do so should report the accident to the police as soon as reasonably practicable, and in any event within 24 hours. The statute provides that failure to carry out the above requirements is an offence.

1.3.2 Duty to act imposed by contract

In the case of *R* v *Pittwood* (1902) 19 TLR 37 the accused was employed as a gatekeeper on a railway crossing. His contract of employment required him to keep the gates shut whenever a train passed. He had opened the gates to let a cart through but omitted to close them and had gone to lunch. Another cart passing over the crossing was struck by a train resulting in the death of a man.

Though Wright J considered the accused's conduct 'gross and criminal negligence' (see para 2.4) his lordship also accepted that criminal liability could arise in the case by regarding the omission to shut the gate as a failure to carry out a duty arising out of the accused's contract of employment. The conviction could be justified upon this ground alone. His lordship relied upon the case of *R* v *Instan* [1893] 1 QB 450. A niece had failed to supply food or in any other way to sustain her elderly and infirm aunt with whom she lived. Her aunt died as a result of that neglect. This failure to care for her aunt was a breach of a legal duty in the words of Lord Coleridge CJ (at p. 454):

> [I]t was the clear duty of the prisoner to impart to the deceased so much as was necessary to sustain life of the food which she from time to time took in, and which was paid for by the deceased's own money for the purpose of the maintenance of herself and the prisoner; it was only through the

instrumentality of the prisoner that the deceased could get the food. There was, therefore, a common law duty imposed upon the prisoner which she did not discharge.

Though the deceased had suffered from gangrene the failure by the accused to summon medical assistance was not considered as an element in the breach of duty, neither did the court have regard to the blood relationship. The basis of the decision appears to be that there was an obligation to supply food by the accused to the deceased because there was a contract which contained an express or implied undertaking to do so. The undertaking arose because the accused had lived with and been supported by the deceased's bounty. The case of *Pittwood* is an example of an undertaking imposed by a contract of employment.

1.3.3 Duty to act imposed by relationship

The common law has long recognised a duty of an adult to maintain a child of tender years, whether that duty arises from parenthood, undertaking, or contract (see *R v Friend* (1820) Russ & Ry 20 a case concerning an apprentice). In *R v Gibbins and Proctor* (1918) 13 Cr App R 134 this duty was extended to a *de facto* parent, though the issue was complicated by the fact that the *de facto* mother had received money from the father of the deceased child for its maintenance, and could be regarded as having impliedly undertaken the care of the child on this basis.

In the case of *R v Stone and Dobinson* [1977] QB 354 it was accepted that a duty of care to maintain the health of a person could exist in relation to an adult. The two accused, a man and his mistress, had accepted the man's sister into their home. The sister was eccentric and failed to look after herself properly. Despite the exhortations of neighbours the two accused did nothing to alleviate the sister's condition, they neither sought medical assistance nor help from the social services. The sister died as a result of this neglect.

It was argued by the defence that no duty to act arose in such cases. The deceased's situation was akin to that of a lodger. In any event her demise was due to her eccentricity of behaviour. It was analogous to the individual coming across a drowning man—there could be no duty to help save an individual in such circumstances. This argument was rejected by the court. The deceased was a relative of the male accused; both he and his co-accused had undertaken to care for her. In such a circumstance the growing infirmity of the deceased brought forth an obligation upon the accused to seek medical help for her. Though the blood relationship was no doubt a pertinent factor, the duty to aid the deceased was imposed upon the accused because they had initially and voluntarily undertaken the task of caring for her. This was the background upon which the subsequent infirmity then created a relationship based upon dependence between the accused and the deceased and which rendered their omissions to deal with the consequences of that dependence criminal. This principle is applicable to many circumstances where such an undertaking provides a condition precedent to potential criminal liability and a resulting dependence may arise which then imposes the duty to act, e.g., in the case of man and wife (see *R v Smith* [1979] Crim LR 251). Whether an adult dependant can voluntarily consent to release an individual from the duty to care for him or her is questionable. It must be a matter of fact whether such a dependant can in the particular circumstances of a case voluntarily and reasonably make such a decision. The difference between the obligation to act which is imposed because of a relationship of dependence and the duty to act imposed in cases like *Pittwood* is that in the latter situation a person voluntarily undertakes to perform all the obligations and terms express and implied in a contractual relationship whereas in the former category the obligation once established is determined by law, i.e., it is imposed irrespective of the individual's willingness to assume it.

1.3.4 Duty to act imposed by office

In *R v Dytham* [1979] QB 722 the accused, a police officer, had observed an altercation outside a night-club during which a man had been beaten to death. The accused made no attempt to quell the disturbance or stop the attack upon the unfortunate victim. When the incident was over, the accused drove away, saying to a bystander that he was due to go off duty.

The accused was charged with misconduct by an officer of justice, in that he had deliberately failed to carry out his duty, by wilfully omitting to take any steps to preserve the Queen's peace, or to protect the person of the deceased or arrest his assailants, or otherwise bring them to justice. The accused contended that there was no such offence known to law, that the misconduct of a police officer required a positive act or an element of corruption but not an omission to act. The court rejected this argument and approved (at p. 727) a passage in Stephen's *Digest of the Criminal Law*, 9th ed. (1950), p. 114, art. 145, which said that:

> Every public officer commits a misdemeanour who wilfully neglects to perform any duty which he is bound either by common law or by statute to perform provided that the discharge of such duty is not attended with greater danger than a man of ordinary firmness and activity may be expected to encounter.

It is emphasised that the failure to act must be wilful and not merely inadvertent. This means that an officer must be aware of the circumstances which give rise to his duty to act. To be criminal, his failure to act must also be blameworthy in the sense that it must be without reasonable excuse or justification. An omission to act would not be blameworthy if the duty to act required an unduly dangerous course of conduct which could not be justified in the circumstances, e.g., with regard to the safety of others.

Though *Dytham* considered the duty of a police officer, it is suggested it is applicable to all office-holders.

1.3.5 Duty to act arising from conduct

In the case of *R v Miller* [1983] 2 AC 161 the accused was a squatter in a house. He fell asleep in a bed, while holding a cigarette. When he awoke he found the mattress smouldering. Though he was aware that the cigarette he had been holding was responsible he took no action to put out the nascent fire. However, the accused did move to an adjoining room and went back to sleep. The house caught fire and was damaged. The accused was convicted of arson contrary to the Criminal Damage Act 1971, s. 1(3). The House of Lords determined that if an individual was totally unaware that his conduct had set in motion a chain of events which could cause or was causing damage to property and, while further damage to property could still be brought about, he became aware of these events and it would be obvious to him, if he had given thought to the matter, that damage or further damage to property could arise (see paras 2.7.2 and 2.7.9) then, if that individual became aware that it was his conduct which had created that risk, a duty (or in the words of Lord Diplock in *Dytham* 'a responsibility') to stop or reduce the further consequence of that conduct would arise.

An example is provided in the scenario by the actions of Edward and John in leaving Rex's home on seeing the arrival of Sarah's parents. They have unintentionally set in course a train of events by knocking over the portable heater which results in damage to property. They later became aware of the fire, and of the fact that they were responsible for it and realised the consequences of their actions. Their failure to stop or reduce the damage caused by the fire is an omission which the law will recognise as an element in the *actus reus* of the statutory offence of criminal damage. The Criminal Damage Act 1971, s. 1(1), provides that: 'A person who without lawful excuse destroys or damages any property belonging to another intending to destroy or damage any such property or being reckless as to whether any such property would be destroyed or damaged shall be guilty of an offence'. (Section 1(2) provides for the more serious offence of damaging property with intent to endanger life or where life is endangered. Section 1(3) provides that damaging property by fire shall be charged as arson.)

The conduct required in the above offence is that property is destroyed or damaged. *Miller* determines that the destruction or damage can be the result of an individual's omission as well as by his commission. (An example of damage by commission is provided in the scenario by Edward and John smashing a window in Rex's house in order to escape.) However, it is suggested that *Miller* is not limited to cases of criminal damage but is of wider application. In the words of Lord Diplock (at p. 176):

> [I] see no rational ground for excluding from conduct capable of giving rise to criminal liability, conduct which consists of failing to take measures that lie within one's power to counteract a danger that one has oneself created, if at the time of such conduct one's state of mind is such as constitutes a necessary ingredient of the offence. I venture to think that the habit of lawyers to talk of *'actus reus'*, suggestive as it is of action rather than inaction, is responsible for any erroneous notion that failure to act cannot give rise to criminal liability in English law.

The *Miller* principle is therefore applicable in any circumstances where an individual becomes aware that his conduct which, though initially innocent, has brought about a situation of danger to persons as well as property. The extent of the duty to act is unclear. Unlike the case of *Dytham* the House of Lords in *Miller* did not consider under what circumstances if any a man may be reasonably excused from undertaking a corrective course of action. In principle the law should not seek to impose too heavy a duty. Failure to act where the conduct required is either too onerous or requires exceptional fortitude or courage should not constitute an omission to carry out a duty.

This point is made in *R* v *Brown* (1841) Car & M 314 where an individual was convicted for failing to assist in maintaining the public peace. He had refused without lawful excuse to help a constable stop an illegal prize-fight. The judgment does not appear to impose an absolute duty on every citizen to help the police restore order but rather it limits this duty to those situations where it is 'reasonably necessary' for such help to have been requested and where there was no 'physical impossibility' or 'lawful excuse' to justify refusal. See also *R* v *Atkinson* (1869) 1 Cox CC 330 where the accused while amongst a crowd of rioters many of whom were his employees refused to exercise his influence to restrain them. He was arrested for failing to assist in maintaining the peace and subsequently charged with riot. He was not convicted. In the relatively recent case of *Albert* v *Lavin* [1982] AC 546, Lord Diplock in an *obiter dictum* at p. 565 says it is not only the right but also the duty of every citizen to take reasonable steps to prevent a breach or threatening breach of the peace, committed or about to be committed in his or her presence.

1.4 STATES OF AFFAIRS AS AN ELEMENT IN THE ACTUS REUS OF AN OFFENCE

There are certain offences where the *actus reus* is constituted by an individual finding himself in a certain state of affairs. In such offences there is no requirement that an individual undertakes a course of conduct or omits to act. Whether the individual is responsible for putting himself into the prohibited situation is legally irrelevant and forms no part of the offence.

One of the clearest examples of such an offence is illustrated by the case of *R* v *Larsonneur* (1933) 24 Cr App R 74. The accused, a French citizen, was permitted to land in the United Kingdom subject to conditions. These were subsequently amended requiring her to leave the country by a certain date. The accused left for the Irish Free State on that date, but was later deported from there. She was brought back to Britain and handed over to the police, who detained her. She was charged with being an alien to whom leave to land in the United Kingdom had been refused and who was *found* in the United Kingdom. In the opinion of the then Lord Chief Justice (at pp. 78–9) the situation was clear:

> She was found here and was, therefore, deemed to be in the class of persons whose landing had been prohibited by the Secretary of State, by reason of the fact that she had violated the condition on her passport.

The *actus reus* of the offence required only that the accused be found in the United Kingdom. In contrast to the case of *Larsonneur* is *Martin* v *State of Alabama* (1944) 31 Ala App 334, 17 So 2d 427. The accused had got drunk in the privacy of his home. The police forcibly entered his house and carried him whilst in a drunken stupor into the highway. He was charged with being in contravention of a statute which prohibited persons from being found drunk in a public place. The court was of the opinion that no offence could be committed under this statute unless an accused acted voluntarily. This requirement of voluntariness could have been demanded by the court in *Larsonneur*—it chose not to do so, though it has been suggested that Miss Larsonneur had voluntarily brought herself into the state of affairs prohibited by her conscious act of going to the Irish Free State where there was a possibility she would be returned to England. She should presumably have returned to France. Though *Larsonneur* has been subject to criticism in so far as it formulated a general principle it has recently been endorsed by the case of *Winzar v Chief Constable of Kent* (*The Times*, 28 March 1983). The accused had been brought to a hospital. The medical staff formed the opinion that he was drunk and fit to leave the hospital. He was asked to leave. Eventually the police were called, he was removed from the hospital and placed in a police car in the hospital forecourt, situated on a road called Westcliffe Road. He was charged with being found drunk on the highway contrary to the Licensing Act 1872, s. 12, which provides that every person who is found drunk on a highway or public place is guilty of an offence. His momentary and involuntary presence on Westcliffe Road while drunk, from the time he was escorted from the hospital to the police car was sufficient to constitute the offence. In the reported words of the court, 'It was enough to show that the appellant had been present in the highway, was drunk and was perceived as such. The words "found drunk" meant "perceived to be drunk"'.

The fact that the accused's presence on the highway was not of his own making or volition made no difference. In the court's opinion the section was intended to deal with persons who were in a state of drunkenness in a public place. The accused satisfied those conditions. The offence with which Winzar was charged is not a serious one, and involves only a fine on conviction. By the Licensing Act 1902, s. 1, a police officer should only arrest an individual for an offence under the Licensing Act 1872, s. 12, when that person is incapable of taking care of himself. The section is concerned to a large extent with the protection of drunken persons from harming themselves by empowering a police officer in such circumstances to take them into custody. If this fact is considered with the minor criminal consequences that follow convictions for an offence under s. 12 then it is suggested that the case of *Winzar* is not a serious inroad into civil liberties, nor a grave exception to the general principle of the criminal law that a person must be aware of his actions before his criminal responsibility can be considered. If, however, *Winzar* is construed in the future as being an authority of general application permitting the extension of *Larsonneur* to crimes of a grave nature then it is to be deplored. It is hoped that *Winzar* will be limited to its facts and to the minor and peculiar offence with which it is concerned.

The scenario discloses another example of these 'state of affairs' or 'situation' offences. By the Road Traffic Act 1972, s. 5(2), it is an offence for a person 'who, when in charge of a motor vehicle which is on a road or other public place, is unfit to drive through drink or drugs.' Though Bruce has been responsible for placing himself within the terms of the offence, would he incur criminal liability if, for example, he had against his will been made drunk by Edward and John and then *placed in* his vehicle by them as a practical joke? It is to be hoped that this would be a defence to any charge under s. 5(2), though it would be open to the courts to construe that the elements of the offence had been made out even in such extreme circumstances. Such offences which are statutory are anomalous in the criminal law but they are long-established and have received the approbation of the judiciary.

1.5 CIRCUMSTANCES AS AN ELEMENT IN THE ACTUS REUS OF AN OFFENCE

The conduct or omission of an individual will rarely constitute in entirety the *actus reus* of an offence. Frequently there is a need for the conduct or omission to take place within the context of relevant circumstances. See, however, the common law offence of battery which requires the infliction of unlawful personal violence upon a victim. (As to whether the requirement that the violence be unlawful is a circumstance see later.)

In the scenario, for Donald's conduct to form the *actus reus* of rape not only must the act of sexual intercourse take place but also the following circumstance must be present. The act of intercourse must be unlawful.

This means that the sexual intercourse must be outside the bonds of marriage (see para. 7.5 for further discussion of this point). Because rape is legally defined in terms of unlawful intercourse it means that generally a man cannot rape his wife. Whether or not this is good law is open to controversial debate and is more a political than a legal issue. One of the arguments militating against changing the law is that it would be difficult to establish in many cases whether a man has raped his wife and this would render such a law difficult to enforce (see para. 7.5.3).

The remaining circumstances that must be present for rape to occur are that the victim is female (see para. 7.5) and that the sexual act has taken place without her consent (see para. 7.5). The *actus reus* of rape has been established in the facts of the scenario.

Edward and John have appropriated property, i.e., they have assumed the rights of an owner. This is the conduct required within the *actus reus* of theft. The circumstance needed to establish fully the external elements of the offence is that at the time Edward and John appropriated the property, it belonged to another. The offences of rape and theft are examples of crimes which require an individual's conduct, or omission, to take place within relevant circumstances. They are sometimes defined as 'conduct crimes', but there is no practical consequence in the use of the term. It has found judicial favour (see, for example, *R* v *Miller* [1983] 2 AC 161), therefore a student should be familiar with its use. The nature of conduct crimes may be determined by reference to their statutory or common law definitions and can be broken down into act or omission and circumstances.

Certain crimes, known as 'result crimes', require that the conduct or omission takes place not only within the relevant circumstances, but also that the event so created has further consequences or a result before the *actus reus* is established. In such offences, there are sometimes elements in the definition of the crime which make express reference to 'circumstances' which are no more than the express negation of defences which are of general application to many offences.

To regard these matters as elements in the *actus reus* of the offence amounting to circumstances is conceptually untidy, for they bear important differences from what may be regarded as circumstances proper. (See, however, para. 6.5.4.)

To take the example of murder (which is a result crime as it requires a consequential death), the conduct required is an act or omission which ultimately causes the death of a human being, i.e., a killing. The definition of murder includes *inter alia* a 'circumstance' that the killing be unlawful. Though expressed in a negative form this element provides that no *actus reus* is constituted if the 'circumstance' of lawfulness is established. This requirement of unlawfulness appears to be as much a circumstance as the requirement that the act of sexual intercourse be unlawful within the *actus reus* of the offence of rape. The 'unlawfulness' requirement in the *actus reus* of the crime of murder, however, is the express but negative reference to situations which if present would amount to a justification of what would otherwise be potentially unlawful, i.e., defences. A killing would not be unlawful for example if it was in self-defence, or was the unfortunate consequence of the application of reasonable force in the prevention of a serious crime (see the Criminal Law Act 1967, s. 3(2), and para. 6.5.4). These defences which negate the 'circumstance' of unlawfulness within the *actus reus* of murder are of general application to offences which involve the use of force or violence against the person. They would still be operative in the case of murder even if the element of unlawfulness was removed from the definition of the crime. The nature of the offence of murder would remain unchanged.

This should be contrasted with the offence of rape. It is a condition of the offence that the act of sexual intercourse be unlawful, i.e., that it is outside the bonds of marriage. It is only then that the circumstance of unlawfulness is established. If this circumstance were removed from the definition of the offence, the ambit and definition of the crime would be altered and widened. A man could in such cases be capable in law of raping his wife if the other requirements of the definition of that offence could be proved. Whether an element in a particular offence is a circumstance proper, or an express reference to the requirement that the applicability of certain generally available defences must be nullified before there can be criminal responsibility depends upon a consideration of that offence as interpreted by case law. This situation is by no means so clear in the judicial mind. Judicial authority is divided as to whether the requirement of 'unlawfulness' in offences such as murder is to be considered as an element (i.e., a circumstance) in the *actus reus* of the offence or not. In the case of *R v Kimber* [1983] 3 All ER 316 at p. 320 it was said that the element of unlawfulness in the offence of battery 'does import an essential ingredient into the offence', i.e., a circumstance (see also *R v Gladstone Williams* (1984) 78 Cr App R 276). This may be contrasted with the view expressed in *Albert v Lavin* [1981] 1 All ER 628 at p. 639 where Hodgson J said:

> It does not seem to me that the element of unlawfulness can properly be regarded as part of the definitional elements of the offence. In defining a criminal offence the word 'unlawful' is surely tautologous and can add nothing to its essential ingredients.

Perhaps the issue of classification is not so important as the realisation of the differences betwen the two kinds of 'circumstance' (see below).

1.6 ABSENCE OF AN ELEMENT IN THE ACTUS REUS OF AN OFFENCE

There may be another distinction between the two forms of 'circumstance' noted above. For example, it may be claimed that an *actus reus* is not established because an element in the *actus reus* is missing, i.e., an individual believes he has brought about all the elements of an offence but in fact has failed to do so. The individual in this situation believes himself to be guilty of an offence which he may have intended or wanted to commit, but in reality (unknown to him) despite his intention and despite performing part of the *actus reus* either he had not performed all of the *actus reus* or else a circumstance required by the definition of the *actus reus* of the offence was not present at the time of his act or omission.

This was the issue raised in *R* v *Deller* (1952) 36 Cr App R 184. The accused was charged with obtaining a motor vehicle from another person by false pretences (see now Theft Act 1968, s. 15, and chapter 8). He had offered in exchange for that vehicle his own vehicle which he had claimed he owned outright. He further maintained it was not subject to a hire-purchase agreement neither was there any money owing on it. The vehicle to be used in the exchange was therefore claimed by the accused to be free from encumbrances.

The vehicle was subject to what appeared to be a hire-purchase agreement. The statements thus made by the accused concerning his own vehicle in order to effect the exchange deal were claimed by the prosecution to be false, and the new vehicle obtained by false pretences. The documents which purported to be a hire-purchase agreement were interpreted by the court as loan agreements, with the loan secured upon the accused's vehicle. As the law stood the loan agreement was void. Due to the accident of circumstance the accused's vehicle was in law free from all encumbrances. The accused had in fact told the truth though believing what he had said was false. There were therefore no false pretences. This circumstance of the offence not being established there was no offence committed.

In such cases as is illustrated by *Deller* it is unnecessary that the individual should be aware of the facts which negate or prevent an element such as a circumstance which forms an element within the *actus reus* of an offence from being formed. In fact as was the case in *Deller* he may believe all the elements of an offence are present (see *R* v *Taafe* [1984] AC 539). However, it is the objective reality of the actual situation which is the crucial factor, the individual's state of mind is legally irrelevant, as far as the elements of the *actus reus* are concerned.

The situation differs where all the elements of an offence are present but for the 'circumstance' which requires the establishing of certain general defences before it can be negated. Such a situation is illustrated by the case of *R* v *Dadson* (1850) 4 Cox CC 358. The accused, a constable, was employed to guard a small forest from which wood had been stolen. He saw one W coming from the forest carrying wood. On being called by the accused to stop, W ran away. Having no other means of stopping W, the accused shot at and wounded him. The accused was convicted of shooting W with intent to do him grievous bodily harm. It was at that time perfectly lawful to shoot an escaping felon (a felon was a person convicted of a felony, i.e., a serious crime—see Introduction). Stealing wood from a forest was not a felony, but by virtue of a statute two convictions of stealing wood from a forest would render a third theft a felony. W had such previous convictions and was therefore a felon. On an objective view of the facts what the accused had done was perfectly lawful, i.e., he had shot someone who was in fact a felon and therefore someone whom he was entitled to apprehend in that way. It could therefore be claimed that this was not an unlawful infliction of a wound. One of the 'circumstances' of the offence was not established. It appeared that as in the case of *Deller* the accused should be acquitted. The conviction however was affirmed. In the words of Pollock CB at p. 359 (emphasis added):

> The [person fleeing from the forest] not having committed a felony *known to the prisoner* at the time when he fired, the latter was not justified in firing at [that person]; and having no justifiable cause, he was guilty of shooting at [that person] with intent to do him grievous bodily harm, and the conviction is right.

The case determines that an element in an offence which amounts to a 'circumstance' which can be negated by the establishing of acts of justification or of general defences requires that an accused is aware of the facts which give rise to the justification or defence. Had Dadson known this was a third-time felon he would have been justified in shooting him, but he did not know that at the time he pulled the trigger.

In the scenario, if Donald had been killed by Rex while Donald was in the act of attempting to kill Sarah, then the killing of Donald by Rex would possibly have been lawful (see *R* v *Duffy* [1967] 1 QB 63 and para. 6.6.1) and therefore not within the requirement that the killing be unlawful. To negate this circumstance Rex would have to be aware of the fact or honestly believe (see para. 6.5.4) that Donald was attempting to kill his daughter. It appears that *Deller* and *Dadson* are in conflict, because of their different conclusions as to guilt, for it can be argued that in neither case was the entire *actus reus* of the respective offences established. Logically both should have been convicted or both acquitted. This is to misunderstand the two cases. What these authorities clearly establish is that the absence of an element of an offence will always provide a specific defence to any crime.

However, an element within an offence which is nullified by establishing independent acts of justification or general defences requires an additional mental element on the part of an individual—he must be aware of the existence of the grounds establishing the particular justification or defence. It is only in such a situation that the justification or defence becomes operative and removes the relevant element (or 'circumstance') of the particular offence. The different decisions in the cases of *Deller* and *Dadson* can be justified alone on the grounds considered above. However, there are in addition strong policy reasons for the different conclusions as to guilt. The law and society can permit the acquittal of individuals like Deller without endorsing or encouraging criminal activity. Furthermore the principle of *Deller* helps the promotion of the policy that only those who are clearly and unambiguously transgressing the criminal law should suffer conviction and punishment. In cases such as *Dadson* it does not seem unreasonable to require individuals who willingly inflict harm upon others to justify their actions other than by fortuitous events outside their control and of which they are ignorant.

1.7 CONSEQUENCES AS AN ELEMENT IN THE ACTUS REUS OF AN OFFENCE

An individual's act or omission can within the context of a set of circumstances constitute the *actus reus* of an offence. Certain crimes require an additional element, that the individual's act or omission results in certain consequences. Such crimes have been considered *supra* and are known as result crimes. In the scenario Donald's murder and the criminal damage caused by Edward and John are result crimes. The *actus reus* of murder has already been considered in this context. The *actus reus* of the offence of criminal damage requires not only a positive act (or in one of the cases in the scenario an omission) to take place within the relevant circumstances but also that the conduct results in or causes physical damage to property.

1.8 THE ACTUS REUS MUST BE CAUSED BY THE CONDUCT OR OMISSION OF AN INDIVIDUAL

It is frequently forgotten that an accused's acts or omissions must not only take place within the prescribed circumstances of an offence, but also that (in the case of result crimes) the consequences of such an offence must have been brought about by those acts or omissions. In all result crimes therefore it must be demonstrated that an individual's conduct or omission has caused the consequences prohibited by the particular offence. Two unusual cases will illustrate this point. In *R* v *White* [1910] 2 KB 124 the accused had put poison into a wineglass containing a lemonade beverage. He intended this to be drunk by his mother. She was found dead with the glass on a small table which was by her side. She had not drunk from the glass (no trace of poison was found in her body). The cause of death was probably due to 'syncope' or 'heart failure'. In any event the quantity of poison in the glass was insufficient to have caused death. The accused was convicted of attempted murder. (For a full discussion of attempts in criminal law see chapter 5.) He could not have been convicted of the full offence, the reason being that though the accused had intended by his actions to bring about the *actus reus* of the offence of murder, one element, namely, the death of the intended victim, his mother, had not been caused or brought about by his conduct. In *R* v *Hensler* (1870) 22 LT 691 the accused sent letters to another begging money and claiming he was a distressed widow. The recipient of the letter knew the falsity of these claims. He nevertheless sent money to the accused. Though the accused was convicted of attempting to obtain money by false pretences, he could not be convicted of the full offence. This was because he had not brought about one essential element of the *actus reus*. The recipient of the letter had not been deceived by the false pretences.

1.9 THE ISSUE OF CAUSATION

It must be established that in cases of result crimes the individual's conduct has brought about the consequences prohibited by the particular offence. This issue of causation is applicable to all result crimes though it has mostly been considered in the light of the crime of murder. Can an individual whose conduct

Scenario

sets in course a train of events, which if uninterrupted could lead to potential criminal consequences claim he is no longer responsible for those consequences, if they are in whole or in part brought about by the intervening acts of others and/or by events over which the individual has no control, i.e., can an individual maintain that in such cases the chain of causation has been broken?

In the case of *R v Jordan* (1956) 40 Cr App R 152 the accused was charged with the murder of the deceased by stabbing him. The stab wound had penetrated the deceased's intestine in two places but his life was not in danger. In fact at the time of death this wound had almost healed. While in hospital the deceased had been treated with Terramycin, an antibiotic. It had become apparent that he was intolerant of this drug. This treatment was nevertheless persisted with.

The deceased was also subjected to the intravenous introduction of abnormal quantities of liquid. His lungs had become waterlogged and pulmonary oedema developed. This resulted in broncho-pneumonia. It was from this condition that he died. It was claimed by the defence that his death was the result of the medical treatment and not the stab wound inflicted by the accused. The chain of causation had been broken, and the accused on this basis was not responsible for the death of the deceased. The court was, however, 'disposed to accept it as the law that death resulting from any normal treatment employed to deal with [an injury resulting from a serious crime] may be regarded as caused by [that] injury' (at p. 157). Beyond this the court was not prepared to lay down any general test as to when causal connection between the infliction of a wound and death could be established or broken. The court accepted the medical treatment in the case had not been normal—on the facts of the case it had been 'palpably wrong'—and these matters produced the symptoms discovered at the post-mortem examination which were the direct and immediate cause of death, namely, the pneumonia resulting from the condition of oedema which was found (at p. 158). In *Jordan* there were sufficient unusual circumstances operating to permit the claim that there had been a break in the chain of causation.

That this case did not lay down a general rule was emphasised in the case of *R v Smith* [1959] 2 QB 35. The accused, a private soldier, stabbed the deceased in a barrack-room brawl. The injuries sustained by the deceased were serious, one of his lungs had been pierced and he was haemorrhaging. The deceased on being carried to the medical reception station was dropped several times. He was given a transfusion of saline solution which proved unsuccessful. When he had breathing difficulties he was given oxygen and artificial respiration. With regard to the deceased's medical condition the treatment the deceased received was 'thoroughly bad' and may have affected his chances of recovery. There was evidence that the deceased's kind of injury tended to heal. If proper medical treatment had been given his chances of recovery would have been as high as 75 per cent. The court considered that the case of *Jordan* 'was a very particular case depending upon its exact facts' (at p. 43). The general principle with regard to the issue of the chain of causation was (at pp. 42–3):

> that if at the time of death the original wound is still an operating cause and a substantial cause, then the death can properly be said to be the result of the wound, albeit that some other cause of death is also operating. Only if it can be said that the original wounding is merely the setting in which another cause

operates can it be said that the death does not result from the wound. Putting it in another way, only if the second cause is so overwhelming as to make the original wound merely part of the history can it be said that the death does not flow from the wound.

In general, therefore, where an individual's conduct or omission has set in course a train of events which may result in consequences forbidden by a criminal offence, he may avoid any potential criminal liability for those consequences only when the actions of others or supervening events are such that the individual's original conduct or omission ceased to be an operative or effective cause in bringing about the relevant consequences, i.e., that the consequences have come about as a result of events or the actions of others which have rendered all previous possible causes redundant. Notwithstanding the requirement in *Smith* that the acts of an individual need to be a 'substantial' cause in bringing about the consequences forbidden by a criminal offence, it appears that this has never been insisted upon. It is only necessary for an individual's actions to be an operative or effective cause in producing the prohibited consequences for the chain of causation to be maintained. In *R* v *Malcherek* and *R* v *Steel* [1981] 2 All ER 422, cases involving victims of violent assaults who were surviving upon life-support machines, the switching off of those machines was not the operative cause of the victims' deaths but the original infliction of the wounds. The chain of causation is not broken in such cases. In *R* v *Blaue* [1975] 3 All ER 466 the deceased, the victim of a brutal assault by the accused, refused medical treatment being a Jehovah's witness and opposed to conventional medicine. She died as a result of this refusal but this did not break the chain of causation, for the assault remained an operative and effective cause of the death, though this case can be explained on the ground that an assailant takes his victim as he finds him with all his attendant characteristics. The question of causation raises itself in the case of Donald's death. Rex has inflicted severe injuries upon him. These injuries may well be an effective cause in Donald's death. The authorities determine that the question of causation is essentially one of fact (see Murphy, *A Practical Approach to Evidence*, para 1.5.1), i.e., a matter for the jury, though the judge has the power to remove the issue of causation where appropriate from it. It would be for the jury to determine whether the events after the infliction of the injuries by Rex upon Donald were such as to render Rex's conduct no longer an operative and effective cause of Donald's death.

The matters to consider are the carrying of Donald out of the house and his being dropped. The failure of Marian to provide prompt medical assistance for him together with Wilma's well-meaning but harmful administering of brandy are no doubt major contributions to Donald's demise. Apart from Wilma's intervention and Marian's failure to seek medical assistance for Donald, Rex has been involved in all the possible causes of Donald's death even those subsequent to the beating he originally inflicted. A reasonable jury could reasonably come to the conclusion that Rex's infliction of injuries upon Donald remained an operative and effective cause of the death, and that the chain of causation was not broken. This issue brings to light the all too often forgotten element of which every student of criminal law must be aware. This is the influence of 'public policy'.

Here public policy dictates that persons should not be able to avoid the legal consequences of their criminal acts simply through the fortuitous intervention of events, circumstances, acts or omissions of third parties. The exception being where the intervention in effect is so overwhelming as to render all prior events superfluous.

1.10 SUMMARY

On examination the scenario discloses the *actus reus* of several offences. Some of these offences are statutory; others have their origins in common law. The constituents of these offences may be determined by reference to the actual wording of the statute and/or the pronouncements of the judges contained in the reported case law. Though criminal offences differ considerably in their actual composition, they share certain common features. The first feature is that generally offences require both external elements known to the law as the *actus reus* of an offence and an accompanying state of mind from the potential criminal known to the law as *mens rea*. The *actus reus* of all offences consist in whole or in part of acts or omissions of an individual generally together with, where specified, surrounding circumstances and consequences. Certain offences require only the establishing of a state of affairs. All offences can be analysed and broken down into various combinations of these factors.

When this analysis is applied to each of the offences disclosed in the scenario the crimes concerned show an underlying uniformity of structure.

(a) *Rape* (a conduct crime, see para. 1.5 onwards). Source: *statutory (Sexual Offences (Amendment) Act 1976, s. 1(1))*. The offence requires that a man have unlawful sexual intercourse with a woman who at the time of intercourse does not consent to it; and *(at the time he knows that she does not consent to the intercourse or he is reckless as to whether she consents to it)*

The actus reus of the offence is composed of:

(i) *A positive act* (see para. 1.2 onwards):

(1) The act required is the act of sexual intercourse.

(ii) *Circumstances* (see para. 1.5 onwards). These include:

(1) The assailant is a man.
(2) That the act of intercourse is unlawful.
(3) That the act of intercourse is with a woman.
(4) That the woman does not consent to the act of intercourse.

(b) *Murder* (a result crime, see para. 1.7 onwards). Source: *common law*. The offence requires the unlawful killing of a human being *(with malice aforethought)* under the Queen's peace, death following within a year and a day of the infliction of the injury.

The actus reus of the offence is composed of

(i) *A positive act* (see para. 1.2 onwards).

    (1) The act required is a killing (see para. 1.2 onwards).

(ii) *Circumstances* (see para. 1.5 onwards). These include:

    (1) That the killing be unlawful (but see para. 1.5 onwards where the view that this is not a true circumstance of the offence is discussed).
    (2) The victim must be a human being.
    (3) The deceased must at the time of death have been under the protection of the Queen's peace.
    (4) The death must occur within a year and a day of the infliction of the injuries by an accused upon the deceased.

(iii) *Consequences*: (see para. 1.7 onwards).

    (1) The death of the deceased must be a result of the accused's acts or omissions (see para. 1.8 and above).

(c) *Theft* (a conduct crime, see para. 1.5). Source: *statutory (Theft Act 1968, s. 1(1))*, which requires *(the dishonest)* appropriation of property belonging to another *(with the intention of permanently depriving the other of it)*.
The actus reus of the offence is composed of:

(i) *A positive act* (see para. 1.2 onwards).

    (1) The act required is the act of appropriation (see para. 1.2).

(ii) *Circumstances* (see para. 1.5). The circumstances are:

    (1) That the act of appropriation be in respect of property which does not belong to the appropriator.

(d) *Criminal damage* (a result crime, see para. 1.7 onwards). Source: *statutory (Criminal Damage Act 1971, s. 1(1))*. The offence requires that an individual: without lawful excuse destroys or damages any property belonging to another *(intending to destroy or damage any property or being reckless as to whether any such property would be destroyed or damaged)*.
The actus reus of the offence is composed of:

(i) *A positive act* (see para. 1.2 onwards):

    (1) The destruction or damage of property.

(ii) *Circumstances* (see para. 1.5 onwards):

    (1) That the act be without lawful excuse. By the Criminal Damage Act 1971, s. 5, the element of without lawful excuse is partially defined. The section

provides a set of circumstances which if established negate this element of the offence. For example, the concept of lawfulness can be established and the element of unlawful excuse nullified if an individual destroys property believing that the owner would consent to the destruction. Section 5 provides particular statutory defences which are applicable to this offence only, without prejudice to the general defences (see chapter 6) which are always available to anyone accused of this offence or any offence.

(2) The property must belong to someone other than the individual damaging it.

(iii) *Consequences* (see para. 1.7 onwards):

(1) The damage or destruction of property must result from the accused's conduct or omission to act.

(e) *Being in charge of a motor vehicle while unfit to drive* (state of affairs offence, see para. 1.4). Source: *statutory (Road Traffic Act 1972, s. 5(2))*. The offence requires that: a person who when in charge of a motor vehicle which is on the road or other public place, is unfit to drive through drink or drugs.

The actus reus of the offence consists entirely of a state of affairs, a set of circumstances only. How the state of affairs has come about does not form an element in the offence (see para. 1.4 onwards).

All the elements of an *actus reus* must be established before there is any possibility of a criminal conviction. Also it must be proved that the accused was responsible for bringing the *actus reus* of an offence into existence (except possibly in states of affairs offences where conduct or lack of it is irrelevant as is usually the state of mind of that person at the time).

Criminal responsibility generally requires that not only are the external elements of an offence established but that the individual concerned has a certain state of mind towards his conduct and the circumstances and consequences of an *actus reus*. This is the element of an offence known as the *mens rea*. This will be discussed in chapter 2. The offences analysed above have had their elements which are the *mens rea* of the particular offences italicised and bracketed, to distinguish these elements from the *actus reus* of each offence. All of them require the element of *mens rea* except the Road Traffic Act 1972 offence. This offence is completed and the accused is liable for it with proof only of an *actus reus*. Such an offence is known as an offence of strict liability; the nature of these crimes will be discussed in chapter 3. It will be clear from this chapter that the majority of criminal offences are created by statute. Equally important is that the significance and meaning of the words used in each statute should be clear, in order that the elements of the *actus reus* which must be proved in each circumstance can be fully appreciated.

1.11 QUESTIONS

1. What is the difference, if any, between circumstances within conduct crimes and the elements which comprise 'state of affairs' offences?

2. In a democratic society what useful function can state of affairs offences have in the criminal law? Should they be abolished?

3. Why is the mental element in the act of appropriation not part of the *mens rea* of the offence of theft?

4. Why is the requirement that a woman should not be consenting to an act of sexual intercourse an element of the *actus reus* and not the *mens rea* of an offence?

5. If an individual publishes an obscene book, is the fact of obscenity a circumstance or a consequence?

2

Mens Rea

2.1 INTRODUCTION

Central to one of the most fundamental aspects of traditional English criminal law is the notion that no one should be punished in criminal proceedings unless the person be proved to have a guilty or blameworthy state of mind. From very early times this concept was stated succinctly in the Latin maxim, *'actus non facit reum nisi mens sit rea'*: 'An act does not make a man guilty of a crime unless his mind be also guilty'. In modern times even in the law the use of Latin has become unfashionable and this element of guilt or blameworthiness has come to be referred to as the internal or mental element of an offence. However, as stated above *'actus reus'* and *'mens rea'* are convenient shorthand and for that reason will be used throughout this book. *Mens rea*, together with the *actus reus* (external or factual elements of an offence discussed in the previous chapter), must generally be proved if a conviction is to be obtained. Virtually every common law offence (public nuisance and criminal contempt of court aside), by tradition, required proof beyond reasonable doubt that the accused was responsible for the *actus reus* of an offence and that also he had the requisite blameworthy state of mind which coincided with the *actus reus*.

Much of the history of England is concerned with the struggle to obtain and maintain the liberty or freedom of the individual within society. Consequently wherever an individual's liberty is threatened by official action as happens when the machinery of the criminal law starts to operate against someone, the judges have acted to check that such a deprivation is fairly warranted. They stated that the prosecution must prove not only that the prohibited facts, consequences, events or omissions occurred and that the accused was responsible for them but also that the accused had a criminal state of mind at that time. That was the traditional position maintained by the judges and to a large extent is still the position. Today, however, there are instances where a person who does not think about what he is doing at all, but should have, will be held liable and there are many offences which have their origins not in common law but in a statute created by Parliament and which appear to be absolute or strict liability offences. This means that the state of mind of the accused appears to be irrelevant with regard to at least one of the elements of the *actus reus* of an offence (see chapter 3). In some instances these modern offences disregard the old tradition by allowing an individual to be deprived of his liberty if the prosecution can prove only the *actus reus*; i.e., that the accused did the prohibited act, or omitted to do what was prescribed or in some instances was found to be involved in a prohibited state of affairs.

With regard to these offences created by statute it is often the case that the statute will use stock words and phrases which expressly or by implication indicate that *mens rea* must be proved. Any words denoting that a certain state of mind is essential to the commission of the crime generally mean that *mens rea* must be proved. Words indicative of the requirement of *mens rea* are 'knowingly', 'maliciously', 'wilfully', 'dishonestly', 'malice', 'intention', 'recklessness', etc. As chapter 3 shows, the inclusion of such words will not guarantee that a section within a statute will be construed as an offence which requires *mens rea* as to all the elements of an offence. Problems also arise for the judiciary when a statute fails to include any of these or similar key, stock words and is silent as to whether or not *mens rea* is an element of that offence. How the judiciary deal with these issues is discussed in the next chapter.

For the present it is sufficient to say that *mens rea* must be proved in relation to virtually all common law offences or generally in relation to serious offences created by statute. When it comes to definition *mens rea* becomes a slippery eel—both difficult to grasp and endowed with the ability to tie itself and the student in complex knots.

2.2 EVIL OR WICKED MIND

It would be nice to be able to say that *mens rea* or the internal element of an offence is simply an evil and wicked mind which invariably must be proved to obtain a conviction. Today it is not clearly an invariable requirement in every instance and where it is required to be proved it is no longer satisfactory simply to think of it as a wicked or evil mind. The inadequacy of that view is highlighted by the not uncommon offence of manslaughter (death of another) caused by gross negligence on the part of the accused. The words guilty mind imply a positive state of mind, negligence is the opposite of that, it is mere inattention or no state of mind at all. But, in this instance, if the fact of causing death and the negligent 'state of mind' are proved, to the extent that it warrants punishment the accused will be able to be convicted and sentenced for manslaughter.

The complexity associated with defining *mens rea* arises from the varieties of states of mind that it is possible for a human being to have in relation to any circumstances, consequence, event or activity and the variety of synonyms which the English language provides to describe these various possible states of mind.

In *DPP for Northern Ireland* v *Lynch* [1975] AC 653 at p. 688 Lord Simon of Glaisdale while dealing with the central issue of duress spoke in passing of the general difficulty that exists in relation to statutory offences because of the number of words used to denote a mental element and the numerous meanings attributed to those words. His words are appropriate not just to ascertaining the mental element in statutory offences but also in relation to ascertaining the mental element or *mens rea* in English criminal law generally, he said:

> A principal difficulty in this branch of the law is the chaotic terminology, whether in judgments, academic writings or statutes. Will, volition, motive, purpose, object, view, intention, intent, specific intent or intention, wish, desire, necessity, coercion, compulsion, duress—such terms, which do indeed

Mens Rea

overlap in certain contexts, seem frequently to be used interchangeably, without definition, and regardless that in some cases the legal usage is a term of art differing from the popular usage. As if this were not enough, Latin expressions which are themselves ambiguous, and often overlap more than one of the English terms, have been freely used—especially *animus* and (most question-begging of all) *mens rea*.

Secondly complexity arises from the fact that the definition of *mens rea* varies from offence to offence and thirdly from the intervention of precedent and public policy.

It is these latter elements of precedent and public policy, which are the most difficult and yet which are the keys to understanding some of the most arcane mysteries of *mens rea*. They explain some of the anomalies which we will come across later in this chapter particularly in relation to the *mens rea* of murder.

2.3 STATES OF MIND

As indicated above, awareness, belief, consciousness, desire, deliberateness, dishonesty, foresight, heedlessness, knowledge, intent, intention, malice, recklessness, wickedness, wilfulness—all imply states of mind some of which are synonyms in the eye of the law, some of which are not. The actual state of mind of the accused at the time of the *actus reus* is vital and the subtle difference between the various possible states of mind and, of course, between those possibilities and that 'non-state of mind' called negligence, is of the utmost significance.

Primarily, and generally speaking, the aim of the criminal law is to hold responsible and subject to some legal penalty those persons who by their acts or omissions consciously and voluntarily behave in an antisocial manner or cause antisocial or proscribed events to occur. No right-thinking person in society would expect a mentally handicapped, retarded, deranged or insane person, or someone who is sleep-walking, to suffer penal consequences for any act or omission. Such persons and their state of mind when they behaved illegally or did a prohibited act are not considered blameworthy.

Voluntariness and various possible defences aside (see chapter 8), a sane person can have differing states of mind which may be legally blameworthy and attract penal consequences.

The scenario can be developed to illustrate the point. On hearing Rex and his wife Marian return to the house, Edward and John flee with the camera, jewellery and silver candlesticks which they have stolen. Assume that Rex sees them, snatches up his loaded shotgun and gives chase. A neighbour is on hand to witness the following possible events.

(a) Rex raises his shotgun, aims it at close range at Edward and John and pulls the trigger killing Edward. In this situation Rex can be said (defences aside) to have desired or wanted, or had as his deliberate aim, the death of Edward. It can be said that that is what Rex intended when he pointed the gun and pulled the trigger. To intend wilfully to do something which is prohibited is very blameworthy in our society. To intend in this sense wilfully or deliberately to kill another human being is one of, if not the most, serious of offences that it is possible to commit in our society. It is murder.

(b) Rex in pursuit is about to fire at Edward and John when, out of the corner of his eye he sees Alf, his next-door neighbour, coming through a hole in the front dividing fence. Rex calculates that although it will be a dangerous shot, provided Alf does not move quickly there should be little risk to him if Rex pulls the trigger. Rex goes ahead and fires. At that very moment Alf had tripped and fallen forward catching the full blast of Rex's shot, and is killed. Here, Rex did not seek or desire the death of Alf. On that basis he is less blameworthy than in the previous case, but he is still sufficiently blameworthy in the eye of the law to warrant the imposition of criminal liability. Rex, in this instance, has been reckless. He knew that there was a risk that Alf might be injured or killed but he went ahead and took that risk. The legal consequence of his recklessness despite the death of Alf cannot be a murder charge (see below for an explanation) but will probably be a charge of manslaughter.

(c) Rex fires one barrel of the shotgun at Edward and John but they escape unharmed. Rex returns to his home from his pursuit via the garden of his other neighbour, Tom. Tom sees Rex and goes to ask what has happened and to steady the wire fence which Rex must climb to reach his own property. To Tom's horror he sees that Rex has not broken the shotgun and that the safety catch is not on. At that moment Rex's foot slips, the gun jolts and goes off. Tom catches the full blast and is killed. Although it is open to debate, it is suggested that in this situation Rex would be less blameworthy than in the previous instances. Here he does not intend Tom's death and he has not been reckless or at least he has not been as reckless as in the previous situation where he knew there was a risk to Alf. Tom's death does not come about, for example, after Rex foresaw a specific risk to him but rather in consequence of a general possibility of harm arising through Rex's carelessness in failing to break the gun barrel. Rex has been negligent rather than reckless. The line, however, between these two concepts often is imperceptible but traditionally negligence is not deemed to be a blameworthy act except in a few restricted instances.

Intention, recklessness, negligence, these are the three basic blameworthy states of mind, proof of any one of which may satisfy the requirement of *mens rea* and when coupled with proof of an *actus reus*, may produce a conviction for that offence. We say proof of any of these three states of mind 'may satisfy' the *mens rea* requirement and 'may produce' a conviction, because of the second complicating factor mentioned above, that proof of a state of mind which would satisfy the *mens rea* requirement for one offence may not do so for another offence. This is illustrated in relation to negligence.

2.4 NEGLIGENCE

Of the three basic blameworthy 'states of mind', negligence is the most wide and objective and therefore in theory the most easy to prove. Proof, however, of a negligent 'state of mind' coupled with an *actus reus* will not make a person liable for every possible criminal offence. At common law a negligent 'state of mind' only was sufficient *mens rea*, if with that 'state of mind', the accused caused the death of another person and then only if the accused was exceptionally negligent. This is one limb of the offence of manslaughter which remains a common law

Mens Rea

offence (see chapter 7 for a discussion of the other limbs, e.g., causing death by an unlawful act). Today there are other offences for which proof of a negligent 'state of mind' will be sufficient *mens rea* such as driving without due care or attention contrary to s. 3 of the Road Traffic Act 1972.

The latter offence is an example of a modern crime created by statute. As such, they are not traditional common law offences and generally are of a far less serious nature and generally proof of simple negligence will suffice.

For the purposes of ascertaining *mens rea* in criminal law, negligence is deemed to be a state of mind even though it is really a state of unawareness or in effect a non-state of mind. Secondly negligence has two definitions depending on the context of the crime in question. On the one hand when it appears in relation to some statutory offences it may carry the same meaning as in the law of civil wrongs or torts. In that instance it means doing something which a prudent, reasonable man would not have done or refraining from doing what he would have done. In a crime such as driving without due care and attention under s. 3 of the Road Traffic Act 1972 that test of simple negligence would probably apply although the standard of proof expected in order to obtain a prosecution would be of a high standard, i.e., beyond reasonable doubt as opposed to the mere balance of probabilities expected in civil actions. In so far as manslaughter is concerned the *mens rea* requirement will be satisfied, if the prosecution are seeking to rely on the accused's negligence by proof of 'gross' negligence. Proof of simple negligence *per se* will not suffice.

In *R* v *Bateman* (1925) 94 LJ KB 791 (at p. 794) where a doctor was prosecuted for the death of a patient the Court of Criminal Appeal said:

> [T]he prosecution must prove the matters necessary to establish civil liability (except pecuniary loss), and, in addition, must satisfy the jury that the negligence or incompetence of the accused went beyond a mere matter of compensation and showed such disregard for the life and safety of others as to amount to a crime against the State and conduct deserving punishment.

In *R* v *Finney* (1874) 12 Cox CC 625 the accused was charged with manslaughter. He was an attendant at a lunatic asylum. He had bathed the deceased and released the water. He intended to put in clean water and had asked the deceased, who was in sufficient possession of his faculties, to get out of the bath. The accused's attention was distracted by another patient and while so distracted he turned on the hot water tap by mistake. The patient who had not yet vacated the bath was scalded and died. Lush J directed the jury on the issue of gross negligence in these terms (at p. 626):

> To render a person liable for neglect of duty there must be such a degree of culpability as to amount to gross negligence on his part. . . . It is not every little trip or mistake that will make a man so liable. . . . Now, if the prisoner, seeing that the man was in the bath, had knowingly turned on the tap and turned on the hot instead of the cold water, I should have said there was gross negligence, for he ought to have looked to see; but from his own account he had told the deceased to get out and thought he had got out. If you think that indicates gross carelessness, then you should find the prisoner guilty of manslaughter;

but if you think it inadvertence not amounting to culpability, or what is properly termed an accident, then the prisoner is not liable.

Though the state of mind of a man who is negligent or 'grossly' negligent is identical, the difference between a negligent man and one who is grossly negligent lies in the existence of various factors which make the lack of prudence and reasonableness in a man's conduct more blameworthy in the latter case. A man who by his training or by experience fails to act in various circumstances may be 'grossly' negligent whereas a man lacking such training or experience may in such cases be merely negligent in failing to act prudently and reasonably. Other factors to consider are the surrounding circumstances, the more the surrounding circumstances of a situation should indicate to a man the need to act in a particular way, the failure to take heed of such circumstances and to act in response to those circumstances may if they are sufficiently serious and numerous render an act not negligent but 'grossly' negligent. It is ultimately a matter of degree. Finally in *Andrews* v *DPP* [1937] AC 576 Lord Atkin suggested that 'reckless' was the adjective that most nearly coincided with the very high degree of negligence required to prove 'gross negligence'.

To sum up, in order to obtain a conviction for gross-negligence manslaughter the prosecution must prove the *actus reus* (the death of a human being) together with the *mens rea* which in this common law crime alone may be satisfied by proof of negligence, but proof of recklessness or intention would equally satisfy the *mens rea* requirement, this is because negligence is the lowest common denominator, the least amount of blameworthiness which will make the accused liable for that offence alone. Clearly proof of a more blameworthy state of mind must equally be sufficient. You have simply surpassed the minimum requirement. Obviously if the prosecution have enough evidence to prove either recklessness or intention then the criminal charge may have been different. If the prosecution prove intention, then the accused could be charged with and convicted of murder. Should the prosecution in such a situation choose for whatever reason to charge manslaughter then proof of intention to kill or reckless disregard for death will produce a conviction for manslaughter but more significantly proof of gross negligence also would do so if necessary. This will not work in reverse. If the offence in question requires proof of intention then proof of that state of mind alone will suffice, proof of recklessness or negligence will not.

2.5 BASIC AND SPECIFIC INTENTION

Leaving aside manslaughter and those statutory offences permitting proof of negligence to satisfy the *mens rea* requirement, all the remaining common law and statutory offences fall into two categories in so far as proof of *mens rea* is concerned. The two categories are:

(a) crimes of specific or ulterior intent, and
(b) crimes of basic or general intent.

In relation to those criminal offences which fall into the former category, i.e.,

Mens Rea

crimes of specific or ulterior intent, the *mens rea* requirement will only be satisfied by proof beyond reasonable doubt that the accused intended to commit the *actus reus*, and in the case of crimes of ulterior intent by proof that the accused *intended* to do some further prohibited act in addition, or ulterior, to the *actus reus* and his intentional (or reckless) commission of the *actus reus* of the offence charged. For crimes in both these categories the position is the same as each requires proof of an extra special intention, and proof of recklessness in relation to that special requirement will be insufficient to obtain a prosecution. It goes without saying that proof of that even weaker and less blameworthy 'state of mind' called negligence will likewise be insufficient. Today since the decision in *R v Moloney* [1985] 2 WLR 648 (see paras. 2.6.2 and 7.6.2) murder, which is a common law offence, has been reaffirmed as a crime of specific intent and the doubts concerning this raised by *Hyam's* case (see paras. 2.6.1 and 7.6.2) have now been dispelled. Murder is the clearest example of a crime of specific intent for all purposes. An accused will be liable only if the prosecution prove he did the act (intentionally or recklessly) which killed or seriously injured the victim *and* that the accused *intended* either to kill or cause such injury. Certain offences of this type, however, are best defined by the term 'ulterior intent offences' (see Lord Simon of Glaisdale in *DPP v Morgan* [1976] AC 182, as modififed in *DPP v Majewski* [1977] AC 443, and para. 6.3.8) because the intent that has to be proved goes beyond the *actus reus*. Examples of ulterior intent offences are burglary with intent under s. 9(1)(a) of the Theft Act 1968 (see chapter 8) and destroying or damaging property with intent to endanger the life of another under s. 1(2)(b) of the Criminal Damage Act 1971 (see *R v Orpin* [1980] 1 WLR 1050, *Metropolitan Police Commissioner* v *Caldwell* [1982] AC 341 and para. 2.7.3). Burglary as defined by the Theft Act 1968, s. 9(1)(a), is defined to include entry into a building by a trespasser with intent to rape any woman therein, or to steal or damage any property therein (see chapter 8). The *actus reus* of burglary has three limbs to be proved (a) entry, (b) of a building and (c) as a trespasser. The *mens rea* of the offence will be satisfied not simply by proof of either intentional or reckless entry of a building as a trespasser but by proof of that, together with proof of the additional specific/ulterior *intent* to rape, thieve or cause damage. The best examples of crimes of specific/ulterior intent are statutory. A close reading of the words of the statute indicate precisely what must be proved. For example, the wording of the Offences against the Person Act 1861, s. 18 (as amended), is as follows:

> Whosoever shall unlawfully and maliciously by any means whatsoever wound or cause any grievous bodily harm to any person, with intent to do some grievous bodily harm to any person, or with intent to resist or prevent the lawful apprehension or detainer of any person, shall be guilty of felony, and being convicted thereof shall be liable to be kept in penal servitude for life. ['Liable to be kept in penal servitude for life now means: liable to be sentenced to imprisonment for life.]

To be found guilty of this offence the accused not only must have intentionally or recklessly wounded (see chapter 7) the victim but he must be proved to have so wounded *intending* to cause grievous bodily harm to the victim (or *intending* to prevent the lawful apprehension of any person). The prosecution may prove that the wound was caused recklessly but that is not enough, in this instance, they are required to go on and show that the intentionally or recklessly caused wound was caused with either of the intents specified. As to this element of the offence proof of intention alone will be sufficient. Proof of recklessness as to whether or not grievous bodily harm was caused will not suffice. The additional element of intent to cause grievous bodily harm or aid another to escape lawful apprehension does not relate to the *actus reus* of wounding, it is an intention additional to and beyond the actual *actus reus*.

Other examples of crimes of specific intent possibly occurring in the scenario are theft and any attempts to commit substantive criminal offences. In the case of theft the Theft Act 1968, s. 1, defines the offence as the dishonest taking of property with intent permanently to deprive another of it, in whose possession it rightfully belongs (see chapter 8). The taking may be intentional or reckless but in addition the prosecution must show the specific intention to permanently deprive by so doing.

A final example of specific intent can be found in the law relating to attempts (see chapter 5). Suffice to say at this point that there is no offence of attempt *per se*. To convict of attempt the law predicates that the accused attempts to commit a recognised substantive offence. For example, the accused must have attempted to rob, murder, rape, damage property, assault or whatever. That is the *actus reus*. The *mens rea* is constituted by showing that the act of actually attempting was done intentionally or recklessly, together with an *intent* to commit the particular substantive offence in question: robbery, murder, rape, etc.

All other offences requiring proof of *mens rea* which on the one hand do not fall in the special category of specifically requiring proof of intention and on the other hand do not fall into the other special category (at the other end of the spectrum) of being able to be proved by evidence of negligence, are offences of basic intent. This simply means that the prosecution having established the *actus reus* may obtain a conviction by proving either intention or recklessness. In relation to crimes of basic intent it is not essential to show a distinction between intention and recklessness because proof of both or either will amount to proof of *mens rea*, e.g., in relation to s. 1(2)(b) of the Criminal Damage Act 1971 mentioned above, provided the accused is charged in the alternative with being reckless as to whether the life of another would be endangered in addition to intending by destruction or damage to property to endanger life, it must be a crime of basic intent because then proof of either state of mind will suffice for a conviction.

To sum up, in the case of certain statutory (generally relatively trivial) offences proof of simple negligence will satisfy the requirement of *mens rea*. In the case of manslaughter proof of gross negligence resulting in the death of another (or proof of recklessness as to death or proof of intention to cause death) will suffice (although if it was obvious that intention to kill could be proved at the outset the prosecution would have charged murder not manslaughter).

In the case of crimes of basic intent only proof of either recklessness or intention will suffice. In the case of crimes of specific/ulterior intent, only proof of intention will suffice to obtain a conviction.

The explanation of negligence above as an aspect of *mens rea* has now been complicated further by the relatively recent redefining of the definitions of intention and of recklessness in particular.

2.6 INTENTION

If negligence is the least form of blameworthiness then the clearest and most serious form of blameworthiness must be the intentional or deliberate doing of something which is prohibited or the intentional or deliberate omission to do something which the accused was bound to do. Historically that intention was synonymous with an evil or wicked state of mind because the accused can be said to have wanted, desired, sought after or aimed at the forbidden consequence for its own sake. The words 'want' and 'desire' are confusing because they can also indicate motive. If the accused had as his conscious aim to behave in a prohibited way (though an accused does not have to appreciate that his conduct is a potential breach of the criminal law) or to bring about a prohibited consequence then, irrespective of his motive, he can be said to be acting intentionally. This is the first and foremost definition of intention for the purposes of *mens rea*.

A clear example of the application of this restricted definition of intention can be seen in *Chandler* v *DPP* [1964] AC 763 and in the case of *R* v *Steane* [1947] KB 997. In the latter case the accused, a Briton living in Germany, made broadcasts which assisted the enemy during the Second World War. The court held that he had no intention to assist the enemy, that his only intention was to save himself and his family from the horrors of incarceration in a concentration camp. What the judge referred to as Mr Steane's intention was strictly his motive. The issue of voluntariness aside, Mr Steane consciously, deliberately or intentionally made the broadcasts. His motive was not to help the enemy but to avoid reprisals but if he made the broadcasts knowing that they would assist the enemy that should have been all that mattered. He had acted intentionally. His motive for doing so should have been irrelevant to the issue of his liability and been considered only in relation to what sentence, if any, his offence might warrant, after defences (in this instance the defence of duress), had been taken into account. The narrow concept of intention (acting deliberately knowing what the result will be) has received judicial approval on a number of occasions and has sometimes been defined as 'direct intention'.

Intention, however, has been given a second, wider definition. If the accused can be shown to be aware that he is acting in a prohibited way (though appreciation that it is contrary to the criminal law is not required), then he can be said to be acting intentionally, likewise if he is aware that a consequence will follow inevitably from his behaviour then that consequence can be said to be intended.

An example of such an intention is provided by the scenario when Edward and John are escaping from the scene of the crime, i.e., Rex's house. Their intention in the sense of their desired aim (i.e. their motive) is to evade capture by Rex and his neighbour Alf (who are standing in the driveway) or by the police. They see that while escaping in Rex's motor car they must speed down his narrow driveway or they will be stopped by Rex and Alf. They are aware that to achieve their liberty they must drive on regardless and the inevitable consequence will be that Rex and/or Alf will be killed or seriously injured. The law has recognised that in such cases Edward and John may be regarded as having intended to injure or kill Rex and/or Alf. This form of intention has been called 'oblique intention'. Its existence was recognised in *Hyam* v *DPP* [1975] AC 55 (see below) and its possible applicability to the offence of attempt was recognised in *R* v *Mohan* [1976] QB 1, and to the offence of wounding with intent to cause grievous bodily harm in *R* v *Belfon* [1976] 3 All ER 46 (see also *R* v *Pearman* [1985] RTR 39). This form of intention, though generally applicable to many offences, is not yet universal and it appears that certain offences may require a direct intention only (see *R* v *Steane* [1947] KB 997). Consequences are only intended in the first sense (direct intent), no matter how inevitable they may be from the accused's conduct, if they are his conscious or deliberate aim, goal or object. That definition makes no allowance for indifference.

The second, wider definition (oblique intent) has no connection with or dependence on the accused's conscious aim or object and that in turn has no necessary connection with the motive of the accused. In the case of oblique intent, if and only if he is aware that a forbidden consequence is certain to follow from his conduct will that consequence in effect be deemed to be intended.

2.6.1 Intention in murder

In relation to murder, however, the concept of intention appeared to have been further extended in what was for 10 years the leading case on the *mens rea* of murder, i.e., *Hyam* v *DPP* [1975] AC 55. Although a significant aspect of that case, namely the defining of *mens rea* for murder, has been overruled in effect by the House of Lords recent decision in *R* v *Moloney* [1985] 2 WLR 648, *Hyam* (like *DPP* v *Smith* [1961] AC 290, see para. 2.14) remains significant in that it helps understand what is, and what is not, intention in the eye of the law. Mrs Hyam, who was having an affair with a man, believed that she had a rival for his affections. She went to the house of this other woman and having poured petrol through the letter-box in the front door of that house she then set light to it. In the ensuing conflagration her supposed rival and one child escaped but two of that woman's children were killed. Mrs Hyam maintained that her purpose in setting fire to the petrol simply was to scare off her supposed rival. She claimed she did not want to kill anyone, not even her rival, let alone that woman's children.

If the only consequences which are to be said to be intentional and therefore blameworthy, are those which are the conscious aims or objects of the accused's conduct or where she is aware that certain consequences are the unavoidable result of her conduct then irrespective of how clearly Mrs Hyam foresaw death as a possible consequence of her activities she cannot be said to have acted intentionally because she did not want death to happen, nor was she aware that the death of the children was the inevitable consequence of her actions. At most she was indifferent as to whether or not death occurred. Her conscious aim or object was to frighten her rival. That was the goal of the enterprise. If, however, only consequences which are the deliberate aim of the accused, or which she is aware are the inevitable result of her conduct, are to be classed as intentional then no liability would attach to those situations where the accused's chance of succeeding in a prohibited aim or object (whether desired or not) is but a possibility which has been foreseen by her as highly probable. Why should such a

Mens Rea

person escape the most serious possible liability simply because the prospect of bringing about a prohibited goal is only a probability even though she has clearly foreseen it? The House of Lords in *Hyam* appeared to determine that in so far as murder is concerned an individual acted intentionally when it was foreseen by that individual that his or her conduct would have consequences which would be 'highly probable', namely, that death or grievous bodily harm was highly probable. After *Hyam* it was thought that in such cases the individual concerned could be said to intend those consequences as a matter of substantive law.

At first sight this multiple definition of intention (direct, oblique and foresight of high probability) for the purposes of proving *mens rea* appears to be summed up by Lord Diplock in the notorious blasphemy case *Whitehouse* v *Lemon* [1979] AC 617 at p. 638 in the following words:

> [W]here intention to produce a particular result was a necessary element of an offence, no distinction was to be drawn in law between the state of mind of one who did an act because he desired it to produce that particular result and the state of mind of one who, when he did the act, was aware that it was likely to produce that result but was prepared to take the risk that it might do so, in order to achieve some other purpose which provided his motive for doing what he did. It is by now well-settled law that both states of mind constitute 'intention' in the sense in which that expression is used in the definition of a crime whether at common law or in a statute. Any doubts on this matter were finally laid to rest by the decision of this House in *Hyam* v *Director of Public Prosecutions* [1975] AC 55.

But two things should be noted. First his lordship seems to equate oblique intention with what was the special intention apparently applicable only to murder arising out of *Hyam's* case. They are similar but not the same. For oblique intent the consequence is foreseen as inevitable, for what was *Hyam* intent the consequence had to be foreseen as highly probable. Secondly by his use of the words 'prepared to take the risk that it may do so' rather than 'foresight that it may do so', Lord Diplock was stating what had been surmised but not stated previously that foresight of consequences as a definition of intention in reality was recklessness being called by another name. As can be seen later in this chapter, one form of recklessness requires foresight of consequences. You can distinguish between oblique intention, what was foresight of consequences in intention (for murder) and foresight of consequences in recklessness (for crimes of basic intent) only on the basis of degrees of probability. It is all a question of degree and it is precisely because it is dependent on so vague and shifting a criterion that Lord Bridge of Harwich in *R* v *Moloney* [1985] 2 WLR 648 (with whom the other Law Lords agreed) declared that foresight of consequences of an act must not be equated with intent to do it. Today intention only exists where the prohibited consequence is proved to be the person's aim, object, purpose, desire or goal or where that individual was aware that his conduct would have the inevitable consequence forbidden by a penal statute. The term 'recklessness' applies to all situations involving foresight of consequences which are less than inevitable. However, in a murder trial or a trial of a crime of specific intent the judge *may* direct the jury, not as a matter of substantive law but as a point of evidence, that in the unusual circumstance of that particular case, they *might* decide that the accused's foresight of the prohibited consequence leads them to the conclusion that the accused intended that consequence to occur.

This seemingly simple solution has now been implemented by the House of Lords in *R* v *Moloney*. The explanation of this lies in public policy and precedent. Society, the judiciary or both, will not countenance the prospect of a person being convicted of murder in a situation where death was caused recklessly. The antithesis to the concept of reckless murder lies in the traditional common law precedents which define murder (see chapter 7) as killing with malice aforethought, which in turn eventually was confined to mean intentional killing.

The introduction of a wider ambit to the definition of intention based on foresight of consequences was the judicial solution to the problem of reckless murder without mentioning the word recklessness.

Consequently in *Hyam* v *DPP* [1975] AC 55, the trial judge described to the jury four states of mind sufficient to constitute malice aforethought, proof of any one of which would satisfy the requirement of *mens rea*. The jury had to be satisfied that when Mrs Hyam set fire to the petrol which she had poured at night into the home of her rival she did so with one or other of these states of mind:

(a) An intent to kill (direct or oblique).
(b) An intention to cause grievous bodily harm (direct or oblique).
(c) Foresight that death was a highly probable consequence of her conduct.
(d) Foresight that grievous bodily harm was a highly probable consequence of her conduct.

Juries deliberate in camera and do not give reasons for their verdicts so although the jury in this case found Mrs Hyam guilty of murder it is not certain which of these four states of mind the members of that panel thought she possessed at the time she set fire to the house and left without warning its occupants. In the trial judge's view, provided she possessed one of these four states of mind it was immaterial which of them she possessed because proof of any of them would suffice to show that she had the necessary *mens rea* to be convicted of murder.

The House of Lords subsequently by a bare majority confirmed the correctness of the trial judge's direction and this appeared to be reaffirmed by the House of Lords in *R* v *Cunningham* [1982] AC 566 (see chapter 7).

The social tension between abhorrence of killing with a desire to punish and the sense of civilisation, sophistication and compassion for human frailty are shown in the judicial attitudes to the state or states of mind acceptable to sustain a conviction for murder. It explains largely the multiple definition of intention that was developed in relation to the *mens rea* requirement of murder. There are practical difficulties associated with the historical definition of murder. For some its scope is too narow and socially dangerous. Until the House of Lords or Parliament will redefine murder clearly to include reckless killing the complexity will remain. The problem and danger associated with that idea, however, should be self-evident. Recklessness is a question of degree or at least the blameworthiness of the conduct depends on society's (or the judge's) perception of the degree of risk involved. The current situation is such that not only does the

Mens Rea

requirement of *mens rea* differ from crime to crime but also it may change in relation to some aspect of a particular crime. Murder, as explained above, illustrates these points.

2.6.2 Murder, foresight and intention

Remember that crimes of specific/ulterior intent require proof of a specified intention. Not just intention to do the prohibited act or produce the prohibited consequence but the intention to do so with the additional specified intention. Only proof of that intention will suffice for a conviction, recklessness will not. Following the decision in *Hyam* v *DPP* [1975] AC 55 and despite the dicta of Lord Diplock in *Whitehouse* v *Lemon* [1979] AC 617 quoted in para. 2.6.1, murder could, for a period of 10 years, be said to fall into a category *sui generis* somewhere between being a crime of specific intent and a crime of basic intent.

Clearly murder is not a crime of basic intent because ostensible proof of recklessness will not satisfy the *mens rea* requirement. Equally it could have been argued that it was not for the past 10 years a crime of specific intent because the *Hyam* decision made it obvious that it was not just proof of intention that would satisfy the *mens rea* requirement but other states of mind as well involving foresight. The *Hyam* multiple definition of intention was not even in that period a general principle applicable to all crimes of specific intent as indeed Lord Diplock appeared to state in the dicta quoted above from *Lemon's* case. Two significant decisions, *R* v *Mohan* [1976] QB 1 and *R* v *Belfon* [1976] 3 All ER 46, had stated categorically that the view of intention according to *Hyam's* case, which requires an individual to foresee that his conduct will make the occurrence of certain consequences a high probability, was not applicable to those statutory assaults which are crimes of specific intent or to the crime of attempt (see also *R* v *Pearman* [1985] RTR 39). For these instances proof of intention (either direct or oblique but in the case of attempts possibly direct only, see *R* v *Mohan*) will satisfy the *mens rea* requirement for those offences, not proof of foresight of consequences or proof of recklessness. It meant that *Hyam's* case did not create a new generally applicable definition of intention.

The complexity produced by defining intention as one of the methods by which *mens rea* may be proved can be reduced to the following propositions:

(a) Crimes of specific/ulterior intent can be proved either by proof of direct intention only, i.e., proof that the accused's object, aim, purpose (call it what you will) was to produce the forbidden consequences, or by proof of an oblique intention on the part of an accused in relation to the requisite specific or ulterior intent.

In such crimes, e.g., murder, *mens rea* can be proved either by proof of a direct intention or an oblique intention. In very rare instances the jury properly directed might infer intention from proof of foresight that the consequences were a highly probable result of the accused's conduct (see *R* v *Moloney* below).

(b) There are crimes of basic intent which can be proved by showing intention, direct or oblique, or recklessness.

(c) There is the crime of manslaughter at common law which can be proved by showing either category of intention (direct or oblique), or recklessness or gross negligence and there are now some modern statutory offences in which proof of negligence *simpliciter* will suffice to satisfy the requirement of *mens rea*.

(d) There are crimes of strict or absolute liability which in theory require proof only of the *actus reus* and that the chain of causation leads back to the accused. An accused's state of mind as regards to some or all of the external elements of the crime in theory is irrelevant. (See chapter 3 below).

There appears to be no difference between foresight of consequences and recklessness and *Hyam's* case appeared to say that for purposes of satisfying the *mens rea* element of murder foresight of death or grievous bodily harm was intention. It looked suspiciously like recklessness but it was not to be called by that name if a conviction for murder was to be achieved.

Today the crime of murder strictly is a crime of specific intent, not simply such a crime for purposes of the defence of voluntary intoxication or self-induced automatism as was thought during the 10 years that *Hyam* was the leading case (see para. 6.3.7).

In the recent case of *R* v *Moloney* [1985] 2 WLR 648 where after a party the accused fired a shotgun as a result of a good-natured but foolhardy contest, killing his stepfather, the House of Lords has reiterated and reasserted the view that foresight or foreseeability are not the same thing as intention and therefore the appropriate direction to be given to juries as to the mental element of murder or other crimes of specific intent would be one explaining direct and oblique intention only. The words of Lord Goddard CJ in *R* v *Steane* [1947] KB 997 were endorsed by their lordships particularly the passage of his judgment (at p. 1004) which reads:

> No doubt, if the prosecution prove an act the natural consequence of which would be a certain result and no evidence or explanation is given, then a jury may, on a proper direction, find that the prisoner is guilty of doing the act with the intent alleged, but if on the totality of the evidence there is room for more than one view as to the intent of the prisoner, the jury should be directed that it is for the prosecution to prove the intent to the jury's satisfaction, and if, on a review of the whole evidence, they either think that the intent did not exist or they are left in doubt as to the intent, the prisoner is entitled to be acquitted.

Today in a murder or other specific intent offence, foresight of probable consequences on the part of the accused should not be treated as equivalent to intent or deemed to satisfy the *mens rea* requirement for that offence. Where the accused foresees that one of the probable consequences of his voluntary conduct will be death or really serious injury to the victim that will not be sufficient *mens rea* as a matter of substantive law. Such foresight, however, in appropriate cases (which will be rare) may be considered as evidence in deducing what the actual intention of that particular accused was in fact at the time of the alleged murder or other offence of specific intent. In such instances if it is necessary to direct a jury by reference to foresight of consequences then it is only necessary for the trial judge to invite the jury to consider two questions:

First was death or really serious injury in a murder case (or whatever relevant consequence had to be proved to have been intended in any other specific intent case) a natural consequence of the accused's voluntary act?

Secondly, did the defendant foresee that consequence as being a natural consequence of his act?

The jury should then be told that if they answered yes to both questions it was a proper inference for them to draw that he intended that consequence.

In other words as a matter of evidence, foreseeability or foresight of consequences could give rise to an inference (after a proper direction) from which a jury *may* conclude that the accused in question did intend (directly or obliquely) to commit that offence. This view coincides with that adopted by the Court of Appeal in relation to a charge of attempt to cause grievous bodily harm contrary to s. 18 of the Offences against the Person Act 1861 (a 'specific' intent offence) in *R v Pearman* [1985] RTR 39, and endorses the principle behind s. 8 of the Criminal Justice Act 1967 (see para. 2.14 and para. 7.6.2).

Generally, apart from explaining the distinction in law between intention and motive, a trial judge should leave what is meant by intent to the jury's good sense unless he is convinced that, on the facts and having regard to the way the case had been presented to the jury in evidence and argument, some further explanation is strictly necessary to avoid misunderstanding. Most trials for murder or wounding with intent will not require any such explanation. If the offence consisted of a direct attack on the victim with a weapon, what further explanation of intent could the jury require except, perhaps, where the accused directed his attack at one person but caused the death of another (see transferred malice, para. 2.10).

To sum up, today, malice aforethought (*mens rea*) of the crime of murder is established by proof that when doing the act which caused the death of another the accused intended to kill or do serious harm. Proof that the accused had foresight: that death or serious harm would probably occur (irrespective of whether or not he desired either of those consequences) will not amount to the necessary malice aforethought.

Lord Hailsham of St Marylebone LC in *Moloney* said it had already been pointed out in *R v Belfon* [1976] 3 All ER 46 that it is not foresight but intention which constitutes the mental element in murder and the undesirability of elaborating unnecessarily on the meaning of intention in all but exceptional cases had already been emphasised by Lawton LJ in *R v Beer* (1976) 63 Cr App R 222 (where the accused had stabbed a woman, a stranger to him, 13 times, killing her). The dictum of that judge has been endorsed since by the Judicial Committee of the Privy Council in *Leung Kam-Kwok* v *R*, 19 December 1984, unreported). Lord Hailsham in *Moloney* went on to emphasise the very unusual nature of the facts in *Hyam*.

The intention of the appellant (Mrs Hyam) was made apparent by two separate sets of facts: (a) that, prior to setting fire to the petrol she ascertained that her lover was not in the house and therefore safe, thus making it plain that *her intention* was to expose those who were in the house to danger to their lives, and (b) that she took elaborate precautions to make sure that her actions did not awake the sleepers in the house making it doubly clear that *her intention* was to expose them to whatever danger would be involved in the fire. Lord Hailsham said that the decision in *Hyam* was not meant to make a person liable for murder where death was the result of criminal negligence or recklessness and not intention, he concluded his judgment by saying (at p. 652):

> I conclude with the pious hope that your lordships will not again have to decide that foresight and foreseeability are not the same thing as intention although either may give rise to an irresistible inference of such, and that matters which are essentially to be treated as matters of inference for a jury as to a subjective state of mind will not once again be erected into a legal presumption. They should remain, what they always should have been, part of the law of evidence and inference to be left to the jury after a proper direction as to their weight, and not part of the substantive law.

However this does not coincide with the view taken by the Privy Council in *Chan Wing-Siu* v *R* [1985] AC 168 which held that all those who had taken part in an unlawful joint enterprise (going with knives to premises with intent to rob and causing injuries to the victim in the process from which he died) had sufficient intent for the offence of murder or causing grievous bodily harm with intent if they had had in mind the possibility that some serious bodily harm might result incidentally during the course of their enterprise. It would be necessary for the prosecution to prove that each of the accused had had in mind such a possibility.

This case, which is in line with *Hyam*, was (a) a decision of the Privy Council and therefore not binding on courts in this country; (b) it was decided before the House of Lords decision in *R* v *Moloney* and (c) it appears to be based on authorities which are primarily concerned with the issue of causation in joint enterprises (see para. 4.8 and para. 1.8), but arguably as causation is an element of the *actus reus* of murder it is principally an evidential matter. In *R* v *Moloney* their lordships said that foresight and foreseeability are matters of evidence from which the jury may draw an inference of intention, they are not deemed as legal presumptions or rules of substantive law to be intention for purposes of murder or any other specific intent offence. As far as the law in England and Wales is concerned that latter view is now the law.

2.7 RECKLESSNESS

Prior to 1981 in relation to those crimes in which the element of *mens rea* could be satisfied by proof of recklessness there was only one definition of a reckless state of mind. For many years and at least since the leading case of *R* v *Cunningham* [1957] 2 QB 396 it was relatively easy to understand. In that case Cunningham's girlfriend lived in a basement flat. Cunningham discovered that the adjoining flat was unoccupied. One night he broke into that adjoining flat and forced the gas meter off the wall in order to steal whatever money it might contain and then he departed. Because he had fractured a pipe, gas escaped into that flat and percolated through the wall into the adjoining flat of his girlfriend who was asleep. The noxious fumes made her very ill. Cunningham was charged with unlawfully and maliciously administering a poison or noxious thing so as thereby to endanger the life of another contrary to the Offences against the Person Act 1861, s. 23.

This being a crime of basic intent the judge said that the prosecution must prove either:

(a) an actual intention to do the particular kind of harm that was done (i.e., show that Cunningham had as his direct intention or desired purpose the asphyxiation of someone in that or any adjoining property), or
(b) recklessness as to whether or not such harm should occur (i.e., that Cunningham had foreseen that harm from asphyxiation might result and yet he had gone ahead despite that awareness to take the risk of it happening).

There was no evidence that Cunningham actively desired to produce the illness, physical injury or death of his girlfriend. Therefore if Cunningham was to be convicted it would have to be on the basis that he foresaw that his conduct would probably produce that consequence. Even though he did not want that to happen if he can be said to have realised that there was a risk that his conduct might bring about that prohibited consequence and he persisted with that conduct and therefore took the risk, then he had sufficient *mens rea* to be convicted of a crime of basic intent.

This definition of such a reckless state of mind can be reduced in effect to the words 'conscious risk-taking'. He who, knowing the risk, is willing to take it must suffer the legal consequences. If the risk materialises into a reality then his reckless indifference to that eventuality is sufficient to satisfy the *mens rea* requirement of any crime of basic intent. Consider what could be the position in cases like *Cunningham* today if the girlfriend had died. If the police had decided to charge the *Cunningham*-type person with clear proof of either deliberate purpose to injure (direct intention), or of awareness that his conduct would produce inevitable injury to a person (oblique intention) or of being reckless, any of these states of mind would result in a conviction for any basic intent offence such as ss. 20 or 47 of the Offences against the Person Act 1861 or common law assault or battery (see chapter 7). If the police decided to charge the *Cunningham*-type person with murder then proof of either conscious purpose (direct intention) to kill (or cause grievous bodily harm) or awareness of the inevitability of such consequences (oblique intention) or in some rare instances foresight of death (or grievous bodily harm) as a highly probable consequence might, not as a matter of substantive law but as a matter of evidence, lead the jury to the inescapable conclusion that in the circumstances the actual accused had malice aforethought and that in effect he intended the death or grievous bodily harm so as to produce a conviction (see *R v Moloney* [1985] 2 WLR 648, discussed in para. 2.6.2 and para. 7.6.2).

2.7.1 Murder, foresight and recklessness

In both instances whether as a matter of substantive law or as an evidential inference, foresight of consequences as proof of *mens rea* will produce a conviction but whereas in the former instance that foresight of consequence may be called recklessness, in relation to murder or any specific/ulterior intent offence, in those rare instances where it is relevant, that same sort of foresight of consequences may not be so called; for the purposes of murder or any specific/

ulterior intent offence, that foresight of consequences may enable the jury to decide that the accused intended the consequence—in effect the jury would be saying that foresight proves the intention of the accused in the circumstances of that case.

The significance of the difference in the degree of probability between intention, recklessness and negligence is discussed in paras. 2.7.2 to 2.7.12 and is discussed in chapter 7 in relation to *Hyam* v *DPP* [1975] AC 55 and the *mens rea* of murder.

Since *R* v *Cunningham* [1957] 2 QB 396, recklessness could be described as conscious risk-taking or foresight of consequences. The words 'conscious' and 'foresight' predicate a certain degree of awareness. Remember that most serious offences in English law can only be committed intentionally or recklessly so that if the person responsible for injury or damage was blissfully unaware that his acts or omissions might injure or damage another then that person should not be held blameworthy and criminally liable. Should this be the case even in a situation where any right-thinking person, any reasonable man, would have been aware that acts or omissions of that sort would be likely to lead to injurious, prohibited consequences? It is in relation to this question that the courts in recent years have developed a second definition of recklessness.

2.7.2 A new aspect of recklessness

In *R* v *Stephenson* [1979] QB 695 the accused appealed having been convicted in the Crown Court of arson contrary to s. 1(1) and (3) of the Criminal Damage Act 1971. The facts were that the accused had gone to a large haystack in a field, made a hollow in the haystack, crept into the hollow and tried to go to sleep. The night was so cold he could not sleep so he lit a fire of straw and twigs inside the hollow. The haystack caught fire and was severely damaged as a result.

The accused admitted to the police what he had done, he said (at p. 698): 'I kept putting bits of straw on the fire. Then the lot went up. As I ran away I looked back and saw the fire . . . getting bigger. I ran off down the road . . . I'm sorry about it, it was an accident.'

If these were the only matters to be considered then, without doubt, a jury would have no difficulty in deciding that he damaged the haystack and that he did so being reckless as to whether the stack would be damaged or not. But the certainty of that conclusion was put into question by medical evidence on the accused's behalf to the effect that he had a long history of schizophrenia and that this affliction would make the accused capable of lighting a fire for warmth even in so dangerous a situation without taking the danger into account.

Given that the accused had no intention to burn down the haystack and given that negligence is not sufficient *mens rea* for a crime of basic intent such as criminal damage then his liability must turn on whether or not the jury were satisfied that he was reckless when he lit the fire. Did the accused consciously take the risk? The medical evidence indicated that he may not have had the same ability to foresee or appreciate risk as a normal person.

The trial judge in his direction to the jury implied that the accused may have been aware of the risk but closed his mind to it, and that there may be many reasons for closing one's mind, schizophrenia being one of them. The accused appealed and the main point in issue was whether the term 'reckless' required proof that the accused actually foresaw the risk of some damage resulting from his actions but nevertheless went ahead (i.e., a subjective test) or whether it would be sufficient simply to prove in order to convict the accused that the risk of damage resulting would have been obvious to any reasonable person in his position (i.e., an objective test).

The appeal court relied on the view of the House of Lords in *Herrington* v *British Railways Board* [1972] AC 877 (at p. 898) which was embodied in the speech of Lord Reid, where he said:

> Recklessness has . . . a subjective meaning: it implies culpability. An action which would be reckless if done by a man with adequate knowledge, skill or resources might not be reckless if done by a man with less appreciation of or ability to deal with the situation. One would be culpable, the other not.

The court considering Stephenson's appeal went on to conclude that recklessness as to whether harm should occur or not arises when the accused has foreseen the risk and the harm that might be done and yet he has gone on to take that risk. In that court's judgment there was a subjective test to ascertain recklessness and this was clear from the then leading authority of *R* v *Cunningham* [1957] 2 QB 396. Further it was stated that it is not the taking of every risk which could be classed as reckless. The risk must be one which it is, in all the circumstances, unreasonable for the accused to take, i.e., the risk must in the particular circumstances be an unjustifiable one.

Clearly, in this court's view, in order to be reckless, knowledge of, or an appreciation of, the risk of damage to property or injury to others must be proved to have entered the accused's mind even though he may have suppressed it or disregarded it.

Stephenson, through no fault of his own, may have been in a mental condition which might have prevented him from appreciating the risk which would have occurred to any normal person. Therefore the trial judge was wrong to imply that he may have closed his mind to obvious facts. Schizophrenia was something which might have prevented the idea of injury, damage, risk or harm entering his mind. The jury should have had the opportunity to acquit him if they thought this was the case. The reaffirmation in *Stephenson's* case of the definition of recklessness established in *Cunningham's* case as the one and only definition of recklessness was short-lived. Two years later in two major decisions the House of Lords reshaped the concept of recklessness by stating a second definition of recklessness and declaring that proof of either form of recklessness would satisfy the *mens rea* requirement of basic intent offences.

2.7.3 The new definition of recklessness

Just as *Hyam* v *DPP* [1975] AC 55 appeared (until *R* v *Moloney* [1985] 2 WLR 648) to have created a second category of intention for purposes of the *mens rea* of murder so *Metropolitan Police Commissioner* v *Caldwell* [1982] AC 341 and *R* v *Lawrence* [1982] AC 510 created a second category of recklessness of general application to basic intent offences. It is however inapplicable to the crime of rape which is a basic intent offence (see chapter 7) and to any statutory offence (such as s. 20 of the Offences against the Person Act 1861) which is expressed in terms of 'maliciously' doing a prohibited act (see paras. 2.7.11, 7.2.2) or to the offence of obtaining by deception under s. 15(1) of the Theft Act 1968 (see para. 8.13.9

2.7.4 Caldwell's case

Here the accused had done some work for the owner of a hotel as a result of which they had quarrelled. The accused had become drunk and then set fire to the hotel out of spite and motives of revenge. The fire was discovered and put out before any serious damage was caused and none of the 10 guests staying in the hotel was injured.

The accused was charged with two counts of arson under s. 1(1) and (2) of the Criminal Damage Act 1971. He pleaded guilty to the first and lesser charge of 'intentionally and recklessly destroying or damaging the property of another' but he pleaded not guilty to the more serious charge of 'damaging property with intent to endanger life or being reckless whether life would be endangered'.

Note that had subsection (2) simply read 'damaging property with intent to endanger life', where an accused is charged with this form of criminal damage it is a crime of specific intent and only proof of a direct/oblique intent, aim or object to endanger life would produce a conviction: see *R* v *Orpin* [1980] 1 WLR 1050. But that subsection goes on to add: 'or being reckless whether life would be endangered'. The word 'reckless' renders this form of criminal damage a crime of basic intent where the accused is charged either with damaging property, being reckless whether life would be endangered or where he is charged in the alternative with intent to *or* being reckless whether life would be endangered. The House of Lords in *Caldwell* stated, concerning the word reckless, that when it is used in a criminal statute such as the Criminal Damage Act 1971 it is used in its popular or dictionary sense meaning 'careless, regardless or heedless of the possible harmful consequences of one's acts' and as such that term encompasses both the following:

(a) a decision to ignore a risk of harmful consequences which the accused has recognised as existing, and
(b) a failure to give any thought to whether there was any risk in circumstances where, if any thought had been given, the risk would have been obvious.

In expounding the new dimension of recklessness the House of Lords appears to be saying that an obvious unreasonable risk arises when an ordinary prudent person would have appreciated the risk of harmful consequences which are not trivial or negligible.

2.7.5 Lawrence's case

In *R* v *Lawrence* [1982] AC 510 the accused was convicted of causing death by reckless driving (see s. 1 Road Traffic Act 1972) in that his motor cycle collided with and killed a pedestrian in a restricted-speed zone. There was a dispute as to the speed of the cycle at the time of the collision.

On appeal the issue concerned whether or not this offence requires *mens rea* and if it does what proof would satisfy that requirement.

The House of Lords held that driving recklessly is an offence requiring proof of *mens rea* and that in order to satisfy that requirement there must be proof that before adopting a manner of driving which involves obvious and serious risk to others the driver either:

(a) recognised that there is some risk and has gone on nonetheless to take it, or

(b) has failed to give any thought at all to the possibility of such a risk.

If the jury are satisfied that the accused drove in such a way as to create an obvious and serious risk of injury or damage and that in so driving he had not given thought to the possibility of any risk *or* having recognised some risk he went ahead, then he is guilty of the offence. 'The jury is to apply the standard of the ordinary, prudent motorist as represented by themselves.'

Traditionally an act or omission of itself was not sufficient for a conviction. the accused had to be shown to have intended or to have known or appreciated or realised or foreseen the risk. If he did not, then no matter how much anyone else might have done so, in other words no matter how much the reasonable, prudent man would have done so, the accused should not be liable. But now the House of Lords would seem to be stating that having created the risk of harmful consequences the accused is guilty even though he just did not think about those consequences or the risk involved. This new limb to the definition of recklessness was stated first in *Metropolitan Police Commissioner* v *Caldwell*. The decision in *Caldwell* was given earlier on the same day as the decision in *Lawrence* but in both cases, after time for consideration.

Today, if a person creates an obvious or unreasonable risk of danger to persons or damage to property it will be with one of the following states of mind:

(a) That person may be aware of the risk.
(b) That person may not have considered whether or not there is a risk.
(c) That person may believe that there is no risk.

If that person is aware of the risk and goes ahead, he is reckless (*R* v *Cunningham* [1957] 2 QB 396). If that person has not considered whether there is a risk or not, he is now deemed to be reckless (*Metropolitan Police Commissioner* v *Caldwell* [1982] AC 341, *R* v *Lawrence* [1982] AC 510). In the former instance he unjustifiably took a risk of which he was aware, in the latter the possibility of risk did not occur to him in circumstances where it should have because the risk was so obvious that, if he had thought about it, it must have impinged upon his mind. Only if the jury accepts that the person who creates an obvious, unreasonable risk believed (having thought about it) that there was no risk will they be entitled to say that he was not reckless. That situation will be rare. Such a person will not be liable under either limb of the definition of recklessness but equally such a person will be an uncommon accused if the risk and its consequences would have been obvious to the ordinary prudent man.

2.7.6 Commentary on the new recklessness

The House of Lords in *Metropolitan Police Commissioner* v *Caldwell* [1982] AC 341 and *R* v *Lawrence* [1982] AC 510 has stated that if the accused created a situation of a gross and obvious risk but gave no thought to the possibility of harmful consequences he now may be convicted of recklessness even though he did not know or appreciate or realise or foresee that risk. It is enough for the jury to consider whether the ordinary, reasonable, prudent man would have done so and on this basis to infer that the failure of an accused to appreciate the risk is in such circumstances reckless. Where a person 'turns a blind eye' to the prospect of risk it is proper for the law to deem that he in fact did know that which he 'pretends' not to know. Often the claim that no thought was given to the prospect of risk simply will not be believable, the inference that he 'turned a blind eye' will be irresistible but now that inference is superfluous, failure to consider the risk is itself reckless. This new test of recklessness is an amalgam of both elements of subjectivity and objectivity. It is subjective in the sense that it is concerned with determining the mind of the accused, and objective in the sense that it uses an objective criterion to assess that mental state. It is suggested, however, that analysing *Caldwell* recklessness as being 'subjective' or 'objective' does not help. It is more important that a student of criminal law is aware (a) of the constituents of the test for determining *Caldwell* recklessness, and (b) that to say a person who gave no thought at all to the possibility of risk is reckless appears to be contrary to traditional concepts of *mens rea* if it is decided purely and totally on objective criteria.

It is suggested that despite the long-standing view that negligence is only sufficient to obtain a conviction for manslaughter at common law, the judiciary have concluded on the basis of public policy that a person who gives no thought to the possibility of a gross and obvious risk is as blameworthy and deserving of punishment as the person who appreciates a risk and decides to take it.

The new, *Caldwell* and *Lawrence* concept of recklessness, it is suggested, is in reality the introduction into English law of a general principle of liability for gross negligence called by another name—'recklessness'.

2.7.7 Recklessness and gross negligence

If *Caldwell*-type recklessness and gross negligence are distinguishable it can only be by way of the degree of inattention or indifference and the significance of the surrounding circumstances in drawing the attention of the ordinary prudent man to the risk and dangers inherent in his action or inaction that resulted in damage or injury.

Clearly crimes of basic intent may have their *mens rea* requirement satisfied by proof of intention or recklessness either of the *Cunningham* (foresight) type or of the *Caldwell* (blissful unawareness) type and while that latter type of recklessness is indistinguishable from gross negligence the conventions of current criminal law preclude one from stating that to be the case in a court of law. In brief the current terminology of the criminal law prevents you from obtaining a conviction for a crime of basic intent by proving gross negligence. You may be in fact doing precisely that and the courts may in fact be punishing for gross

Mens Rea

negligence but it must not be called gross negligence. In relation to basic intent offences it must be referred to as recklessness of the *Caldwell* type.

Whatever the kind of recklessness envisaged, all share one common factor. The risk which is foreseen or which ought to have been foreseen must be an unjustifiable risk in all the circumstances of the case, and this must be determined by the jury.

2.7.8 Risk taking and social utility

In so far as recklessness and indeed gross negligence are concerned, liability will depend on an almost mathematical formula. If the social utility of the action or inaction, judged objectively, is as great, or greater than, the sum of the risk plus the kind of injury or damage likely to result, then the accused will probably not be liable. So the surgeon probably will not be liable who foresees, but proceeds, or fails to foresee when he should have foreseen, that there is a good chance his patient might die during an operation. He will only be liable for old *Cunningham*-style recklessness if he took an unjustifiable risk which depends on the social utility of his actions. If, for example, the surgeon was consciously aware of the risk to a female patient's life but for a large sum of money still performed plastic surgery to try to 'beautify' her bust, he would be serving no socially useful purpose and might be held to be reckless.

Rex, who shoots at Edward and John, who are fleeing with items of his property, knowing the risk to his neighbour Alf, is performing an act of little if any social utility, because it would seem that risk and likelihood of serious injury to his companion outweigh the pleasure of revenge. If on the other hand we add some facts (even though they may be improbable) to the effect that Rex happens to be a police officer who recognises Edward and John as escaped criminal lunatics of the most dangerous type or if he knew they were carrying a deadly disease which would devastate the population of Britain, then Rex's shooting at them despite the risk to his neighbour might be considered socially useful and would possibly outweigh the risk and resulting injury to his neighbour. It is likely that even in an improbable situation such as the one just outlined no one, not even a police officer, would escape liability for shooting at Edward or John (although the unusual facts may mitigate the penalty imposed for doing so) and likewise he would be liable for taking the risk of hitting Alf, the neighbour. The point to be taken is, however, that in some circumstances social utility may justify taking a risk.

Likewise in relation to both new-style *Caldwell* recklessness and to gross negligence the question of social utility is significant. Whereas the surgeon or (with regard to the scenario) the police officer going about his ordinary or proper duties might avoid being made liable for consequences he did not contemplate, Rex would not. What distinguishes old from new-style recklessness and new-style recklessness from gross negligence, and gross negligence from negligence *simpliciter* is simply a question of degree. Is the risk of injury or damage highly probable, probable, possible, very remote, virtually impossible? There is no clear answer of general application in every case. The social utility of the accused's conduct together with the degree of risk will decide whether or not he is blameworthy in the sense of being reckless (in either sense) or negligent or without blame.

2.7.9 Mental defect and recklessness

In every situation involving *mens rea* (i.e., intention, recklessness or negligence) the mentally ill (like Mr Stephenson) the congenitally retarded and the incurably insane should not be liable either because of the defence of insanity or because they lack *mens rea*. In so far as recklessness is concerned it is immaterial, for example, whether such an individual thought about the risk of lighting a fire inside a hollow in a haystack and decided it was safe or whether he did not give the matter any thought at all: he does not have *mens rea*. His schizophrenia, for example, precludes him from either coming to a reasonable answer or from considering the matter.

Mental illness or retardation aside the acceptable explanations for failing to think about the risk will be infinitesimal. Anger, inexperience, tiredness, drink or drugs—none of these will excuse a failure to consider risk. The reasonable, prudent man does not undertake dangerous activities or exercises with attendant potential harm to others when in such states. The mentally ill person on the other hand may be in a state in which he cannot realise either that there is a risk or, even if he is aware of the risk, cannot assess the potential dangers so as to be able to avoid the harmful consequences of that risk. Having said that, recent decisions show that a youth, or even a person with the handicap of some degree of mental retardation coupled with youth and tiredness, can be held to be reckless in the *Caldwell* sense of that word.

In *R* v *R (SM)* (1984) 79 Cr App R 334 the Court of Appeal held that the reckless man (for purposes of the Criminal Damage Act 1971 at least) is not to be defined by reference to a particular defendant's sex, age and other characteristics. It stated that the trial court was not obliged to equate the ordinary prudent man to one who shared the sex, age and other particular characteristics of the defendant which might affect his forethought or recognition of risk. In that case the accused, a boy of 15 years, committed several burglaries. He was arrested as a result of a 'tip-off'. A few days later the accused threw petrol bombs through the windows of houses of those whom the accused believed responsible for his arrest. He claimed, on trial for arson with intent, that he intended to frighten, not to injure. In *Elliott* v *C* [1983] 1 WLR 939 the accused was a girl aged 14 years who was mentally backward. She stayed out one night without sleeping and in the early hours of the following morning she started a fire with inflammable liquid in a shed. The shed and its contents were destroyed. She was charged under the Criminal Damage Act 1971, s. 1(1), with destroying that property being reckless as to whether it would be destroyed or not.

The magistrates found (a) that she had given no thought to the possibility of a risk that the shed and contents would be destroyed and (b) that even if she had given any thought to the matter the risk would not have been obvious to her. Therefore, they found her not guilty because in their view *Caldwell's* case stated in effect that the accused should only be held to have acted recklessly by her failure to give any thought to an obvious risk that property would be destroyed where such a risk would have been obvious to *her* if she had given any thought to

Mens Rea

the matter. Like Mr Stephenson who lit a fire inside a haystack the magistrates were saying that she did not have the mental capacity to appreciate the risk whether or not she considered it.

The prosecution appealed and the Divisional Court stated what was to be the correct interpretation of the new definition of recklessness as expounded in *Metropolitan Police Commissioner* v *Caldwell* [1982] AC 341 and affirmed in *R* v *Lawrence* [1982] AC 510 and *R* v *Miller* [1983] 2 AC 161 (see chapter 1) in so far as the Criminal Damage Act 1971, s. 1, is concerned. In their view it means that a risk is obvious if it is one which must have been obvious to a reasonable, prudent person, not necessarily to the particular accused and therefore it is not a defence to say that because of limited intelligence or exhaustion the accused would not have appreciated the risk even if she had thought about it.

In the light of the decisions in *Lawrence*, *Miller* and *Elliott* v *C* [1983] 1 WLR 939, the fact that Miss Elliott's application for leave to appeal was rejected by the House of Lords and the Court of Appeal's decision in *R* v *R (SM)* (1984) 79 Cr App R 334, which held that the reckless man is not to be defined by reference to a particular defendant's sex, age and other characteristics, it seems clear that the Divisional Court's interpretation of *Caldwell* recklessness in *Elliott* as requiring the application of purely objective criteria is the correct one. The case of *R* v *Mohammed Bashir* (1982) 77 Cr App R 59, which supported the more subjective interpretation that the risk must have been obvious to the accused, (despite being a decision of the Court of Appeal), must be taken now to have been wrongly decided except in relation to the offence of rape (see para. 7.5.2). In so far as rape is concerned the Court of Appeal in *R* v *Satnam and Kewal* (1984) 78 Cr App R 149 has made it clear that *Caldwell* recklessness has no part to play. Judges are to direct juries in rape trials on the basis of s. 1 of the Sexual Offences (Amendment) Act 1976 and *DPP* v *Morgan* [1976] AC 182 *without* regard to *Caldwell* or *Lawrence* which, the court said, are concerned with recklessness in a different context and under a different statute. Subsequently the Court of Appeal has added that in order to convict in a reckless rape case the jury must be directed to convict only if they find the accused could not care less whether the complainant was consenting: *R* v *Breckenridge* (1984) 79 Cr App R 244.

2.7.10 Avoiding Caldwell recklessness

The one route left open by the *Caldwell* definition for avoiding criminal liability is to argue that the accused had given thought to the prospect of risk but decided wrongly that there was no risk. This argument was not open to Miss Elliott because she had stated that she did not consider the prospect of risk at all. This only leaves an accused like Miss Elliott or possibly Mr Stephenson with the defence of insanity (see chapter 6). The stigma and repercussions of a successful plea of insanity, however, are for many people as bad and possibly more daunting than any penalty the criminal law might impose. Furthermore, it now appears that mental illness short of insanity will do no more than explain the state of mind of a reckless man. The fact of recklessness may thus be inferred from an accused's conduct (see *R* v *Bell* [1984] 3 All ER 842). This case is a clear indicia of the wide scope of the mental state of recklessness as now interpreted by the courts.

2.7.11 Limiting Caldwell recklessness

Given that the subjective interpretation of *Caldwell* in *R* v *Mohammed Bashir* (1982) 77 Cr App R 59 is wrong except in relation to reckless rape (see para. 7.5.2) and that the objective interpretation in *R* v *Lawrence* [1982] AC 510, *R* v *Miller* [1983] 2 AC 161, *Elliott* v *C* [1983] 1 WLR 939 and *R* v *R (SM)* (1984) 79 Cr App R 334 is correct in law the effect is wide-ranging but arguably it does not extend (in addition to rape), to any statutory offence, albeit a crime of basic intent, where the word 'maliciously' is part of the definition of the offence. For example, in the case of malicious wounding under the Offences against the Person Act 1861, s. 20 (which is a crime of basic intent), that word limits recklessness as part of the *mens rea* to *Cunningham*-type recklessness (knowing the risk or foreseeing the harm but going ahead to take the risk despite that). This limitation at least on the ambit of *Caldwell* as objectively interpreted has been confirmed as correct in the recent case *W* v *Dolbey* [1983] Crim LR 681.

2.7.12 The wide scope of Caldwell recklessness

That expectation aside the wide-ranging scope of the new recklessness was supposedly confirmed in *R* v *Seymour* [1983] 2 AC 493. The accused and his cohabitee had an altercation; the accused drove off in his 11-ton lorry and his cohabitee gave chase driving the accused's car. She managed to pull in front of and force him to stop the lorry. She alighted to continue the quarrel, he drove the lorry forward to ram his car out of the way. During the course of his manocuvre his cohabitee was crushed to death between the lorry and the motor car. The accused was charged with manslaughter. His defence was that she was crushed by accident and that he would plead guilty to causing death by reckless driving, an offence carrying with it a less serious penalty. The prosecution insisted that the trial proceed on the issue of manslaughter. The judge directed that a conviction could be reached on proof of gross negligence. The accused was found guilty and sentenced to five years' imprisonment. Given that gross negligence and *Caldwell*-type recklessness (as objectively interpreted) coincide, then proof of either will be sufficient. So proof that death was caused by taking a risk which the accused failed to consider at all will be sufficient, whether or not that occurs in the course of an otherwise perfectly legal activity.

Significantly the House of Lords in *Seymour* appear to have declared that the *Caldwell* definition of recklessness (presumably as objectively interpreted) incorporates what previously was termed gross negligence. In *Andrews* v *DPP* [1937] AC 576 Lord Atkin had suggested that 'reckless' was the adjective that most nearly coincided with the very high degree of negligence required to prove gross negligence but he had not said they were one and the same. Since *Seymour* those two terms have been equated and made synonymous in the criminal law of England. This new definition, their lordships held, may apply to common law offences of recklessness such as manslaughter, and it may not be limited to statutory offences of recklessness such as the Criminal Damage Act 1971 or the Road Traffic Act 1972, ss. 1 and 2. If correct this may mean that in relation to all crimes of basic intent (except rape and those statutory offences in which the word 'malicious' appears) the *mens rea* requirement will be satisfied either by proof of

Mens Rea

intention (direct or oblique) recklessness within the *Cunningham* sense or by proof of gross negligence but under the name and guise of 'recklessness'.

Caldwell as interpreted in *Elliott* v *C* [1983] 1 WLR 939 and confirmed in *Seymour* shows how far away from notions of a guilty mind the concept of *mens rea* has developed. Whether it is a good or bad development from society's point of view is a very open question. The other view is shown in such cases as *R* v *Satnam and Kewal* (1984) 78 Cr App R 149, *W* v *Dolbey* [1983] Crim LR 681 and *R* v *Kimber* [1983] 1 WLR 1118.

The person who considers the prospect of, but wrongly concludes that there is no risk is either mentally ill (in which case because of the decision in *Elliott* only the defence of insanity is available) or else that person genuinely has no *mens rea*. He does not intend the harmful eventuality, he does not have foresight of it, he is not reckless in the sense of having seen the risk and decided to take it and yet he did consider the prospect of risk. If he is blameworthy at all it must be on the basis of negligence but unless he has killed someone (manslaughter) or breached a statutory provision making negligence sufficient for liability, he should not be held criminally liable.

The avoidance of liability on the basis of having thought about the risk but coming to a wrong decision as to its existence or probabilities, however, depends on whether or not the jury accept as true the accused's assertions that he did consider the risk but genuinely made a wrong decision as to the prospect of any danger or harm being caused. Had Miss Elliott raised this the magistrates as the tribunal of fact could have said that she did not have *mens rea* because her mental condition prevented her from properly appreciating the risk and therefore she should not be liable. If, for example, the risk in all the circumstances is obvious to any ordinary person and is an unreasonable one for the accused to take, while that may not be conclusive proof that he knew the risk and really chose to take it or that he wrongfully turned a 'blind eye' to it, yet it may lead the tribunal of fact or the jury (depending on the mode of trial) to conclude that his claim that he considered the prospect of risk and decided wrongly but genuinely that there was none is untrue. The tribunal of fact or the jury is entitled to conclude that the risk was known and appreciated by him and he wrongfully closed his mind to that obvious fact, suppressed it, drove it out of his mind or turned a 'blind eye' to it. The tribunal of fact or the jury could then conclude that such a person is intentional or reckless in the old *Cunningham* sense of that word.

In relation to the amended scenario the situation where Rex sees the risk of his neighbour Alf coming between his gun and the fleeing thieves (Edward and John) has been discussed above but what if Alf was not visible to Rex and Rex gave no thought to the prospect that Alf (or anyone else for that matter) might come between his gun and Edward and John at whom he was firing?

2.8 MENS REA AS TO CIRCUMSTANCES

Where a circumstance forms an element in the *actus reus* of an offence, and that offence requires the establishing of *mens rea* as to such elements; then the mental states which constitute *mens rea* for the consequences of an offence are generally applicable to its circumstances. An individual cannot, however, 'intend' a circumstance but he can be aware of its existence, or so close his mind to its existence that he wilfully blinds himself to its occurrence. These are the equivalents of direct or oblique intention with regard to consequences. A man may be reckless as to the existence of a circumstance be it either *Cunningham* or *Caldwell* recklessness. Equally a man may be negligent with regard to the presence of circumstances. Which of the above mental states are sufficient with regard to such elements in particular crimes is dependent upon the definition of those crimes and their interpretation by the judiciary.

2.9 COINCIDENCE OF ACTUS REUS AND MENS REA

Generally speaking *actus reus* and *mens rea* must coincide and must be related. In the application of both of these principles the law appears to allow a degree of flexibility. That flexibility, however, does not lie in the application of these rules but rather in the width of the concepts of *actus reus* and *mens rea*.

In the scenario Edward and John see the owners of the house return so they smash a window and flee. If we assume that Rex, the home-owner, snatched up his shotgun, gives chase and eventually shoots at Edward and John, then the principles of coincidence and relationship can be illustrated.

If we assume that Rex shoots at Edward and John intending to kill them or cause them grievous bodily harm, then if he hits them and they die Rex could be convicted of murder. If they are injured he could be convicted of attempted murder or of one of the statutory assaults. If he misses Edward and John he could be convicted of an attempt to do any of those things but missing them gives rise to three further issues.

First, suppose that, having shot at and missed Edward and John, Rex returns home but a week later when driving home drunk his car skids out of control and crashes into a bus queue killing three people, two of whom coincidentally happen to be Edward and John, the very two whom Rex intended to kill the previous week. Rex had no idea that there would be a bus queue, that he would crash or that Edward and John would be present. Should Rex be convicted of their murder? The answer must be that he cannot be convicted of that offence because the *actus reus* (the killing) does not coincide with the *mens rea* (the intention to kill formed the previous week). Rex may be convicted of some offence other than murder, such as manslaughter, reckless driving, causing death by reckless driving, a statutory assault, battery at common law or some other statutory offence relating to the use of a motor vehicle. Two cases are often cited to show that this rule is flexible and can be stretched. It is not, however, the rule that is flexible but rather the court's view of the width of the *actus reus*.

In *Fagan* v *Metropolitan Police Commissioner* [1969] 1 QB 439 the accused was parking his motor car. He managed, quite by chance or accident, to stop on a policeman's foot. He did not respond immediately to the policeman's request to move the vehicle off his foot. Clearly the facts disclose that Fagan was responsible for the *actus reus* of one of the statutory assaults or battery at common law but at the time he caused the *actus reus* (i.e., caused unlawful physical violence) he did not have the necessary associated *mens rea*. He did not intend to assault or batter the policeman and he was not reckless. He did not see a risk of stopping on the policeman's foot and choose to chance it and whether or not he thought about the risk it may not have been obvious to a reasonable man

Mens Rea

in those circumstances that the car would stop on a policeman's foot.

Subsequently when the accused realised what had happened and yet refused to move it, it could be argued that he then had the *mens rea* (i.e., he intended to cause unlawful, physical violence) but that now there was no *actus reus* to coincide with that *mens rea*. The actual infliction of the unlawful, physical violence had finished.

The court took the view that the *actus reus* (i.e., infliction of unlawful physical violence) in relation to all offences involving assault or battery was a continuing one. The *actus reus* did not start and finish at the point when he drove on to the policeman's foot. It started then and only finished when he drove off the policeman's foot. If he could be shown to have *mens rea* (intention or recklessness as to the infliction of unlawful, physical violence) at any time from the moment he drove on to the foot until he drove off the foot, then he could be convicted. This does not mean that the rule of coincidence of *actus reus* and *mens rea* has been compromised it means simply that the *actus reus* in assault and battery based crimes is capable of being a continuing *actus reus*.

Today a similar conclusion would be reached in light of the decision in *R v Miller* [1983] 2 AC 161 (see chapter 1). In that case the House of Lords held that where a person puts another person or property belonging to another in danger of injury or damage and then omits to rectify that situation or seek to divert the consequences he is guilty of any offence of basic intent which is appropriate in the circumstances. Such a person in effect has been reckless in one or other of the two senses now applicable to that word. Realising that the car is on the policeman's foot and deciding to do nothing, in the light of *Miller's* case, may be both *actus reus* and *mens rea*.

The case of *Thabo Meli v R* [1954] 1 WLR 228 appears to be similar but is different to *Fagan v Metropolitan Police Commissioner* [1969] 1 QB 439 in that there the accused had the *mens rea* of murder when they attacked the victim but failed to produce the *actus reus* of murder at that time because they did not injure the victim sufficiently to kill him. Subsequently they pushed the supposed 'corpse' of the victim over a cliff in an attempt to make it appear that the victim had died from an accidental fall. In fact the actual cause of the victim's death was exposure at the foot of the cliff. Again the *actus reus* and the *mens rea* do not appear to coincide.

The trial judge in that case had said to the jury:

> Unless you find that something happened in the course of this evening between the infliction of the injuries and the decision to throw the body into the water, you may undoubtedly treat the whole course of conduct of the [accused] as one.

An appeal against this direction to the Privy Council was dismissed. Their lordships expressed the opinion that it was impossible to divide up what was really one transaction into the initial attack and the pushing off the cliff neither of which directly caused death, and the leaving for dead, exposed at the foot of the cliff which did cause death. In the opinion of the Privy Council it was stated (at p. 230) that:

There is no doubt that the accused set out to do all these acts in order to achieve their plan and as parts of their plan; and it is much too refined a ground of judgment to say that, because they were under a misapprehension at one stage and thought that their guilty purpose had been achieved before in fact it was achieved, therefore they are to escape the penalties of the law (at p. 230).

In so far as murder is concerned the point made in *Thabo Meli* has been rendered superfluous by subsequent cases. Since *R* v *Vickers* [1957] 2 QB 664 and especially since *Hyam* v *DPP* [1975] AC 55, the single-transaction argument should be immaterial at least in so far as murder is concerned. Both *Vickers* and *Hyam* (which have been confirmed in *R* v *Cunningham* [1982] AC 566) assert that proof of intention to cause grievous bodily harm will be sufficient *mens rea* (if the victim dies) to convict of murder. If the accused has the intention to kill or cause grievous bodily harm then so long as death results from an attack with one of those intentions then it must be immaterial when the death occurs provided it is within a year and a day (see chapter 7) from the accused's causative act or omission. It is irrelevant whether or not the victim is dead when the accused pushes the supposed 'corpse' of the victim over the cliff.

If the decision in *Thabo Meli* has any significance for crimes other than murder then the discussion in that case of acting with *mens rea* during the course of a continuing transaction may have some significance.

To sum up, where the *mens rea* comes first and the *actus reus* occurs later in time the position appears to be as follows:

(a) In the case of murder provided the prosecution can show one of the two intents (*mens rea*) specified in *R* v *Moloney* [1985] 2 WLR 648 then death (the consequence aspect of the *actus reus*) need not be instantaneous and may occur any time up to a year and a day after the act of causing grievous bodily harm (the conduct aspect of the *actus reus*).

(b) Alternatively in the case of murder and definitely in cases other than murder it can be argued that the separated *mens rea* and *actus reus* relate to and are part of 'one transaction' or event. As long as the *mens rea* is continuing the *actus reus* can combine with it.

Where the *actus reus* occurs first and the *mens rea* comes later in time the position appears to be as follows:

(c) In crimes involving assault or battery the *actus reus* can be continuing. Formation of a *mens rea* at any point during the continuation of the *actus reus* will be sufficient to produce a conviction.

(d) In the case of crimes of basic intent proof of a failure of an individual to prevent or to warn others of the harmful consequences that might happen to persons or property from a danger which that individual has set in motion will produce a conviction.

The *actus reus* of criminal damage by setting fire to property (even unintentionally) can be joined now with the blameworthy state of mind of failing to do anything about putting out that fire.

In the scenario Edward and John commit the *actus reus* of criminal damage by knocking over the heater in Rex's house (albeit unintentionally and without any old *Cunningham*-type recklessness on their part) and their fleeing from the scene knowing of or being aware of the fire and realising their responsibility for it without doing anything to try to put it out is now recognised as a blameworthy state of mind. Their failure to act to contain or stop the fire is reckless and that *mens rea* combines with the *actus reus* to make them liable to a charge (on the facts in the scenario) of criminal damage (see *R v Miller* [1983] 2 AC 161).

2.10 TRANSFERRED MALICE

In the scenario Edward and John have gone upstairs in Rex and Marian's home and are in the process of stealing when they see the owners of the house return. They smash a window to make their escape.

Assume first that they are making their escape when Rex snatched up his shotgun and gave chase. He aimed his shotgun at Edward and John intending to kill them, or at least cause them grievous bodily harm. He pulled the trigger. The shots missed the two culprits for whom they were intended and happen to hit a passing cyclist, killing him.

In such a situation there are two possible philosophies for any legal system to choose between. On the one hand Rex only intended to kill Edward or John; he had no *mens rea* in so far as the passing cyclist was concerned and therefore should not be convicted of the cyclist's murder. While it could be argued that Rex has been reckless or grossly negligent as to the prospect of his shots killing other persons, recklessness or gross negligence will not be sufficient *mens rea* for murder. If Rex was to be charged it would have to be for some offence less than murder.

On the other hand, by consciously trying to kill Edward and John, Rex has unlawfully caused the death of the cyclist and the law could deem that he be treated as if he has killed Edward or John. On this view Rex could be guilty of the murder of the cyclist irrespective of whether or not he knew of the cyclist's presence.

It is this second view of the matter which has been applied by the English common law system for several centuries since *R v Salisbury* (1553) 1 Plow 100, and reaffirmed in *R v Latimer* (1886) 17 QBD 359. In effect the malice (i.e., intention) or *mens rea* that Rex had towards Edward and John is deemed to be transferred to the cyclist. That *mens rea* coupled with the *actus reus* of shooting and the consequential death of the cyclist mean that Rex may be found guilty of murder.

Assume for the moment that Edward and John have climbed out of Rex's window and are in the process of running down the road when Rex fires his shotgun at them intending to kill or seriously injure them but this time his shot misses them (and misses the hapless passing cyclist) but strikes a neighbour's parked car causing serious damage. In the previous example the *mens rea* that Rex had towards Edward and John at the time he shot the cyclist could be deemed to be transferred to the cyclist with only a little use of mental dexterity. To say that Rex's *mens rea* in relation to Edward and John can be joined with the *actus reus* of criminal damage to a neighbour's property would require indulging in mental gymnastics. The law has not gone this far. In *R* v *Pembliton* (1874) 12 Cox CC 607, there was a brawl outside a public house during the course of which the accused picked up a stone and threw it at a fellow combatant who was standing in front of a plate-glass window. The stone missed the adversary but went on to smash the window behind his intended victim. Pembliton was convicted on a charge equivalent to the modern offence of criminal damage but that conviction was quashed on appeal. The appeal court clearly stated that the *mens rea* of one offence involving persons could not be joined with the *actus reus* of offences against property and vice versa.

When this judgment is applied to the scenario it does not mean that Rex will escape criminal liability where damage to the parked car occurred. Whether or not he will be liable will depend on the charges brought against him. For example, he could be convicted of attempted murder (see chapter 7), manslaughter, statutory assault or common law assault or battery by firing the gun at Edward and John. In these cases actual damage to the car is irrelevant.

Alternatively he could be convicted of criminal damage to the parked car on the grounds that he was reckless. Even though he had no intention to damage the car, if he foresaw the risk to the car and still fired the gun, or if he did not even consider the risk to the car (which would have been obvious if he had given any thought to the matter), then he would be liable for the damage. His intention to kill or injure Edward and John becomes irrelevant to this charge and there is no need to consider even trying to transfer Rex's malice because the *mens rea* requirement for criminal damage can be satisfied by proof of Rex's recklessness.

2.11 BURDEN OF PROOF

There are two well-known and related maxims of English law to the effect that (a) everyone is presumed innocent until proved guilty and (b) that 'He who alleges must prove'. They mean that the burden or onus is placed on the prosecution to prove beyond reasonable doubt that the accused created, caused or committed the *actus reus* of an offence together with proof of a requisite coincidental *mens rea* (see Murphy, *A Practical Approach to Evidence*).

Prior to the famous decision in *Woolmington* v *DPP* [1935] AC 462 it was thought that murder provided an exception to the general rule stated above. It was believed, in other words, that where the accused had caused the death of another the burden or onus was placed upon him to prove his innocence to the satisfaction of the jury or else to prove some mitigating factor which would justify a verdict of the less serious offence of manslaughter rather than murder.

In that case the accused had caused the death of his wife. He had gone to visit her intending to induce her to return to live with him. He had taken a rifle with him and it was a bullet from this gun which killed her. He claimed that he pulled the trigger involuntarily while threatening to shoot himself as a means of inducing her to return to him. The trial judge's direction to the jury given at pp. 465–6 was as follows:

The Crown has got to satisfy you that this woman . . . died at the prisoner's hands . . . If they satisfy you of that, then he has to show that there are circumstances . . . which alleviate the crime so that it is only manslaughter, or which excuse the homicide altogether by showing that it was pure accident.

Woolmington was convicted. The Court of Criminal Appeal dismissed his appeal but his further appeal to the House of Lords was successful and he was then acquitted. In the House of Lords Viscount Sankey LC rendered one of the great judgments of English law in the course of which he said (at p. 480):

> [I]f it is proved that the conscious act of the prisoner killed a man and nothing else appears in the case, there is evidence upon which the jury may, not must, find him guilty of murder. It is difficult to conceive so bare and meagre a case, but that does not mean that the onus is not still on the prosecution.

If at the end and on the whole of the case, there is a reasonable doubt created by the evidence of the prosecution or the accused as to whether he killed with a malicious intention, the prosecution has not made out its case. As Lord Sankey LC said, at p. 481 (emphasis added):

> Throughout the web of the English criminal law one golden thread is always to be seen, *that it is the duty of the prosecution to prove the* prisoner's guilt subject to . . . the defence of insanity and subject also to any statutory exception.

Since this decision there has been created a further exception in the form of the rule in *R v Edwards* [1975] QB 27 (see Murphy, *A Practical Approach to Evidence*). Lord Sankey LC concluded:

> No matter what the charge or where the trial, the principle that the prosecution must prove the guilt of the prisoner is part of the common law of England and no attempt to whittle it down can be entertained.

Secondly not only must the prosecution prove its allegations it must also be prepared to negate every defence which might be raised by an accused in a trial, including such defences as duress, self-defence and non-insane automatism (see *R v Bone* [1968] 2 All ER 644, *R v Lobell* [1957] 1 All ER 734 and *Bratty v Attorney-General for Northern Ireland* [1961] 3 All ER 523, respectively).

The one exception to the general rule stated above at common law is that the accused must prove that he is insane if he is to avail himself of that defence (see *M'Naghten's Case* (1843) 10 Cl & F 200): everybody is presumed sane until the contrary is proved. The prosecution therefore does not have to prove a person is sane. Other exceptions have a statutory origin, e.g., the defences of provocation and diminished responsibility within the Homicide Act 1957, ss. 2 and 3 (see chapter 7).

What has been said above is of course a simplification. In virtually every instance the accused will have what is sometimes known as the tactical burden of introducing the prospect of a defence. Where this amounts to a denial of *actus reus* or *mens rea* that is all he has to do. Then the legal burden is on the prosecution to negate that suggestion. In other instances where the defence is separate from a denial of one of the two central elements, e.g., duress or self-defence (see above), then the accused has not only the tactical burden to satisfy but also he must satisfy the so-called evidential burden by adducing sufficient evidence to make the defence a live issue fit and proper to be left to the jury (see *R v Gill* [1963] 1 WLR 841 at p. 846). If the accused does satisfy both burdens then the prosecution is bound to negate such defences beyond reasonable doubt.

2.12 STANDARD OR LEVEL OF PROOF

The quality, level or standard of proof expected from the prosecution is 'beyond reasonable doubt'. What that means in law is best explained in *Miller v Minister of Pensions* [1947] 2 All ER 372 at p. 373 where it was said:

> proof beyond a reasonable doubt does not mean proof beyond the shadow of a doubt . . . if the evidence is so strong against a man as to leave only a remote possibility in his favour which can be dismissed with the sentence:
> 'of course it is possible but not in the least probable' the case is proved beyond reasonable doubt, but nothing short of that will suffice.

Where the burden of proving a defence is placed on the accused as in insanity or diminished responsibility the standard expected is less onerous. The accused in such instances only has to prove the defence on the civil law standard, i.e., on a balance of probabilities, and not the higher criminal law standard of beyond reasonable doubt, see *R v Patterson* [1962] 2 All ER 340.

2.13 PROOF OF ACTUS REUS

From the previous chapter it should have been evident that the *actus reus* of most crimes can be perceived, witnessed and testified about in court. Witnesses can state what happened, what they saw and heard and felt. Expert witnesses can testify as to fingerprints and types of various bodily secretions and footprint size and similarity etc. which may implicate the accused.

2.14 PROOF OF MENS REA

What a man does or fails to do can be witnessed but how do you witness what goes on in a man's mind? Unless the accused confesses what he was thinking it would appear to be impossible to prove a man's state of mind and therefore impossible to prove *mens rea*.

The law, however, is practical. Common sense dictates that from the factual evidence attested by witnesses the jury will be able to infer the state of a man's mind at the time of the *actus reus*. The jury may be invited by the judge to draw its own conclusions as to the accused's state of mind from what was said and done by him together with a consideration of the surrounding circumstances, any motive found, any explanation offered by him.

Taking the scenario as an illustration. If Rex (the home-owner) shot at Edward and John (the fleeing thieves) then, if the blast from Rex's shotgun had hit and killed either of them, Rex might be charged with murder. Once the prosecution has proved he fired the gun and hit the deceased then if Rex offers no explanation the jury may properly draw the inference that he was aware of what he was doing and the consequences of doing it and therefore that he did intend to kill or cause serious bodily harm. If the jury considered that he foresaw the normal consequences of his conduct as highly probable then it might properly infer that he intended to murder one or both of the fleeing thieves.

This inference which the jury is entitled to draw is otherwise known as the presumption that a man intends the natural consequences of his conscious acts. But it is only a presumption. The jury, while entitled to reach that conclusion on the facts, is never bound to do so. It would be wrong for a judge mandatorily to direct a jury that once the accused's act or behaviour was proved the jury must find that the accused intended the natural consequences of that act or behaviour unless he disproved that he so intended.

In the notorious decision of the House of Lords in *DPP* v *Smith* [1961] AC 290 a constable directed the accused to stop the car which he was driving and which the constable suspected to contain stolen goods. When it looked as though the car would not stop the constable dived on to its bonnet in an attempt to make the accused stop. The accused then drove in an erratic manner, swerving about in an effort to dislodge the constable. He succeeded but the result was that the constable fell on to the road and was run over by an oncoming vehicle receiving injuries from which he subsequently died. The accused was convicted of murder. On appeal this was reduced to manslaughter but the House of Lords restored the murder conviction.

The effect of the House of Lords decision would seem to be that a jury could be directed that it must, not simply that it could, infer that the accused foresaw what a reasonable man would have foreseen. Viscount Kilmuir LC said (at p. 327):

[I]t matters not what the accused in fact contemplated as the probable result or whether he ever contemplated at all, provided he was in law responsible and accountable for his actions, that is, was a man capable of forming an intent, not insane within the M'Naghten Rules and not suffering from diminished responsibility. On the assumption that he is so accountable for his actions, the sole question is whether the unlawful and voluntary act was of such a kind that grievous bodily harm was the natural and probable result. The only test available for this is what the ordinary responsible man would, in all the circumstances of the case, have contemplated as the natural and probable result. That, indeed, has always been the law.

This means, of course, that it does not have to be proved that the accused intended death or grievous bodily harm (proof of foresight will now only be sufficient evidence in a case from which the jury *may* be invited to infer intention). He could be convicted if a hypothetical reasonable man could have foreseen that death or grievous bodily harm was the natural and probable consequence of his acts.

The general public's reaction was that this went against the whole tenor of traditional principles of English law and was wrong. In response Parliament abrogated the effect of *Smith's* case by passing s. 8 of the Criminal Justice Act 1967.

That provision says nothing about *when* intention is to be proved, its sole concern is with *how* intention is to be proved. It reads as follows:

> A court or jury, in determining whether a person committed an offence:
> (a) shall not be bound in law to infer that he intended or foresaw a result of his actions by reason only of its being a natural and probable consequence of those actions; but
> (b) shall decide whether he did intend or foresee that result by reference to all the evidence, drawing such inferences from the evidence as appear proper in the circumstances.

It is obvious from the wording of this provision that it applies only to crimes which require proof of intention or foresight. It has been shown above that the law of murder requires that the accused intended death or grievous bodily harm; therefore the Criminal Justice Act 1967, s. 8, will apply and will dictate how the jury is to decide that issue. Manslaughter, however, does not necessarily require proof that the accused intended or foresaw death or any other result and therefore in such circumstances s. 8 has no application.

In instances (like murder and specific intent offences) where s. 8 does come into operation the jury is not precluded from inferring that the accused did intend the natural and probable consequences of his acts, it simply prevents the trial judge from directing it to come to that conclusion. If after considering all the evidence the jury believes that the accused was honestly mistaken about the consequences of his acts then it should not convict him irrespective of what the hypothetical reasonable man would have thought or foreseen.

In relation to crimes of basic intent where proof of *Caldwell* recklessness, and manslaughter where proof of either *Caldwell* recklessness or gross negligence, will suffice then on an objective assessment what the ordinary, reasonable man would have thought, foreseen, done or refrained from doing does become a proper consideration for the jury.

2.15 SUMMARY IN LIGHT OF THE SCENARIO

The *actus reus* or external elements of each of the crimes disclosed in the scenario has been outlined at the end of the previous chapter. The *mens rea*, internal elements, or requisite state of mind which may be proved and which must coincide with the *actus reus* of each offence are as follows:

(a) *Rape of Sarah* (a crime of basic intent, (see chapter 7).
The *mens rea* of this offence is composed of:

(i) With regard to conduct (the fact of unlawful sexual intercourse):

(1) An intention (direct) to have intercourse. Donald must be shown to have had as his deliberate goal, sexual intercourse with Sarah. Only proof of *Steane*-type (direct) intention will suffice.

(ii) With regard to the circumstances (i.e., that the unlawful intercourse be with a woman who at the time of intercourse does not consent to it and at the time

Mens Rea

he knows that she does not consent to the intercourse or he is reckless as to whether she consents to it), proof of any of the following states of mind will satisfy the *mens rea* requirement:

(1) that sexual intercourse without consent was the accused's conscious aim, object or desired goal, or
(2) that the accused was aware that the woman was not consenting, or
(3) that the accused knew that there was a risk that the woman was not consenting but he opted to take the risk.

On the facts in the scenario a jury could be satisfied that Donald either intended to have sexual intercourse with Sarah irrespective of whether or not she consented or at least that he knew there was a risk she was not consenting and yet he went ahead and had intercourse irrespective of that risk.

(b) *The death of Donald:* murder (prior to *R* v *Moloney* [1985] 2 WLR 648 this was a *sui generis* offence; now it is and has been clearly reasserted by the House of Lords to be a specific intent offence defined as the unlawful killing of a human being with *malice aforethought*).

Malice aforethought or *mens rea* of murder is composed of proof of either of the following:

(i) Intention to kill (direct or oblique).
(ii) Intention to cause grievous bodily harm (direct or oblique).

In some rare instances consideration by a properly directed jury of the accused's foresight of death or grievous bodily harm may lead them to the inescapable conclusion that the accused did intend death or grievous bodily harm. Intention can be either direct or oblique, i.e., either that the death (or grievous bodily harm) was the deliberate object or that death (or grievous bodily harm) was known to the accused to be morally certain from his conduct.

On the facts in the scenario the jury must be satisfied that Rex either intended to kill Donald or cause him grievous bodily harm. Foresight would not be an issue and it would be confusing for the trial judge to mention foresight at all to the jury, see *R* v *Beer* (1976) 63 Cr App R 222 discussed in para. 2.6.2.

Assume that the scenario's facts are altered slightly for the moment so that Rex returns home, sees the lifeless body of Donald on the floor and the distressed state that Sarah is in and assumes that Sarah has killed Donald. Assume that Rex takes what he believes to be Donald's corpse out into the back garden. Assume that Donald in fact was alive but dies through exposure to the bitter night air. Then Rex could be charged with manslaughter (see chapter 7).

(c) *Theft by Bruce, Donald, Edward and John* (a crime of specific intent). The dishonest (appropriation of property belonging to another) with the intention to permanently deprive the rightful possessor of it.

The *mens rea* requirement will be satisfied by proof of all of the following states of mind:

(i) As to the appropriation either intention (direct or oblique) or recklessness (*Cunningham* or *Caldwell* type). In the scenario Bruce, Donald, Edward and John all have direct intention to appropriate property belonging to Rex. They all deliberately or consciously intend that as their goal.

(ii) Dishonesty, i.e., the intention (direct) to act fraudulently.

(iii) The specific intention (direct or oblique) to permanently deprive another of that property.

(d) *Criminal damage by Edward and John* (a crime of basic intent). (To destroy or damage property without lawful excuse belonging to another) intending to destroy or damage any such property *or* being reckless as to whether any such property would be destroyed or damaged.

The *mens rea* requirement will be satisfied by proof of either of the following states of mind:

(i) intention (direct or oblique) to destroy or damage the property of another, or

(ii) intentional or reckless (*Cunningham* or *Caldwell*-type) conduct which destroys or damages the property of another.

In the scenario Edward and John intentionally damage the window with the motive of effecting an escape from Rex with property they have stolen from him. Their knocking over of the heater may well be accidental but in accordance with *Miller's* case by allowing damage to result or continue they can be said obliquely to have intended that damage or at least been reckless (*Cunningham* or *Caldwell* type).

(e) *Statutory offence of being in charge of a motor vehicle while unfit to drive by Bruce.*

This is what is known as a strict liability or absolute offence which probably does *not* require proof of any *mens rea* or blameworthy state of mind in order for the prosecution to obtain a conviction (see chapter 3).

2.16 QUESTIONS

1. The surgeon who foresees that there is an even chance that his patient might die on the operating table takes a risk if he goes ahead. Is he reckless if he does and death results? If he is, can he be convicted of murder?
2. If recklessness is equated with unjustified risk-taking, how great must the risk be to incur criminal liability?
3. If the handbrake, which you had properly applied when parking your car in a car parking building, slipped and your car rolled back trapping someone against the wall, would you incur any criminal liability if having realised that person's predicament you did nothing to release him or her?

3

Strict Liability Offences

SCENARIO

Bruce will find that his presence in the car will cause him further problems irrespective of the fact that he is drunk and incapable and slumped in the driving seat. Unbeknown to him his vehicle is a veritable den of potential criminal liability. Bruce's car has a defect in the braking system which was not readily apparent from its being driven to Rex's home but is now obvious from the position of the vehicle. It has rolled down Rex's driveway and has only been stopped by the gatepost. It now abuts on the highway. The application of the handbrake or footbrake having no effect. The vehicle is due to have its MOT test, which would instantly disclose this defect in the mechanical soundness and safety of the car.

Though Bruce obtained a road tax licence and affixed this to his vehicle, it had, during the course of the evening become detached from the windscreen. When the police arrived and found amongst the confusion Bruce in his unfortunate condition they discovered the excise licence hidden below the front passenger seat.

They examine the vehicle and in the glove compartment in a packet of cigarettes they find a minute quantity of LSD (lysergic acid diethylamide). The police question Bruce about the drugs, excise licence, roadworthiness of his car and Bruce though drunk understands the questions but is evasive in his responses.

The police enter Rex's home and see that Donald and Sarah had been smoking cannabis. On the walls of the home Rex has a collection of firearms, all of which are flintlocks. Though apparently antique they are in full working order. (Some, however, are modern reproductions though this is unknown to Rex.) Rex does not possess a firearms certificate. He does not believe that he needs one since he never intends to use the firearms.

The issue in this scenario will be to consider the possible criminal offences that may have been committed by the various parties and whether their intentions, or mental state or lack of it is of any legal significance.

3.1 THE NATURE OF STRICT LIABILITY OFFENCES

Offences of strict liability (sometimes known as offences of absolute prohibition) are crimes where an accused need not have *mens rea* with regard to one or more of the elements of the *actus reus*, i.e., the circumstances or consequences of an offence (see chapter 2). Though strict liability offences have a respectable pedigree (see, for example, *R* v *Woodrow* (1846) 15 M & W 404, 'the innocent and unintentional possession of adulterated tobacco') an early and illustrative example of the nature of such an offence is to be found in the case of *R* v *Prince* (1875) LR 2 CCR 154. The accused was charged with having unlawfully taken an unmarried girl being under the age of 16 out of the possession and against the will of her father. This was contrary to the Offences against the Person Act 1861, s. 55 (see now Sexual Offences Act 1956, s. 20). This section provided that it was an offence to 'unlawfully take . . . any unmarried girl, being under the age of 16 years, out of the possession and against the will of her father or mother, or of any other person having the lawful care or charge of her'. The accused was convicted. It had been found by the jury that the girl, though 14, looked very much older than 16 and it was found upon reasonable evidence that before the accused had taken her away she had told him she was 18. The accused believed her statement in good faith and on reasonable grounds.

The issue before the appellate court was could the conviction be upheld? The majority of their lordships affirmed the conviction, though on slightly differing grounds and views. It was no defence to a charge under the section that the accused believed in good faith and on reasonable grounds that the girl was over 16. On this basis he had lacked *mens rea* with regard to that particular element of the offence. Bramwell B was of the opinion that (at p. 175): 'The legislature has enacted that if anyone does this wrong act, he does it at the risk of the [girl] turning out to be under 16.'

It was clear that the court was enforcing a policy which was aimed at the protection of young unmarried girls. This policy was considered by the court to be of such primary importance that it was not prepared to accept that it would be a defence for an individual to claim that he lacked any semblance of knowledge that a girl in his possession was below the age of 16. If she was in his possession and the other elements of the offence could be established, then in such circumstances the offence may have been constituted. The court had construed the section as creating an offence of strict liability, i.e., that at least one of the elements of the offence (the age of the girl) did not demand any mental requirement on the part of the accused. The court, however, was of the view that the other elements of the offence did require *mens rea*. If Prince had taken the girl while honestly believing (though wrongly) that he had the parent's or guardian's consent, or that the girl was in no one's possession or care or charge or was married he could not have been convicted. Furthermore the tenor of the judgments suggest that if Prince had believed he had a lawful excuse in taking the girl (which presumably would have to be based on honest and reasonable grounds see para. 6.5.4) this would also have been a defence. In addition it must be established that an individual intended to take possession of such a girl. If she had, for example, without his knowledge hidden herself at his usual place of abode and had then been discovered he could not be convicted.

Most strict liability offences therefore require a considerable mental element on the part of an accused. (Cases such as *R* v *Larsonneur* (1933) 24 Cr App R 74 and *Winzar* v *Chief Constable of Kent* (*The Times*, 28 March 1983) (see para 1.4) which involved offences which are constituted entirely by 'states of affairs' require no mental element whatsoever on the part of an accused. Such crimes are, however, very rare. The general form of strict liability offences is similar to that of *Prince*.

3.2 STRICT LIABILITY OFFENCES AT COMMON LAW

Strict liability offences, though almost entirely creatures of statute can also be found in the common law. It has been suggested that contempt of court (as modified by the Contempt of Court Act 1981), public nuisance and criminal libel (as modified by the Libel Act 1843) are examples of common law strict liability offences. However, the situation with regard to these offences is not as clear as it has been claimed (at least with regard to the two latter offences). These latter offences are more realistically to be considered as examples of crimes of vicarious liability (the nature of which will be considered in para 4.16.1). Nevertheless any doubts as to the judiciary's ability to create strict liability offences was removed, it is suggested, by the controversial case of *Whitehouse* v *Lemon* [1979] AC 617.

The accused were the editor and publishers of a magazine known as *Gay News*. On sale to the general public it was mainly of interest to homosexuals. There was published in the magazine a controversial poem which described homosexual acts committed upon the body of Jesus Christ and ascribed to him during his lifetime homosexual practices with the apostles and others. The co-accused were charged with blasphemous libel, in that they had unlawfully and wickedly published or caused to be published a poem which blasphemed the Christian religion in vilifying the life and crucifixion of Christ. The jury had been directed that if they considered the poem blasphemous it was only necessary for the prosecution to establish the intention by the accused to publish the poem. It was not a requirement of the offence that the accused must have intended to produce a blasphemous libel; the finding that the poem was itself a blasphemy would suffice. The House of Lords by a bare majority held that the offence of publishing a blasphemous libel did not depend upon the accused having an intent to blaspheme. It was sufficient for the prosecution to establish only that the publication of the poem had been intentional and that it had been blasphemous. The majority of their lordships denied that they were interpreting the offence as being one of strict liability. However, it is suggested that the opinion of the minority—that, by denying that an intention to blaspheme was an element of the offence, the House of Lords were creating a crime of strict liability—is to be preferred. The requirement that the publication be blasphemous was a consequence which amounted to an element of the *actus reus* of the offence. The determination by the majority of their lordships that there was no necessity for an individual to have any state of mind with regard to this element of the offence renders the decision indistinguishable from the situation found in *Prince*. Even if the majority were not prepared to classify the crime of blasphemous libel as one of strict liability it shares all the characteristics of such an offence.

Perhaps the reasons for attaching of what is to all intents and purposes a strict liability tag to the offence of blasphemous libel lies in the promotion of certain policies by the court. The clearest expression of one such policy is to be found in the speech of Lord Scarman, where his lordship was of the opinion (at p 665) that:

It would be intolerable if by allowing an author or publisher to plead the excellence of his motives and the right of free speech he could evade the penalties of the law even though his words were blasphemous in the sense of constituting an outrage upon the religious feelings of his fellow citizens. This is no way forward for a successful plural society.

His lordship expressed the hope that the offence of blasphemous libel would be extended to all religions which exist in the multiracial, multicultural Britain of today. Such a crime would help cement, strengthen and protect the religious and cultural bonds in our society. It cannot be doubted that such policies and aims are laudable and desirable, and were determining factors in the formulation of the views of the majority of their lordships. Nevertheless it should be asked could these aims and policies have been promoted just as vigorously with the requirement that an individual either intended or was reckless as to whether his written or published views could possibly be blasphemous. Though Lord Scarman expressed the opinion that the writer's or publisher's motive should not permit an excuse from criminal liability, the issue was not whether motive is pertinent to criminal responsibility, for generally it is not. The issue in the case was whether an individual's lack of intention or lack of reckless indifference in producing what was objectively a blasphemous libel should nevertheless provide a defence. Furthermore, his lordship was of the opinion that claims to rights of free speech could result in an evasion of criminal liability. It is suggested that the right to free speech is consistent both with the promotion of the religious freedoms of a plural society and with a requirement that a society should only impose criminal liability for blasphemous libel when it can be established that an individual intended or was recklessly indifferent in producing such a consequence. A society which is truly mature should possess sufficient discriminating qualities to discern between the criminally mischievous and the insensitive or tactless, and the ability to tolerate the latter. The majority of the House of Lords in wishing to promote certain policies needlessly widened the ambit of a criminal offence and unnecessarily classified the offence of blasphemous libel in effect as a crime of strict liability.

3.3 STRICT LIABILITY IN STATUTORY OFFENCES

The practical reality of strict liability is that it is almost exclusively a creature of statute. Once the nature of strict liability offences are understood the principal issue is to determine whether a given penal section in a statute constitutes a strict liability offence or not. The first factor to consider are the actual words of a section.

3.3.1 The words of a section

The presence of words in a section of a statute such as 'knowingly', 'wilfully', 'maliciously', 'using' or 'permitting' which by definition import a mental element would seem to suggest that such a section could not be interpreted as creating an offence of strict liability. Nevertheless such a word or words might be interpreted as not applying to all the elements of the *actus reus* of the offence. Furthermore

Strict Liability Offences

what interpretation is to be given to a section within a statute when there is a total absence of such words? An examination of the authorities shows a confusing and contradictory pattern.

Certain statutory offences contain the word 'knowingly'. In *Roper v Taylor's Central Garages (Exeter) Ltd* [1951] 2 TLR 284 at p. 288 Devlin J expressed the opinion that 'All that the word "knowingly" does is to say expressly what is normally implied'. Though this statement has not received universal judicial approval it seems to be supported by the case of *Sherras v De Rutzen* [1895] 1 QB 918. The accused was the licensee of a public house which was situated opposite a police station. His premises were frequented by off-duty police officers. He served a uniformed constable whom he honestly and reasonably believed to be off duty, by reason of the absence of an armlet which was only worn by an officer while on duty. The officer had wrongfully removed the armlet, however, and was still on duty. The accused was convicted at first instance of an offence under the Licensing Act 1872, s. 16(2), which provided that a licensed person who 'Supplies any liquor or refreshment whether by way of gift or sale to any constable on duty unless by authority of some superior officer of such constable . . . shall be liable to a penalty'.

The accused appealed contending that an offence under s. 16(2) could only be constituted where the licensee had knowledge that the police constable was on duty or had at least closed his eyes to this possibility. The appellate court was of the opinion that the conviction be quashed. The accused had acted innocently in the words of Wright J (at pp. 922–3):

> It is plain that if guilty knowledge is not necessary, no care on the part of the publican could save him from a conviction under s. 16(2), since it would be as easy for the constable to deny that he was on duty when asked, or to produce a forged permission from his superior officer, as to remove his armlet before entering the public house.

The imposition of strict liability would in the court's opinion have served no purpose. The court considered that in general and subject only to certain limited exceptions (see later), the law should require *mens rea* as to all the elements of the *actus reus* of an offence. This presumption applied even where words which import *mens rea* were absent from a section of a statute. In the opinion of Day J the fact that the Licensing Act 1872, s. 16(1), which made it an offence for a licensee 'knowingly' to suffer a constable who is on duty to remain on his licensed premises (in contrast to s. 16(2) which did not contain the word 'knowingly') did not render the two subsections different as to their essential nature. Section 16(1) by using the word 'knowingly' with regard to the offences of either harbouring or suffering a constable on duty to remain on licensed premises, obviously required *mens rea*. The absence of 'knowingly' or any word which generally imports *mens rea* in s. 16(2) had only (in his lordship's opinion) the effect of shifting the burden of proof (see Murphy, *A Practical Approach to Evidence*). In the words of Day J (at p. 921):

> In cases under s. 16(1) it is for the prosecution to prove the knowledge, while in cases under s. 16(2) the defendant has to prove that he did not know. That is

the only inference I draw from the insertion of the word 'knowingly' in the one subsection and its omission in the other.

(As to the effect of this opinion on later case law see para. 3.9.)

The case seemed to suggest that *mens rea* would be required as to all the elements of an offence where an accused would be liable to a penalty if convicted. The absence of words which generally import *mens rea* were of no legal significance.

In total opposition to this view is the case of *Cundy* v *Le Cocq* (1884) 13 QBD 207. The accused was a keeper of licensed premises. He had served an individual with intoxicating liquor; that individual was drunk. This was an offence contrary to the Licensing Act 1872, s. 13. The individual concerned gave no indication that he was drunk, and the accused was at no time aware of this fact. The accused argued that in the absence of knowledge of the condition of the individual concerned he could not be convicted. This was rejected by the court. In the words of Stephen J (at p. 209):

> I am of opinion that the words of the section amount to an absolute prohibition of the sale of liquor to a drunken person, and that the existence of a bona fide mistake as to the condition of the person served is not an answer to the charge.

His lordship considered that the policy of the section was to suppress drunkenness and to this end the offence was to be one of strict liability. There is a great temptation for publicans in the interests of their trade to serve alcohol without regard to the sobriety of their customers. Endorsing this offence as one of strict liability would ensure that a licensee took great care in ascertaining whether his customers were drunk or not.

As to the fact that the section did not contain any words which generally import *mens rea* his lordship was of the opinion (at p. 209) that though:

> Some of these [the sections of the Licensing Act 1872] contain the word 'knowingly', as for instance s. 14, which deals with keeping a disorderly house, and s. 16, which deals with the penalty for harbouring a constable. Knowledge in these and other cases is an element of the offence; but the clause we are considering says nothing about the knowledge of the state of the person served.

In the absence of any such words which imported *mens rea*, the offence was to be classified as one of strict liability. The situation is therefore confusing and contradictory. There is no general presumption that in the absence of words which are generally considered to import *mens rea* a section of a penal statute will be construed as either an offence requiring *mens rea* or as an offence of strict liability. Unfortunately the situation where a section within a penal statute does contain words which suggest that an individual is required to have a state of mind or attitude to the elements of the *actus reus* of an offence is equally confusing.

The Police Act 1964, s. 51(3), provides that it is an offence for an individual wilfully to obstruct a police officer in the execution of his duty. The importance

Strict Liability Offences

of this section for the principle of strict liability lies in the fact that the section determines that the obstruction should be 'wilful'. Judicial consideration of this requirement has failed to display a consistent interpretation. Authority is divided as to whether the term wilful determines the offence as requiring *mens rea* as to all elements of the *actus reus* of the offence or as a crime of strict liability.

Authorities beginning with *Betts v Stevens* [1910] 1 KB 1 and culminating in *Willmott v Atack* [1977] QB 498 suggested that the requirement that the obstruction of a police officer be wilful made the offence one requiring full *mens rea*. An individual needed to be aware of or at least reckless to the fact that his conduct obstructed a police officer in the execution of his duty. However, recent decisions, in particular *Ricketts v Cox* [1982] Crim LR 184, *Hills v Ellis* [1983] QB 685 and *Lewis v Cox* [1984] 3 WLR 875 endorsing *Rice v Connolly* [1966] 2 QB 414, merely require an accused to act deliberately. If his conduct then gives rise to a factual obstruction within the terms of s. 51(3) the offence is made out. Since an accused on this interpretation does not require any mental element with regard to the circumstances of the offence, it is a crime of strict liability. This interpretation seems to be based on the promotion of the policy that an accused interferes in police affairs at his own peril.

The situation with regard to other offences which require the element of wilfulness is more clear. In the case of *R v Sheppard* (1981) 72 Cr App R 82, for example, the House of Lords determined that the offence of 'wilful' neglect of a child contrary to s. 1 of the Children and Young Persons Act 1933 required a mental element. A person 'wilfully' neglects a child if he omits to provide care for it and either he is aware at the time of the failure to act that the child's health might be at risk or his lack of awareness of the child's physical condition was due to his indifference.

This review of the above authorities shows that the courts have followed no discernible pattern in their interpretation of statutes. It cannot be said that a penal section of a statute which does not contain a word which generally imports *mens rea* will necessarily be construed as an offence of strict liability. More importantly the inclusion of such words does not guarantee in all instances that an offence will be construed as one requiring *mens rea* as to all the elements of the *actus reus* of an offence. Though the words 'knowingly' and 'wilfully' have been considered in relation to particular offences the same ambiguity exists with regard to other words in many other statutes. Whether in a given instance a word within a section of a penal statute imports *mens rea* into a particular offence can only be determined by reference to judicial decisions. Words such as 'malicious' generally import *mens rea* into an offence (see *R v Vickers* [1957] 2 QB 664, a leading case relating to murder) as does the word 'permit' (see *James & Son Ltd v Smee* [1955] 1 QB 78, a case concerning the permitting of the use of a road vehicle in contravention of vehicle construction and use regulations—see later). However, in *Green v Burnett* [1955] 1 QB 78, a case which was heard at the same time as *James & Son Ltd v Smee*, the fact that the accused was charged under the same regulations of having actually 'used' a motor vehicle on which a certain part of the braking system fitted thereto was not maintained in good and efficient working order produced a different conclusion. The fact that the accused were charged with having 'used' the vehicle while in breach of the vehicle construction and use regulations determined that the offence of 'using' was one of strict liability. There are many words (which it would be pointless to set out) which on a literal interpretation would seem to suggest that if contained in a section of a penal statute, that section should require *mens rea* as to all the elements of the *actus reus* of an offence. However, it is certain that whether a section which contains such words is nevertheless and notwithstanding their inclusion to be determined in a given instance as creating an offence of strict liability can only be ascertained by reference to judicial authority. If there is any principle upon which a penal section within a statute can be determined as creating an offence of strict liability prior to any judicial pronouncement it lies otherwise than in its constituent words.

3.4 FACTORS UTILISED BY THE COURTS IN DETERMINING OFFENCES AS CRIMES OF STRICT LIABILITY

3.4.1 Quasi-criminal or regulatory offences

The issue that must be considered is whether extrinsic factors are taken into account by the judiciary in their interpretation of statutes. That is to say can a court in promoting certain policies which are independent of and unrelated to a penal statute, determine that in a given case a section within that statute should be determined as creating an offence of strict liability? Consideration must be given as a starting-point to a part of the judgment of Wright J in *Sherras* v *De Rutzen* [1895] 1 QB 918 which expressly considered this issue. His lordship was of the view (at pp. 921-2) that the exceptional cases when a section within a statute can be presumed to be one of strict liability: 'may perhaps be reduced to three. One is a class of acts which, in the language of Lush J in *Davies* v *Harvey* (1874) LR 9 QB 433, are not criminal in any real sense, but are acts which in the public interest are prohibited under a penalty.' His lordship then gave certain examples which are principally of historical interest. These examples have modern equivalents.

Clear examples of such modern offences, which can truly be regarded as not criminal in any real sense can be seen in statutes which seek to gain revenue from the carrying out of certain activities. Such an example can be seen in the case of the Vehicles (Excise) Act 1971. Section 12(4) of this Act provides that any individual who owns a motor vehicle which is used on the public roads and upon which he should pay duty (road tax) shall display a licence indicating that the road tax has been paid. By virtue of regulations made under s. 12(4) this licence must be displayed on the near-side lower corner of the windscreen, so that all the particulars upon the licence are clearly visible in daylight from the near side of the road. In the case of *Stowager* v *John* [1973] RTR 124 the accused locked his car and left it on a public road. There was a current vehicle excise licence in a plastic holder exhibited entirely in accordance with s. 12(4) and the relevant regulations made thereunder. Within a matter of hours and unknown to the accused the holder fell from the windscreen and into the car. The accused was convicted at first instance of an offence under s. 12(4) of having failed to exhibit a current excise licence affixed to his vehicle in accordance with the relevant regulations. It was held by the final appellate court, the Divisional Court of the Queen's Bench that the offence created by s. 12(4) of the Vehicles (Excise) Act 1971 was an

Strict Liability Offences

offence of strict liability. Furthermore this offence required no mental element on the part of the accused whatsoever with regard to any part of the *actus reus*. The accused was convicted though he had acted innocently and no fault or negligence could be attributed to him. The rationale of the decision was that the accused was responsible for his car and its accessories. It was entirely in his control and was his responsibility. The court, however, left open the issue whether the accused would have had a defence to a charge under s. 12(4) if the failure to exhibit the licence was due to its theft by a third party. The fact that the court was not totally willing to accept that cases of theft of an excise licence could provide a defence to a charge under s. 12(4) clearly indicates the extent to which it was prepared to construe the section as being one of strict liability. This was because in the opinion of Lord Widgery CJ (at p. 128) the case came clearly within the situation of offences envisaged by Wright J in *Sherras* v *De Rutzen* and was not really criminal in the true sense. In such cases the courts are willing, and always have been, to impose strict liability.

In the scenario therefore Bruce is criminally responsible for the failure of his vehicle to display an excise licence in accordance with s. 12(4) of the Vehicles (Excise) Act 1971 and the regulations made thereunder. It is irrelevant that the failure to comply with the requirements of the Act arose from an accident of circumstance which may have been inevitable and that he was not even negligent.

One of the more fruitful grounds for the expansion of this factor of quasi-criminality as a justification for the imposition of strict liability can be found in the area of consumer protection.

In the case of *Smedleys Ltd* v *Breed* [1974] AC 839 the accused were food manufacturers. In a particular season of about seven weeks they could expect to can 3,500,000 tins of peas in a single factory. They supplied to a retail store a tin of peas which was found by the purchaser to contain a caterpillar. It was similar in colour, size, density and weight to the peas in the tin. It was sterile and could not have constituted a danger to health if consumed. The accused were charged with an offence under s. 2(1) of the Food and Drugs Act 1955 which provided that if 'a person sells to the prejudice of the purchaser any food . . . which is . . . not of the substance . . . demanded by the purchaser, he shall . . . be guilty of an offence' (see now Food Act 1984, s. 2(1)).

The accused relied upon s. 3(3) of the Act which provided a defence to a charge under s. 2(1) if the presence of the extraneous matter was an unavoidable consequence of the process of collection or preparation of the food. At first instance it had been found that the accused had taken all reasonable care to prevent the presence of the caterpillar in the tin of peas. The accused company was nevertheless convicted. On final appeal to the House of Lords the conviction was upheld. It was no defence to show that the accused had taken all reasonable care in their preparation of the food. The defence under s. 3(3) was to be construed strictly. It was only available to the accused if the presence of the caterpillar was an unavoidable consequence of the food processing. The caterpillar could have been detected by visual inspection.

Their lordships accepted that the offence was one of strict liability. Furthermore the defence under s. 3(3) was of little practical importance. Though there had been only four complaints involving extraneous matter in the production of some $3\frac{1}{2}$ million tins of peas by the accused during 1971 this was regarded by the court as irrelevant to the issue of criminal liability.

The purpose of imposing strict liability and construing the statutory defence in such a restrictive manner was that the protection of the consuming public was paramount. In the words of Lord Hailsham of St Marylebone LC (at p. 851) though it was possible to:

> sympathise . . . with a manufacturer with a reputation and record as excellent as that of [the accused], to construe the Food and Drugs Act 1955 in a sense less strict than that which I have adopted would make a serious inroad on the legislation for consumer protection which Parliament has adopted and by successive Acts extended, over a period, now, of more than a century.

That the public as consumers must be protected from the more harmful aspects of the modern manufacture of products is a matter which must be considered axiomatic. The promotion of this policy is guaranteed by the prevalence of numerous statutes which though criminal in form have been reduced by the courts to an intricate system of strict liability offences that regulate the processes of manufacture and distribution of goods to consumers. These offences may demand an impossibly high standard of care on the part of manufacturers as has been illustrated by the case just considered. Such regulatory offences are the natural development of the views of Wright J in *Sherras* v *De Rutzen* and his classification of certain strict liability offences as 'not criminal in any real sense, but . . . acts which in the public interest are prohibited under a penalty'.

The ambit of such offences is not limited to food manufacture.

In *Pharmaceutical Society of Great Britain* v *Logan* [1982] Crim LR 443 the sale of medicine by a person who was not qualified and while unsupervised by a pharmacist and which was contrary to s. 52 of the Medicines Act 1968 was held to be a strict liability offence. The justification for the imposition of strict liability was the promotion of safety for the general public in the handling of medicines and drugs. (See also *Pharmaceutical Society of Great Britain* v *Storkwain* (*The Times*, 9 May 1985). The sale of a controlled substance without a prescription is also a strict liability offence (s. 58(2) the Medicine Act 1968).

Other statutes which regulate modern activities include s. 1 of the Trade Descriptions Act 1968, which provides *inter alia* that it is an offence for a retailer to apply a false or misleading trade description to any goods in his stock. This offence has been determined as being one of strict liability. Many statutory provisions relating to road traffic regulation create strict liability offences, as does the legislation which promotes minimum standards of safety and health for employees in shops and offices. These areas are far too complicated and extensive for detailed discussion in this book. It can be seen that strict liability offences encompass all aspects of life in the 20th century. They regulate *inter alia* the manufactaure of the products we consume or use, the means of travel available to us, and our safety and health in the activities we undertake, be it in our leisure time or in the course of our employment. The importance of such statutes lies in the fact that in their absence many aspects of modern life would be rendered dangerous or even impossible. It is the belief by the courts that strict liability helps advance the aims and policies inherent in such regulatory statutes that ensures its continued existence and growth in these areas of law, which are

Strict Liability Offences

concerned with the general promotion of modern social welfare and the well-being of the general public. This area of strict liability has expanded in ways that could scarcely have been foreseen by Wright J when he expounded it in *Sherras* v *De Rutzen*.

3.4.2 Public nuisance

In *Sherras* v *De Rutzen* [1895] 1 QB 918 Wright J considered a second exception to the common law presumption that statutory offences required *mens rea* as to all the elements of their *actus reus*. In his lordship's opinion this exception included 'some, and perhaps all, public nuisances' (at p. 922). His lordship cited the case of *R* v *Stephens* LR 1 QB 702 which involved nuisances caused by the workmen of an employer who had expressly forbade such conduct and who was entirely unaware of his employees' actions. This exception was confirmed, it is suggested, by the House of Lords in the case of *Alphacell Ltd* v *Woodward* [1972] AC 824. The accused were paper manufacturers. Their manufacturing process produced effluents which were run into two settling tanks and then recirculated and reused. The accused's premises were adjacent to a river. The lower settling tank had an overflow system into the river, but an actual overflow was prevented by two pumps, one automatic, the other a manual standby. This equipment was frequently examined and well maintained. Nevertheless due to the intakes of each pump becoming blocked by vegetation the lower settling tank overflowed and caused the discharge of effluent into the river. The accused were charged with causing polluting matter to enter the river contrary to s. 2(1) of the Rivers (Prevention of Pollution) Act 1955 (see now in addition the Control of Pollution Act 1974, ss. 32 and 33). The accused maintained that they should have been acquitted since the overflow had taken place without their knowledge and without negligence on their part.

This argument was rejected by the House of Lords. The offence required that the accused caused pollutant to enter the river. The accused had so 'caused' the pollution and no element of *mens rea* was to be imported into the offence by virtue of the term 'caused'. In the words of Lord Wilberforce (at pp. 834–5):

> In my opinion, this is a clear case of causing the polluted water to enter the stream. The whole complex operation which might lead to this result was an operation deliberately conducted by the [accused] and I fail to see how a defect in one stage of it, even if we must assume that this happened without their negligence, can enable them to say they did not cause the pollution. In my opinion, complication of this case by infusion of the concept of *mens rea*, and its exceptions, is unnecessary and undesirable. The section is clear, its application plain.

See also *F.J.H. Wrothwell Ltd* v *Yorkshire Water Authority* [1984] Crim LR 43.

One further justification for the imposition of strict liability upon this offence was that it would be almost impossible for the prosecution to establish that the pollution was caused by the intentional or negligent act of an accused (see Viscount Dilhorne at p. 839). Viscount Dilhorne and Lord Salmon justified the imposition of strict liability in this case on the basis that the offence was not criminal in any real sense but an act prohibited under a penalty. Lord Pearson, however, was prepared to impose strict liability on the basis that offences of this kind are in the nature of a public nuisance. It is suggested that this is the more appropriate ground for determining the nature of the offence, for even Lord Salmon was of the view that 'It is of the utmost public importance that our rivers should not be polluted. The risk of pollution, particularly from the vast and increasing riparian industries is very great.' However, the case illustrates that an offence can be determined as one of strict liability on more than one ground.

3.4.3 Criminal proceedings which enforce a civil right

Wright J in *Sherras* v *De Rutzen* [1895] 1 QB 918 gave his final example of a situation where a criminal offence could be determined as one of strict liability in the following vein (at p. 922):

> Lastly, there may be cases in which, although the proceeding is criminal in form, it is really only a summary mode of enforcing a civil right. See per Williams and Willes JJ in *Morden* v *Porter* 6 CB (NS) 64 as to unintentional trespass in pursuit of game; *Lee* v *Simpson* 3 CB 871 as to unconscious dramatic piracy; and *Hargreaves* v *Diddams* LR 10 QB 582, as to a bona fide belief in a legally impossible right to fish.

The factor has been mentioned for the sake of completeness. Unlike the other exceptions considered by Wright J it has not been of recent practical importance (apart perhaps from unconscious dramatic piracy).

3.5 GRAVE SOCIAL DANGER

Wright J in *Sherras* v *De Rutzen* [1895] 1 QB 918 did not lay down a definitive list of the factors that would be taken into account by a court in deciding whether to construe a penal section in a statute as one of strict liability. Since *Sherras* v *De Rutzen* the law has recognised new factors as justifying the imposition of strict liability in certain given cases. One such factor is that a statute seeks to prevent (by imposing criminal liability) a course of conduct which if unchecked could give rise to grave social danger, or serious harm to the general welfare of the public. In such cases the courts are prepared to dispense with the requirement of *mens rea* at least with regard to one element of the *actus reus* of such an offence. There are many examples of acts which are a source of grave social danger to the public. The decision to impose strict liability in the case of *Alphacell Ltd* v *Woodward* [1972] AC 824 could also be justified on this ground.

The scenario discloses three examples of road traffic offences which are crimes of strict liability, and which can be justified as offences of that kind on the principle that they each seek to prevent a grave social danger.

The Road Traffic Act 1972, s. 40, empowers the Secretary of State for Transport to make regulations concerning *inter alia* the construction and use of road vehicles, for the promotion of greater road safety. The current regulatons made under this section are the Motor Vehicles (Construction and Use) Regulations 1981 (SI 1981 No. 1017). Regulations 13 and 64 make provision for

Strict Liability Offences

hand and foot brakes on a motor car to be in full and efficient working order.

By s. 40(5) of the Road Traffic Act 1972 it is an offence to be in breach of these regulations. These are strict liability offences.

In the scenario Bruce has thus committed two separate offences under these regulations. In addition he is also criminally liable under s. 5(2) of the Road Traffic Act 1972. This offence was considered in chapter 1. It is a crime which is constituted entirely by a state of affairs. The offence is also one of strict liability. All the elements of the offence are present. He is in charge of a motor vehicle, which is on a public road, and he is unfit to drive through drink. Unless he can establish the statutory defence under s. 5(3) that he is so unfit through drink that he is incapable of driving the vehicle and therefore is to be deemed not to be in charge of it for the purpose of s. 5(2) he will be found to be criminally responsible. There is no requirement in the offence for Bruce consciously or recklessly or even negligently to have placed himself within the terms of the offence. The grave social dangers which can result from inadequately maintained road vehicles and drivers who are incapable through alcohol or drugs are manifest. Though many road traffic offences are no more than regulatory it cannot be said that drunken drivers or vehicles with inoperative braking systems are any less than a potential and hazardous source of death and severe injury upon the roads.

Nevertheless a paradox is apparent. The imposition of strict liability is sometimes justified on the ground that it is applicable to offences which are not truly criminal in any real sense and are no more than a means of maintaining and regulating certain socially desirable ends: yet when an offence is considered so serious that it seeks to prevent death or serious injury or some other grave social harm to the fabric of society, then this is also considered a justification for the imposition of strict liability. Some of the factors which are used to justify strict liability are complementary and it may well be that the courts can determine an offence as being one of strict liability on the basis of more than one factor, see *Alphacell Ltd v Woodward* [1972] AC 824. Nevertheless the factors of non-criminality and grave social harm are in total contradiction. They exist at entirely opposite ends of the criminal spectrum. It can be argued that when offences are no more than regulatory there is no significant injustice done to an accused in dispensing with the requirement of *mens rea* with regard to at least one element of the *actus reus* of an offence. This argument all but disappears when an offence is considered which purports to deal with a case of a grave social evil. The very fact that it is a serious offence carrying with it a considerable social stigma (and possible grave penal consequences) for an accused should suggest that only those who intend to carry out the offence or who are at least reckless should be convicted. The reality of the situation is that the fact that an offence may be a serious one dealing with the suppression of a grave social harm is used to justify the imposition of strict liability in certain cases. It can be seen therefore that there are no crimes which cannot potentially be brought within the confines of strict liability offences, and justified as such on grounds which are in conflict with other equally recognised factors which are themselves used to vindicate strict liability in other offences.

An examination of the scenario will disclose further strict liability offences all of which are considered by the judiciary to be crimes which combat grave social evils. Rex has in his possession a number of firearms, all of which he honestly and reasonably believes to be antiques. The possession of firearms is regulated by the Firearms Act 1968. Section 1(1)(a) of the Act provides that it is an offence to possess, purchase or acquire a firearm without holding a current firearms certificate. By virtue of s. 58(2) of the Act there is no requirement for an individual to have a firearms certificate, if the firearms he possesses are antiques and they have been sold, transferred, purchased, acquired or possessed by him as a curiosity or ornament.

Unknown to Rex a number of his firearms though apparently antiques are modern reproductions and are fully working models. On an objective assessment of the facts Rex should possess a current firearms certificate in relation to these weapons. He has committed the *actus reus* of the offence under s. 1 and the defence under s. 58(2) of the Act is unavailable to him.

His only defence is to claim that his honest belief as to the nature of the firearms in his possession should determine that he lacks *mens rea* (see para. 6.5.4).

The scenario matches almost exactly the facts of *R v Howells* [1977] 3 All ER 417. In that case the accused's argument that the offence under s. 1(1)(a) of the Firearms Act was an offence requiring *mens rea* was rejected.

The court considered the section should be construed strictly, the reason for imposing strict liability was, in the words of Brown LJ (at p. 425), because:

[T]he danger to the community resulting from the possession of lethal firearms is so obviously great that an absolute prohibition against their possession without proper authority must have been the intention of Parliament when considered in conjunction with the words of the section. . . . [T]o allow a defence of honest and reasonable belief that the firearm was an antique . . . would be likely to defeat the clear intention of the Act. (But see para. 6.5.4).

A supplementary argument of the accused was that if the offence was construed as being one of strict liability then his honest and reasonable belief in the nature of the firearm precluded him from 'possessing' the firearm within the terms of s. 1(1)(a) of the Act (but see para. 6.5.4. It now appears that such a belief need not be based on reasonable grounds). The basis of this argument was that even in an offence of strict liability, the fact of possession requires a mental element. The accused could not 'possess' the firearm unless he was aware of its principal qualities. He could, on the basis of his honest and reasonable belief, possess only an antique firearm. If such was the case an essential element of the offence was missing. This argument was also rejected by the court. The accused had custody and control of the firearm and his honest and reasonable belief that the weapon was a genuine antique when it was a modern reproduction did not prevent him possessing it. The accused's conviction was affirmed. The accused was aware that it was a firearm, he was merely mistaken as to its age, he therefore possessed it within the terms of the Act. On the face of it Rex has no answer to a charge under s. 1(1)(a) of the Firearms Act. An offence of this kind is one which is considered to be a potential danger to the well-being of society. On this basis it has been construed as an offence of strict liability.

The police have evidence of a much more serious offence, the discovery of a

Strict Liability Offences

minute quantity of LSD (lysergic acid diethylamide) in Bruce's car. It is an offence contrary to s. 5 of the Misuse of Drugs Act 1971 for an individual to be in unlawful possession of a controlled drug. LSD is such a drug. In *Warner* v *Metropolitan Police Commissioner* [1969] 2 AC 256 the House of Lords considered the nature of this offence and the concept of possession. The case concerned the offence of unlawful possession within s. 1(1) of the Drugs (Prevention of Misuse) Act 1964 (now s. 5 of the 1971 Act). The majority of their lordships (Lord Reid dissenting) were of the opinion that the offence was one of strict liability. All of their lordships were cognisant of the dangers to society of the misuse of drugs and of the trafficking in such substances. Unless the offence was one of strict liability wholesale evasion of criminal responsibility under the Act would render the Act a nullity. The offence therefore totally forbade the unauthorised possession of any controlled drug.

However, the offence required the prosecution to establish the element of possession of a controlled drug by an accused. Lord Pearce, accepting the opinion of Lord Parker CJ in the case of *Lockyer* v *Gibb* [1967] 2 QB 243, considered ([1969] 2 AC 256 at p. 305) that:

a person did not have possession of something which had been 'slipped into his' bag without his knowledge. One may, therefore, exclude from the 'possession' intended by the Act the physical control of articles which have been 'planted' on him without his knowledge.

His lordship further considered what was meant by possession. It did not require the prosecution to prove that an individual was aware of the name and nature of the drug. His lordship thought that the concept of possession was satisfied:

[B]y a knowledge only of the existence of the thing itself and not its qualities, and that ignorance or mistake as to its qualities is not an excuse. This would comply with the general understanding of the word 'possess'. Though I reasonably believe the tablets which I possess to be aspirin, yet if they turn out to be heroin I am in possession of heroin tablets. This would be so I think even if I believed them to be sweets. It would be otherwise if I believed them to be something of a wholly different nature.

As to the difference between nature and quality with regard to a substance, though it may only be a matter of degree, his lordship expressed the hope that a jury would sensibly determine when an individual had made a mistake as to the quality of a substance, which will not provide a defence, and which will not negate possession and a mistake as to nature which might preclude an individual from possessing the substance within the terms of the Drugs Act. The extent of this possible defence was left unclear and seems to have been reduced to a vanishing point by later authorities. In *R* v *Marriott* [1971] 1 All ER 595, a case involving some 0.03 grains (about 2 milligrams) of cannabis which forensic tests had established were affixed to the blade of a penknife, it was held that to establish the fact of possession it was only necessary to show that the accused had reason to know that there was foreign matter on the knife. It was only necessary for him to be aware of the existence of the substance. Though *Warner* v *Metropolitan Police Commissioner* was cited to the court the case of *R* v *Marriott* made no reference to the possibility of a mistake by an individual as to the nature of a substance negating its possession. In the case of *Searle* v *Randolph* [1972] Crim LR 779 the accused was found to have some 36 cigarette ends on his person. One cigarette contained three milligrams of cannabis and traces of this drug were found in two other ends. The court though purporting to apply the test of possession as determined by Lord Pearce in *Warner* v *Metropolitan Police Commissioner* considered that the difference between a normal tobacco-filled cigarette end and the one in the possession of the accused was akin to the difference between an aspirin and heroin tablet, i.e., a mistake as to quality. The prosecution needed to establish only that the accused knew that he had on his person the cigarette end and it was not necessary for him to be aware that the cigarette end also contained cannabis.

In one circumstance the defence that an individual may not possess a controlled drug if he is entirely unaware of its true nature is still available to an accused. The application of the defence seems to be limited to cases when the controlled drug is in a container. In *Warner* v *Metropolitan Police Commissioner* the accused was driving a van in the back of which were three cases. Two of these cases contained scent bottles and another a plastic bag containing 20,000 amphetamine tablets. The accused had made deliveries of cases containing scent for one B on previous occasions. His defence was that he believed that this delivery also on B's behalf was also of scent. He had no conception that one of the cases contained a controlled drug. A majority of the House of Lords were of the opinion that if an individual possessed a container, i.e., he had physical control of it and was aware of its existence, then prima facie he also possessed its contents. However, if an individual was entirely mistaken as to the *nature* of the contents of a container to the extent that if he had known what was really in the container he would not have taken physical possession of it, then he could not be regarded as being in possession of its contents. If an individual was only mistaken as to the *quality* of the contents of a container, i.e., he believed it contained aspirin when in fact it contained heroin, then he would be deemed to be in possession of the contents. If an individual takes physical possession of a container and is unaware of the true nature of its contents, i.e., a controlled drug, and has no reason to suspect that fact, then in the absence of a legal right to open the container it cannot be said that an individual is in possession of those controlled drugs.

Where either an individual has reason to suspect that a container may contain controlled drugs and/or the individual has a right to and a reasonable opportunity to examine its contents, then he shall be considered to be in possession of those contents i.e. drugs as well as the container, irrespective of whether he has examined the contents or not. The fact that an individual is voluntarily intoxicated will not negate the fact of his possession of controlled drugs (see *R* v *Young* [1984] 1 WLR 654 and para. 6.3.2). It cannot be said that this is a satisfactory state of affairs. It is difficult to determine the difference between a mistake as to nature and a mistake as to quality of a substance. Furthermore Lord Pearce (in *Warner*) seems to suggest that a belief by an individual that he has in his possession sweets which are in fact heroin tablets would not be a mistake as to the nature of the substance. On this basis it would be difficult to conceive of any case where the defence would be available. This unnecessary complication of the concept of possession as applicable to the contents of a container can lead to the very worst examples of strained legal reasoning and the most absurd results, see *R v Irving* [1970] Crim LR 642.

Nevertheless it cannot be doubted that the courts take their duty of protecting both the individual and society from grave social evils seriously. If the judiciary consider that a section within a penal statute which purports to defend society from serious dangers can only be made effective by construing it as an offence of strict liability, then they will not shun from so interpreting and applying it (see *Gammon (Hong Kong) Ltd v Attorney-General of Hong Kong* [1985] AC 1).

The issue as to whether Bruce is in unlawful possession of the LSD contrary to s. 5 of the Misuse of Drugs Act 1971 is fraught with difficulties.

It cannot be doubted that the cigarette packet is a container, and on this basis the case of *Warner v Metropolitan Police Commissioner* is applicable.

Nevertheless the question of whether Bruce is in possession of the LSD may differ depending upon various circumstances.

If the LSD were mixed with the tobacco in the cigarettes, then irrespective of any belief that Bruce may have as to the nature of the contents of the cigarette packet, he may be deemed to be in possession of the LSD. This will be so where Bruce is aware of the cigarette packet and is also aware that the packet has contents, i.e., tobacco (or so he believes).

The difference between tobacco and LSD is not, according to *Warner v Metropolitan Police Commissioner*, a difference as to nature but quality. On this basis as Bruce is aware that the packet has contents he possesses those contents.

If the LSD forms a separate entity from the cigarettes within the cigarette packet then Bruce may claim that rather like the accused in *R v Irving* [1970] Crim LR 642 he may not 'possess' the LSD. In this case the accused possessed a medicine bottle which contained stomach pills and unknown to him a single amphetamine tablet, part of a prescription for his wife. It was held by the appellate court that the accused was in possession of the bottle and the stomach pills but not in the circumstances the amphetamine tablet. Bruce could therefore argue that he was not in possession of the LSD but only of the cigarettes. The situation would be different perhaps if there were circumstances which would have either aroused in Bruce's mind the suspicion that there was a quantity of controlled drugs in the packet and/or he had a legal right and reasonable opportunity to examine the contents of the cigarette packet but had not done so.

If the packet contained only LSD then Bruce would possess the drug if he was aware or believed that the packet had something in it, though he thought the contents to be only tobacco. For in such a case his belief that he possesses tobacco is a mistake as to the quality of the contents and not to its nature. He would also possess the LSD if he believed or knew the cigarette packet had contents other than tobacco, dependent upon those contents differing from LSD only as to quality and not as to nature, e.g., sweets. If Bruce believed the packet to be empty then he could not be in possession of the actual contents, i.e., the LSD. If, however, he either became suspicious that the cigarette packet might contain a controlled drug and/or he had a legal right to and a reasonable opportunity to examine the inside of the cigarette packet then he might be considered to possess the LSD.

Such solutions to the problem of drug possession are needlessly artificial. They are the result of the promotion of the policy that seeks to prohibit and penalise any unauthorised possession of controlled drugs. It is seen as a necessary weapon in society's struggle with the drug trafficker.

3.6 PRESUMPTION AGAINST THE IMPOSITION OF STRICT LIABILITY

In the case of *Sweet* v *Parsley* [1970] AC 132 the accused was charged under s. 5(b) of the Dangerous Drugs Act 1965 with the offence of being a person 'concerned in the management of premises' which were 'used for the purpose' of smoking cannabis. The accused was a subtenant of a farmhouse which she had further sublet to others. She had ceased to live there, and only visited the farmhouse to collect post and rent. It was conceded by the accused that the premises had been used for smoking cannabis. It was accepted by the prosecution that the accused had no knowledge that the farmhouse had been used for this purpose. The accused was convicted. On appeal to the House of Lords it was determined that s. 5(b) did not create a strict liability offence, and that the conviction should be quashed. In the words of Lord Morris of Borth-y-Gest (at p. 154), 'If someone is concerned in management there must at least be knowledge of what it is that is being managed'. The House of Lords unanimously considered that the words 'used for the purpose' within the offence both referred to and were interconnected with the actual management of premises and clearly inferred *mens rea* into the offence. An accused must manage premises and be aware that the premises are being used for the purpose of smoking cannabis. Without more the effect of *Sweet* v *Parsley* would have been to determine that the above-mentioned offence was one requiring *mens rea*. However, their lordships considered the function and place of strict liability offences in the criminal law. Lord Pearce (at p. 156) rejected the argument of the prosecution that an offence of such social gravity must be one of strict liability; to encourage those concerned in managing premises to exercise greater vigilance, and to prevent the guilty from going free.

Lord Morris was content to approve the opinion of Lord Goddard CJ in *Brend* v *Wood* (1946) 175 LT 306 at p. 307 where his lordship had approved the principle that a statute should in the interests of civil liberties impose strict liability only where this is clearly or by implication the construction the statute bears.

Lord Morris stated ([1970] AC 132 at p. 155):

It is said that the intention of Parliament was to impose a duty on all persons concerned in the management of any premises to exercise vigilance to prevent the smoking of cannabis. If that had been the intention of Parliament different words would have been used.

This presumption against imposing absolute standards was emphasised by Lord Reid. His lordship considered that though Parliament could with a clear intention create an offence of strict liability, in cases where there was no such clear intention in a statute certain factors had to be taken into account in determining whether an offence was to be construed as one of strict liability or

Strict Liability Offences

not. His lordship accepted that quasi-criminal regulatory offences could be the legitimate subject of strict liability where silence as to *mens rea* could be so interpreted but that: 'It does not in the least follow that when one is dealing with a truly criminal act it is sufficient merely to have regard to the subject-matter of the enactment. One must put oneself in the position of a legislator.' His lordship was of the opinion that consideration should be given to the fact of the grave consequences, social and penal, that would follow a conviction of a serious crime. The innocent should not be punished so that more of the guilty could be convicted. Such situations bring the law into disrepute. Nevertheless his lordship observed 'that in some recent cases where serious offences have been held to be absolute offences, the court has taken into account no more than the wording of the Act and the character and seriousness of the mischief which constitutes the offence' (at p. 156).

In *Sweet* v *Parsley* the House of Lords determined that there is a general presumption (which may be displaced by the clear intention of Parliament) favouring the importation of *mens rea* to all the elements of the *actus reus* of an offence. This presumption is most clearly applicable where the offence is one with serious consequences for an accused who is convicted, e.g., social stigma or severity of punishment, though the fact that such an offence is concerned with an issue of public concern may displace the presumption (see *Gammon (Hong Kong) Ltd* v *Attorney-General of Hong Kong* [1985] AC 1).

In so far as offences which seek to prohibit grave social harms or evils are determined by virtue of *Sweet* v *Parsley* to be offences requiring *mens rea* there is an apparent conflict with cases such as *Warner* v *Metropolitan Police Commissioner* [1969] 2 AC 256. This latter decision determines that serious offences which have as their purpose the prohibition of conduct or states of affairs which result in, e.g., grave social dangers can be justified as strict liability offences upon this basis. This line of authority, it is suggested, has not been deprived of any vitality and there seems nothing in principle from deterring a court from imposing strict liability on this basis notwithstanding *Sweet* v *Parsley*.

It is suggested that where a court considers that Parliament clearly intended to impose strict liability then, notwithstanding the decision in *Sweet* v *Parsley*, it will in the future be free to do so and may justify the imposition on the principle that the offence under particular consideration is, e.g., a crime which seeks to regulate and prohibit conduct or a state of affairs which may give rise, e.g., to a grave social harm or danger. On this basis it can be argued that *Warner* v *Metropolitan Police Commissioner* and *Sweet* v *Parsley* are not in conflict. *Sweet* v *Parsley* affirms that in cases of serious offences the imposition of strict liability is no longer to be considered as a process merely of questioning, e.g., whether the offence concerned is one involving grave social danger. The emphasis is against the imposition of strict liability in such cases but this is not the same thing as suggesting that the courts will always require *mens rea* in cases of serious offences. Two cases will illustrate the point.

The spirit of *Sweet* v *Parsley* was applied in *R* v *Phekoo* [1981] 3 All ER 84 a case concerning the unlawful harassment of residential occupiers of property, contrary to s. 1(3)(a) of the Protection from Eviction Act 1977. The appellate court quashing the conviction of the accused was of the opinion that the offence being of a serious nature, e.g., tantamount to blackmail, which provided for substantial penal consequences required *mens rea* as to all the elements of the *actus reus*. The accused would have to have intended to harass and be aware that his harassment was in relation to the occupiers of the house concerned and that those occupiers were residential occupiers as required by the Act and not mere squatters.

However, in the case of *R* v *Champ* (1981) 73 Cr App R 367 the accused was charged with the unlawful cultivation of cannabis contrary to s. 6 of the Misuse of Drugs Act 1971. This offence carried the maximum penalty on conviction of 14 years' imprisonment. Nevertheless the court did not consider that this factor justified imposing the burden upon the prosecution of proving that the accused had *mens rea* as to all the elements of the *actus reus* of the offence.

3.7 WILL THE IMPOSITION OF STRICT LIABILITY ENHANCE OR ASSIST THE ENFORCEMENT OF AN OFFENCE?

In *Lim Chin Aik* v *R* [1963] 1 All ER 223 the accused, who was living in Singapore, was charged under an immigration ordinance which prohibited a certain class of individuals, which included the accused, from actually entering or remaining in Singapore. There was no evidence that he was aware of the existence of this ordinance. Though convicted at first instance of breaching this provision, his conviction was quashed by the Judicial Committee of the Privy Council. Lord Evershed giving the opinion of the Privy Council considered that (at p. 228):

> [I]t is not enough . . . merely to label the statute as one dealing with a grave social evil and from that to infer that strict liability was intended. It is pertinent also to inquire whether putting the defendant under strict liability will assist in the enforcement of the regulations. That means that there must be something he can do, directly or indirectly, by supervision or inspection, by improvement of his business methods or by exhorting those whom he may be expected to influence or control, which will promote the observance of the regulations. Unless this is so, there is no reason in penalising him. . . . Where it can be shown that the imposition of strict liability would result in the prosecution and conviction of a class of persons whose conduct could not in any way affect the observance of the law, their lordships consider that, even where the statute is dealing with a grave social evil, strict liability is not likely to be intended.

Thus as a corollary where a statutory offence has been interpreted as one of strict liability, one of the determining factors may be that by imposing strict liability individuals are encouraged to greater vigilance to prevent the commission of the prohibited act (see *Gammon (Hong Kong) Ltd* v *Attorney-General of Hong Kong* [1985] AC 1). Despite the attractive logic of the principle endorsed in *Lim Chin Aik* v *R* it has been more honoured in the breach than in the observance. It is not a question which seems to be taken seriously into account by the judiciary in this country in determining whether to impose strict liability. It has been argued that the case of *Harding* v *Price* [1948] 1 KB 695 is an early example of an authority which adopted the philosophy inherent in *Lim Chin Aik* v *R*. In *Harding* v *Price* the accused had been responsible for a road accident in which another vehicle had been damaged. The accused did not stop or report the

Strict Liability Offences

accident to the police as he was required to by statute. It was found as a fact that due to the noise of a trailer which was attached to his vehicle he had not heard the collision and was not aware of the accident. On appeal the accused's conviction was quashed. In the words of Lord Goddard CJ (at p. 701) of the report:

> [I]f a statute contains an absolute prohibition against the doing of some act, as a general rule *mens rea* is not a constituent of the offence; but there is all the difference between prohibiting an act and imposing a duty to do something on the happening of a certain event. Unless a man knows that the event has happened, how can he carry out the duty imposed? If the duty be to report, he cannot report something of which he has no knowledge. . . . Any other view would lead to calling on a man to do the impossible.
>
> I should, however, add that the authorities show that, even where the statute imposes what is apparently an absolute prohibition, an absence of guilty knowledge may in some cases be a defence; *Sherras* v *De Rutzen* [1895] 1 QB 918 is one instance. . . . Such cases depend on the wording and purpose of the particular statute.

It is instructive to note that in *Harding* v *Price* Humphreys J regarded the offence as being regulatory and Singleton J considered that the absence of any word importing *mens rea* merely placed the burden of establishing the lack of *mens rea* on the accused (see para. 3.3.1).

Though *Harding* v *Price* bears a resemblance to *Lim Chin Aik* v *R* [1963] 1 All ER 223 it can be justified on more narrow grounds. It is accepted that a great number of strict liability offences require a considerable mental element. *Harding* v *Price* can be seen as a case which unlike 'states of affairs' offences (see chapter 1) determined that as a condition precedent to criminal liability the accused must have been aware of or intended or been reckless as to the bringing about of certain fundamental elements of the offence, i.e., the factual element of a road accident. This is the same as Lemon publishing the poem in *Whitehouse* v *Lemon* [1979] AC 617 or Prince in *R* v *Prince* (1875) LR 2 CCR 154 consciously taking an unmarried girl into his charge. It cannot be denied, however, that the case may simply be an instance of judicial benevolence.

3.8 THE MITIGATION OF STRICT LIABILITY OFFENCES

Though a statutory offence may be one of strict liability, parliamentary draftsmen may provide in such a statute a special and particular defence or defences which generally mitigate the harsh reality of strict liability. Virtually all such defences may be classified as of two principal kinds or an amalgam of both. Two examples will suffice to illustrate the general position.

Section 24 of the Trade Descriptions Act 1968 provides an accused with a possible defence where he is charged with an offence under this Act, e.g., applying a false trade description to goods which he has offered for sale. The full details of the defence are that:

(a) The accused must first prove (s. 24(1)(a)) 'that the commission of the offence was due to a mistake or to reliance on information supplied to him or to the act or default of another person, an accident or some other cause beyond his control'.

Though this paragraph sets out clearly the circumstances which may in part provide a defence for an accused, they are in essence factors which suggest that the offence was due to the actions of third parties or matters over which the accused had no control.

(b) An accused must also prove that (s. 24(1)(b)) 'he took all reasonable precautions and exercised all due diligence to avoid the commission of such an offence by himself or any person under his control'.

This additional requirement provides that an accused must in practical terms establish that neither he nor anyone in his employ or control has been negligent.

Section 24 provides an apt illustration of the two principal defences that are made available to an accused in the case of statutory strict liability offences. Namely, defences of 'no negligence' or fault due to the actions of a 'third party'. In the Trade Descriptions Act 1968 these defences were amalgamated into a combined statutory defence.

An example of a pure 'no negligence' defence is provided by the Misuse of Drugs Act 1971. An individual who has been found to be in unlawful 'possession' of a controlled drug within the meaning of *Warner* v *Metropolitan Police Commissioner* [1969] 2 AC 256 contrary to s. 5(2) may establish a defence by virtue of s. 28 of the Act that he 'neither knew of nor suspected nor had reason to suspect the existence of some fact alleged by the prosecution which it is necessary for the prosecution to prove if he is to be convicted of the offence charged.'

The accused is placed under a legal burden to satisfy a jury on a balance of probabilities (see Murphy, *A Practical Approach to Evidence*) that he did not know or suspect or have reason to suspect that he had in his possession a controlled drug. It is thus a defence for an individual *inter alia* to establish that he has taken reasonable care to ensure that he is not in possession of a controlled drug but does not impose upon him any greater duty of care. It is not generally a defence within the section for an accused to establish that he possessed a controlled drug but that he neither knew nor suspected nor had reason to suspect that the substance or product in question was a different controlled drug from that which is the subject of a prosecution for unlawful possession.

There are many examples of statutory defences which are unique to particular statutory strict liability offences. It would be pointless to give any illustrations of such defences. However, in this chapter an example has already been considered. By virtue of s. 3 of the Food and Drugs Act 1955 it was a defence to a charge under s. 2 of the Act (selling food not of the substance demanded by a customer due to the presence of extraneous matter) for an accused to establish that the extraneous matter was an 'unavoidable consequence of the process of collection or preparation of the food', (see now Food Act 1984, s. 3). The nature of this defence has already been considered in outline above.

3.9 THE MITIGATION OF STATUTORY STRICT LIABILITY OFFENCES: POSSIBLE COMMON LAW SOLUTIONS

In *Sweet* v *Parsley* [1970] AC 132 Lord Reid (at p. 150) considered that an

Strict Liability Offences

improvement upon the blanket imposition of strict liability would be the substitution in appropriate cases of the requirement for the prosecution to establish that an accused had been grossly negligent with regard to the *actus reus* of an offence. In addition to this suggestion his lordship also looked favourably upon the principle that:

> Parliament has not infrequently transferred the onus as regards *mens rea* to the accused, so that, once the necessary facts are proved, he must convince the jury that on balance of probabilities [see Murphy, *A Practical Approach to Evidence*] he is innocent of any criminal intention.

This suggestion as an alternative to the imposition of strict liability has found judicial favour, e.g., Singleton J in *Harding* v *Price* [1948] 1 KB 695 at p. 704 and, in particular, Day J in *Sherras* v *De Rutzen* [1895] 1 QB 918 (see para. 3.3.1).

Neither suggestion as an alternative to the imposition of strict liability has, however, found much judicial favour or general application. The suggestion as to the transfer of the onus of proof is contrary to the balance of established authority and appears to be irreconcilable with the celebrated House of Lords decision in *Woolmington* v *DPP* [1935] AC 462 which determined that in general it is for the prosecution to prove beyond reasonable doubt the guilt of an accused and not for a defendant to establish his innocence (see Murphy, *A Practical Approach to Evidence*).

Lord Reid also seemed to suggest that on the basis of an Australian authority, *Proudman* v *Dayman* (1941) 67 CLR 536, another alternative to strict liability would be to permit an accused (presuming the prosecution had proved the commission of the offence) to establish that he had 'an honest and reasonable belief in a state of facts which, if they existed, would make the [accused's] act innocent' and thus afford 'an excuse for doing what would otherwise be an offence'.

This has been interpreted as requiring the accused to establish on a balance of probabilities that he was not negligent and that in addition he also lacked *mens rea* in relation to at least one of the elements of the *actus reus* of an offence. The prosecution would in such cases be relieved from the burden of establishing the *mens rea* of the accused. Whatever the interpretation ascribed to Lord Reid's suggestion in this instance it would seem this particular alternative to the imposition of strict liability is subject to the same objections considered above. It appears to be irreconcilable with *Woolmington* v *DPP*. This authority was also one of Lord Pearce's principal objections in *Sweet* v *Parsley* [1970] AC 132 (at pp. 157–8) to the implementation of his suggested alternatives to the imposition of strict liability, which were similar to those of Lord Reid.

Lord Diplock (at p. 164), taking the approach as he understood it of Dixon J in *Proudman* v *Dayman* (1941) 67 CLR 536 expressed the opinion that: 'the accused does not have to prove the existence of mistaken belief on the balance of probabilities; he has to raise a reasonable doubt as to its non-existence'. His lordship considered that this belief had to be both honestly and reasonably held (see *R* v *Tolson* (1889) 23 QBD 168).

This alternative to the imposition of strict liability has been interpreted as requiring an accused to adduce sufficient evidence to raise the issue before a jury or tribunal of fact that he has an honest and reasonable belief in a state of facts which would if they existed provide a defence to a charge under such a statutory offence. This in essence would be the establishing of an evidential burden (see Murphy, *A Practical Approach to Evidence*) by the accused that he was not negligent and that he lacked *mens rea*. Following this the prosecution would then have to prove beyond reasonable doubt that the accused was negligent and where appropriate that he had acted with the required *mens rea*. Until the establishing of this evidential burden by an accused the only burden imposed upon the prosecution would be the proof beyond reasonable doubt of the commission of the *actus reus* of the offence concerned by the accused.

None of the alternatives to strict liability considered above has as yet been implemented by judicial decision. Though it can be suggested that the courts have accepted a limited concept of a no-negligence defence at common law. In *Warner* v *Metropolitan Police Commissioner* [1969] 2 AC 256 it was determined that an accused may negate the fact of possession of a controlled drug which is in a container by establishing that there were no circumstances which aroused his suspicions that he had in his physical possession such a substance and the fact that though he may have had a legal right to examine the contents within a container it was not reasonable for him to do so. These facts, if established, amount in effect to a defence that an accused was not negligent in being in possession of a controlled drug but that his possession of the substance concerned was the product and result of an honest and reasonable but mistaken belief as to its true nature.

3.10 THE JUSTIFICATION FOR THE IMPOSITION OF STRICT LIABILITY

The principal arguments for the imposition of strict liability have been most clearly expressed by Dickson J in *R* v *City of Sault Ste Marie* (1978) 85 DLR (3d) 161, where (at p. 171) he expressed the opinion that there were two principal justifications for the imposition of strict liability. The first was that the high standards of care exacted by such offences ensure that social interests would be protected and individuals who undertake activities which may cause harm to individuals would be encouraged to maintain those standards if they know that mistake or ignorance would not excuse them. The second justification is administrative efficiency, the need to prove fault in so many cases (many of which are merely regulatory offences) would place too great a burden upon the prosecution in terms of time and money, apart from permitting many guilty individuals to escape criminal responsibility.

The arguments against the imposition of strict liability are that it violates fundamental principles of criminal law. In addition it is argued that the assumption that it promotes high standards of efficiency and care have not been established. It can of course be argued that it has not been demonstrated that the imposition of strict liability does *not* encourage or help to create higher standards of care and efficiency upon individuals. Furthermore it has been argued that the prosecution frequently need to establish the *mens rea* of an accused for the purpose of the consideration of his sentence thus depriving strict liability of its principal advantage to a prosecutor. No doubt where the prosecution in a given

Strict Liability Offences

case has evidence of *mens rea* possessed by an accused it will no doubt adduce it and such a matter will be a cogent factor in the decision to prosecute. In any event it is frequently forgotten that in cases of strict liability the prosecution are usually only relieved from establishing *mens rea* with regard to one element of the *actus reus* of an offence, though, of course, this may be in relation to an important element. In such circumstances the argument that *mens rea* needs to be established in strict liability offences is no more than a recognition of their usual nature. Nevertheless there is an advantage to a prosecuting authority in cases of strict liability in being relieved in part or in whole from the *need or obligation* to establish *mens rea* in relation to at least one aspect of the *actus reus* of an offence. (For it does ease the administrative burden of many prosecuting authorities.) It is suggested therefore that the argument that *mens rea* frequently needs to be established by the prosecution in order that the court may consider an appropriate sentence in a given case is for the reasons given above not a strong one in justifying the rejection of strict liability. The issue of sentence is not a problem for the prosecuting authority but for the judge or bench.

It cannot be doubted that the judiciary regard strict liability offences as a necessary evil in the protection of society from a multitude of dangers which emanate from numerous sources. The various prosecuting authorities find their administrative and prosecution burdens considerably eased by the existence of strict liability offences. These cogent factors which are steeped in practical reality are important because, whether they are valid or not, they are generally believed to be valid by those who adhere to them. On this basis the arguments of academics as to the injustice and non-effectiveness of the imposition of strict liability seems to be views which are fated to be ignored.

Despite the opinions expressed by the House of Lords in *Sweet* v *Parsley* [1970] AC 132 exhorting the introduction of alternatives to strict liability, its continued existence in statutory offences will remain for a considerable time notwithstanding the lamentations of academics. The presence of strict liability offences is a fact of life that must be accepted by every lawyer be they practising, student or academic.

3.11 QUESTIONS

1. The Law Commission Report on the Mental Element in Crime (Law Com. No. 89) recommended *inter alia* in a draft Bill that any statutes which created criminal offences and which come into force after the passing of this draft Bill could only create strict liability offences expressly. If such a future statute was silent as to the requirement of *mens rea*, the offence would not be presumed to be one of strict liability.

Why is this draft Bill not retrospective in effect?

Would such a Bill if it became a statute guarantee the future extinction of judicially created strict liability offences?

How does the draft Bill differ in its treatment of strict liability offences from the alternatives to strict liability suggested by their lordships in *Sweet* v *Parsley*?

2. How strict is a strict liability offence?

3. Should the law distinguish strict liability offences committed by companies from those committed by individuals?

4. What is the principal purpose or purposes of strict liability offences?
   If there is such a purpose or purposes is the criminal law the most appropriate mechanism to promote it or them?

5. Is the present argument that strict liability offences are unjust overstated?
   Are there appropriate areas of the law where strict liability has a valid function?
   If so what are those areas?
   Why do you think the imposition of strict liability in those areas is or would be beneficial, and to whom?

6. Can Rex be held criminally responsible for Sarah's and Donald's smoking of cannabis in his home? If so, would the prosecution have to establish the fact that he was aware of this incident or, that he was recklessly indifferent to it, or that he should have been aware of it?

4

Participation in Criminal Offences

SCENARIO

Edward and John have made their escape from Rex's home using his car. They abandon it on the outskirts of town. They hail a taxi driven by Ron. They do not intend to pay the fare. They alight from the taxi in the centre of town and seek to avoid paying Ron. There is an altercation and a fight develops. William and Henry, two passers-by, watch this spectacle with interest though Henry remains a mere passive spectator. William, however, recognises Ron as the individual he had had a very unpleasant argument with in a local public house over a spilt drink. He goes over to the scene of the fight and holds Ron while Edward and John continue to rain blows upon the unfortunate taxi-driver. Edward having been badly hurt by Ron (his right arm is fractured) loses all self-control and draws a knife. Neither John nor William knew of the existence of this weapon. Edward slashes Ron's cheek, a wound which will require a dozen stitches.

Edward and John make their second escape of the evening in Ron's taxi. Only Edward can drive a motor vehicle and since his arm has been fractured he is forced to operate the foot pedals and John the steering-wheel. Together they drive the vehicle near to Edith's home. Edith is Edward's mother. They are welcomed by Edith; she conceals the stolen goods and drives Edward, in her own car, to the hospital explaining the fractured arm as an injury caused in the home.

A few days later the police arrive at Edith's home and though they question her for a considerable time, she insists that Edward and John stayed at her home during the night in question. After an extensive search of the premises the police find the stolen articles. Edith explains that she bought them in good faith from a peripatetic market trader.

4.1 PRINCIPAL PARTICIPATION

This chapter will consider the various ways in which the law attributes criminal responsibility to parties who are directly or indirectly involved in the commission of a criminal offence, dependent upon those parties having the prescribed *mens rea*. An individual whose acts or omissions have been directly responsible for the bringing about of the *actus reus* of an offence with the prescribed *mens rea* will be considered by the law as a principal offender. Examples in the scenario of such individuals are numerous. Donald is a principal offender in his theft of alcohol from Rex's home and more importantly in the rape of Sarah. Rex's infliction of grievous bodily harm upon Donald and Donald's murder are both offences for which Rex stands as principal offender. These examples will suffice; though the scenario discloses further illustrations.

The law has always recognised that there may be more than one principal offender with regard to a crime. If two or more individuals embark upon a common enterprise and their conduct is such that either (assuming that they each have the prescribed *mens rea*) could have brought about the particular offence, then both may be convicted as principal offenders. Some of Edward and John's enterprises may be viewed in this light, e.g., their theft of the camera, jewellery and candlesticks and their causing the criminal damage to Rex's house. Either could have been convicted of those offences independently of the other. However, where one or more individuals embark upon a joint enterprise and act in concert (then dependent upon all concerned possessing the minimum degree of *mens rea*) all may be convicted as principal offenders, even though each individual's conduct viewed in isolation could not have brought about the offence concerned. In the scenario we see that Edward and John, because of Edward's disablement, are both driving Ron's taxi-cab from the scene of their most serious crimes. On this basis both may be convicted of an offence under s. 12 of the Theft Act 1968, i.e., taking a motor vehicle or other conveyance without authority or possibly theft of the vehicle (contrary to s. 1 of the Theft Act 1968 (see chapter 8). Their driving of the vehicle when both are palpably unfit to do so will doubtless amount to reckless driving contrary to s. 2 of the Road Traffic Act 1972. Neither Edward nor John alone could have committed the offences considered above, yet since the offences have been brought about by the common enterprise of both of them they are rightly convicted as joint principals of those crimes. In the case of *R* v *Tyler and Whatmore* [1976] RTR 83 it was determined by the Divisional Court of the Queen's Bench that the two accused were jointly driving a motor vehicle when one was operating the foot pedals and the other was leaning across and steering. Both accused could be convicted as joint principals with regard to the offence of 'driving' a motor vehicle without having proper control of that vehicle contrary to s. 40 of the Road Traffic Act 1972 and the regulations made thereunder, though neither could have been convicted as sole principals of the full offence.

What is the situation where individuals each contribute to the commission of the *actus reus* of an offence but the offence is not the consequence of their joint enterprise, but the result of the spontaneous and unrelated conduct of each party which in combination is responsible for bringing about the external elements of the offence? If the actions of each individual would when considered in isolation be insufficient to cause the *actus reus* of the crime, then even if all the individuals intended to bring about the offence they could not be convicted as joint principals of the full crime though they may be convicted as joint principals of an attempt (see chapter 5). Such a situation will be very rare and may prove impossible to establish, for it will be a natural inference for a jury to determine that such individuals are in fact engaged upon a joint enterprise.

4.2 THE PRINCIPAL OFFENDER AND THE INNOCENT AGENT

An individual may still be regarded by the law as a principal offender though he may not have been directly responsible for bringing about the *actus reus* of a crime. This is where an accused has instigated another to bring about the external elements of an offence but the latter is not criminally responsible for his conduct (see the case of *R v Butt* (1884) 15 Cox CC 564). A macabre example of this principle is provided by the case of *R v Michael* (1840) 9 C & P 356. The accused left her child of nine to ten months in the care of one S. She purchased laudanum and directed S to give her child a spoonful of this concoction every night, representing it to be a medicine, though for a child of such tender years it was a poison. She intended thereby to kill her child. S did not administer the laudanum to the child believing it to be unnecessary. While S was absent one of her children innocently administered the drug to the accused's child who died as a result. Alderson B had directed the jury at first instance that if the poison had been administered to the child while the accused's original criminal intention (i.e., *mens rea*) subsisted then even though it had been through an innocent unconscious agent, 'the death of the child, under such circumstances, would sustain the charge of murder' (at p. 358). The appellate court unanimously agreed with the direction. The administering of the poison by S's child 'was, under the circumstances of the case, as much, in point of law, an administering by the [accused], as if the [accused] had actually administered it with her own hand' (at p. 359). It is pertinent to note that the doctrine of innocent agent will apply even in cases where the agent's conduct (which has brought about the *actus reus* of an offence) has not been influenced or instigated by the principal offender, though such instigation or influence will certainly suffice. The commission of the external elements of the offence may thus merely be the result of an unfortunate accident of circumstance, brought about by the actions of the innocent agent, which brings to fruition the principal offender's nascent but continuing criminal intentions.

Since an individual can only be convicted as a principal offender in the above cases because the *actus reus* of the offence had been brought about through the conduct of an innocent agent it is important to be aware what constitutes an innocent agent in the eyes of the law. In argument in the case of *R v Manley* (1844) 1 Cox CC 104 counsel for the accused suggested that an innocent agent was a person 'who, from age, defect of understanding, ignorance of the fact, or other cause, cannot be *particeps criminis*' (i.e., party to the crime). If an agent is held responsible for his conduct, i.e., he suffers from none of the above-mentioned defects, disabilities or delusions, then if his conduct is accompanied by an appropriate *mens rea* it is he and he alone who can be convicted as principal offender.

Thus an individual will be deemed an innocent agent where, though he has brought about the elements of an offence which has been the object of another, he can establish one or more of the following defences, (see chapter 6):

(a) That he lacks *mens rea* with regard to the *actus reus* of the offence.
(b) That he is not of sufficient age to form a criminal intent.
(c) That he is insane or suffering from non-insane automatism.
(d) That he is under a reasonable and/or honest mistake of fact which if true would have justified his actions.
(e) That the individual has been forced to commit the *actus reus* of the offence while under duress.

In the scenario if it had not been Donald who had raped Sarah but Bruce, and the latter had been induced by Donald to have intercourse with Sarah, then if Donald intended to see that Sarah was subjected to unlawful sexual intercourse without her consent he could still be convicted as principal offender to her rape. This, however, would be dependent upon Bruce being established as an innocent agent. Any of the above situations would constitute Bruce such an individual, e.g., if he acted under duress (see chapter 6).

It has been suggested that the doctrine of innocent agent is inapplicable to offences involving assaults or which require a direct personal causal link or involvement between the commission of the *actus reus* and the actual perpetrator. Though it is accepted that certain offences of this kind can only be committed personally and not through an innocent agent, e.g., the crime of bigamy, it is nevertheless submitted that the crime of rape is capable of being committed through the act of an innocent agent. In the case of *R* v *Cogan and Leak* [1975] 2 All ER 1059 Lawton LJ was of such an opinion, though this part of his lordship's judgment was *obiter*, for the accused in the case was convicted on a different basis (see para. 4.6). Apart from this judicial authority, it does not seem unreasonable as a matter of policy to determine that those who seek to inflict serious physical and/or mental harm upon others should be held criminally responsible for such harm whether they are directly involved or have achieved their ends through indirect means which include the use of an innocent agent. The law recognises participation in offences other than as a principal. It is to these matters that consideration must now be given.

4.3 SECONDARY PARTICIPATION

The Accessories and Abettors Act 1861, s. 8 (as amended by the Criminal Law Act 1977), states that:

> Whosoever shall aid, abet, counsel, or procure the commission of any indictable offence [see Introduction] whether the same be an offence at common law or by virtue of any Act passed or to be passed, shall be liable to be tried, indicted, and punished as a principal offender.

The Magistrates' Courts Act 1980, s. 44, makes a similar provision with regard to offences tried summarily (see Introduction).

The Accessories and Abettors Act (for convenience reference will be made only to the 1861 Act) determines that individuals whose participation in a criminal offence comes within the terms of the section will be treated by the law for all purposes as if they were principal offenders to that offence though they are in reality secondary parties to the crime. Individuals bring themselves within the mischief of the section where they have 'aided', 'abetted', 'counselled' or 'procured' the commission of an offence. It is these terms that must now be considered in turn.

4.3.1 Aiding

An individual aids the commission of an offence when (with the necessary *mens*

Participation in Criminal Offences

rea) he gives help, support or assistance to the principal offender in the carrying out of the crime in question. A person may aid another in the commission of an offence even though he is not present at the scene of the crime. In the scenario, if Edward's mother, Edith, had telephoned Rex, inviting him and his wife to meet her at the local public house in order to facilitate Edward and John's theft of the camera, jewellery and candlesticks from the house she would, dependent upon her having the required *mens rea*, be guilty of aiding that theft. An individual may aid another in the commission of an offence by being in the vicinity of the crime but not present at the actual scene, for example by driving the principal offender to the locality of the offence, see *DPP for Northern Ireland* v *Lynch* [1975] AC 653 or by acting as a look-out. (See *R* v *Betts and Ridley* (1930) 22 Cr App R 148.) A person may aid a principal offender directly at the scene of a crime by providing immediate physical help, support or assistance, e.g., by restraining a victim of a rape in order to facilitate the completion of the criminal act, see *R* v *Clarkson* [1971] 3 All ER 344. In the scenario William has gone to aid Edward and John in their serious 'assault' upon Ron, the taxi driver. William's active physical intervention is conduct which amounts to aiding Edward and John's criminal activities. This illustrates the point that aiding does not require that the principal offender ask for assistance, nor be aware that he has been aided by the acts of another.

The most readily apparent form in which the aiding of a criminal offence may take place is the supplying of materials or tools by the aider to the principal offender. In the case of *R* v *Lomas* (1913) 9 Cr App R 220 the accused had supplied a jemmy to one King who had committed a burglary while using it. Undoubtedly this was an act which could be regarded as aiding King in his criminal activities. The issue was complicated by the fact that the jemmy was the property of King and it was argued that returning the jemmy could not amount in law to a positive act of assistance, it was merely returning to King what was lawfully due to him and could not in the circumstances amount to aiding the commission of the offence. This was accepted by the Court of Criminal Appeal (the ancestor of the Court of Appeal Criminal Division) as being a point of some validity by Devlin J (as he then was) in *R* v *Bullock* [1955] 1 All ER 15 (at p. 17).

In *National Coal Board* v *Gamble* [1959] 1 QB 11 this point was further explained and accepted as the law by Devlin J (at p. 20) as follows:

> A person who supplies the instrument for a crime or anything essential to its commission aids in the commission of it; and if he does so knowingly and with intent to aid, he abets it as well [see para. 4.3.2] and is therefore guilty of aiding and abetting. I use the word 'supplies' to comprehend giving, lending, selling or any other transfer of the right of property. In a sense a man who gives up to a criminal a weapon which the latter has a right to demand from him aids in the commission of the crime as much as if he sold or lent the article. But this has never been held to be aiding in law: see *R* v *Lomas* and *R* v *Bullock*. The reason, I think, is that in the former case there is in law a positive act and in the latter only a negative one. . . .[A] man who hands over to another his own property on demand, although he may physically be performing a positive act, in law is only refraining from detinue [a civil wrong of wrongfully detaining property rightly belonging to another].

Though this principle has been subjected to academic and judicial criticism, see Lord Parker CJ in *Garrett* v *Arthur Churchill (Glass) Ltd* [1969] 2 All ER 1141 at p. 1145, it is still the law, though it is difficult to conceive of any useful policy that is promoted by its continued existence.

The aid which is given to a principal offender must take place before or at the time of the commission of the crime in question. In the case of *Thambiah* v *R* [1966] AC 37, an accused who *inter alia* opened a bank account as a preliminary to the presentation by one R of forged cheques for payment into the account was held criminally liable in aiding R's offence of the fraudulent use of forged cheques. Any assistance, help or support given to a principal offender after the commission of an offence cannot in law amount to aiding, though it may constitute an offence under the Criminal Law Act 1967 (see para. 4.11). Though it appears as a matter of abstract reasoning easy to distinguish the point at which an offence is completed, it may be more difficult in practical terms especially in cases of offences which continue or may continue over a considerable period of time, e.g., theft (see chapter 8).

4.3.2 Abetting

It was once thought that abetting was synonymous with aiding or that it described the mental element which was necessary to constitute a secondary party's conduct criminal. This appears to coincide with the view expressed by Devlin J in *National Coal Board* v *Gamble* [1959] 1 QB 11 quoted in para. 4.3.1. High judicial support for this view can also be found in *DPP for Northern Ireland* v *Lynch* [1975] AC 653 at p. 698 per Lord Simon of Glaisdale. However, in the case of *Attorney-General's Reference (No. 1 of 1975)* [1975] 2 All ER 684 (at p. 686) Lord Widgery CJ was of the opinion that if s. 8 of the 1861 Act used the four different words 'aid', 'abet', 'counsel', 'procure' to describe the ways in which an individual could constitute himself as a secondary party to a crime then:

> [T]he probability is that there is a difference between each of those four words and the other three, because, if there were no such difference, then Parliament would be wasting time in using four words where two or three would do. Thus, ... we approach the section on the footing that each word must be given its ordinary meaning.

This latter opinion has much to commend it and seems to have been accepted as the true interpretation of s. 8 of the 1861 Act. On this basis, 'abetting' should be construed as a separate independent form of activity from that of aiding and from any other form of activity which may be undertaken by a secondary party to a crime. It is thought to involve any form of countenance, incitement, instigation or exhortation of a principal offender to commit an offence (dependent of course upon the secondary party having the required *mens rea*). A clear example of such activity can be seen in the scenario. Marian is actively encouraging her husband Rex to beat Donald severely. She is abetting his conduct and may, dependent upon her having the necessary *mens rea* (see later), be convicted of abetting either the infliction of grievous bodily harm by her husband upon Donald or even his murder. It is generally thought that such encouragement, incitement etc. must

Participation in Criminal Offences

take place at the time of the commission of the offence and usually therefore at the scene of the crime. This particular requirement distinguishes abetting from the third form of activity which is prescribed in the 1861 Act, that of 'counselling'.

4.3.3 Counselling

It is now thought that although 'counselling' encompasses the same form of activity as is covered by the term 'abetting' it is to be limited to such conduct carried out by a secondary party (together with the prescribed *mens rea*) which takes place before the commission of the offence and therefore usually at some distance from the scene of the crime.

Both abetting and counselling by necessity require that the exhortations, instigation, incitement or countenance of the secondary party impinge upon the mind of the principal offender, i.e., there must be a meeting of the minds of both parties.

4.3.4 Procuring

The nature of procuring was examined in the case of *Attorney-General's Reference (No. 1 of 1975)* [1975] 2 All ER 684. The accused had surreptitiously laced his friend's drink with a double measure of spirits, knowing that his friend would shortly be driving his car home. His friend drove his vehicle with an excess quantity of alcohol in his body and was convicted of the offence under s. 6(1) of the Road Traffic Act 1972 (see now the new s. 6(1)(a) and (b) substituted by the Transport Act 1981, s. 25 and Sch. 8). This section provided that it was an offence for a person to drive or to attempt to drive a motor vehicle on a road or public place with a blood alcohol concentration above the prescribed limit. Though acquitted at first instance of any involvement in this offence as a secondary party the question for the court was whether the accused should have been convicted. The court was of the opinion that the accused had procured the commission of the offence.

In the words of Lord Widgery CJ (at p. 686):

> To procure means to produce by endeavour. You procure a thing by setting out to see that it happens and taking the appropriate steps to produce that happening. We think that there are plenty of instances in which a person may be said to procure the commission of a crime by another even though there is no sort of conspiracy [see chapter 5] between the two, even though there is no attempt at agreement or discussion as to the form which the offence should take.

His lordship had accepted that the principal offender had driven with an excess quantity of alcohol in his blood without being aware of that fact. The commission of the offence had followed and was the consequence of the introduction of the alcohol into his bloodstream by way of the laced drink. The issue of causation was crucial to the act of procuring, his lordship was of the opinion that (at p. 687):

You cannot procure an offence unless there is a causal link between what you do and the commission of the offence.

Procuring thus takes place when a secondary party (with the necessary *mens rea*) helps a principal offender bring about the commission of a crime and the secondary party's conduct is a causative factor in bringing about the *actus reus* of the offence. This is a unique characteristic of this form of secondary participation. It is not a requirement of any other form of secondary participation e.g. counselling (see *R* v *Calhaem* (1985) 129 SJ 331). The four ways in which an individual may as a secondary party involve himself in the commission of an offence have now been discussed. There are however some additional matters which need consideration before the mental state required of a secondary party to a crime can be fully examined.

4.4 PRESENCE AT THE SCENE OF THE CRIME AND THE INACTIVITY OF A SECONDARY PARTY

It appears that generally an individual does not aid or abet an offence merely by being a passive spectator. This can be seen from the case of *R* v *Clarkson and others* [1971] 3 All ER 344. The accused were serving soldiers in Germany. They had all been drinking and returned to the barracks. The accused hearing a girl's screams had entered the barracks where other soldiers were raping a girl. They watched this appalling incident. The accused said nothing which gave encouragement to the rapists nor did they actively participate in the principal offence. On appeal by the accused against their conviction it was held that their conduct could not amount to aiding or abetting the commission of the rape of the girl. Though they had entered the room because they had heard the girl scream and had remained there, this alone could not constitute aiding the commission of the offence, the law required the accused to perform some positive physical acts which assisted the principal offenders in their appalling endeavours.

It was also determined, on the facts, that the accused's presence at the scene of the crime did not encourage the principal offenders in their carrying out of the rape of the girl. Their conduct could not on this basis amount to abetting. Megaw LJ referred to *R* v *Coney* (1882) 8 QBD 534, a case concerning the presence of the accused at an illegal prize-fight, in which the Divisional Court of the Queen's Bench decided that mere presence at the scene of a crime was not conclusive evidence of aiding or abetting the criminal offences (assaults by the prize-fighters on each other). Megaw LJ approved the statement of Hawkins J in *R* v *Coney* (at pp. 557–8) that:

> [T]o constitute an aider and abettor some active steps must be taken by word, or action, with the intent to instigate the principal, or principals. Encouragement does not of necessity amount to aiding and abetting, it may be intentional or unintentional, a man may unwittingly encourage another in fact by his presence, by misinterpreted words, or gestures, or by his silence, or non-interference, or he may encourage intentionally by expressions, gestures, or actions intended to signify approval. In the latter case he aids and abets, in the former he does not. It is no criminal offence to stand by, a mere passive

spectator of a crime, even of a murder. Non-interference to prevent a crime is not itself a crime. But the fact that a person was voluntarily and purposely witnessing the commission of a crime, and offered no opposition to it, though he might reasonably be expected to prevent and had power so to do, or at least to express his dissent, might under some circumstances, afford cogent evidence upon which a jury would be justified in finding that he wilfully encouraged and so aided and abetted. But it would be purely a question for the jury whether he did so or not.

The issue is complicated by his lordship's combining of the offences of aiding and abetting. In so far as his lordship appears to differentiate these elements he seemed to suggest that an individual can generally only aid in the commission of an offence when he is present at the scene of a crime by his positive physical intervention. However, an individual's passive presence may, without more, encourage, incite or instigate a principal offender in committing an offence, and to this extent mere physical presence of a secondary party at the scene of a crime may amount to abetting that crime, dependent upon that individual having the necessary *mens rea*. Whether in a particular instance a principal offender is so incited or encouraged to commit an offence is a matter of fact. This may explain the many conflicting authorities upon this point which come to different conclusions as to whether mere presence of a secondary party at the scene of an offence can result in criminal liability.

In the scenario Henry's passivity at the scene of the serious assault by Edward and John upon Ron, would probably not amount to abetting the commission of that offence though he is fully aware of the criminal nature of the activity. It would be a matter of fact for a jury to consider (see *Smith* v *Baker* [1972] Crim LR 25). One case where it was suggested that mere passivity could have amounted to abetting the commission of an offence was *Wilcox* v *Jeffery* [1951] 1 All ER 464. An alien gave an illegal musical performance at a jazz club contrary to his condition of entry into the UK. The accused had been present at this performance. However, the conduct of the accused in this case both in helping the alien enter the country and in his subsequently writing a laudatory article for a jazz magazine upon the musical performance was cogent evidence that his presence at the scene of the offence though passive was encouraging the alien in his illegal performance and this was capable of amounting to abetting. There is nothing to suggest that Henry has by his presence encouraged Edward and John and thus abetted the commission of the serious assault by them upon Ron.

There are two situations where an individual's passivity at the scene of a crime may amount to abetting the commission of an offence by a principal offender. The first situation is where the secondary party is present at the scene of the crime pursuant to an antecedent agreement between him and the principal offender to that effect. Such an agreement should be sufficient evidence for a jury to infer that the secondary party's subsequent presence at the scene of the crime (even though it is passive) amounts to an encouragement of the principal offender and therefore an abetting of the offence.

The second situation is where the secondary party stands in a position of authority in relation to the principal offender. The fact that a secondary party is in such a position impliedly encourages (and therefore abets) the principal offender in the commission of his offence where he refrains from exercising his authority in controlling the conduct of the latter. Examples of such relationships are parent and child, employer and employee (see *Cassady* v *Reg Morris (Transport) Ltd* [1975] Crim LR 398 and perhaps in a more controversial sense considering the position of women in present-day society the relationship of man and wife. In the case of *Du Cros* v *Lambourne* [1907] 1 KB 40 this principle was extended to the owner of a motor vehicle in permitting another to drive his vehicle in a manner dangerous to the public. It was also held applicable to the licensee of a public house who took no action in restraining individuals from consuming alcohol on his premises after drinking hours, an offence contrary to s. 59(1) of the Licensing Act 1964, see *Tuck* v *Robson* [1970] 1 All ER 1171.

A person may under the same situations discussed above also aid the commission of an offence though he is merely a passive spectator at the scene of the crime. It is a matter of fact dependent upon the circumstances of each case, though it will be easier to establish the fact of aiding where the secondary party is present at the scene of a crime pursuant to an antecedent agreement. It will be difficult to conceive of situations where mere presence at the scene of a crime without a prior agreement could be determined by a jury as conduct which aided another in the commission of an offence, even when the secondary party stands in a position of authority with regard to the principal offender, see *R* v *Clarkson* [1971] 3 All ER 344. The ways in which an individual may involve himself in a criminal offence as a secondary party have now been considered. Such conduct amounts to the *actus reus* which is committed by the secondary party. As in most serious offences a secondary party must have *mens rea* in relation to his conduct and it is this factor that must now be considered.

4.5 THE MENS REA OF A SECONDARY PARTY

4.5.1 Mens rea as to consequences

A secondary party must intend that his actions either assist, help, encourage, incite, instigate or bring about the commission of an offence. See *R* v *Clarkson* [1971] 3 All ER 344. This intention may be a direct intention (see chapter 2), i.e., the aim or object of the secondary party is to see that his conduct so aids, abets, counsels or procures the commission of an offence by a principal offender. In *DPP for Northern Ireland* v *Lynch* [1975] AC 653 (at p. 699) Lord Simon of Glaisdale, who considered that aiding and abetting were synonymous terms, was of the opinion that the 'offence' of aiding and abetting was:

> a case where 'specific intent' [as a name] is justified for all its ambiguity [see chapter 2]. but the *mens rea* involved does not seem to admit of the approach adopted in *Hyam* v *DPP* [1975] AC 55. I think that the 'intent' in *Steane's* case [[1947] KB 997] should probably be construed as the mental element involved in performing an act with the object that a particular consequence should ensue—i.e., virtually, motive or purpose.

It would not on this view be sufficient *mens rea* for a secondary party to be reckless as to whether his conduct aids, abets, counsels or procures the commission of an offence—direct intention alone would suffice.

However, his lordship also approved the opinion of Devlin J in *National Coal Board* v *Gamble* [1959] 1 QB 11 which suggests that oblique intention will also suffice to affix the criminal liability of secondary parties in their involvement in an offence, i.e., an awareness on the part of the secondary party that his conduct will aid, abet, counsel, or procure the commission of an offence by a principal offender. In *National Coal Board* v *Gamble* Devlin J had been of the opinion that:

> [A]n indifference to the result of the crime does not of itself negative abetting. If one man deliberately sells to another a gun to be used for murdering a third, he may be indifferent about whether the third man lives or dies and interested only in the cash profit to be made out of the sale, but he can still be an aider and abettor.

However, Lord Simon in *DPP for Northern Ireland* v *Lynch* [1975] AC 653 suggested that with regard to the act of supplying an instrument for a crime or anything essential to its commission, 'it must be foreseen that the instrument or other object or service supplied will probably (or possibly and desiredly) be used for the commission of a crime' (at pp. 698-9). This opinion appears to suggest that a secondary party may recklessly aid a principal offender on the basis of his foresight of the consequences of his conduct with regard to the principal offence (see chapter 2). This statement conflicts with the balance of authority including that of Lord Simon himself in the latter part of his judgment (see above). The law clearly requires that a secondary party must intend to aid, abet, counsel or procure the commission of an offence, and that intention may be either direct or oblique.

Nevertheless it is suggested that neither policy nor logic should preclude the law from determining that a man can aid the commission of an offence recklessly, be it *Cunningham*-style or *Caldwell* recklessness (see chapter 2). The application of *Caldwell* recklessness to such cases seems justified on the basis of *R* v *Seymour* [1983] 2 AC 493 (see chapter 2). The secondary party should be criminally responsible for the consequences of his conduct where a reasonable man would have appreciated that it was a gross and obvious risk that his actions could only aid the principal offender in the commission of the offence. It is suggested that this principle should be equally applicable to the other forms of secondary participation in crimes, namely, abetting, counselling and procuring.

4.5.2 Mens rea as to circumstances

The facts which comprise the *actus reus* of the offence which is ultimately committed by the principal offender constitute the material circumstances which a secondary party must in some part be aware of before his conduct with regard to that offence can be rendered criminal. It is not necessary, however, that the secondary party is aware that the principal offender is committing a criminal offence.

Awareness of or wilful blindness (i.e., the deliberate closing of the mind) to the existence of the facts which constitute the *actus reus* of the offence committed by the principal offender will found the required *mens rea* as (or so it appears) will subjective *Cunningham*-type recklessness i.e., reckless indifference as to the existence or non-existence of one or more of the material circumstances. In *Carter* v *Richardson* [1974] RTR 314 where the accused was convicted of aiding and abetting a learner-driver to drive a motor vehicle with blood alcohol level above the prescribed limits contrary to s. 6(1) of the Road Traffic Act 1972, (see now the new s. 6(1)(a) and (b) substituted by the Transport Act 1981, s. 25 and sch. 8). Lord Widgery CJ approved the opinion of the magistrates at first instance that:

> it was impossible for the defendant to know exactly how many milligrams of alcohol there were in a millilitre of Collin's [the learner-driver's] blood and that it sufficed that an aider and abettor was aware that the principal had consumed an excessive amount of alcohol or was reckless as to whether he had done so.

It is suggested that *Caldwell*-type recklessness should also be sufficient to satisfy the requirement of *mens rea* in relation to secondary parties with regard to the circumstances which constitute the *actus reus* of the offence committed by the principal offender (as has been suggested above with regard to the consequences of a secondary party's conduct).

Though a secondary party may be affixed with knowledge of the material circumstances of the *actus reus* perpetrated by the principal offender, it is not necessary that he be aware of all the peculiar facts which constitute the particular offence which is committed by the principal offender, it is sufficient that he is aware of the type of offence which is to be committed. This is the effect of the decision of the Court of Criminal Appeal in *R* v *Bainbridge* [1959] 3 All ER 200. The accused had purchased oxygen cutting equipment on behalf of one Shakeshaft. He was fully aware that the equipment would be used for illegal purposes. He alleged that he believed the cutting equipment would be used for breaking up stolen goods and not for breaking into a bank. The judge at first instance had directed the jury that:

> The knowledge that is required to be proved in the mind of [the accused] is not the knowledge of the precise crime. In other words, it need not be proved that he knew that the Midland Bank, Stoke Newington branch, was going to be broken and entered, and money stolen from that particular bank, but he must know the type of crime that was in fact committed. In this case it is a breaking and entering of premises and the stealing of property from those premises. It must be proved that he knew that that sort of crime was intended and was going to be committed. It is not enough to show that he either suspected or knew that some crime was going to be committed, some crime which might have been a breaking and entering or might have been disposing of stolen property or anything of that kind. That is not enough. It must be proved that he knew that the type of crime which was in fact committed was intended.

On appeal Lord Parker CJ approved the correctness of this direction. Counsel for the accused had argued that a secondary party must be aware of the 'particular crime' to be committed by the principal offender at the time when he

Participation in Criminal Offences

renders assistance, i.e., not only the type of crime but its location and date. This was rejected by the court, though it was accepted that knowledge that some illegal venture was intended was insufficient.

In *DPP for Northern Ireland* v *Maxwell* [1978] 3 All ER 1140, this rather restricted view of the minimum mental requirement that should be possessed by a secondary party with regard to the peculiar facts which comprised the principal offence was extended. The accused had directed others to a public house by driving his car there, the principal offender and others following in their own transport. The principal offender had subsequently attempted to bomb that public house. The accused was convicted of being a secondary party to the offence of doing an act with intent to cause an explosion likely to endanger life, and with being in possession of a bomb with the same intent. It was held by the House of Lords that a secondary party aids or abets the commission of an offence, even when he lacks prior knowledge of the actual crime intended, if he contemplated the commission of one of a limited number of crimes by the principal and with the required *mens rea* lent his assistance in the commission of one or more of those crimes. It was irrelevant that at the time of rendering assistance the secondary party was not aware of the actual crime or crimes the principal will commit, it was sufficient if it or they were within the general 'type' of offences which were within his contemplation. In the words of Lord Hailsham LC (at p. 1147):

> The fact that, in the event, the offence committed by the principals crystallised into one rather than the other of the possible alternatives within his contemplation only means that in the event he was accessory to that specific offence rather than one of the others which in the event was not the offence committed.

His lordship further considered that there must be

> limits to the meaning of the expression 'type of offence' . . . but it is clear that if an alleged accessory is perfectly well aware that he is participating in one of a limited number of crimes and one of these is in fact committed he is liable under the general law at least as one who aids, abets, counsels or procures that crime even if he is not actually a principal. Otherwise I can see no end to the number of unmeritorious arguments which the ingenuity of defendants could adduce.

One issue still remains unsolved, how wide will the ambit of offences within a given 'type of offence' be construed? Furthermore will a secondary party, e.g., be considered to have aided a robbery when he contemplated rendering assistance to a principal offender only in respect of a theft? Since robbery has, as one of its constituent elements the necessity for a theft, will his liability be limited to aiding the commission of the theft element within the full offence of robbery?

Returning to the scenario—if Edith had telephoned Rex and his wife in order to get them out of their house and so aid her son, Edward, and his friend, John, in their criminal activities, her liability would depend upon the 'type of offences' which were within her contemplation as being the possible crimes that could be committed by the two young men. Edith must have contemplated theft as one offence that Edward and John would carry out. It would be unnecessary for her to know the actual objects that are ultimately stolen. It might be possible to construe an offence of burglary (see chapter 8) as being within the 'type of offence' contemplated by Edith as being a crime which might be committed by Edward and John, especially if it involves the form of burglary that is comprised by their entry into the house as trespassers in order to steal (see chapter 8). It is probable that their committing the offence of criminal damage, however, is not within the 'type of offence' contemplated by Edith. On this basis she should not be considered a secondary party to those incidents.

4.5.3 Secondary participation in strict liability offences

A principal offender may be convicted of an offence of strict liability (see chapter 3) though he may lack *mens rea* with regard to at least one element of the *actus reus*. However, authority has determined that secondary participation in a criminal offence, as a creation of the common law, requires full *mens rea* as to all its elements. When the secondary party therefore renders assistance procures or gives encouragement in relation to a strict liability offence, he will need to have full *mens rea*, both as to the consequences of his conduct and with regard to the *actus reus* of the principal offence, see *Callow* v *Tillstone* (1900) 83 LT 411.

4.6 THE NEED FOR THE COMMISSION OF AN ACTUS REUS BY THE PRINCIPAL OFFENDER

A secondary party cannot aid, abet, counsel or procure a principal offender unless that individual ultimately commits an *actus reus* of an offence. In *Thornton* v *Mitchell* [1940] 1 All ER 339, the driver of an omnibus was charged with driving his vehicle without due care and attention and with driving without reasonable consideration for others contrary to s. 12(1) of the Road Traffic Act 1930 (see now s. 3 Road Traffic Act 1972). The conductor had been charged with aiding and abetting the driver to commit these offences. The driver had reversed his vehicle into some passengers who had just alighted from the bus with fatal consequences. The driver being unsighted because of the bus's construction had relied upon the conductor's instructions and signal in reversing. It was reasonable for him to do so. At first instance the driver was acquitted of both offences. Because of the interpretation of the statute, only the actual driver of the vehicle could be convicted as principal offender, and on this basis the conductor could only be a secondary party to the offences. The conductor was convicted of aiding and abetting the offence of driving without due care and attention. On appeal it was held that the conductor could not be so convicted because the driver had not committed any offence. There was no *actus reus*. By relying on the signal of the conductor which was reasonable having regard to the vehicle's construction the driver had driven with due care and with reasonable consideration for others. The court adopted the view expressed by Avory J in *Morris* v *Tolman* [1923] 1 KB 166 (at p. 171) where his lordship had said that:

Participation in Criminal Offences

[I]n order to convict, it would be necessary to show that . . . [the conductor] was aiding the principal [the driver], but a person cannot aid another in doing something which that other has not done.

These authorities determine that where an individual's conduct has not brought about the *actus reus* of an offence, then, irrespective of the mental state of that individual there is no criminal activity which a secondary party can aid, abet, counsel or procure. In such cases criminal participation by a secondary party is a legal impossibility.

Where the principal offender has committed the *actus reus* of an offence (with full *mens rea*) but he may not be prosecuted, because, e.g., he cannot be found, or ascertained, or, though there is evidence of his guilt, the law will not permit such evidence to be presented to a court of law, there is no bar to another being convicted of aiding, abetting, counselling or procuring that principal offender in the commission of that offence. Mere procedural or practical restrictions to the prosecution of a principal offender do not negate the fact that such an individual may be responsible for the commission of an offence in which another may render assistance as a secondary party. It is not the fact of prosecution which makes an individual guilty of a criminal offence but his responsibility for bringing about the *actus reus* of a crime with the prescribed *mens rea*. See *R v Davis* [1977] Crim LR 542 and *R v Humphreys and Turner* [1965] 3 All ER 689.

The *mens rea* of a principal offender when he brings about the *actus reus* of an offence is generally irrelevant to the secondary party's criminal liability. Though where the principal protagonist who commits the *actus reus* of an offence lacks *mens rea* and this is known to the party rendering assistance, the latter may, if he seeks to bring about the crime through the medium of the former be held responsible as principal offender through the doctrine of innocent agent (see para. 4.2). The fact that a principal offender has brought about the *actus reus* of an offence, however, is crucial. If the secondary party (with the prescribed *mens rea*) has rendered assistance to another and that other has brought about the external elements of an offence then the secondary party is guilty as an aider, abettor, counsellor or procurer of that *actus reus*. This remains so even if the perpetrator of the *actus reus* lacks *mens rea* and could not be convicted as a principal offender. Such is the consequence of *R v Cogan and Leak* [1975] 2 All ER 1059. Cogan was convicted of rape and Leak of aiding and abetting that rape. Cogan appealed against his conviction contending that he honestly believed the victim (who was Leak's wife) had consented to the act of intercourse, though there were no reasonable grounds for that belief. Leak also appealed *inter alia* on the ground that if Cogan was acquitted as principal his conviction as a secondary party could not stand. Cogan's appeal was allowed on the basis that his belief that the victim was consenting deprived him of *mens rea* notwithstanding that his belief was not reasonable (see *DPP v Morgan* [1976] AC 182 and chapter 6). It was held by the appellate court that Leak as a secondary party could nevertheless be convicted of aiding and abetting Cogan to have sexual intercourse with the victim, knowing that she did not consent. This in law amounted to aiding and abetting the *actus reus* of a rape. It made no difference that the victim had been the wife of Leak (see para. 7.5.3.). The case of *R v Cogan and Leak* determines that if an individual has brought about the *actus reus* of an offence, and the secondary party affixed with knowledge of this fact, has with full *mens rea* rendered assistance to that individual in his commission of that *actus reus*, then he is rightly convicted of aiding, abetting, counselling or procuring the commission of that *actus reus*. In essence the *actus reus* brought about by the perpetrator is married with the *actus reus* and *mens rea* of the secondary party and this brings the secondary party's conduct within the mischief of s. 8 of the Accessories and Abettors Act 1861. A secondary party may thus be convicted though the principal offender has been acquitted of any offence. This is the case wherever the perpetrator of the *actus reus* of an offence has a defence, even in cases where the defence does not negate *mens rea*. In *R* v *Bourne* (1952) 36 Cr App R 125 a man compelled his wife to commit the offence of buggery with a dog. He was convicted of aiding and abetting that offence though the wife was not charged as principal offender.

It was accepted by the Lord Chief Justice, Lord Goddard, that the wife could have established the defence of duress (see chapter 6) though his lordship did not make clear whether duress would have deprived the wife of the required *mens rea* or not.

Following the House of Lords decision in *DPP for Northern Ireland* v *Lynch* [1975] AC 653 it appears that duress excuses an individual from criminal liability, but does not negate either the *actus reus* of the offence or the *mens rea* of the offender.

4.7 CONVICTION OF SECONDARY PARTY OF AN OFFENCE DIFFERENT FROM THAT OF THE PRINCIPAL OFFENDER

It appears logical that where a secondary party shares with the principal offender a common intent to bring about an offence then both may be convicted of that crime, one as principal the other as an aider, abettor, counsellor or procurer (see *R* v *Murtagh and Kennedy* [1955] Crim LR 315).

Where a secondary party has an intent to aid a principal offender but only intends to render assistance in relation to a less serious offence than one actually committed, he may be convicted of secondary participation in that less serious offence. In the scenario William aids Edward and John in their assault upon Ron the taxi-driver. If he intended only to aid in the infliction of a common assault or an assault occasioning actual bodily harm contrary to s. 47 of the Offences against the Person Act 1861 (see chapter 7) then he may be convicted as an aider of such offences. However, he may not as the law stands at present be convicted of aiding and abetting the infliction of the grievous bodily harm upon Ron (including the stabbing) by Edward and John.

However, there are two situations where a secondary party may incur greater criminal liability than a principal offender. The first is where the principal offender has a partial defence which though not excusing him entirely from criminal responsibility has the effect of mitigating the gravity of his offence. In the scenario Marian is abetting Rex in his savage assault upon Donald. Though Rex may well be convicted of murder, he may be able to claim the defence of provocation (see Homicide Act 1957, s. 2 and chapter 7). The effect of this defence is to reduce the offence committed by a principal offender from murder to voluntary manslaughter (see chapter 7). This remains so even when the individual claiming the defence has the prescribed *mens rea* for murder. If Rex could claim that the defence was applicable to his case, he could only be convicted of the manslaughter of Donald. This defence is unavailable to a secondary party. It follows from this that if Marian is seeking to encourage Rex to kill or inflict grievous bodily harm upon Donald she is rightly convicted of abetting his murder (see chapter 7).

A secondary party may also be convicted of a greater offence than the actual perpetrator of a crime when he renders assistance to a principal offender in the commission of an offence and possesses a greater *mens rea* with regard to that crime than the perpetrator. In the scenario if Rex intended to inflict actual bodily harm upon Donald and is found to have caused his death he may be convicted of the crime of involuntary manslaughter (see chapter 7). If Marian was aware that Donald was in such a vulnerable physical state that Rex's attack must produce his demise, then if she encouraged the attack knowing of its inevitable fatal consequence she is rightly convicted of abetting Donald's murder, and not the offence of involuntary manslaughter.

However, it appears that a counseller (i.e., a secondary party who encourages a principal offender to commit an offence prior to its commission and who is not present at the scene of the offence) may not be convicted of a greater offence than the actual perpetrator.

In *R v Richards* [1973] 3 All ER 1088 the accused, in order to regain her husband's affection, paid a sum of money to two men to attack him. On the day of the attack she had put the principal offenders on notice by a pre-arranged signal which she gave them from her house as her husband left for work. The assault on her husband by the two men produced a laceration to his scalp which required two stitches. The principal offenders were charged with wounding with intent contrary to s. 18 and unlawful wounding contrary to s. 20 of the Offences against the Person Act 1861 (see chapter 7). They were convicted of the latter and less serious offence. However, the accused was convicted of abetting the more serious offence under s. 18. On appeal it was held that the accused could not be convicted of a more serious offence than the principals, and a conviction of counselling an offence under s. 20 was substituted. This was based upon the court's view that the position of a counsellor differed from other secondary participants, who were generally at the scene of the crime. Relying upon a passage in Hawkins's *Pleas of the Crown* the court considered that a secondary party who was absent from the scene of a crime (i.e., generally a counsellor) could not be convicted of an offence greater than that actually committed by a principal offender. The principle in *R v Richards* is not it is suggested limited to counsellors but to any secondary party who is not present at the scene of a crime.

The court rejected the general rule governing the criminal responsibility of secondary parties formulated in *DPP v Merriman* [1973] AC 584 which determined that a secondary party's ultimate criminal liability in relation to an offence should be governed by his particular *mens rea* with regard to the *actus reus* committed by the principal offender. It seems wrong in principle that a secondary party's fundamental criminal liability is dependent upon the fact of presence or absence at the scene of the principal offence. *R v Richards* has produced an unnecessary and illogical distinction as regards potential criminal liability between individuals whose mental state and involvement in an offence are identical and cannot be justified on either policy or logic.

4.8 LIABILITY OF PRINCIPAL OR SECONDARY PARTY FOR UNFORESEEN CONSEQUENCES

The authority of *R* v *Anderson and Morris* (1966) 50 Cr App R 216 determined that where individuals embark upon a joint enterprise (in whatever capacity) then each is liable be they principal or secondary party for all the consequences of that joint enterprise, even though those consequences are brought about in an unusual way and are unforeseen by the parties. This is dependent upon the parties having the required *mens rea* (see *Chan Wing-Siu* v *R* [1985] AC 168 and *Davies* v *DPP* [1954] AC 378). Where, however, one co-adventurer goes beyond and outside that which has been agreed and contemplated with the others they may escape criminal liability for the consequences that result from that *unauthorised* act. Lord Parker CJ in *R* v *Anderson and Morris* (at p. 223) justified this rule on the doctrine of causation (see chapter 1). The sudden *unauthorised* action of one co-adventurer in his lordship's words may constitute:

> an overwhelming supervening event which is of such a character that it will relegate into a matter of history matters which could otherwise be looked upon as causative factors.

If a co-adventurer commits a crime which happens to differ only in the method of execution from that contemplated and agreed by all the parties to the crime, all are rightly convicted in their respective capacities. Only where a co-adventurer commits a crime altogether different from that authorised or instigated as the common enterprise will all the other parties escape criminal liability for the completed act see *R* v *Saunders and Archer* (1576) 2 Plow 473, and *R* v *Creamer* [1966] 1 QB 72.

This restricted defence appears to be inapplicable to individuals who contemplate the infliction of serious violence upon a victim and all have the *mens rea* applicable to murder (see chapter 7 and *R* v *Kelly* (unreported) 5 April 1984 (Court of Appeal) and *R* v *Williams and Blackwood* (1973) 21 WIR 329).

In the scenario both Edward and John attack Ron the taxi driver. William aids them in this enterprise. As all three individuals contemplate the use of some violence they are liable for all possible offences that may be committed where the infliction of actual bodily harm forms an element in the offence (even when the offences have been brought about in an unforeseen way), e.g., an assault occasioning actual bodily harm contrary to s. 47 of the Offences against the Person Act 1861.

If when Edward drew a knife John and William were unaware of its existence and Edward with the intention to kill stabbed Ron to death, he would stand as a principal to the offence of murder. However, John being unaware of the knife or its use by Edward would neither be a principal nor a secondary party to the offence of the murder of Ron. This would also be the case with regard to William who could not be a secondary party to the killing (see *Davies* v *DPP*).

Participation in Criminal Offences

4.9 REPENTANCE

Can a secondary party avoid all criminal responsibility for his complicity in a criminal offence by his withdrawal from the enterprise, at least if his withdrawal is made before the commission of the offence by the principal offender? The leading case upon this issue is that of *R v Becerra* (1975) 62 Cr App R 212. The accused had broken into a house with two others, C and G, with the intention to steal from it. While in the house they were surprised by a tenant. The accused at this point who had previously handed a knife to C called to the others 'Let's go'. He departed along with G. C, however, stabbed the tenant to death. The accused was charged *inter alia* with the tenant's murder. He was convicted. He appealed on the ground that though there may have been a common enterprise to kill or inflict grievous bodily harm upon a person should the need arise, he had by his words and departure from the scene of the crime withdrawn from that joint enterprise before the attack on the tenant. He was not an agent in the chain of causation which resulted in the tenant's death. He was therefore no longer a cause of or responsible for the commission of the murder and not liable to conviction for it.

The Court of Appeal accepted that withdrawal from a common enterprise could, if it was made *before* the commission of an offence, provide a defence to a charge of complicity in such a crime. The court carefully reviewed the case law upon the subject as to when and under what circumstances an individual may successfully claim that he has withdrawn from a common enterprise.

It has been accepted since *R v Saunders and Archer* (1576) 2 Plow 473 that an individual's withdrawal from a common enterprise could be made by giving a clear, effective and timely warning to the other parties involved of such intention. The court in *Becerra* seemed to accept that such conduct was sufficient to excuse individuals from criminal liability where they had merely counselled others in the preparatory stages of a criminal offence. Where communication to the other parties is not possible then it is presumed communication or notice of withdrawal should be made to the police. *Becerra* suggests that where an individual is at the scene of the crime he would have to intervene physically to prevent the offence happening, and communication to the other co-adventurers of his intention to withdraw from the common enterprise at such a stage would no longer be sufficient to excuse him from criminal responsibility for all the consequences that flow from the conduct of all the co-adventurers. Whether an individual has successfully withdrawn from the common enterprise in a given case is a matter of fact (see Murphy, *A Practical Approach to Evidence*) and should be left to the jury (see *R v Grundy* [1977] Crim LR 543 and *R v Whitefield* [1984] Crim LR 97.

4.10 VICTIMS OF CRIMES AS SECONDARY PARTIES

The case of *R v Tyrrell* [1894] 1 QB 710 determined that a girl below the age of consent could not be convicted as an aider or abettor of a man who committed the offence of having unlawful sexual intercourse with her. (see now s. 6 of the Sexual Offences Act 1956). Though Mathew J was of the view that this principle was gained from the interpretation of the relevant statute, Lord Coleridge CJ based his view of the law on the principle that this particular legislation was concerned with the protection of young women from sexual abuse, despite their inclinations or desires. The policy of the Act could not be endorsed if those very women could be held criminally responsible for their conduct. In *R* v *Whitehouse* [1977] 3 All ER 737 this policy was applied to the case of incest where it was accepted that since a girl below the age of 16 was incapable in law of committing such an offence (see Sexual Offences Act 1956, s. 11) then she could not aid or abet such a crime. Though this appears to be the general principle applicable to most offences which seek to provide a protective element to the victims of certain sexual abuses and practices, there are exceptions at common law. It appears that in law a woman may be charged with aiding or abetting her own illegal abortion (see *R* v *Sockett* (1908) 1 Cr App R 101) in practice prosecution of such persons is rare.

4.11 ASSISTING OFFENDERS

We have seen in the scenario that Edith has misled the police as to the whereabouts of her son Edward and his companion John. She may on such conduct have committed an offence under s. 4(1) of the Criminal Law Act 1967. This provides that where an individual has committed an arrestable offence (see Introduction) then another who without lawful authority or any reasonable excuse does any act with intent to impede that individual's apprehension or prosecution shall be guilty of an offence.

Edward and John have committed a number of arrestable offences, e.g., the theft of the camera, jewellery and candlesticks. Edith knowing this does not commit an offence under s. 4 if she refrains from answering the police questions as to the whereabouts of Edward and John or their involvement in the various criminal activities. However, her lies as to the location of Edward and John on the evening in question and, e.g., her removal of their fingerprints from the stolen goods and concealing the same, would amount to an offence under the section (see *R* v *Brindley and Long* [1971] 2 QB 300). Such conduct must be carried out with the intent that it impedes the apprehension or prosecution of offenders and this appears to be satisfied by a direct intent only (see chapter 2).

4.12 SECONDARY PARTICIPATION AND INCHOATE OFFENCES

It now appears that there is no offence of attempting to aid, abet, counsel or procure an offence—see s. 1(4)(b) of the Criminal Attempts Act 1981. In the scenario consider the situation if Edith had telephoned Rex inviting him and his wife for a drink at a local public house in order to get them out of the house and assist Edward and John in their criminal activities. If Rex and his wife had left the house not in consequence of that call but to make a dinner appointment with friends then Edith would have failed to aid Edward and John in their criminal activities. Such a case can amount only to an attempt to aid, which is not an offence. It also appears that it is no offence to conspire (see chapter 5) to aid and abet (see *R* v *Hollinshead* [1985] 2 WLR 761). However, the case of *R* v *Dunnington* [1984] Crim LR 98 determined that an individual may aid (and presumably abet, counsel or procure) a principal offender who is responsible for an attempted crime (see chapter 5). If Edith had succeeded in getting Rex and his wife out of the house by her telephone call, but Edward and John had been disturbed in their criminal activities and had fled the house empty-handed then Edith could be convicted of aiding Edward and John in their attempted theft. This is logical and differs from the situations discussed above. Edith has done all that is necessary to assist the principal offenders, and they have committed an offence known to law, i.e., attempted theft (see chapter 5).

4.13 SUMMARY

The law of complicity in criminal offences is marred by a confusion of terminology. Notwithstanding the decision of the Court of Appeal in *Attorney-General's Reference (No. 1 of 1975)* [1975] 2 All ER 684, the courts still do not clearly distinguish between the various ways in which a secondary party may render assistance to another, e.g., between aiding and abetting (see para. 4.3.2). However, the factor which produces the greatest difficulty in understanding this aspect of criminal law is that the law once used different terms to describe the same kinds of secondary participation in an offence, which was dependent upon whether the principal offence was a felony or a misdemeanour (see Introduction).

The Criminal Law Act 1967, s. 1, abolished the classifications of and differences between felonies and misdemeanours and as regards participation in criminal offences adopted the terms and definitions that had been used with regard to misdemeanours. These are the terms which have been discussed in this chapter. Since 1967 therefore all participants in a criminal offence are principals or by virtue of s. 8 of the Accessories and Abettors Act 1861 (which had reformed the law of complicity in crimes with regard to misdemeanours) to be treated as principals, where they are aiders, abettors, counsellors or procurers with regard to an offence.

The old terms and definitions that were applicable to felonies must still be familiar to the criminal law student, however, for the pre Criminal Law Act case law cannot be understood without an acquaintance with the relevant terms. These authorities are no longer binding upon the courts, but they remain useful and illustrative examples of the ways in which individuals may participate in criminal activity.

4.14 PARTICIPANTS IN A FELONY

The principal offender or offenders with regard to a felony were defined as 'the principal(s) in the first degree', an example in the scenario being Rex and his assault upon and murder of Donald.

Individuals who rendered assistance at the time of the commission of the offence, irrespective of whether they were present at the scene of the crime were defined as 'the principal(s) in the second degree'.

Such individuals were generally the equivalent of aiders, abettors or procurers and both Marian and William are examples of individuals who would have been regarded as principals in the second degree.

Individuals who rendered assistance to a principal offender prior to the commission of an offence were known as 'Accessory(ies) before the fact'.

The modern equivalent to such an individual could be either a counsellor (the most common instance) or a procurer or aider. An example in the scenario of what would once have been an accessory before the fact would be Edith telephoning Rex to get him and his wife out of their house to aid Edward and John in their proposed criminal activities.

The law relating to felonies recognised a secondary party assisting a principal offender *after* the commission of an offence. Such a person was known as an 'accessory(ies) after the fact'.

This form of participation in a criminal offence was abolished by the Criminal Law Act 1967. However, it is in essence preserved as a substantive offence by s. 4 of that Act, which has been considered above. This offence is applicable to cases where the principal offender has committed an arrestable offence (see Introduction).

4.15 CORPORATE LIABILITY

4.15.1 The rationale of corporate liability

Though criminal offences are principally committed by individuals, the criminal law has for a considerable period of time extended responsibility for the commission of crimes to organisations, which though they have no separate physical existence from the human beings who form their administrative and operative bodies are nevertheless considered by the law to be entirely independent entities from such individuals.

Thus the law recognises that a company registered under the Companies Act 1985, local authorities or a corporation created by royal charter or Act of Parliament, e.g., a nationalised industry, have an independent legal existence from the individuals who are employed by them or direct their activities. The law attributes to these bodies all the faculties and legal responsibilities of a living person. As regards criminal law, entities such as a company registered under the Companies Act 1985 may thus be subject to the same criminal liability as a human being. In terms of numbers companies registered under the Companies Act 1985 are the most important, and it is such a type of corporation which will be considered in the discussion of the concept of corporate liability for criminal offences. There are two principal situations where a company will be held criminally responsible.

4.15.2 Statutory construction

Where a penal statute expressly or by implication includes a company within the class of individuals who may commit an offence, a company may then be held criminally responsible. Such offences are by practical necessity usually ones of strict liability or offences which it is possible to conceive as being committed by an entity which has no real physical existence. This limits the kinds of crimes that can be committed on this basis to offences which impose liability on individuals who are the occupiers of property, or who carry on businesses or trades, or who manufacture products. This was first recognised by the courts in the case of *R* v *Birmingham & Gloucester Railway Co.* (1842) 3 QB 223.

This doctrine is inapplicable where the statute or common law offence requires

Participation in Criminal Offences

conduct on the part of the principal offender which it is impossible for a company to execute, for example, fraud. It is clear in such cases that the offence requires *mens rea*. It would seem that a company cannot be held criminally liable in cases where an offence requires the principal offender to have a particular mental state with regard to the *actus reus* of a crime. The courts have surmounted this problem by the doctrine of identification.

4.15.3 The doctrine of identification

In the celebrated case of *H.L. Bolton Engineering Co. Ltd* v *T.J. Graham & Sons Ltd* [1957] 1 QB 159 the doctrine of identification, that the conduct and *mens rea* of an individual associated with a company could be ascribed to a company for the purposes of imposing criminal responsibility upon it was explained and rationalised by Denning LJ (as he then was) as follows (at pp. 172-3):

> A company may in many ways be likened to a human body. It has a brain and nerve centre which controls what it does. It also has hands which hold the tools and act in accordance with directions from the centre. Some of the people in the company are mere servants and agents who are nothing more than hands to do the work and cannot be said to represent the mind or will. Others are directors and managers who represent the directing mind and will of the company, and control what it does. The state of mind of these managers is the state of mind of the company and is treated by the law as such. . . . ([See] *Lennard's Carrying Co. Ltd* v *Asiatic Petroleum Co. Ltd* [1915] AC 705). . . . [I]n cases where the law requires a guilty mind as a condition of a criminal offence, the guilty mind of the directors or the managers will render the company itself guilty. That is shown by *R* v *ICR Haulage Ltd* [1944] KB 551 . . . in which the court said (at p. 559): 'Whether in any particular case there is evidence to go to a jury that the criminal act of an agent, including his state of mind, intention, knowledge or belief is the act of the company . . . must depend on the nature of the charge, the relative position of the officer or agent, and the other relevant facts and circumstances of the case'.

The kinds of individuals who would be regarded as the mind and body of a company depends upon the facts of each case. Such an individual as the 'directing mind' of the company stands in these cases not in the capacity of an agent, he is regarded as the company and his liability is also that of the corporation he represents.

This latter point was clearly endorsed by the House of Lords in *Tesco Supermarkets Ltd* v *Nattrass* [1972] AC 153 in which the dictum of Denning LJ quoted above was approved. In *R* v *Andrews Weatherfoil Ltd and Others* [1972] 1 All ER 65 the Court of Appeal stated as a general proposition that the individual whose conduct and mental state were relevant for the purpose of the doctrine of identification had to have the status and authority which in law would make his acts the acts of the company. Through a circular statement it emphasises that reference should be made not to the titles that a man bears, e.g., manager, general manager etc. but to his power and ability to influence company policy and conduct, a person of lesser status is as regards the doctrine of identification legally of no significance.

Thus a supermarket manager of one store in a company which owned several hundred such stores was not a directing mind of the company (see *Tesco Supermarkets Ltd* v *Nattrass*). In this case the company had delegated total responsibility to the individual concerned to carry out particular duties, his failure to execute his responsibilities bringing about the potential criminal liability. This case illustrates the point that the fact that a company has delegated certain duties to an individual does not in law affix a company with that individual's conduct or mental state for the purposes of the doctrine of identification and is irrelevant to corporate liability under that doctrine. It is, however, of significance to the concept of vicarious liability which will be considered below.

4.15.4 Summary

The doctrine of identification determines that a company may incur criminal responsibility through the commission of an offence by an individual who is recognised in law as being the persona of that company. This will include individuals employed under a contract for services, i.e., independent contractors as well as employees (see *Worthy* v *Gordon Plant (Services), The Times* 19 March 1985). It must not be forgotten that the individual in addition remains criminally responsible in his own capacity. The doctrine of identification, though widening the ambit of corporate liability in crime, cannot, it is thought, be extended to cover certain crimes. Offences such as assaults, rape or murder can it seems be committed only by a human being and cannot be ascribed to a company under any circumstances, this is because of their non-physical nature. Furthermore where an offence prescribes imprisonment as the only form of punishment, it appears that such an offence cannot be committed by a company. However, this is more a recognition of the fact that a prosecution in such cases would serve no practical purpose, for a company cannot be imprisoned. The usual form of sanction against a company is to impose a fine, and thus offences which permit such a course of action are, subject to the limitation discussed above, crimes for which a company can be held accountable. The practical situation is that corporate liability, be it imposed by virtue of statutory construction or by the doctrine of identification, is generally concerned with offences connected with economic activity and its existence must be considered in this light.

4.16 VICARIOUS LIABILITY

4.16.1 Vicarious liability at common law

The general principle of English law is that a person (which includes a corporation) cannot be held criminally responsible for the acts of subordinates which are carried out without that person's knowledge or authorisation—see *R* v *Huggins* (1730) 2 Ld Raym 1574. There are, however, exceptions to this general principle. At common law an employer was liable vicariously for the acts of his employee in causing a public nuisance or in publishing a criminal libel.

Participation in Criminal Offences

4.16.2 Vicarious liability imposed by statute

Vicarious liability, i.e., being held criminally responsible for the actions of others is most commonly found in statutory offences. It is applicable to the relationship of employer and employee, principal and agent and between partners (which is regarded for the purposes of vicarious liability as the same form of relationship as principal and agent). Vicarious liability may be imposed upon an individual by virtue of the express terms of a statute, e.g., by providing that an individual will be held criminally liable within the terms of such a statute where either he, his servant (employee), agent etc. have been responsible for bringing about the particular prescribed conduct.

4.16.3 Statutory construction (extensive construction)

Vicarious liability may be imposed upon an individual within a statutory offence by implication. In the case of *Coppen v Moore (No. 2)* [1898] 2 QB 306, an employee of the accused sold to a customer a ham which he described as a Scotch ham. The accused had given express warning to all his shop assistants not to apply such a description to any hams sold by them. The description so given to the meat was false and the application of such a trade description was an offence contrary to s. 2(2) of the Merchandise Marks Act 1887. It was held by the Divisional Court of the Queen's Bench that the accused as employer of the shop assistant was criminally liable for the latter's conduct in applying the false trade description.

Lord Russell LJ was of the opinion that liability should be imposed vicariously in this case because (at p. 314):

> The [accused] . . . carries on an extensive business as grocer and provision dealer, having, it appears, six shops or branch establishments, and having also a wholesale warehouse. It is obvious that, if sales with false trade descriptions could be carried out in these establishments with impunity so far as the principal [i.e., the accused] is concerned, the Act would to a large extent be rendered nugatory.

In his lordship's opinion an accused could only be held vicariously liable for the conduct of his employees or agents where:

> the conduct constituting the offence was pursued by such servants [employees] and agents within the scope or in the course of their employment.

This principle of ascribing the conduct of an employee or agent to an employer or principal is applicable wherever the statute concerned requires conduct such as 'selling' or 'using'. It is not an abuse of such terms to consider that when, e.g., an employee carries out such conduct within the course of his employment and on behalf of his employer that such conduct should be considered to be that of his employer.

For reasons which are not clear this principle of statutory interpretation sometimes known as 'extensive construction' seems applicable only to offences where the conduct prescribed does not require any *mens rea*, i.e., offences of strict liability. The courts have developed an alternative principle to impose vicarious liability upon an individual in cases of offences which require *mens rea* as to all their elements. This is the principle of delegation.

4.16.4 Delegation

According to Lord Parker CJ in *R* v *Winson* [1969] 1 QB 371, the principle of delegation is only applicable:

> in cases where, although the statute uses words which import knowledge or intent such as . . . 'knowingly' or in some other cases 'permitting' or 'suffering' and the like, cases to which knowledge is inherent, nevertheless it has been held that a man cannot get out of his responsibilities which have been put upon him by delegating those responsibilities to another.

As in all cases of vicarious liability, the person actually responsible for the commission of the offence must be an employee or agent of the person ultimately held criminally liable. In addition the employee or agent must bring about the offence within the scope or course of his employment or authority.

The delegation principle seems applicable only in cases where the employer or principal has the right or duty to perform certain activities by virtue of his particular status. In cases of delegation the employer or principal has entrusted a subordinate with the execution of the duties that usually he must or is empowered to perform by virtue of that status. The law as a matter of policy has determined that such a delegation does not excuse an employer or principal from criminal liability merely because the offence has been brought about by the actions of a subordinate.

In *Allen* v *Whitehead* [1930] 1 KB 211 the accused, the owner of a café, delegated the running of that establishment to one of his employees. Though the accused was unaware that the premises were being used by prostitutes, this was known to the employee. The accused was convicted of an offence under s. 44 of the Metropolitan Police Act 1839 of knowingly permitting or suffering prostitutes to remain in a place where refreshments are sold and consumed. The actions and *mens rea* of the employee were ascribed to the accused.

What kind of conduct by an employer or principal will constitute delegation in a given instance was considered by the House of Lords in *Vane* v *Yiannopoullos* [1965] AC 486 (though their lordships determined that on the facts of the case there had been no delegation). The House of Lords without clearly approving the principle of delegation seemed to suggest that it could only be applied where all the authority possessed by an individual by virtue of his status had been entrusted to a subordinate. The accused was the licensee of a restaurant and many of the cases upon delegation seem confined to situations where the employer or principal is possessed of a licence to sell alcohol. Their lordships seemed to suggest that a licensee would have to be absent from the premises and to have left the management of those premises entirely in the employee's hands before delegation could be regarded as having taken place.

In *Howker* v *Robinson* [1973] QB 178 it was determined that the licensee of a

Participation in Criminal Offences

public house had delegated his control and authority to sell alcohol under his licence to an employee, though he had remained on the licensed premises. The sale of alcohol by the employee to a person under 18 years of age contrary to s. 169(1) of the Licensing Act 1964 had taken place in one of two bars. At the time of the illegal sale the accused had been absent from that particular bar and had been serving in the other. Whether delegation has taken place is according to *Howker* v *Robinson*, in essence a matter of fact (see Murphy, *A Practical Approach to Evidence*) and it cannot be said that a particular state of affairs can never constitute an act of delegation. It has been decided in the case of *Linnett* v *Metropolitan Police Commissioner* [1946] KB 290 that the imposition of vicarious liability based upon the principle of delegation is not limited to the relationship of employer and employee or principal and agent but is also applicable to cases of co-licensees.

4.16.5 Liability of employee or agent

In the cases which have imposed vicarious liability upon an employer or principal through the medium of delegation, the actual perpetrator of the offence may not be convicted as a co-principal. This is because the offences concerned require that only persons of a particular status, e.g., licensees, may be convicted as principals. The law, however, somewhat illogically permits the employee or agent in such cases to be convicted as a secondary party, i.e., as aider of his employer or principal who has been convicted as principal vicariously.

However, in cases of the imposition of vicarious liability by way of 'extensive construction' there is no objection to finding the actual perpetrator a co-principal to the offence for which his employer or principal has been found vicariously responsible.

4.16.6 Defences

In *Coppen* v *Moore* [1893] 2 QB 306 the statute concerned provided the employer with a defence if he could have established his good faith, and the fact that he had taken all reasonable precautions to prevent the occurrence of the offence, e.g., by the adequate supervision of his staff. Many statutes today which have been interpreted as imposing vicarious liability have similar defences, e.g., the Trade Descriptions Act 1968, s. 24. Where a statute which is interpreted as imposing vicarious liability does not expressly contain such a defence then it will not be deemed to apply to that particular statute by implication.

4.16.7 Abetting or attempting an offence and vicarious liability

Vicarious liability is not applicable in cases where the employee's or agent's conduct amounts to abetting a third party to commit an offence—see *Ferguson* v *Weaving* [1951] 1 KB 814. In *Gardner* v *Akeroyd* [1952] 2 QB 743 it was also accepted that an employer or principal cannot be held vicariously responsible for conduct on the part of a subordinate that amounts to only an attempted crime.

4.16.8 Summary

Vicarious liability, however imposed, is a creature of convenience. It is principally restricted to cases of statutory offences which are concerned with the regulation of commercial activities. Vicarious liability prevents the owner of such enterprises or the individual primarily concerned in their management from escaping responsibility for breaches in the criminal law by claiming that the commission of an offence was the result of the actions of a subordinate. Since vicarious liability is generally concerned with commercial activities its existence poses no real infringements to civil liberty and helps the effective enforcement of many such modern mercantile and social activities through the threat of penal sanction. Though criticised it will continue to survive and is a more realistic answer to the problem of enforcing responsible managerial conduct than pious hopes of reforming, effective and creative parliamentary activity in this area of the criminal law.

4.17 QUESTIONS

1. What is the difference between a person held criminally responsible through the doctrine of innocent agent, and an individual who is regarded by the law as a secondary party?

2. Why was the conductor in *Thornton* v *Mitchell* not convicted?

   (a) as a principal, or
   (b) as a secondary party?

3. How does vicarious liability differ from strict liability?

4. Should the rule in *R* v *Richards* which determines the ultimate criminal responsibility of a counsellor with regard to an offence be generally applicable to all secondary parties? If not, why not?

5. Should a secondary party's criminal responsibility ever be determined by reference to that of the principal offender?

6. It has been held in the recent case of *R* v *Clarke* [1985] Crim LR 209 that if a secondary party's conduct with regard to a principal offence is 'overall calculated and intended not to further but to frustrate the ultimate result of the crime', the secondary party may have this matter considered in his defence.

   Is this recognising a defence of motive or merely that a secondary party may lack *mens rea*?

5

Inchoate Offences

5.1 INTRODUCTION

In the earlier chapters it was pointed out that in relation to most serious offences the prosecution is bound to prove in addition to the *actus reus*, the accused's guilty mind or *mens rea*. This can be achieved either by showing a positively blameworthy state of mind such as intention or recklessness in the sense of conscious risk-taking, or by showing one of the negative but blameworthy 'states of mind' such as recklessness in the sense of failing to think about an obvious risk or varying degrees of negligence.

In chapter 2 emphasis was placed on the fact that in general the *mens rea* must coincide with and relate to the *actus reus*. In chapter 3 it was shown that in some instances today proof of *actus reus* alone or more commonly proof of *actus reus* and some degree of *mens rea* as to some but not all the elements of the *actus reus*, will suffice for a conviction. So far the converse has not been mentioned. We have not yet discussed the question of liability for *mens rea* alone or for *mens rea* together with proof of some, but not all the elements of the *actus reus*.

5.2 LIABILITY FOR MENS REA ALONE

It will be a sad day for freedom and civil liberties in this country when an individual is held criminally liable for having 'evil' or prohibited thoughts or to put it another way, if a person is convicted in proof of *mens rea* alone. As of yet in our society there are no 'thought police'. What you feel or think currently cannot, and should never be able to, make you liable to punishment (at least not in this life) whether or not it is morally good or bad, legal or illegal, in or out of line with the views of the government of the day. Ethically your thoughts may be such as to brand you as morally or ethically bad or guilty but the law always requires proof of an *actus reus* to accompany the thoughts before the label 'criminal' will be attached to any person. In brief thoughts without deeds will not make you a criminal but beware once one's thoughts or feelings are reflected in external conduct the prospect of criminal liability may arise. For example, even though our society avowedly adheres to the principle of freedom of speech (as well as of thought) yet the expression of certain views (for instance those which are seditious, or blasphemous, or in breach of the Official Secrets Act, or likely to cause a breach of the peace, or defamatory or discriminatory), especially if in public, may constitute a criminal offence. In those circumstances, however, the law maintains that a person is being made liable not for the views he holds but for the intentional or reckless or negligent expression of those views which produce or are likely to produce prohibited consequences.

Shortly in this chapter the offence of conspiracy will be discussed. At first sight this offence appears to be an exception to what has been stated in the previous paragraph because conspiracy is simply a state of mind. It is constituted by a meeting of two or more minds in agreement to engage in criminal pursuits and it is clear that a conviction may be obtained without proof of any positive external conduct having been taken to achieve the agreed goal. But with a moment's reflection it becomes clear that mental telepathy being as of yet unperfected, conspiracy cannot be a purely *mens rea* offence, there must be some external activity or conduct by way of communication between the various parties to the conspiratorial agreement. So even in conspiracy a person is not being punished for thoughts alone but for the communication of thoughts or for overt acquiescence in or agreement with the criminal thoughts or intentions of another.

If two men independently conceive of a plan to burgle the same bank at the same time and in the same way but each is apprehended before they can achieve their goal then each may escape criminal liability depending on whether or not they had done anything by way of conduct towards achieving that goal. One thing is clear, there is no possible liability for conspiracy. If on the other hand there was evidence that these two men had communicated in writing, words, signs or gestures and agreed together to act in concert to burgle the bank then they would both be liable for a criminal conspiracy whether or not they had taken any other steps towards achieving their joint venture.

A person cannot be made liable for criminal thoughts alone but it does not mean that he can only be liable for the completed *actus reus* of his desired antisocial conduct. These two positions are two ends of a spectrum. At one end proof of *mens rea* alone will not make a person liable; at the other end, proof of having committed all the *actus reus* elements of a substantive offence (with *mens rea*) will make that person liable for that completed offence. Between these two extremes are various possible and perceivable activities by which the inner thoughts are made manifest by external conduct.

5.3 THE SCENARIO

Assume that the facts in the original scenario are slightly altered and the following events actually occur:

(a) Donald conceives in his mind an idea to burgle Rex's house knowing that Rex and Marian will be away. If by chance their daughter, Sarah, is at home Donald intends to have sexual intercourse with her by force if needs be.

(b) Donald approaches Bruce and tells him his plans. He asks Bruce to go with him to steal valuables while he is having intercourse with Sarah.

(c) Donald encourages Bruce to help him to find two other persons to take

Inchoate Offences 127

part in the intended burglary.

(d) Bruce agrees to go along with this and they formulate a plan in collaboration with Edward and John who were recruited by Bruce.

(e) On the night in question, Donald, Bruce, Edward and John arrive at Rex's house. There is a light on. They ring the doorbell but Sarah has been smoking cannabis and is in a deep sleep. Bruce then renders the alarm on Rex's home inoperative.

(f) John breaks a window and all four of them enter Rex's house. They 'raid' Rex's liquor cabinet and Donald subsequently violates Sarah while Edward and John are collecting valuables which they intend to steal.

(g) Rex and Marian return home. Bruce, Edward and John flee causing damage to Rex's house in doing so.

A reading of s. 9 of the Theft Act 1968 which defines the offence of burglary (see para. 2.5 and para. 8.12.1 onwards) makes it clear that at stage (f) of the proceedings described above the four youths have committed and completed the offence of burglary. That occurs the moment they deliberately entered Rex's house ('a building') without authority ('as trespassers') with intent to steal or damage Rex's property or to rape Sarah.

If the crime of burglary could not be established alternative charges are available. Donald could be charged with rape (see para. 7.5 onwards) or theft or being party to theft (see para. 8.1 onwards) and the others with theft and/or criminal damage, or possibly each with being a party to rape.

Consideration must now be given to the events leading up to the unlawful entry. Should the young men be liable for some offence even though some intervening event prevents them from ever reaching stage (f), the entering of the house? What if the presence in the vicinity of Rex's house of a policeman had deterred them from entering the house, or what if their tools for housebreaking were inadequate or what if they realised the morally reprehensible nature of their proposed conduct and they changed their minds and went home? Events such as these could prevent the proposed unlawful entry into Rex's house from ever taking place. Should that be an end to the matter?

5.4 INCHOATE OFFENCES

Clearly any legal system would be defective if criminal liability only arose when substantive offences such as burglary, rape, murder, theft, criminal damage etc. have actually been committed. Imagine the dilemma if, being aware that these four young men intended to steal Rex's property and rape Sarah, the police had to choose between preventing the offences from occurring in the knowledge that then Donald, Bruce, Edward and John could not be prosecuted, or waiting, helpless, and then prosecuting the four offenders after the burglary, theft, rape and acts of criminal damage had been completely performed. Neither situation would be satisfactory. While it would be wrong to prosecute anyone simply for having criminal thoughts or dreaming up criminal plans, it would be equally intolerable if antisocial persons could only be prosecuted after fully perpetrating one of the substantive offences.

A sophisticated legal system such as our own will contain in its armoury, to protect society from the activities of such antisocial persons as Donald, Bruce, Edward and John, offences sometimes known as inchoate and sometimes as preliminary offences. These offences provide a penalty, deterrent or punishment even though the desired substantive offence to which they relate is not committed for some reason. These offences are available to be charged as soon as a person begins to commit overt acts which evidence his intention to put his criminal thoughts or plans into operation. These overt acts may be sufficient to constitute one of the inchoate offences even though the intended substantive offence has not yet been committed and probably now will not be committed by that person.

The inchoate or preliminary offences are three in number and they arise as follows in the scenario:

(a) When Donald suggests that Bruce steals from Rex's house and that he recruit others to assist in stealing from that house Donald is *inciting* Bruce to commit an offence. Donald, in making such a suggestion which encourages Bruce to commit an offence, is himself committing the preliminary or *inchoate offence of incitement* which is a common law offence.

(b) When Donald and Bruce agree to proceed with the burglary (and subsequently when Edward and John agree to join in) they are committing the preliminary or *inchoate offence of conspiracy*. This is in the main a statutory offence contrary to the Criminal Law Act 1977, but some conspiracies remain criminal by reason of the common law (see para. 5.7.2 onwards).

(c) Where Donald, Bruce, Edward and John, with no lawful excuse, commence taking steps to achieve their goal of burgling Rex's house they have committed the preliminary or *inchoate offence of attempt* provided the steps taken by them are more than merely preparatory. Attempt is now a statutory offence contrary to the Criminal Attempts Act 1981.

(d) Once the four young men have entered Rex's home unlawfully they have *completed the offence of burglary*, there is no need to worry about charging them with any of the three inchoate offences. They can be charged and convicted for the more serious substantive offence. The lesser inchoate offences become irrelevant or at least subsumed in the greater offence.

If for whatever reason they never do enter Rex's house then there is no liability at stage (a) of the amended scenario; Donald will not be punished for his thoughts and plans no matter how 'wicked' or criminal. Likewise there would be no liability at stage (b); Donald is at liberty to approach Bruce and tell him of his ideas. The mere disclosure of his nefarious thoughts would not constitute an offence. At stage (c), however, Donald has incited Bruce to commit the criminal offence of burglary and Bruce subsequently incites Edward and John to do likewise. At stage (d) the agreement between all four of them to burgle Rex's home constitutes a criminal conspiracy. If at stage (e) the police or Rex intervene or something else prevents the burglary then all four probably could be charged with the offence of attempted burglary.

From society's point of view the beauty of the inchoate offences lies in the fact that they allow more than 'one bite of the cherry' especially where more than one person is involved in antisocial behaviour. Take Donald as an example. If he cannot be charged with the *complete offence* of burglary or rape or theft then he

Inchoate Offences

might be charged with *attempted* burglary at least. If he has not done enough to satisfy the legal requirements for attempt he may be charged with *conspiracy* to burgle and/or with *incitement* of others to burgle.

One of the first and foremost features which must be grasped relating to all three inchoate offences is that they do not exist 'in the air' or on their own. A person should not be charged with incitement, or conspiracy or attempt. He should only be charged in relation to, and by reference to, an intended, substantive offence. To do otherwise would be improper. Why? First the accused is entitled to know what crime he is alleged to have incited, conspired, or attempted and secondly to incite, conspire at or attempt something which is not a criminal offence cannot itself be an offence, inchoate or otherwise, simply by reason of the incitement, conspiracy or attempt. Because the inchoate offence must be charged in relation to an intended substantive offence all three inchoate offences can be described as crimes of specific intent. Donald, for example, intentionally incites and conspires with Bruce with the specific intention of burgling, or causing to be burgled, Rex's house.

5.5 ACTS OF PREPARATION

If at stage (b), before he incites Bruce, Donald had gone to a hardware shop and bought tools which were to be used to break into Rex's house and if he had gone and photographed Rex's house to see where the burglar alarms were sited, it is clear that he is preparing for the burglary. At this point he has incited no one; he has conspired with no one and as we will see shortly, he has not attempted to burgle Rex's house. If apprehended leaving the shop with the tools, or while photographing the house, should he be liable for some offence? In some societies these acts of preparation would in themselves constitute an offence but that does not appear to be the case in English law. The notions of attempt, conspiracy and incitement do each involve preparatory conduct to some extent but those offences aside, preparation is not punishable. In other legal systems it may be that the inchoate offences, and especially attempts, are defined in such a way as to include all preparatory conduct on the way towards the preparation of the intended substantive offence but, again, that is not the case in English law. Here there is a supposedly clear distinction between acts of preparation and acts of perpetration. Liability attaches only to the latter but as you will see later in this chapter it is not easy to say where the line between the two is to be drawn. Even at their widest ambit the current law of attempt, conspiracy and incitement cannot catch every preparatory act.

There is one reported case, however, which stands as an authority (albeit not a strong authority) for the proposition that acts of preparation for the commission of a criminal offence are in themselves offences at common law. The facts of *R v Singh (Gurmit)* [1966] 2 QB 53 were that the accused had procured a rubber stamp which would print the words 'Magistrate 1st Class, Jullumpur'. He intended to use this stamp to forge a document with the aim of defrauding another. He was charged with 'unlawfully procuring a rubber stamp with intent to defraud' and the trial judge was asked whether or not this was an offence recognised at common law. The judge ruled that what Gurmit Singh had done did amount to the indictable offence of preparation. If that ruling is correct and represents a general principle of common law then there is an inchoate offence prior to incitement, conspiracy or attempt. It would mean that Donald in the scenario would have committed an offence by purchasing the tools or by photographing Rex's house with intent to burgle. But it is very doubtful that there is any such common law preparatory offence at all short of attempt, conspiracy or incitement. The decision in *Gurmit Singh* to the contrary stands alone. It is a judgment at first instance and of little consequence in so far as the doctrine of precedent is concerned. Furthermore if there was an offence of preparation at common law, Parliament would not have had to create, as it has done, specific statutory offences of preparation, one of the best examples of which is to be seen in s. 3 of the Criminal Damage Act 1971. That provision reads as follows:

A person who has anything in his custody or under his control intending without lawful excuse to use it or cause or permit another to use it:

(a) to destroy or damage any property belonging to some other person; or
(b) to destroy or damage his own or the user's property in a way which he knows is likely to endanger the life of some other person;

shall be guilty of an offence.

This offence is punishable by up to 10 years' imprisonment.

Another example is s. 25(1) of the Theft Act 1968 which reads:

A person shall be guilty of an offence if, when not at his place of abode, he has with him any article for use in the course of or in connection with any burglary, theft or cheat.

This offence is punishable on indictment (see Introduction) by up to three years' imprisonment.

In the scenario Donald took photographs of Rex's house and purchased implements to be used to facilitate entry into Rex's house. The possession of the implements (not the photographs) might be caught within s. 3 but only if the prosecution could prove *an intention to use them* (or to permit Bruce, Edward or John to use them) *to cause criminal damage*. On the facts that may not be possible, as their intention appears to be burglary and/or rape and theft. However, both the possession of the housebreaking implements and of the photographs beyond the confines of Donald's residence or the residences of the other three youths, would probably be caught by s. 25 of the Theft Act 1968. The term 'article' as used in that provision clearly is wide enough to encompass not only the tools or implements but also photographs which show the position of burglar alarms and points of likely access to the building and escape routes from it. *The provision is specifically aimed to catch acts preparatory to burglary, theft, criminal deception and the taking and driving away of any vehicle* provided it can be proved that the accused *intended to use any article in the course of, or in connection with any of those four offences*. This may be difficult but not impossible depending on when and where he was apprehended, the type of 'article' and the

Inchoate Offences

reasonableness of any explanation.

The ambit of this section is extremely wide and subject to proof of possession and intention, anything, even everyday items, could make a person liable provided it is something that he would not have had with him at that time but for the intention to commit a substantive offence. To have something out of the ordinary in the circumstances with no explanation would warrant a charge under this section. So, for example, to be apprehended on a balmy summer's night with woolly gloves or on a bitter, winter's night with thin, rubber gloves could be sufficient as in either case they could be worn to avoid leaving fingerprints. Apprehending Donald at night in the vicinity of Rex's house with photographs of that house, or apprehending him with housebreaking implements or tools could bring him and the other three within s. 25. The test, it is submitted, must be the abnormality of the possession in the circumstances.

Proof of *mens rea* requires in this instance first, proof of knowledge that one possesses the article and secondly, proof of an intention to use the article in the course of or in connection with any of the four specified offences. Because of the words 'in the course of or in connection with', the photographs in Donald's possession or anything else that, while they may necessarily be used in the actual perpetration of the substantive offence, might be used before or after its commission, can bring the possessor within the section. It will be sufficient to incur liability under the section if the article is for future use by Donald or one of the others, and even if it is not possible to show that Donald intended the article to be used in connection with the burglary of Rex's house, because the section only requires proof of his intention to use it in connection with 'any' burglary, theft or cheat.

Section 25(3) states that if, for example, Donald is so apprehended and then charged under s. 25:

> proof that he had with him any article made or adapted for use in committing a burglary, theft or cheat shall be evidence that he had it with him for such use.

In such a situation an evidential burden is placed on Donald. If he offers no explanation then the judge is entitled to tell the jury that there is evidence upon which they may find that he had the necessary intention provided they are satisfied beyond reasonable doubt that he had that intention in fact. (See para. 2.14 for a discussion of a comparable section, s. 8 of the Criminal Justice Act 1967). Where an explanation is offered the jury must decide whether or not it may reasonably be true and where the article possessed is not made or adapted for one of the four specified offences then unless there is proof of other incriminating circumstances to accompany it, there is not a proper case to leave to the jury.

If the possession of the photographs or the taking of them by Donald are not caught by s. 25 and if, as submitted above, there is no general common law offence of preparation then Donald will not be liable for any offence until he does something further such as inciting or conspiring or attempting to burgle Rex's house.

In so far as the prospect of a general offence of preparation at common law is concerned one final point should be made in relation to the decision in *Gurmit*

Singh's case. The Criminal Attempts Act 1981, s. 6, abolishes the offences of attempt at common law together with any offence at common law of procuring materials for crime. In so far as the decision in *Gurmit Singh's* case dealt with the 'unlawful procuring of implements for the commission of a crime' the judge's view may now be rendered otiose and irrelevant, but s. 6, by its wording, is limited to 'procuring materials for crime' and makes no mention of acts of preparation (an example of which would be taking photographs) other than procuring materials. Despite s. 6 of the Criminal Attempts Act 1981 and despite the other arguments above to the contrary, there is still the possibility, albeit slight, that acts of preparation are an offence chargeable at common law. The most cogent argument against the existence of such an offence at common law, however, is the definition of attempt contained in the common law cases on the subject and in s. 1(1) of the Criminal Attempts Act 1981 which is the current law. It is to that offence and the two other established inchoate offences that we now turn. They are dealt with below in the following order: attempts, conspiracies and finally incitements.

5.6 ATTEMPTS

5.6.1 Reasons for uncompleted crimes

The analysis of criminal conduct generally reveals four distinct stages: (a) the formation of the *mens rea*, (b) the preparation (both (a) and (b) have been discussed above), (c) the attempt (falling short of completion) and (d) the successful completion of the intended offence. As already indicated, while *mens rea* is very material it does not incur criminal liability in itself and it is doubtful whether preparation (with *mens rea*) constitutes an offence at common law but clearly once an intended substantive offence has been successfully completed the person responsible is liable for that offence not for attempt.

Anyone who sets out to commit a crime may, for a number of reasons, fail to complete the commission of that crime. In the scenario, for example, the four young men set out with the intention to burgle Rex's home but they may not achieve that goal. Why?

(a) *They may simply change their minds before committing any overt act sufficiently connected with the intended offence* as to amount to an attempt. Right up to the point of trying to 'break in' or at least up to the point of entering on to the property belonging to Rex it may be argued that they have not committed an attempt and if they change their minds they are not liable. The only overt acts were merely preparatory and not so immediately connected with the complete offence as to amount to an attempt to commit it. But they may have changed their minds too late to deny that they had gone so far as an attempt. To have broken the door lock or a window in Rex's house and then to change their minds about entering would leave them liable to a charge of attempted burglary. As we will see these acts are immediately and irrevocably connected with the complete offence, they are more than merely preparatory, and therefore constitute an attempt.

(b) *They may be prevented by someone from doing some act necessary to complete the commission of the crime* as, for example, where a police constable or

Inchoate Offences

the home owner interrupts their activities while they are trying to force open a door or window but before they have entered the premises. Generally they will be liable for attempted burglary although it may depend on the precise point at which the interruption or intervention occurs. If the intervention occurs too soon (for example, while Donald, Bruce, Edward and John are still in the street outside Rex's house) then they may escape liability for attempted burglary at least. Some other charge, perhaps s. 25 of the Theft Act 1968 may be appropriate (see para. 5.5).

(c) Although the four young men are not interrupted *they may fail* to complete the commission of the intended crime *through their own incompetence or inadequate means*. For example, Bruce may fail to disarm the burglar alarm system or the jemmy which Donald bought may not be strong enough to force open the door. Again, if they have tried, if they have taken a step that is more than merely preparatory towards the complete offence, then they are liable for a criminal attempt.

(d) *They may discover that it is impossible to commit the intended offence*, not because of insufficient or inadequate means or incompetence on their part but *because for some reason it is physically not possible whatever means they employ*. For example, if Rex's house has burnt down in the interim or if on opening a window in Rex's house they can see that Rex's family has moved meanwhile and the house is now empty. In such situations the four young men are ready, willing and able to burgle but it is now physically impossible for them to do so because of supervening events. Should they be liable for something? Should the pickpocket who puts his hand into the pocket of another only to discover it is empty, be liable? Should the man who fires a bullet at, and hits, what he thinks is someone he hates, be liable even though it was in fact a tree stump? What if it was the body of the man he hated but he had already died of a heart attack? In all these instances it is physically impossible to produce the desired or intended criminal consequence, there is nothing to steal and no one alive to wound or kill. There could have been, however, but for the unexpected intervening event.

(e) They may *complete what they intended to do but contrary to their belief, what they have done is not a crime*. The four young men do break into the house intending to steal but (to take a very fanciful example), unbeknown to Donald, Rex turns out to be Donald's long lost father and he has died in the interim leaving this house and all its contents to Donald.

Should Donald (and his compatriots) be saved from criminal liability by the fact that what he has done, contrary to his own belief at the time, does not, after all, amount in law to a crime? What he intends to steal is already his own and therefore incapable of being stolen by him. Can Donald be liable for attempt if caught doing something which he thinks and intends to be criminal but which in fact is not, not because it is physically impossible but because it is legally impossible?

The law relating to the problems of defining attempt and the effect of physical and legal impossibility are discussed below in more detail.

5.6.2 The law of criminal attempts

The Criminal Attempts Act 1981 contains the current law on attempts. Section 6 of that Act abolishes the common law offence of attempt and replaces it with the statutory offence defined in s. 1(1) as follows (emphasis added):

> If, with intent to commit an offence to which this section applies, a person does *an act which is more than merely preparatory to the commission of the offence*, he is guilty of attempting to commit the offence.

At common law there had to be a positive act of perpetration which nevertheless fell short of the intended, substantive crime. It was summed up by Parke B in the old case of *R* v *Eagleton* (1855) Dears CC 515 when he said (at p. 538):

> The mere intention to commit [an offence] is not criminal. Some act is required, and we do not think that all acts towards committing [an offence] are indictable. Acts remotely leading towards the commission of the offence are not to be considered as attempts to commit it, but acts immediately connected with it are.

What was sufficiently connected with the crime so as to constitute an attempt to commit it depended on the facts and the ingredients necessary to constitute the completed, substantive offence together with the application of one or more of a number of tests to show the sufficiency of the connection between the overt acts and the intended offence. These tests, to which we will turn shortly, comprised: (a) proximity, (b) equivocality, (c) *locus paenitentiae*, (d) impossibility, (e) social danger.

Today, in England and Wales attempts are no longer governed by the common law but by the Criminal Attempts Act 1981 but, as at common law, the dividing line is to be drawn between acts of preparation (to which it is submitted no liability attaches—at least not for an inchoate offence, see para. 5.5) and acts of perpetration (being steps which are more than merely preparatory and therefore attempts for which a person may be liable). The Criminal Attempts Act 1981 is the law but s. 1(1) does not really help the judge, the lawyer or the student to say exactly where the line between acts of mere preparation and punishable perpetration is to be drawn in any given case. Leaving aside specific, statutory offences of preparation like s. 25 of the Theft Act 1968 (see para. 5.5), at what point has Donald in the scenario taken the step which is more than merely preparatory? When he buys the housebreaking tools? When he photographs Rex's house? When he sets off in the dead of night with the tools in his pocket towards Rex's house? When he arrives in the street in which the house is situated? When he enters Rex's property? When he takes the tools from his pockets? When he inserts a tool into the door lock or between the window and the frame? Where is the line to be drawn? According to *R* v *Ilyas* (1984) 78 Cr App R 17 reference may still be had, despite the Criminal Attempts Act 1981, back to the old common law cases to provide assistance to decide this issue.

5.6.3 Attempt at common law

The tests discussed in the old common law cases possibly do provide some assistance although there is a certain amount of ambiguity and conflict in those cases. They show three things in particular, however, first that there are a number of tests or methods developed to help draw the dividing line, secondly that some of these tests produced unsatisfactory results, and thirdly they illustrate that there is a very narrow line between preparation and perpetration or attempt.

Proximity At common law the most common test of an attempt was *proximity*. In *R v Robinson* [1915] 2 KB 342 at 348 Lord Reading CJ said:

> acts remotely leading to the commission of the offence are not to be considered as attempts to commit, but acts immediately connected with it are.

If the act was sufficiently proximate to the crime intended then it was an attempt. If it was the penultimate act or possibly the act preceding the penultimate act, then it was likely to constitute an attempt.

The cases, however, illustrated the unsatisfactory nature of this test and show why other tests were developed. In *R v Button* [1900] 2 QB 597, the accused was convicted of attempting to obtain prize money by false pretences in that he had entered handicap races under another person's name so as to conceal his own past winnings, with intent to defraud. In *R v Robinson* [1915] 2 KB 342 a jeweller hid his stock, summoned the police and pretended his shop had been broken into. He intended to make a fraudulent claim against his insurance company. He was held not guilty of an attempt to obtain money by false pretences. What distinguishes these two cases is the fact that Button had done all he could towards the commission of the defrauding (in that instance deceiving the race organisers) whereas Robinson had not. He had not made an insurance claim although he intended to do so.

In *Comer v Bloomfield* (1970) 55 Cr App R 305 the accused hid his van then wrote to his insurance company enquiring whether or not he could claim. He was held not guilty of an attempt to obtain property by deception on the basis that such a letter was not sufficiently proximate to the obtaining of compensation.

In *DPP v Stonehouse* [1977] 2 All ER 909, the accused, a well-known politician who was in financial difficulties, tried to fake his death and assume a new identity in the Antipodes. He had provided for his wife, who was not a party to his plans, by previously insuring his life for a large sum of money. His wife had not made a claim on the policy when he was discovered alive in Australia. Stonehouse was convicted of attempted fraud on the basis that his faked drowning was sufficiently proximate to the commission of the fraudulent claim. What distinguishes *Comer v Bloomfield* from *Stonehouse* presumably is that Stonehouse had done all he could to commit the complete offence (apart from avoiding detection) whereas in *Comer v Bloomfield* the accused still intended to make an insurance claim himself but had not yet done so. There was still something more he could do towards the commission of the offence. In *Stonehouse* there was nothing more he could do although it was up to his next of kin to make a formal claim on the life insurance policy. Stonehouse had produced the circumstance which entitled his wife or other relatives to make a claim.

At common law then an act was sufficiently proximate if the accused had done the 'last act' needed to commit the complete offence even if something more still remained to be done by another person. That was the position in *Button* and *Stonehouse* but not in *Robinson* or *Comer* v *Bloomfield*. In the latter two cases the accused's conduct was still in the pre-penultimate stage and therefore classifiable as mere preparation. It may well be that today if charged in a situation similar to that in *Robinson* or in *Comer* v *Bloomfield* a jury properly directed (without reference to those cases) would find the steps taken to be more than merely preparatory and therefore an attempt within s. 1(1) of the Criminal Attempts Act 1981.

Equivocality A second test for attempt at common law was *the equivocality test* which was based on ascertaining from the facts and circumstantial evidence the clear and unambiguous intention of the accused. If his acts showed beyond reasonable doubt the criminal end towards which they were directed then it could be said to be an attempt. Two cases illustrate the operation of this test. In *Davey* v *Lee* [1968] 1 QB 366, the accused's conviction was upheld for attempting to steal copper from the South Western Electricity Board. He had cut the wire fence surrounding the Board's premises near to the place where the copper was stored and he had been apprehended attempting to climb through the fence. The court took the view that if the acts of the accused were immediately, and not merely remotely connected with the completed crime, and if the doing of those acts could not reasonably be thought of as having any other purpose than the commission of the intended substantive offence then an attempt would be proved. The act speaks for itself—no other explanation is possible.

In *Jones* v *Brooks* (1968) 52 Cr App R 614, the accused had been seen trying to open car doors. He admitted intending to drive home in one of the cars. He was convicted of attempting to take and drive away a motor vehicle. On appeal the court upheld that conviction based on the equivocality test despite the fact that the trying of door handles was equivocal; it could have been a step towards any of the following: (a) theft of the car; (b) theft of its contents; (c) damage to the car or its contents, or (d) some innocent purpose such as sheltering from the rain, or going to sleep in it. The Court of Appeal, however, felt able to disregard the equivocal nature of the accused's acts because they, together with his express intention, could show that the *actus reus* of attempt was committed. The *equivocal* nature of his acts did not mean that he could not be convicted. In the words of the judge: 'intention is relevant when the act concerned is equivocal, in order to see towards what the act is directed'.

Where the act is *unequivocal* then there is clearly an attempt. Leaving aside s. 9 of the Criminal Attempts Act 1981 which creates a special new offence of interfering with motor vehicles, would either the accused in *Davey* v *Lee* and *Jones* v *Brooks* be guilty of attempt today?

Locus paenitentiae At common law the third test, that of *locus paenitentiae*, applied only where the accused had voluntarily changed his mind and given up the idea of proceeding towards the commission of the substantive offence. In such a case according to this test his actions would only be preparation if they were completely harmless. Repentance alone would not prevent his uncompleted, but sufficiently connected, acts amounting to an attempt. They

Inchoate Offences

were an attempt if they came close to completing the offence and if any harm, injury or damage had been caused.

Impossibility   The fourth test at common law was the *impossibility test*. If it was impossible in fact to achieve the intended substantive offence then for some time it was the law that no liability attached to a person who attempted to achieve that impossible goal. In *R* v *McPherson* (1857) Dears & B 197 it was held that a person could not be convicted for attempting to steal when he broke into a building to steal articles which were not there. In *R* v *Collins* (1864) 9 Cox CC 497, it was held that where a person puts his hand into the pocket of another with intent to steal but the pocket is empty, he cannot be convicted of attempting to steal. Later these cases were overruled as mistaken. In *R* v *Brown* (1889) 24 QBD 357 a pregnant woman believing that she was taking a noxious drug to procure her own miscarriage took something which in fact was harmless but she was held guilty of an attempt to procure an abortion. In *R* v *Ring* (1892) 17 Cox CC 491, which involved identical facts relating to pickpocketing as in *Collins* the decision was exactly the opposite and Ring was found guilty of attempted theft even though the pocket in question was empty. The old general impossibility test was changed and for many years the propostiion held sway that a plea of physical impossibility was no bar to a charge of attempt. However, the law relating to impossibility took another turn in the case of *Haughton* v *Smith* [1975] AC 476, and this led subsequently to Parliament's passing the Criminal Attempts Act 1981. Those developments are discussed in detail below.

Social danger   The fifth test at common law was not often referred to openly but clearly the consideration of it lay behind the application of the other tests. This was *the social danger test*. Here the seriousness of the intended crime and the social danger apprehended from it were factors that caused judges to consider certain acts as attempts which otherwise might have been treated as mere preparation. Again, as is so often the case in law, this so-called test was more often than not simply a means of rationalising the judges' opinion of the harmfulness or danger of such acts. Nowhere were any criteria laid down to ascertain social danger; there was no touchstone to reckon the social impact of any acts. Nevertheless judges did use it to decide whether or not an attempt had occurred—for example, in *R* v *Brown* (1889) 24 QBD 357 Darling J thought that the social danger of quack physicians supplying, or of pregnant women administering to themselves, medicine to induce abortion, even though the medicine turned out to be innocuous, was sufficiently serious to warrant conviction of such persons for attempt to procure an abortion. The judge's and the jury's view on the social danger of the completed offence may dictate whether or not in their view the proximity or equivocality or *locus paenitentiae* tests have been satisfied and a step taken which is more than merely preparatory.

5.6.4   Mens rea of attempt

A conviction for an attempted crime can only be secured if the prosecution show intention to commit the completed offence. Edmund Davies LJ in *R* v *Easom* [1971] 2 QB 315 put it this way: '[I]t is implicit in the concept of an attempt that the person acting intends to do the act attempted'. *Easom* is instructive because the accused there had picked up a policewoman's handbag in a darkened cinema and having gone through its contents he replaced it without having taken anything. He could not be guilty of theft having taken nothing and it was thought that he could not be guilty of attempted theft 'unless it were established that he was animated by the same intention permanently to deprive [the woman] of the goods enumerated in the particulars of the charge [her handbag and its contents] as would be necessary to establish the full offence'. That intention could not be shown in relation to any of the contents. (For the position today see the discussion of conditional intent, para. 8.11).

If attempt involves proof of intention as to a consequence then there must be proof that the accused did intend (directly or obliquely) or that he did foresee the consequence of his acts as resulting in the crime in question. Also it must be proved that he intended those consequences even though a lesser degree of *mens rea* might suffice if he were charged with the completed crime rather than an attempt at it.

In the scenario when Rex returns home to find the aftermath of Donald's drunken debauchery and then attacks the prone body of the incapacitated Donald, Rex may be guilty of murder. His assault kills Donald and even though at the time of the assault he intended simply to cause Donald grievous bodily harm (see the *mens rea* of murder, para. 7.6.2) that can suffice to satisfy the mental element of murder whereas if Rex was only charged with *attempted* murder then the prosecution would have to prove Rex's intention to kill. A lesser intent will not suffice according to *R v Whybrow* (1951) 35 Cr App R 141 where it was held to be a misdirection to tell the jury that if the accused intended to kill *or* to cause grievous bodily harm an attempt to kill had been proved. The Court of Criminal Appeal said: '[I]f the charge is one of attempted murder, the intent becomes the principal ingredient of the crime'.

An example can be illustrated by the scenario. If Rex assaulted the supine body of Donald but the attack did not kill him, then Rex could be convicted of unlawful wounding contrary to s. 20 of the Offences against the Person Act 1861 either because he intended the harm *or* because he was reckless as to whether or not he caused harm to Donald. If, however, Rex was charged only with attempted unlawful wounding then the prosecution would only obtain a conviction if it proved that Rex intended to cause such harm, i.e., intended to wound Donald. (This is the same specific intent as is required to obtain a conviction under s. 18 of the Offences against the Person Act 1861 for the more serious offence of causing grievous bodily harm with intent to do so.)

To ascertain what exactly is meant in law by those words 'intended to' you should refer back to para. 2.6, and in relation to attempt the case of *R v Mohan* [1976] QB 1. There the accused was charged with an attempt to cause bodily harm: He had been driving when a pedestrian policeman signalled him to stop. The accused slowed down initially and then accelerated driving at the policeman who managed to jump out of the path of the vehicle. The accused drove away. In the Court of Appeal James LJ said that in relation to the *mens rea* of attempt, 'intention' means '"specific intent"' and can be defined as "a decision to bring about a certain consequence" or as the "aim"'. Having considered *Hyam v DPP* [1975] AC 55 (which at that time was significant, see paras. 2.6.1, 2.6.2 and 7.6.2)

Inchoate Offences

the Court of Appeal held that despite that case (which has since been superseded by *R v Moloney* [1985] 2 WLR 648) the *mens rea* of attempt could *not* be satisfied by proof that the accused 'knew or correctly foresaw that the consequences of his act unless interrupted would "as a high degree of probability", or would be "likely" to . . . [bring about] . . . the commission of the complete offence'.

James LJ went on to say:

> In our judgment, evidence of knowledge of likely consequences, or from which knowledge of likely consequences can be inferred, is evidence by which intent may be established but it is not, in relation to the offence of attempt, to be equated with intent.

And he added that since attempt is a crime of specific intent it requires proof of:

> a decision to bring about, in so far as it lies within the accused's power, the commission of the offence which it is alleged the accused attempted to commit, no matter whether the accused desired that consequence of his act or not.

There is no doubt that attempts are crimes of specific intent but what that means is difficult to say with any certainty in this instance. The opening words of the last quotation suggest that proof of direct intention of the *Steane* type (i.e., proof that that was what the accused deliberately aimed to achieve) alone will suffice. On the other hand the concluding words of that quotation suggest that proof of oblique intention (knowledge of the inevitablility or virtual certainty of the consequence) will suffice. The term 'specific intent' generally is used to encompass both direct and oblique intention but it is submitted that attempts are exceptional. Only proof of direct (*Steane*-type) intention (see para. 2.6), should satisfy the *mens rea* requirement for an attempt.

If you fling out your hand towards a priceless Ming vase with the intention of smashing it, but cannot quite reach, you can be said to have attempted to break that vase. Were you to know that if you stretched out your hand the inevitable consequence would be that the Ming vase would break, even though you do not want it to break, can you be said to have attempted to break that vase if apprehended in the process of stretching out an arm (possibly to revive the circulation or ward off cramp)? It is submitted that 'virtual certainty' is not, and should not be, sufficient to satisfy the *mens rea* of attempt and that that is the construction intended by the judges in *Mohan's* case.

There is an argument that what *Mohan's* case said is rendered immaterial anyway by the Criminal Attempts Act because s. 6(1) abolishes the offence of attempt at common law 'for all purposes'. If this applies to *Mohan's* case then the meaning of the word 'intent' in s. 1(1) of the Criminal Attempts Act 1981 may be interpreted afresh free of what was held in *Mohan's* case. Even if that is so and there is now a prospect of oblique (virtual-certainty) intent being included in the ambit of s. 1(1), there is no doubt that the word 'intent' precludes foresight of consequence as highly probable, probable or likely as well as being reckless as to consequences (see now *R v Pearman* [1985] RTR 39). The Court of Appeal stated there in relation to the specific intent offence of attempting to cause grievous bodily harm (see para. 7.3.3) that although foresight of the consequences of an act might be something from which a jury could infer the intent to cause those consequences, such foresight was not to be equated with intent to do the act. This view coincides precisely with that recently expressed by the House of Lords in relation to the meaning of intention for the purposes of the *mens rea* of murder (see *R v Moloney* [1985] 2 WLR 648 discussed in paras. 2.6.1, 2.6.2 and 7.6.2).

5.6.5 Reckless attempts

What of recklessness? Can the *mens rea* for attempt be satisfied by proof of recklessness? In relation to this question James LJ had this to say in *R v Mohan* [1976] QB 1:

> We do not find in the speeches of their lordships in *Hyam v DPP* [1975] AC 55 anything which binds us to hold that *mens rea* in the offence of attempt is proved by establishing beyond reasonable doubt that the accused knew or correctly foresaw that the consequences of his act unless interrupted would 'as a high degree of probability', or would be 'likely' to, be the commission of the complete offence. Nor do we find authority in that case for the proposition that a reckless state of mind is sufficient to constitute the *mens rea* in the offence of attempt. . . .
> In our judgment, evidence of knowledge of likely consequences, or from which knowledge of likely consequences can be inferred, is evidence by which intent may be established but it is not, in relation to the offence of attempt, to be equated with intent. If the jury find such knowledge established they may and, using common sense, they probably will find intent proved, but it is not the case that they must do so.

While that quotation from *Mohan* may be the law in so far as the *mens rea* of attempts is concerned it is an area of law which is not free of controversy. It can be argued, for instance, that there is no rational reason why, if a complete, substantive crime may be committed intentionally, recklessly or negligently, an attempt to commit such a crime should not be committed respectively with intent, recklessness or negligence as sufficient state of mind. An attempt, irrespective of the state of mind of the attempter is as dangerous to society and its right-thinking and right-acting members as the complete offence and therefore as deserving of a deterrent-inducing penalty as the complete offence.

Imagine the situation where in an international competition a rival pole-vaulter saws part way through the pole of the major contender for the title, or in the Winter Olympics if one competitor tampers with the binding mechanism that keeps the world champion's boots attached to his skis? In both instances if the pole snaps or the ski detaches and the champion is injured the person should be liable for *recklessly assaulting*, even though there was no intent to injure but merely to win. If the tampering is discovered before the pole is used or before the skier sets off down the precipitous slope why should the person who tampered with them escape liability for *attempt to assault* simply because he was reckless rather than intentional. When either state of mind will suffice for the full offence, why not for the attempt at that offence?

5.6.6 Negligent attempts

Likewise it can be argued, there is no good reason why a person should not be liable for a negligent attempt where negligence would suffice for the full offence. If a professional, skilled or trained person such as an anaesthetist could be liable for the manslaughter of a patient where his gross negligence during an operation resulted in the patient's death, then why should he escape liability for attempt if his gross negligence is ascertained first, prior to the operation which would have resulted in death but was then postponed?

Despite the cogency of such arguments the law on the issue of *mens rea* in attempts is as stated in *R* v *Mohan* [1976] QB 1 and it is submitted that the views expressed in that case are correct and apply today irrespective of s. 6 of the Criminal Attempts Act 1981 (see *R* v *Pearman* [1985] RTR 39). It should be remembered that generally in the case of attempts no harm or at least less harm is involved than in the case where the substantive crime is complete. Also the person convicted of attempt is to a larger degree than in substantive crimes being punished for his *mens rea* and therefore proof of only the best and highest form of *mens rea* (namely intention) should suffice. *Mohan's* case was correct in insisting that intention must be proved for an attempt. This view has been endorsed by Parliament in the statutory enactment that now governs the law of attempt because the Criminal Attempts Act 1981, s. 1(1), opens with the words: 'If, *with intent* to commit an offence', (with no mention of recklessness or negligence) and continues: 'to which this section applies, a person does an act which is more than merely preparatory to the commission of the offence, he is guilty of attempting to commit the offence'.

Clearly irrespective of the varying permissible states of mind that could be proved to obtain a conviction for the complete offence and even if the complete offence is one of strict liability, s. 1(1) requires proof of direct intention to commit the complete offence if a conviction for attempt is to be sustained.

5.6.7 Circumstances in relation to attempts

It must be remembered that the *actus reus* of a crime generally can be divided into acts, consequences and circumstances. So far in relation to the *mens rea* of attempt we have been concerned to show that the accused must intend to produce the prohibited consequences but in relation to relevant surrounding circumstances what *mens rea* is required to be proved? The Criminal Attempts Act 1981, s. 1(1), requires proof of intention to bring about the consequences together with proof of knowledge of the factual circumstance required by the definition of the substantive offence.

Section 1(3) provides for the situation in which the accused's state of mind would not amount to an intention to commit the full offence because of a lack of knowledge of necessary circumstances, e.g., if the accused intends to have sexual intercourse with a girl believing she is under age but without knowing that to be definitely the case. The attempt requires proof of intention to have intercourse with a girl under the legal age. He does not know her age and therefore would not have the necessary intention but for s. 1(3) which states:

In any case where:

(a) apart from this subsection a person's intention would not be regarded as having amounted to an intent to commit an offence; but
(b) if the facts of the case had been as he believed them to be, his intention would be so regarded,

then, for the purposes of subsection (1) (i.e. s. 1(1)), he shall be regarded as having had an intent to commit that offence'.

By that provision the person who believes, but who does not know for certain, is deemed to have the intention to commit the offence and therefore can be liable for attempting to commit that offence. That concession aside the section does not state that proof of any other state of mind in relation to circumstances, such as recklessness, will suffice unless acting on a belief can be said to be acting recklessly. But even if that argument could be sustained it would not include *Caldwell*-type recklessness (see para. 2.7.4) as to circumstances because that type of recklessness is so defined as to be incompatible with, and to preclude, the prospect of any thought or belief having been given to the relevant circumstances. Intention as to consequences plus knowledge or belief as to circumstances are the states of mind that must be proved. Proof of intention as to consequences and mere recklessness as to circumstances will not suffice. This would appear to be the current law despite Professor Glanville Williams's persuasive argument to the contrary in [1983] Crim L R 365. He maintains that recklessness as to a necessary circumstance is sufficient for an attempt or at least should be. In his view 'no case *decides* that intention requires knowledge of (as opposed to recklessness as to) circumstances in cases of attempt'. He argues that in *Gardner* v *Akeroyd* [1952] 2 QB 743 at p. 747 when Parker J said 'So far as an attempt is concerned, . . . knowledge and intent are clearly necessary' he was not expressly considering 'whether recklessness might not be an alternative to knowledge for an attempt; the point was not before the court'. Williams goes on to support his view by showing that in one pre Criminal Attempts Act case, *R* v *Pigg* [1982] 2 All ER 591 the Court of Appeal did hold that attempted rape could be committed by a person who was reckless as to the woman's consent (i.e., reckless as to a circumstance). But as has already been stated above, Parliament did not take the opportunity in enacting the Criminal Attempts Act to canonise clearly those views of the Court of Appeal and of Professor Williams as to the position then at common law. Therefore, as the law stands today proof of knowledge of circumstance should be necessary to convict for attempt where circumstances are a relevant part of the substantive offence in question.

5.6.8 Attempting the impossible

The historical changes in the law on this topic were outlined above (para. 5.6.3). At one time if the complete offence was impossible there was no liability for attempting it. Then the law changed so that a person in those circumstances could be liable for attempt and in 1975 in the leading modern case on the common law's attitude to attempting the impossible the House of Lords held in

Haughton v *Smith* [1975] AC 476 that no liability for attempt would arise if it was physically or legally impossible for the complete offence to be committed. That decision provoked such a reaction that Parliament passed the Criminal Attempts Act 1981 to abrogate it and make it clear that a person may be convicted for attempting the impossible. Whether it achieves that goal and extends liability to all forms of impossibility is discussed below.

In para. 5.6.1 the five reasons why a person may fail to complete the commission of an intended substantive offence were set out. Apart from the first (changing his mind or repentance) and the second (the intervention of a third party or prevention), there were *three* other possible reasons for failure to complete a substantive offence all of which involve degrees of aspects of impossibility.

Of these the third was that the accused failed because of his incompetence or because the implements used were inadequate. For example relying on an ordinary tin-opener to open a tungsten steel safe. In the scenario if Bruce was apprehended trying to lever open a window or door into Rex's house with a toothpick rather than a jemmy, that would be a combination of incompetence and inadequate implements. Such people are attempting the impossible in the sense that it is impossible to cut open the safe or break into Rex's house in the way that the accused was trying to achieve his aim. In *Haughton* v *Smith* their lordship's view was that this type of activity, even though it involved an aspect of impossibility, did constitute an attempt because the desired or intended end could have been achieved but for incompetence or ineffectiveness.

The fourth reason given for failing to complete the intended crime was labelled factual or physical impossibility. The classic example of this is being caught in the act of trying to steal from another's empty pocket. In *Haughton* v *Smith* the House of Lords maintained that there could be no conviction for attempted theft in such circumstances (strictly their lordships were concerned with an issue of legal impossibility and so their views on the law in relation to factual impossibility are *obiter dicta* but subsequent cases, e.g., *Partington* v *Williams* (1975) 62 Cr App R 220, accepted their lordship's views as *ratio decidendi*).

The fifth reason for failing to commit the complete offence was labelled legal impossibility. The classic example is of a person leaving a restaurant and taking an umbrella from the rack thinking it belongs to someone else, and if that belief was correct theft would have been committed, but the reality of the situation is that the umbrella belongs to the person who has taken it even though he does not know that at the time. This is a rare and strange situation because unlike the other four instances mentioned, in this case the person who intended to steal the umbrella has achieved his goal but since there is no complete offence with which he can be charged (because in reality he has stolen nothing), the question arises— should he be liable for attempting to steal?

The facts of *Haughton* v *Smith* were that the accused was charged with attempting to handle stolen goods (see para. 8.14 onwards) knowing or believing them to be stolen. However, before the accused had taken possession of the goods they had been seized by the police who, in order to catch the accused in the act, had had the goods driven to the place where they were to be received by him. But this ploy was a disaster because since the goods were in police custody they were no longer stolen for the purposes of a charge of handling. When the accused received the goods he was not handling *stolen* property and the House of Lords held that he could not be convicted of attempting to handle stolen goods even though he thought they were stolen because in reality they were no longer stolen—it was legally impossible for any complete offence to be committed.

To convict for attempt in this instance or in the instance involving the umbrella would be to convict simply for *mens rea*, for the evil, wicked thought, the mere intention to handle stolen goods or to steal someone else's umbrella. Remember also that in each of the other instances, had the accused not failed to achieve his intended aim he would have committed a substantive offence whereas in these latter situations involving legal impossibility the aim or goal actually is achieved but no substantive crime could ever be committed.

5.6.9 The position at common law

Haughton v *Smith* [1975] AC 476 determined that where the intended crime was impossible to complete because the accused used inadequate means he was guilty of an attempt. If the accused failed because of physical impossibility (e.g., the pocket was empty) or if it was legally impossible to commit the intended offence then there would be no liability for attempt.

Obviously, after *Haughton*, falling on the right side of the dividing line was crucial and yet in many situations the facts could fall into either category. In the scenario when Bruce uses a toothpick to try to lever open a locked door or window in Rex's house, is it impossible because of insufficiency of means or is it physically impossible for a toothpick ever to lever open a locked door or window?

Which side of the line the unfortunate accused ended up depended largely on the persuasiveness of his counsel and the mood of the judge. The courts, however, did not move significantly towards seeing all of these situations as involving insufficiency of means as illustrated by the other important case prior to the Criminal Attempts Act 1981.

In *DPP* v *Nock* [1978] AC 979 the accused tried to make or extract a controlled drug out of chemicals which could not produce that controlled drug. The House of Lords held it to be a case of physical impossibility rather than inadequacy of means and therefore there was no liability for attempting to produce the drug. Was it not equally open to the court to say this was a case of inadequacy of means (materials) and according to *Haughton* declare the accused guilty of attempt? Generally dissatisfaction with *Haughton* v *Smith* and its consequences led Parliament to enact the Criminal Attempts Act 1981. On the question of attempting the impossible it declares in s. 1(2):

> A person may be guilty of attempting to commit an offence to which this section applies even though the facts are such that the commission of the offence is impossible.

And in s. 1(3).

In any case where:

Inchoate Offences

(a) apart from this subsection a person's intention would not be regarded as having amounted to an intent to commit an offence; but

(b) .if the facts of the case had been as he believed them to be, his intention would be so regarded,

then, for the purposes of subsection (1) above, he shall be regarded as having had an intent to commit that offence.

Subsection (2) is clear, it purports to abolish the dicta in *Haughton* v *Smith* which stated that attempting the factually or legally impossible was not an offence.

Subsection (3) relates to those crimes which require proof of intention as to consequences together with knowledge (or belief, in those instances where knowledge is inappropriate, e.g., in relation to falsehood for purposes of deception) of circumstances. The aim of this subsection is to ensure that the accused cannot argue that he had no intention to commit the offence because he lacked knowledge of non-existent circumstances. Now an accused who has tried to achieve an object when necessary circumstances are absent can no longer claim only to have intended to achieve the innocent result which was possible.

Liability under s. 1(2) depends on the successful application of s. 1(3). The former provision declares a person may be liable for an attempt even where the facts are such that the commission of a substantive offence is impossible. Section 1(3) aims to attribute a fictional intention where his actual intention could not amount to an intent to commit an offence. So where supervening events occur making the commission of the complete offence impossible s. 1(3) provides that person with the *mens rea* for an offence under s. 1(1) provided he has done acts which are more than merely preparatory towards the commission of a substantive offence. This covers the 'empty pocket' situation and removes the physical or factual impossibility defence. But what of legal impossibility?

5.6.10 Legal impossibility today

It is suggested that nothing in s. 1 of the Criminal Attempts Act 1981 removes the defence of legal impossibility. Section 1(3) deals only with *mens rea* and not *actus reus* and that is significant because s. 1(1) requires that a person must intend and act toward the commission of an *'offence'*. It was and still is the case that the inchoate offences, attempt included, do not exist 'in the air'. They must be connected with and related to a specific substantive offence (see paras. 5.4 and 5.6.1). Therefore, if a person intends to carry out an act which even if completed would not amount to a criminal offence because no *actus reus* can be established, there must be no offence. It necessarily follows that that person is incapable of attempting because there is no substantive offence to attempt. In the case of legal impossibility (where you intend to take an umbrella believing it is someone else's and it is in fact your own) there is no *actus reus* and no amount of inferring of intention by way of s. 1(3) will create an *actus reus*.

With physical impossibility the notional removal or negation of the physical impediment will make the accused's act criminal because the way is clear for him notionally to complete his intended offence and therefore it is possible to consider him capable of attempt in those circumstances. In the case of legal impossibility the person may hope, think, desire or believe he is committing or attempting to commit an offence but in reality he is not doing so. To make him liable for attempt would be to convict him for his criminal thoughts, for *mens rea* alone, and that is not acceptable in any democratic society. If Parliament had intended to impose liability for criminal thoughts alone it should have stated clearly that such a radical innovation was being introduced or at least it should have defined the word 'offence' so that for the purposes of criminal attempts it would be clear that attempting to do what is legal can in some instances amount to the offence of attempt.

If this view of the law is correct (see Ryan and Scanlan, 'Attempted impossibility dead or alive?' (1983) 80 LS Gaz 1902 and see [1984] Crim LR 584 where the views expressed here and in the authors' article were canonised by Professor Hogan) it means that since the introduction of the Criminal Attempts Act 1981 the dividing line for purposes of liability for attempt is now drawn between physical impossibility (which no longer provides the accused with a defence) and legal impossibility (which does). Earlier (see para. 5.6.9) at the time when the dividing line was drawn between incompetent/ineffective impossibility and physical impossibility it was said that *Nock's* case (the attempt to make a prohibited drug from chemicals which could never produce it) could have fallen on either side of the line. If the accused was incompetent he was liable. If it was accepted as being physically impossible in reality to produce that drug from them, he was not liable at that time but would now be liable in light of s. 1(2) and (3) of the Criminal Attempts Act 1981. Might it not have been possible to argue that that case really concerned legal impossibility? If the accused produced a substance, a drug but not a controlled drug, then he had not committed a substantive offence and if he could not be liable for a full offence why should he be liable for attempt? If legal impossibility still is a defence then the dividing line is crucial and yet there are no guidelines or criteria to say on which side of the line a case must fall.

5.6.11 Summary of legal impossibility

Notwithstanding the above, two recent cases cast doubt upon the view that legal impossibility was still a defence. In *Anderton* v *Ryan* [1985] 2 WLR 23 and *R* v *Shivpuri* [1985] 2 WLR 29 it was held that a person was liable for attempt under the Criminal Attempts Act 1981 where, if the facts were as that person believed them to be, the full offence would have been committed by him but where, on the true facts, *the offence* which he set out to commit was in law impossible. However, the views expressed above in para. 5.6.10 relating to legal impossibility appear now to have been endorsed on appeal by the House of Lords in *Anderton* v *Ryan* [1985] 2 WLR 969. There the accused received a video recorder believing it to be stolen. She was charged with dishonestly attempting to handle a stolen video recorder contrary to s. 1(1) of the Criminal Attempts Act 1981 (see para. 8.14.1 onwards). On appeal the prosecution conceded that the recorder was not stolen. Quashing the conviction the House of Lords held by a majority that the Criminal Attempts Act was concerned with the issue of *mens rea* not *actus reus* but for a conviction for attempt both elements must be present. Since the recorder was not stolen,

Inchoate Offences

there was no *actus reus* and no crime had been committed despite the guilty state of the accused's mind. Whatever Parliament's intention may have been in passing the Criminal Attempts Act, the majority in the House of Lords seem to be of the opinion that in situations akin to the facts in *Anderton* v *Ryan* there can be no liability for attempt on the current wording of the statute. It may have been intended to catch those persons who dishonestly handled goods *mistakenly* believing that they were stolen goods but it is ambiguous as it stands and it does not clearly provide for that situation. The decision however has been severely criticised by Professor Glanville Williams in (1985) 135 NLJ 502, but despite what he thinks the law should be, the fact is that some judges and legal commentators consider the statute unclear. A better redrafting of s. 1 will be needed to achieve what may well have been intended. Furthermore, the majority in the House of Lords do not appear to have differentiated between legal and physical impossibility so that in future argument may arise as to whether or not both categories of impossibility will now provide a defence. It is hoped that their lordships will address their minds to this particular issue in *R* v *Shivpuri* which is currently on appeal.

5.6.12 Practical and procedural points

In relation to the scenario the police, having apprehended Donald, would weigh up the possible charges in light of the facts. If they chose to charge Donald with burglary contrary to s. 9 of the Theft Act 1968 then the possible outcomes of the trial are: (a) acquittal; (b) guilty of the substantive offence (burglary); (c) guilty of an attempt to commit burglary.

A verdict of guilty of attempt is always an alternative verdict to the charge of any substantive offence and generally the prosecution does not need to prosecute it on the indictment (see Criminal Law Act 1967, s. 6(3) and (4)). But this concession does not apply where an indictable matter is triable in the magistrates' court. There the prosecution must charge attempt. Magistrates are not able to convict for attempt if the completed offence is charged (see *Pender* v *Smith* [1959] 2 QB 84 at p. 89). The need specifically to charge attempt does not arise in relation to such indictable offences as burglary which are triable in the Crown Court but if the police consider that there is no chance to obtain a conviction for the completed offence they will simply charge the attempt to commit it. In such an instance there cannot be a conviction then for the completed offence but the Criminal Law Act 1967, s. 6(4), provides for the accused to be convicted of attempt even though at the trial he is conclusively proved guilty of the completed offence (see *Webley* v *Buxton* [1977] QB 481).

5.7 CONSPIRACY

5.7.1 The rationale of conspiracy

As with the law of attempts conspiracy was a common law offence but whereas attempts are now governed completely by the Criminal Attempts Act 1981 conspiracy is only partially governed by a statute, the Criminal Law Act 1977, and the rest remains at common law.

So far in this chapter we have shown that even if a person's intention to commit a crime can be proved that in itself is not a crime. Likewise at common law proof of the intention of two or more persons together was not an offence but if it could be shown that they had come to an agreement amongst themselves to engage in unlawful conduct that could amount to the offence of conspiracy to do what was agreed. In theory nothing more was needed although in reality the difficulty of proving the agreement necessitated proof of some further step or overt act to obtain a conviction.

In the scenario if Bruce purports to conspire with Donald to burgle Rex's house but in fact Bruce has no intention of going through with the plan there is no liability because for a conspiracy there must be a genuine agreement; a genuine meeting of minds, a compact. Telling another of one's plans and negotiating with another to participate also fall short of *an agreement* and are not conspiracy. Likewise if Bruce helped Donald, even though he knew of Donald's criminal purpose (e.g., by supplying Donald with housebreaking implements) this may make Bruce liable *as a party* to the burglary of Rex's house but Bruce could not be said to have agreed with Donald to burgle Rex's house simply because he supplied equipment for that purpose.

Where there are more than three parties, for example, if there was an agreement between Donald, Bruce, Edward and John to burgle Rex's house then they do not all have to agree at the same time and they do not have to have communicated with all the other parties. For each to know that they are joining a venture which involves others is sufficient provided there is a link between them.

As soon as the parties 'agree', there is a conspiracy if what they agree to do is forbidden by law. Likewise as soon as persons agree to join an enterprise forbidden by law which they know involves others, they become conspirators. Once the prohibited agreement is made the offence is complete, it does not matter what happens after that and it is immaterial if details are still to be settled or provisions made or conditions still to be met. It is irrelevant that a party does not intend to carry out all that he has agreed to execute by virtue of the conspiracy. An individual by entering into an irrevocable conspiracy commits an offence, even if he had intended only to execute part of what he had agreed, for it is certain the other parties may fully execute the agreement in any case (see *R* v *Anderson* [1984] Crim LR 550).

The reason why such agreements are declared to be inchoate offences probably lies in the fact that it is more likely that planned activities will be carried out. The resolve of the conspirators is strengthened by mutual support, pride and 'face-saving'. Furthermore the combining of skills and resources can bring more ambitious and more complex criminal activity within the sphere and reach of individuals who would not have bothered even attempting such activities on their own. If true, conspiracies can be seen to constitute a greater danger to society than the criminal aspirations of individuals. In modern complex societies organised crime is equally complex and pernicious; the offence of conspiracy can be used as a net to prevent the commission of substantive offences by numerous persons who are spread far apart and who are planning varying degrees of participation.

Like the accomplice and the inciter, the conspirator who organises the commission of crime is a menace to society, in fact often he is more of a danger

Inchoate Offences

than a principal offender because he may remain hidden and less exposed to detection. The perpetrators often are insignificant in comparison with the organisers who plan and give the instructions and orders. Conspiracy can be used to strike at the organisers.

Having said that, it should be noted that of all the offences conspiracy has a width and vagueness about it that permits it to be abused often at the expense of civil liberties. Picketers and demonstrators who would not be convicted of substantive offences (e.g., of affray) can all too easily be charged with conspiracy to cause an affray or some other serious offence, when a lesser charge would have been appropriate or even where no charge at all was warranted. (But see now *R* v *Bonsall* (1985) Crim LR 150).

5.7.2 Common law definition: actus reus

The classic definition as applied in cases like *Mulcahy* v *R* (1868) LR 3 HL 306 showed that a criminal conspiracy could arise (a) from an agreement to do an unlawful act or (b) from an agreement to do a lawful act by unlawful means. This two-limbed definition embraced agreements to commit serious crimes, summary offences, torts, frauds, acts tending to corrupt public morals and acts tending to outrage public decency. The very wide scope of the common law definition ultimately led to agitation for reform, particularly in light of the decision in *Kamara* v *DPP* [1974] AC 104. There the House of Lords held that an agreement to commit the tort of trespass to land, if accompanied by an intent to inflict more than merely nominal damage, was an indictable conspiracy. It was this notion that a person could be criminally liable if he agreed to commit a *civil wrong* that prompted the intervention of Parliament.

Initially it was proposed that in the new legislation only agreements to commit crimes would be indictable. But there was a stumbling-block to this sensible proposal. At common law it had been decided that there could be a conspiracy to defraud even though there was no agreement to commit a crime. This is best illustrated by *Scott* v *Metropolitan Police Commissioner* [1975] AC 819 where several individuals together made copies of films without the consent of the copyright holders intending to make a profit by showing the films for a fee but without paying the copyright holders anything. Because they did not steal anything from, or deceive, the copyright holders, the accused probably could not have been convicted under the Theft Act 1968 (see para. 8.1 onwards) but the court held that they had *conspired to defraud at common law*. In the recent case of *R* v *Lloyd and others* [1985] 3 WLR 30 the reasoning in *Scott* was applied though this case was not referred to. The facts of *Lloyd* were similar to those in *Scott's* case. The accused executed an agreement to borrow feature films owned by another, copy them, sell those copies and return the original films to the owners. The accused could not conspire to commit the offence of theft as there was no intention permanently to deprive the owners of their goods (i.e., the films), but merely to borrow them (see para. 8.10). However, there may have been a conspiracy to commit an offence under the Copyright Act 1956. It was accepted that the accused could have been charged with a conspiracy to commit an offence under this Act. However, for reasons noted below (see in particular *R* v *Ayres*) a conspiracy to defraud at common law could not in the circumstances lie.

Consequently when Parliament passed the Criminal Law Act 1977 creating as a statutory offence of conspiracy the agreement to commit criminal offences, it included a provision that agreements which amounted at common law to conspiracies to defraud should also be criminal conspiracies. Furthermore for reasons of political expediency the government of the day included two other categories of criminal conspiracy, namely, conspiracy to corrupt public morals and conspiracy to outrage public decency. Section 5(1) of the Act abolishes the offence of conspiracy at common law subject to the exceptions already mentioned and specifically retained in s. 5(2) (conspiracy to defraud) and in s. 5(3) (the conspiracies to corrupt public morals and outrage public decency). We find ourselves today in the position of having to contend both with statutory conspiracy and those three remaining common law conspiracies. However, it has recently been held that where the evidence supports a conspiracy which contemplated the commission of a substantive offence, the accused must be charged with having committed a statutory conspiracy (see later under s. 1(1) of the 1977 Act) and not one of the common law conspiracies, e.g., to defraud, preserved by s. 5(2) and (3) (see *R* v *Ayres* [1984] 1 All ER 619 and *R* v *Tonner and Evans* [1984] Crim LR 618).

5.7.3 Conspiracy to defraud

In *Scott* v *Metropolitan Police Commissioner* [1975] AC 819 Viscount Dilhorne defined this conspiracy as:

> an agreement by two or more by dishonesty to deprive a person of something which is his or to which he is or would be or might be entitled and an agreement by two or more by dishonesty to injure some proprietary right of his.

An indictment for conspiracy to defraud at common law must state the means by which the fraud is to be carried out (see *R* v *Hollinshead* [1985] 1 All ER 850). The Court of Appeal in this decision appeared to accept the proposition (in the absence of contrary authority or justification) that where two or more persons agree to carry out a course of conduct which would not in itself be unlawful, the fact that a stranger to the agreement may by his conduct execute that agreement in a fraudulent manner will not necessarily constitute that agreement a common law conspiracy to defraud. The court gave leave to appeal to the House of Lords on this point.

5.7.4 Conspiracies relating to public morals and decency

The leading cases are respectively *Shaw* v *DPP* [1962] AC 220 and *Knuller (Publishing, Printing & Promotions) Ltd* v *DPP* [1973] AC 435. In the former the accused was charged with conspiracy to corrupt public morals. He had published a magazine called the *Ladies' Directory* which contained the names, addresses, photographs and the propensities of prostitutes. He was convicted despite the fact that until then no such offence was generally known to exist. The House of Lords maintained that the courts have the power to preserve the moral welfare of the State, and that they are the guardians of the public's morals. In *Knuller's* case

Inchoate Offences

the accused was convicted of conspiracy to outrage public decency by the publication of advertisements relating to, and encouraging, certain homosexual practices. Here the House of Lords affirmed the decision in *Shaw's* case stating that such conspiracies can be committed even by encouraging conduct which although in itself is not illegal (e.g., prostitution or homosexual practices by adults in private with consent) might be likely to result in corruption of that kind. Lord Simon said:

> the words 'corrupting public morals' conduct which a jury might find to be destructive of the very fabric of society, and the term 'outraging public decency' goes considerably beyond offending the susceptibilities of, or even shocking, reasonable people.

Because of the wide criticism of *Shaw's* case, their lordships in *Knuller* concurred that while the earlier decision was correct, there was no general or residual power at common law for the courts to create any new offences of this type.

5.7.5 Mens rea of conspiracy

In *Churchill* v *Walton* [1967] 2 AC 224 the *mens rea* of conspiracy at common law was stated to be an intention to carry out the agreement and knowledge of those facts which make that agreement unlawful. The Criminal Law Act 1977, s. 1, is complex but in effect it reiterates the common law view, as expressed in *Churchill's* case, of the *mens rea* that is required for a conviction.

The section reads as follows:

> (1) Subject to the following provision of this Part of this Act, if a person agrees with any other person or persons that a course of conduct shall be pursued which, if the agreement is carried out in accordance with their intentions, either:
>
> (a) will necessarily amount to or involve the commission of any offence or offences by one or more of the parties to the agreement, or
> (b) would do so but for the existence of facts which render the commission of the offence or any of the offences impossible,
>
> he is guilty of conspiracy to commit the offence or offences in question.
>
> (2) Where liability for any offence may be incurred without knowledge on the part of the person committing of any particular fact or circumstance necessary for the commission of the offence, a person shall nevertheless not be guilty of conspiracy to commit that offence by virtue of subsection (1) above unless he and at least one other party to the agreement intend or know that that fact or circumstance shall or will exist at the time when the conduct constituting the offence is to take place.
>
> (3) Where in pursuance of any agreement the acts in question in relation to any offence are to be done in contemplation or furtherance of a trade dispute

(within the meaning of the Trade Union and Labour Relations Act 1974) that offence shall be disregarded for the purposes of subsection (1) above provided that it is a summary offence which is not punishable with imprisonment.

(4) In this Part of this Act 'offence' means an offence triable in England and Wales, except that it includes murder notwithstanding that the murder in question would not be so triable if committed in accordance with the intentions of the parties to the agreement.

The aim of s. 1(1) is to make it clear that the alleged conspirators must be proved to have agreed on a course of conduct which will undoubtedly result in the crime they conspired to commit if their agreement is carried out in accordance with their intentions. Conspiracy, like attempt, is an intentional crime—a specific intent offence. This requires proof of direct intention to perpetrate an agreed crime. What this means can be illustrated by reference to the scenario. If it could be proved that Donald, Bruce, Edward and John had agreed to rape Sarah they would be guilty of conspiracy to rape. If it could be proved that they had agreed to kill Sarah or Rex, they would be guilty of conspiracy to murder. If it could be proved that they agreed (for some reason) to break Sarah's arm (perhaps as revenge on, or a warning to, Rex) they have conspired to cause grievous bodily harm but what if the shock of having her arm broken is such that Sarah dies?

According to *R v Moloney* [1985] 2 WLR 648 (see para. 2.6.1) the four youths can be convicted of murder (proof of intent to cause grievous bodily harm or inferring such intent from the fact of foresight that it is highly probable now are sufficient to satisfy the *mens rea* of murder). If, for some reason (possibly evidential), the prosecution chose in this instance to charge the youths not with murder but with *conspiracy to murder* there could be *no* conviction because what Donald, Bruce, Edward and John have agreed to do *will not necessarily* result in Sarah's death. For a conspiracy charge to succeed in this instance an agreement specifically to kill Sarah would have to be proved, alternatively they should have been charged with conspiracy to cause grievous bodily harm or to assault.

Section 1(2) makes it clear that even if the complete substantive offence may be committed without knowledge of a 'particular circumstance' there can be no conviction for the inchoate offence of conspiracy unless that fact or circumstance is known to the persons charged with conspiring.

In the scenario assume that Sarah (Rex's daughter) is aged 15 and that Donald and the others do not intend to rape her but, believing her to be 17, they intend to induce her to go with them out of the possession and control of Rex and Marian—her parents. If Donald had taken Sarah away with him then according to *R v Prince* (1875) LR 2 CCR 154 (see para. 3.1) he would be liable for taking a girl under 16 out of the possession of her parents irrespective of his belief as to her age.

Had Donald been apprehended, having done an act that was more than merely preparatory towards taking Sarah away but not yet having completed the offence, the issue of attempt arises. Assume the *actus reus* is able to be proved, what of the *mens rea*? The law requires proof of intention (direct only) to achieve the consequence of taking her from her parents but in addition knowledge of the requisite circumstances that Sarah is under the prohibited age. Donald believes

Inchoate Offences

she is 17; she is only 15 in fact. Donald may have been reckless but he does not have 'knowledge' that she is under 16 and therefore should not be liable for attempt. Section 1(2) and (3) of the Criminal Attempts Act 1981 is irrelevant.

Where Donald has agreed with Bruce, Edward and John to take Sarah out of the custody of her parents and they all believe Sarah is over 16 none of them could be convicted of conspiracy to abduct her. Section 1(2) of the Criminal Law Act 1977 makes it certain there can be no conviction for conspiracy in these circumstances unless the relevant fact or circumstance (in this instance, her age) is known to the accused charged with conspiracy.

5.7.6 Further actus reus points

We have said that the *actus reus* of conspiracy is an agreement:

(a) to commit a crime;
(b) to defraud;
(c) to corrupt public morals;
(d) to outrage public decency.

The first is governed by the Criminal Law Act 1977 and the latter three by the common law and in each instance there must be an agreement between two or more persons. There are, however, certain specified individuals who do not qualify as another person for conspiracy purposes.

First the common law in *Mawji* v *R* [1957] AC 526 and the Criminal Law Act 1977 s. 2(2) state that one spouse cannot be convicted of conspiracy with the other spouse if they are the only parties to the agreement. This only applies where the parties are married at the time of the agreement. In the scenario Rex and Marian would not commit the crime of conspiracy in agreeing to murder Donald when they return home and find the chaos and him on the floor incapable through drink. If, however, Sarah also agreed that all three of them murder Donald then all of them (Rex, Marian and Sarah) are guilty of conspiracy.

Secondly, there can be no conspiracy according to s. 2(2) in the following circumstances:

(a) If the only other party is a person *under the age of criminal responsibility* (see para. 6.4.1) i.e., under 10 years, but a conspiracy can be formed with a child between the age of 10 and 14 years if that child can be shown to have a 'mischievous discretion' (see para. 6.4.2).

(b) If the only other party is a '*victim*' or an '*intended victim*' of the offence. For purposes of this provision a person is a victim if the complete offence in question is one which exists for the protection of that person. The same rule applies in the case of parties to offences (see *R* v *Tyrrell* [1894] 1 QB 710 and see para. 4.10).

Assume in the scenario that Donald (an adult) only agreed to burgle Rex's house with Bruce and Edward, both of whom were under 10 years of age. In that instance there would be no conspiracy (but see the discussion of innocent agents, para. 4.2). If all three of them agreed with John, aged 13, to steal from Rex's house then there may be a conspiracy between Donald and John provided John could be shown to know that what he had agreed to do was 'wrong'. If Donald and the three others are adults and they agreed not to rape Sarah (aged 15 years) but to take her away from Rex and Marian, they would have conspired at child-stealing contrary to s. 56 of the Offences against the Person Act 1861 which has now been repealed by s. 11 of the Child Abduction Act 1984 but preserved as an offence by virtue of s. 2 of that Act. But if only Donald had agreed with Sarah to take her away there would be no conspiracy to do so because Sarah is 'the victim' whom that statute is designed specifically to protect. Also even if Sarah aids, abets, counsels or procures Donald with full knowledge to take her away she would not be a party to the complete offence for which Donald would almost certainly be convicted irrespective of what he believed Sarah's age to be (see *R* v *Prince* (1875) LR 2 CCR 154 para. 3.1). If Donald had agreed with Marian (Sarah's mother) to take Sarah away it appears from the case of *R* v *Duguid* (1906) 21 Cox CC 200 that if Donald took Sarah he could be convicted of the full offence which is now contained in s. 2 of the Child Abduction Act 1984, but Marian could not (she is exempted being the mother) and short of that Donald could be convicted of conspiracy to commit that offence. Marian, though exempt from the full offence, can be convicted of conspiring to 'kidnap' her own child, see *R* v *B* [1984] Crim LR 352 (see also *R* v *Burns* (1984) 79 Cr App R 173). If it could be argued that Marian is 'the victim' that s. 56 of the 1861 Act aimed to protect, would she escape liability for conspiring because then she would have been exempted by s. 2(2) of the 1977 Act?

(c) If the only purported parties to the agreement are a registered company (see para. 4.15) and a sole director of that company. In *R* v *McDonnell* [1966] 1 QB 233 it was held that in this instance to say the company was a separate entity or a separate mind was unrealistic even though the company itself could have been convicted of the substantive offence if the director responsible had been acting as the mind of the company at the time of the offence and presumably there had been another director to conspire with. In such a case both the directors and the company could be convicted of conspiracy. A company *can* also be liable for conspiracy where it conspires with one of its own directors *and* someone else (e.g., another company through the doctrine of identification, see para. 4.15.3, or a director of another company or any individual who is capable of conspiracy), i.e., where it conspires with another company or with any other person other than one of its own directors.

(d) If the only other party to the purported agreement is someone who is mentally disordered (see para. 6.1). Section 1(1) of the Criminal Law Act 1977 requires an agreement and such a person may be incapable of forming the *mens rea* for the substantive offence, in which case there is no agreement within the section. If, however, the disordered person is able to form the *mens rea* the normal party should be liable for conspiracy because the agreement (which there is) will amount to the commission of an offence by *one* of the parties. For policy reasons the disordered person should not be liable.

Where there are but two accused, each charged with conspiring with the other, it does not necessarily follow that the acquittal of one *must* lead to the acquittal of the other. It is for the judge to determine on the evidence whether, as a matter of

Inchoate Offences

law, it is possible for one accused to be acquitted and the other convicted. This is justified where there is a marked or substantial difference between their cases and the evidence that is admissible against them (see *R* v *Roberts* (1984) 78 Cr App R 41). If, however, one in such cases is acquitted because he has not committed the substantive offence of conspiracy then the other must also be acquitted of conspiracy, by analogy with *R* v *McDonnell* for there is no one to conspire with.

5.7.7 Conspiracy to do the impossible

The Criminal Attempts Act 1981, s. 5(1), amended s. 1(1) of the Criminal Law Act 1977 so as to bring the law relating to conspiring to do the impossible into line with the law now governing attempts to do the impossible. So an agreement to pursue a course of conduct which, if carried out as intended, will necessarily amount to the commission of any offence by any one party or if it would do so but for the existence of facts which render the commission of the offence impossible, it shall amount nevertheless to a conspiracy to commit the offence in question. This amendment abolishes the decision in *DPP* v *Nock* [1978] AC 979 where the accused was held not liable for attempting and conspiring to produce a prohibited drug from chemicals which could never produce it. Now a person charged on these facts would be liable on both counts even though what he attempted or conspired to do was impossible (see para. 5.6.9).

5.8 INCITEMENT

5.8.1 Essence of incitement

A person will be liable for the inchoate offence of incitement if he endeavours to persuade or induce another to participate in a crime or to commit any act which, if committed by that person would amount to a criminal offence. While the incitement must be to the commission of a substantive offence yet it is irrelevant whether or not the incitement is successful in fact. So if, before meeting Bruce, Donald was in the crowded bar of a public house and he shouted out 'Rex's house is full of gold. Go and get it, lads!', Donald could have committed incitement whether or not any of the patrons who heard him, acted on the exhortation.

5.8.2 Actus reus of incitement

Proof is required that by word or deed the accused encouraged another to commit a crime. It does not matter whether the encouragement or exhortation is to one person, or to a group, or to the world at large. Of course, if anyone goes and commits the crime incited then the inciter can be charged not only for incitement but also as a secondary party (see paras. 4.3.2 and 4.3.3) to that completed, substantive offence. The principal must commit the offence or one similar to the one incited to affix the secondary party with criminal responsibility in such cases, see *R* v *Leahy* [1985] Crim LR 99.

5.8.3 Mens rea of incitement

It must be proved that the accused intended (directly) that as a result of his persuasion, encouragement or exhortation another person would commit an act or bring about a consequence that was criminal. As long as what he incited was a crime in fact, then irrespective of whether or not he knew it was a crime, he will be liable for incitement.

5.8.4 Inciting the impossible

Prior to the Criminal Attempts Act 1981 it was not an offence to attempt or conspire to commit an offence if it was physically or legally impossible to commit it (see paras. 5.6.9 and 5.7.7), but in so far as incitement was concerned the fact that the crime incited could not in the circumstances be committed was irrelevant and the accused could be liable: *R* v *McDonough* (1982) 47 Cr App R 37.

The Criminal Attempts Act 1981 and the Criminal Law Act 1977 (as amended by the 1981 Act) now declare that a person who attempts or conspires at the commission of an offence even if it is physically impossible (and arguably if it is legally impossible—see paras. 5.6.9 to 5.6.11 and 5.7.7) may be liable for attempt or conspiracy which brings the law in these areas into line with what it always was in relation to inciting the impossible.

The common law of incitement in relation to physically impossible offences is contained in two cases. In *R* v *McDonough* (1962) 47 Cr App R 37, the accused was convicted for inciting the handling of stolen lamb carcasses even though there were no stolen carcasses at that time. So even though it was physically impossible to handle the stolen goods he was held rightly convicted, whereas if he had conspired to handle them or attempted to handle them he would *not* have been liable according to *Haughton* v *Smith* [1975] AC 476 and *DPP* v *Nock* [1978] AC 979 (see paras. 5.6.9 and 5.7.7). Under the 1981 legislation (and its amendment to the 1977 Act), which brought all three inchoate offences into line on this aspect of the law, he would have been liable today whichever the charge—incitement, conspiracy or attempt. That unity, however, has been upset by a recent case dealing specifically with inciting the physically impossible.

In *R* v *Fitzmaurice* [1983] 1 All ER 189 the facts were complex but in essence there were two separate conspiracies. Those in the first conspiracy planned to 'set up' the dupes in the second conspiracy in that having (through the accused) induced the second group to embark on a crime, those involved in the first group would report the dupes' intended crime to the police and claim whatever reward money was available for so doing. The accused's role was to procure the men who would conspire to carry out the suggested but, unbeknown to them and the accused, bogus robbery of a woman. Supposedly that woman would be carrying money from a business to a bank. The dupes thought they were to rob this woman but what they did not know was that a security van would arrive at that bank at that time. It was planned that the dupes would be caught by the police, who had been 'tipped off', in circumstances which would make it appear that they were about to rob the security van. The dupes were charged with conspiracy and the accused with incitement 'to rob a woman' but while the intention was to rob a particular woman, in fact no such woman existed. Because the facts

Inchoate Offences

occurred in 1980 the pre-1981 law applied and consequently those charged with conspiracy were not guilty but the accused who incited was held guilty.

To uphold this conviction the Court of Appeal stated that the decision in *McDonough* was correct but the judges went on to say that it did not mean that in every instance, if the crime incited cannot be committed in the circumstances, that that fact is irrelevant. In the court's view *McDonough's* case was correctly decided on the facts but only because while there were no stolen carcasses at that time, it was not impossible that some time in the future the stolen lamb carcasses would be available. The effect of this would seem to be that if it was absolutely, physically impossible for any such goods ever to be available, then there could be no conviction, at common law, for incitement. Despite that, the court upheld Fitzmaurice's conviction and yet what the accused had incited was a 'mere charade', something that was impossible—the robbery of money from a woman who would not appear on that day. The Court of Appeal, however, felt that 'By no stretch of the imagination was that an impossible offence to carry out and, ... therefore, ... [he] was rightly convicted'. But what Fitzmaurice incited was the robbery of a specific woman, a recognised identifiable woman and no other, and she could not be robbed in the way incited because she was a sham with no possibility of being present at the time of the incited wages snatch. The accused therefore was being convicted for the possibility that that woman might be robbed at some other time and place. That was not what the accused incited.

It seems to follow from the judgment that if it was absolutely impossible for any woman ever to be in that place then, in that very limited situation, the defence of physical impossibility would be available to the inciter. If that is to be the law then that case dissects physical impossibility in a way that is not available for attempts or conspiracies. In those instances, the only defence now is to argue that what was involved was legally impossible. In the case of incitement, however, it is submitted that not only will there be a defence if the thing incited is legally impossible (i.e., no offence), but also if it is absolutely, physically impossible as opposed to being simply impossible at the time of the incitement.

5.9 INCHOATE INCHOATE OFFENCES

At common law an attempt to incite was recognised as an offence, see *R v Banks* (1873) 12 Cox CC 393, and given that incitement is an indictable offence this is still the law. Section 1(4) of the Criminal Attempts Act 1981 states that the law of attempt applies to *any* offence which, if it were completed, could be triable in England as an *indictable* offence. Although certain offences are exempt, incitement is not one of them. Therefore it is an offence to *attempt to incite* the commission of a crime.

It is not possible *to attempt an attempt*—acts of that type would be 'merely preparatory' in terms of s. 1(1) of the Criminal Attempts Act 1981.

Section 1(4) of that Act makes it clear that now a person cannot be held liable for *attempting to conspire*.

At common law, according to *R v Cromack* (1978) Crim LR 217, there is an offence of *inciting another to incite*, and also an offence of *inciting another to attempt* the commission of a substantive offence. Despite the various statutory intrusions and the law of attempt and conspiracy this aspect of the law of incitement seems to remain unchanged.

Section 5(7) of the Criminal Law Act 1977 states that it is *no* longer an offence to *incite either a statutory or a common law conspiracy*.

In our law there are some statutes which create separate, special offences of incitement. Apart from the fact that generally such offences (e.g., s. 54 of the Criminal Law Act 1977 which makes it an offence for a man to incite to have sexual intercourse with him a girl under 16 whom he knows to be his granddaughter, daughter or sister) have a special penalty attached to them, the other significant feature of such offences is that they are substantive offences. Therefore, despite anything said to the contrary above, such offences can be incited, conspired at or attempted.

5.10 INCHOATE OFFENCES AND PARTICIPATION

Section 1(4) of the Criminal Attempts Act 1981 makes it clear that now a person cannot be held liable for attempting to aid, abet, counsel, procure or suborn the commission of an offence or to attempt offences under s. 4(1) or 5(1) of the Criminal Law Act 1967 (i.e., assisting offenders and accepting consideration for not disclosing information about an arrestable offence respectively). If, however, aiding or abetting etc. is the principle offence as in s. 2(1) of the Sexual Offences Act 1961 then an attempt to aid or abet etc. is a possible offence because then the accused is attempting an offence and not simply attempting to aid an offence.

5.11 PENALTY FOR INCHOATE OFFENCES

If the prosecution successfully obtains a conviction for any of the inchoate offences then the penalty is at the discretion of the court but must not exceed that which the court could impose for the completed substantive offence, according to the Powers of Criminal Courts Act 1973, s. 18(2), Criminal Law Act 1977, s. 3, and Criminal Attempts Act 1981, s. 4. Sometimes a statute may impose a maximum penalty for an attempt which differs from the maximum imposable for the complete offence. For example, in the case of rape the Criminal Law Act 1977 imposes a maximum of seven years for attempted rape whereas rape itself can be punished by up to life imprisonment.

6

Defences

This chapter will consider the existence of various defences which are available to an accused charged with a criminal offence. They may be subsumed under the following general classifications:

(a) Defences relating to the incapacity of an accused to formulate any mental element including the *mens rea* of an offence.
(b) Defences based upon the fact that the accused, though he has brought about the external elements of an offence with the prescribed *mens rea* has certain beliefs as to the existence of facts which constitute his conduct lawful.
(c) Mistaken belief by the accused in the existence of certain facts so that the accused lacks the mental element in an offence.
(d) Defences with no underlying unifying factor, other than that of the elusive principle of public policy. The law accepts these defences in the public interest.

6.1 INSANITY, INSANE AUTOMATISM

6.1.1 Introduction

An individual may suffer from such a defect of his reason that the law does not hold him responsible for his actions. A special example is the defence of insanity. The outlines of this defence were first laid down in *M'Naghten's case* 10 Cl & F 200. This was an advice sought by the House of Lords from the judges following the acquittal of M'Naghten of the murder of Sir Robert Peel's private secretary following the finding that he was insane. The case determines that it is a defence to any criminal charge for an accused to establish:

(a) that he was suffering from a disease of the mind and as a consequence of this,
(b) he was labouring under a defect of reason, and as a consequence of this,
(c) he did not appreciate the nature or quality of his actions *or* if he did appreciate the nature or quality of his actions he did not know that his conduct was wrong.

The judges also determined that if an accused through a defect of reason arising from a disease of the mind suffers from an insane delusion, his criminal liability should be assessed on the basis that the facts as he believes them to be are true. For example, if an accused through an insane delusion had believed another was about to attack and kill him, then the killing of that other should be regarded as a possible act of self-defence (see para. 6.6.1). If, however, the insane delusion resulted in an accused believing another was stealing his wallet, then even if those facts were deemed to be true, the killing of the imagined thief would not be excused (unless the accused did not appreciate his conduct was wrong, see later) since the law does not recognise such conduct as being justified.

Consideration must now be given to the various elements which must be established before the defence of insanity can be raised.

6.1.2 Disease of the mind

The leading authority upon the meaning of this term is *R* v *Sullivan* [1984] AC 156. The House of Lords endorsing the nature of the defence of insanity proposed in *M'Naghten's case* determined that 'mind' within 'disease of the mind' was to be understood in its ordinary sense, of the mental faculties of reason, memory and understanding. A disease of the mind was any condition which impaired those faculties so severely as to produce a defect in reason (see below). Only then could an individual claim the defence of insanity. It did not matter whether the cause of this impairment was organic, e.g., epilepsy or arteriosclerosis, see *R* v *Kemp* [1957] 1 QB 399, or functional, e.g., a mental illness such as paranoia, or a psychosis. Neither did it matter whether this impairment was permanent or transient and intermittent, provided that the impairment subsisted at the time of the commission of the offence. It is also irrelevant whether the impairment is curable or incurable (see *R* v *Kemp*). This latter point emphasises that the defence of insanity which is now governed by legislation (see later) is concerned with ensuring that individuals who suffer from such a condition are subject to control and confinement by society. The public must be protected from individuals who are subject to such recurrent states of mind under which they may undertake dangerous antisocial activities.

The principal characteristic of a disease of the mind within the defence of insanity is that its cause lies internally within the physiology or psychology of the individual concerned and is not brought about by external sources, e.g., drugs, concussion, etc. When an individual becomes the victim of an autonomic state brought about by external factors he may claim an altogether different defence from insanity (see *R* v *Bailey* [1983] 2 All ER 503 and later).

Defect of reason The disease of the mind must produce a defect of reason in an accused. This is more than a temporary bout of forgetfulness or absent-mindedness, see *R* v *Clarke* [1972] 1 All ER 219. An individual must be incapable of exercising any semblance of normal reasoning power. In such instances the individual is incapable of accepting legal responsibility for his conduct because either:

(a) he cannot appreciate the nature or quality of his act, or

(b) though he may appreciate the nature or quality of his act he did not know his conduct was wrong.

Defences

The nature and quality of an act refers to its physical nature, see *R v Codere* (1916) 12 Cr App R 21.

Examples include:

(a) An individual acting as an automaton, i.e., without conscious appreciation of his conduct.

(b) An individual incapable of realising the consequences of his actions, e.g., strangling a small child without realising it will cause his or her death and seeking only to impose parental punishment.

(c) An individual may not know the nature or quality of his act because he is unable to appreciate the circumstances in which his conduct takes place. A rather prosaic example would be the case of an individual who fired his shotgun at what he believed, because of a defect of reason, to be a scarecrow but was in fact his next-door neighbour.

If an individual who was suffering from a defect of reason was unable to appreciate some aspect of the consequences of his conduct or the circumstances in which his conduct took place which did not relate to the nature or quality of his actions, the defence of insanity would be unavailable to him. Thus if an individual (because of a defect of reason) killed a woman thinking his victim to be his wife whom he wrongly believed to be an adulteress, these delusions would not relate to the nature and quality of his act; he would be aware he was killing a human being, the fact of adultery even if true would not justify his conduct.

Even where an individual is aware of the nature or quality of his act he may not, because of a defect of reason, be aware that his conduct is wrong. In such circumstances an accused may be able to claim the defence of insanity. In the case of *R v Windle* [1952] 2 QB 826 the Court of Criminal Appeal considered what this requirement meant within the terms of the M'Naghten rules. It was argued that if a person, because of a defect of reason, believed that what he was doing was beneficial or kind, or praiseworthy and therefore morally justified, his conduct should be excused, as it could not be said to be wrong within the provisions of the M'Naghten rules. This would still be so even if he was aware that his actions were contrary to the law. This was rejected by the court. 'Wrong' within the M'Naghten rules meant simply contrary to the law. Thus if an accused was aware that his conduct breached the criminal law, he could not claim the defence of insanity, notwithstanding his deluded moral beliefs. Though *R v Windle* has been subject to frequent criticism it undoubtedly represents the law upon this point.

The narrowness of the concept of defect of reason in the M'Naghten rules fails to take into account the greater understanding of the human mind which has been brought about through recent discoveries in psychology and psychiatry. It fails to take into account the fact that an individual may appreciate the nature or quality of his conduct and know that he is in breach of the law and yet find that he is unable to prevent himself from acting as he did, see *R v Kopsch* (1925) 19 Cr App R 50. Such an 'irresistible impulse' may well constitute an 'impairment of mental responsibility' within the defence of diminished responsibility, however (see chapter 7).

6.1.3 Evidence and procedural matters

The M'Naghten rules determine that a man is presumed sane unless the contrary is proved. Insanity is one of the few defences that an accused must establish (see *Woolmington* v *DPP* [1935] AC 462). He must prove on a balance of probabilities that he is insane (see Murphy, *A Practical Approach to Evidence*)—only then does the prosecution have to negate the defence, though they must prove the contrary on the basis of the normal standard of proof borne by the prosecution; by establishing the accused's sanity beyond reasonable doubt (see Murphy).

Where an accused raises the issue of his mental capacity, it does not matter that he has not pleaded the defence of insanity expressly. If the evidence adduced by an accused amounts in effect to a plea of insanity he bears the burden of establishing it, and where the evidence is insufficient the judge must as a matter of law (see Murphy) withdraw the issue of the accused's possible insanity from the jury. Where such evidence is sufficient to constitute the accused's insanity a fit and proper issue for a jury to consider, the judge as a matter of law must leave that issue to the jury. He must direct that the plea of insanity has been raised, and further direct the jury as to the burden of proof borne by the accused, and the constituents of the defence, see *Bratty* v *Attorney-General for Northern Ireland* [1963] AC 386. In exceptional cases the judge on his own volition may raise the issue of the accused's insanity (see *R* v *Dickie* [1984] 1 WLR 1031).

6.1.4 The verdict of insanity

At common law a verdict of insanity was an acquittal. By statutory intervention in the 19th century the verdict of a jury in cases of insanity was to be 'guilty but insane'. The verdict still amounted to an acquittal since it was not an unambiguous verdict of guilty, see Trial of Lunatics Act 1883. Even before the passing of the aforementioned Act all individuals found insane were liable to be detained. By s. 1 of the Criminal Procedure (Insanity) Act 1964, the verdict of a jury is now the more logical 'not guilty by reason of insanity'. Nevertheless by virtue of s. 5 of the 1964 Act an individual found insane is still to be ordered to be detained in a hospital by the Home Secretary until he is satisfied that this is no longer necessary for the protection of the public.

The grave consequences for an individual following a verdict of 'not guilty by reason of insanity' would be even harder to bear for an accused if he could establish other defences which would justify an acquittal. Accordingly by s. 12 of the Criminal Appeal Act 1968 (see originally s. 2 of the 1964 Act) an accused has a right of appeal upon certain grounds from such a verdict. This does not mean that in such cases an accused must go free, for the finding of insanity still stands.

The grave dangers to society of individuals who are insane is such that the law permits the prosecution to adduce evidence of an accused's insanity with all its attendant consequences though the prosecution in essence seeks an acquittal through the verdict of 'not guilty by reason of insanity'. There are two situations where this course of action is permitted.

(a) *By statute.* By s. 6 of the 1964 Act where an accused charged with murder has raised the defence of diminished responsibility (see chapter 7) the

Defences 163

prosecution may seek to prove the accused's insanity beyond reasonable doubt.

(b) *By common law*. Where an accused has raised the issue of his mental capacity, e.g., by claiming that he was a non-insane automaton (see later) the prosecution may try and establish the accused's insanity. It would appear that the prosecution (in accordance with the general rule as to the burden of proof which it bears in criminal cases) must establish the accused's insanity beyond reasonable doubt. Though there is a dictum suggesting that in such a circumstance the burden of proof borne by the prosecution is but on a balance of probabilities (see *Bratty* v *Attorney-General for Northern Ireland* [1963] AC 386 per Lord Denning).

Insanity pre-trial An individual in custody pending trial may be found to be suffering from mental illness or severe mental impairment. If this opinion is founded on the reports of two medical practitioners the Home Secretary may order the individual concerned to be detained in a hospital without trial if it is expedient to do so and is in the public interest see Mental Health Act 1983, ss. 47, 48 and 51, and Criminal Procedure (Insanity) Act 1964, s. 4.

Where an accused on arraignment is found unfit to plead, such that he is unable *inter alia* to understand the nature of the charge against him or to conduct his defence he may be committed to hospital without being tried. The issue of fitness to plead on arraignment may be raised by an accused, the prosecution or judge, if the issue is in doubt it must be tried by a specially empanelled jury (see Criminal Procedure (Insanity) Act 1964, s. 4).

Where an accused is suffering from hysterical amnesia such that he cannot recall his actions or events at the time of the commission of the offence, but his mental state is otherwise normal he is regarded as being fit to plead on arraignment see *R* v *Podola* [1960] 1 QB 325.

Though by s. 4 the issue of whether an accused is fit to plead should be determined as soon as it arises, the trial judge has a discretion to delay consideration of this issue at any time up to the opening of the case for the defence (see Murphy, *A Practical Approach to Evidence*). This should provide an accused with the opportunity to test the sufficiency of the prosecution case and to be acquitted if it is lacking, and preserves his right to raise any specific defences that may be applicable to his case. It is irrelevant that even if acquitted because of the operation of s. 4 he would nevertheless be detained in a hospital because of his mental state, see *R* v *Burles* [1970] 2 QB 191. The discretion to postpone consideration of the issue of fitness to plead should not be exercised where it is obvious that the prosecution case is overwhelming and the accused would surely be convicted. In such a case it may be expedient to consider immediately the issue of the accused's fitness to plead.

6.1.5 Insanity: Summary

Insanity, though a defence available in respect of any charge, is infrequently encountered today. Because of the severe consequences for an accused following a verdict of 'not guilty by reason of insanity', the defence was in practice restricted to cases of murder (where the penalty was death). Since the abolition of the death penalty and the availability of the defence of diminished responsibility (see chapter 7) to an accused charged with murder the defence of insanity is of no practical importance.

6.2 NON-INSANE AUTOMATISM AND INVOLUNTARY CONDUCT

6.2.1 Involuntary conduct

It is a defence for an accused to establish that though he has been the principal protagonist in the *actus reus* of an offence, he has been an involuntary agent in its commission (see chapter 1). In *Hill* v *Baxter* [1958] 1 QB 277 it was accepted as an example of involuntary conduct that a man could not be convicted of any offence, which involved driving a vehicle, where while he was in the driving seat, he had been attacked by a swarm of bees. In such a case the swarm of insects produced an involuntary reflexive response, and it was this involuntary action that was responsible for driving the motor vehicle. The driver's conduct would also have been involuntary if his car had been propelled forward, though stationary and lawfully parked, by another vehicle crashing into its rear.

6.2.2 Non-insane automatism

An individual's conduct may also be involuntary because he is an automaton, i.e., not conscious of the circumstances surrounding him nor of the consequences of his conduct. This has exactly the same meaning as being an automaton within the rules relating to insanity (see above). Thus an individual conscious of his actions but unable to exercise control over his behaviour, because of an irresistible impulse (see *Bratty* v *Attorney-General for Northern Ireland* [1963] AC 386) or unable to exercise moral restraint, or where his mind was not working effectively (see *R* v *Isitt* [1978] Crim LR 159) is not an automaton. In *R* v *Sullivan* [1984] AC 156 it was determined that the difference between automatism produced by insanity (sometimes called insane automatism) and non-insane automatism lay in their causes. Whereas insane automatism has an 'internal' cause produced by organic or functional factors in the human body or mind (see above) non-insane automatism occurs, according to Lord Diplock (at p. 172) when:

> temporary impairment [of the mental faculties] *(not being self-induced by consuming drink or drugs)* [see later] results from some external physical factor such as a blow on the head causing concussion or the administration of an anaesthetic for therapeutic purposes. [Emphasis added.]

(See also *R* v *Quick and Paddison* [1973] 3 All ER 347.) Examples of such external factors which produce a temporary mental impairment apart from those noted above are sleepwalking and hypnosis, or in the case of a diabetic, the taking of too much insulin by injection or failure to take any or sufficient food following such an injection, see *R* v *Bailey* [1983] 2 All ER 503.

If this defence is established an accused must be acquitted, there is no question of his being detained either in a hospital or institution; like all general defences and in contrast to insanity an accused bears only an evidential burden in

Defences

establishing it (see Murphy, *A Practical Approach to Evidence*). Thus once an accused has raised the issue of non-insane automatism and has adduced sufficient evidence for it to be left to the jury (see *Moses v Winder* [1980] Crim LR 232) it becomes a matter of fact for them to determine whether it has been established. The prosecution can only negate the defence by evidence which satisfies the tribunal of fact beyond reasonable doubt that an accused was not an involuntary agent through non-insane automatism.

Where the accused raises the issue of non-insane automatism, but the prosecution adduce evidence of his insanity, or the judge is satisfied that the accused has in essence done so (see para. 6.1.3), he must direct the jury on the basis that the defence of insanity has been raised see *R v Kemp* [1957] 1 QB 399 and *Bratty v Attorney-General for Northern Ireland*.

Non-insane automatism is not available as a defence to an accused where he has intentionally or recklessly (or in some instances negligently) brought about his autonomic state. However, even a self-induced autonomic state may provide a defence in certain circumstances to an accused, and consideration must now be given to this and related issues.

6.3 ALCOHOL AND DRUGS

6.3.1 Self-induced automatism and voluntary intoxication

An individual may voluntarily enter an autonomic state either:

(a) by knowingly or recklessly (see later) taking alcohol or drugs (see *R v Lipman* [1970] 1 QB 152) or, in cases of medically prescribed drugs, by knowingly or recklessly taking the medication in excess of the dosage advised, or

(b) in the case of a diabetic by knowingly or recklessly taking too much insulin or omitting to counteract its effects by an adequate intake of food (see *R v Bailey* [1983] 2 All ER 503).

An individual may, however, after taking drugs or alcohol merely deprive himself of the ability to perceive fully the circumstances in which his actions took place or to foresee the consequences of his conduct (sometimes called voluntary intoxication). In such cases he may lack *mens rea* with regard to the *actus reus* of an offence though he is not an automaton. Though both states of mind considered above are radically different (see para. 1.2) they do share one common element: they may, even where self-induced, provide a defence to a criminal charge. To this extent they are to be regarded as identical.

6.3.2 Crimes where self-induced automatism or voluntary intoxication is not a defence: Crimes of negligence

In *Moses v Winder* [1980] Crim LR 232 the accused was charged with driving without due care and attention contrary to s. 3 of the Road Traffic Act 1972 (a crime which in essence amounts to negligent driving). He was a diabetic and put forward a defence of automatism. It was held that since the accused had not taken all the precautions he ought to have taken to deal with the threat of diabetic coma, i.e., he had taken only palliatives and then proceeded to drive his car, he was rightly convicted. The case was decided in part upon public policy, that individuals should not be allowed to endanger life or limb by claiming a defence of automatism in such situations. However, it would seem that the most pertinent justification for the decision is that the accused drove without due care and attention, i.e., negligently, not because of the dangerous way in which he drove, but because he drove the vehicle without taking the precautions to combat diabetic coma which were necessary to ensure he drove with due care and attention. This was the negligent element necessary to constitute the offence.

It is the voluntary deprivation of the ability to control one's future conduct through the intentional or reckless taking of alcohol or drugs which is itself negligent. An offence which is satisfied by negligence is then completed by the commission of the *actus reus* by an accused, even in cases where at the relevant time he is an automaton. By analogy this principle is also applicable to crimes which may be committed recklessly, i.e., offences of basic intent (see chapter 2). It would also appear to be no defence for a person to be voluntarily intoxicated or a self-induced automaton where the offence is one of strict liability (see *R* v *Young* [1984] 1 WLR 654 and para. 3.5).

6.3.3 Offences of basic intent

In *DPP* v *Majewski* [1977] AC 443 the accused had voluntarily taken a considerable quantity of drink and drugs. He then committed various offences comprising assaults upon police officers and members of the public (see chapter 7). He had no subsequent recollection of the incidents, nor at the time was he aware of his actions. He was convicted at first instance, but appealed on the ground that because of his condition at the time of the commission of the offences he was incapable of forming the intent necessary to constitute his conduct criminal (i.e. that he lacked *mens rea*). It was determined by the House of Lords that unless the offence was one which required proof of a specific or ulterior intent (see later), it could not be a defence to a criminal charge that as a result of voluntarily intoxication an accused carried out an offence which he did not intend to bring about. This means that where an offence is one of basic intent (see above), i.e., it can be committed recklessly, then irrespective of whether an individual as a result of voluntary intoxication or self-induced automatism is incapable of carrying out the *actus reus* of the offence intentionally or even consciously, he will nevertheless be guilty of the offence. Since the case of *R* v *Bailey* [1983] 2 All ER 503 this principle is applicable to cases of diabetics who through their intentional or reckless actions and/or omissions have induced themselves into a state of automatism (i.e. a diabetic coma).

It has been argued that to convict individuals of serious offences when they are in a state of self-induced automatism where they are not conscious of their actions or voluntarily intoxicated and incapable of forming the *mens rea* of a crime is to convert such offences to ones of strict liability or to contradict fundamental principles of criminal law. It is suggested that both viewpoints are misguided not only in principle but are contrary to the authority of *DPP* v *Majewski*. In the words of Lord Elwyn-Jones LC (at pp. 474–5):

If a man of his own volition takes a substance which causes him to cast off the restraints of reason and conscience, no wrong is done to him by holding him answerable criminally for any injury he may do while in that condition. His course of conduct in reducing himself by drugs and drink to that condition in my view supplies the evidence of *mens rea*, of guilty mind certainly sufficient for crimes of basic intent.

This is because in the words of Stroud quoted by Lord Edmund-Davies (at p. 496):

The true explanation is, that drunkenness is not incompatible with *mens rea* . . . because mere recklessness is sufficient to satisfy the definition of *mens rea*, and drunkenness is itself an act of recklessness.

The law therefore establishes a conclusive presumption against the admission of proof of voluntary intoxication for the purposes of disproving *mens rea* in crimes of basic intent or in admitting the defence of automatism where this state is self-induced. Where this presumption applies it does not make either 'drunkenness' or automatism a crime (though either state may have been voluntarily entered into) but the drunkenness or automatism once voluntarily entered into, constitutes an integral part of the offence as forming, together with the other unlawful conduct charged against the defendant, a complex act of criminal recklessness.

It was argued before the House of Lords in *DPP* v *Majewski* that by virtue of s. 8 of the Criminal Justice Act 1967 (see chapter 2) an accused had a right to have the issue of his intoxication or automatism considered in determining whether he had the necessary *mens rea* with regard to an offence, even a crime of basic intent. This was irrespective of whether such states were self-induced or not. On this basis, it was argued, the substantive rule of law discussed above was abrogated or qualified by that section. This was based on the premise that the section provides that a jury or court should make reference to all the evidence in drawing any inference as to an accused's intention or foresight, i.e., his *mens rea* as regards offences even of basic intent. This it was suggested is inconsistent with determining that an act of self-induced automatism or voluntary intoxication is to be regarded as a reckless act, for it should by virtue of s. 8 of the 1967 Act be possible for the tribunal of fact to conclude in such cases that an accused lacked any intention or foresight with regard to the *actus reus* of an offence, and should therefore be acquitted. This argument as to the effect of s. 8 was rejected by the House of Lords. In their lordships' opinion the purpose and effect of s. 8 was merely to alter the law of evidence. The section determines *how* a tribunal of fact may infer an accused's mental state, including whether he was reckless in a given instance by reference to all the evidence. It cannot affect the substantive law, however, which determines *when* recklessness is an element in an offence, or *what* may constitute recklessness in a given offence.

The fact that the House of Lords in *DPP* v *Majewski* determined that self-induced automatism or voluntary intoxication was not a defence to an offence of basic intent is to a large extent a policy decision which has been clothed by their lordships in the language of recklessness. It is instructive to note the opinion expressed by Lord Simon of Glaisdale that to permit a defence for an accused in such cases would leave the victim 'legally unprotected from unprovoked violence' (at p. 476). However, the clearest expression as to the policy basis of the decision in *DPP* v *Majewski* is to be found in the speech of Lawton LJ in the Court of Appeal (at p. 447) who, considering the frequency with which an accused may raise the issue of his self-induced mental state as a defence, was of the view that:

> The facts are commonplace—indeed so commonplace that their very nature reveals how serious from a social and public standpoint the consequences would be if men could behave as the [accused] did and then claim that they were not guilty of any offence.

6.3.4 Self-induced automatism and voluntary intoxication in statutory offences

In *R* v *Woods* (1982) 74 Cr App R 312 the Court of Appeal considered s. 1(2) of the Sexual Offences (Amendment) Act 1976 which applies to the crime of rape (a basic intent offence). This subsection provides that in determining the issue of an accused's *mens rea* as to his victim's consent to sexual intercourse the jury should in conjunction with all 'relevant matters' have regard to the presence or absence of reasonable grounds in assessing that state of mind.

The court determined that the accused's voluntary intoxication or self-induced automatism could not be taken into account under the head of 'relevant matters' in assessing an accused's beliefs as to the issue of consent since the fact of voluntary intoxication (or self-induced automatism) was not a legally 'relevant matter', thus endorsing *DPP* v *Majewski* [1977] AC 443.

Where a statute provides for a defence based upon an accused's belief as to the existence of certain facts which needs only to be honestly held and is not dependent upon the presence or absence of reasonable grounds then it appears an accused's voluntary intoxication or self-induced automatism may be taken into account in assessing whether the accused truly and honestly possessed that belief. This is the consequence of the Divisional Court case of *Jaggard* v *Dickinson* [1981] QB 527, which considered the defence of honest belief in a lawful excuse to destroy another's property contained in s. 5 of the Criminal Damage Act 1971, see para. 1.10. *Majewski* is thus inapplicable to such offences. It is pertinent to note that the crime to which the defence related is the offence of criminal damage contained in s. 1 of the Criminal Damage Act 1971, which is primarily a basic intent offence (see later).

6.3.5 Possible common law exceptions to the rule in Majewski

The common law also recognised that in certain circumstances a mistaken belief though induced by the accused's voluntary intoxication could provide a defence, e.g. where an individual acted under the misapprehension that he was acting in self-defence or the prevention of crime (see, e.g., *R* v *Wardrope* [1960] Crim LR 770). These authorities cannot, it is suggested (at least with regard to offences of basic intent), survive the House of Lords decision in *DPP* v *Majewski* [1977] AC 443.

Non-dangerous drugs In the recent Court of Appeal decision of *R* v *Hardie* [1984] 3 All ER 848, it was accepted that where an accused was a self-induced automaton or voluntarily intoxicated through the taking of a drug (with or without medical prescription) which had merely a soporific or sedative effect, he may be able to claim that he lacked the *mens rea* for an offence of basic intent or that he was an automaton. Though affirming the general principle of *Majewski* the court accepted that the taking of sedatives etc. such as Valium even in excessive quantities, could not in the ordinary way raise a conclusive presumption that proof of intoxication (or automatism) was not to be admitted for the purpose of showing the absence of *mens rea* or in establishing the defence of automatism. Thus if an accused took such a drug and as a consequence at the time of the commission of the offence he lacked *mens rea* or was an automaton he would be entitled to an acquittal whether the offence concerned was one of basic or specific intent. However, if the taking of the drug was itself reckless (either in the *Cunningham* or *Caldwell* sense, see chapter 2), e.g., before setting out upon a car journey, or before undertaking any activity which requires complete mental awareness, then in such circumstances the taking of the drug would constitute the reckless element in an offence of basic intent. This principle is also recognised in cases of self-induced automatism where the accused is a diabetic. In *R* v *Bailey* [1983] 2 All ER 503 it was accepted that where an accused entered an autonomic state through hypoglycaemia either as a consequence of taking too much insulin, or failing to counteract its effects by eating food, he may nevertheless have a defence to a subsequent criminal act (be it an offence of basic or specific intent) unless the taking of the insulin or omission to counteract its effects was itself a reckless act, having regard to the surrounding circumstances prevailing at the time.

6.3.6 Insanity and voluntary intoxication

Where an accused through drink or drugs has produced in himself a disease of the mind, e.g., delirium tremens, such as to produce a defect of reason he may be able to claim the defence of insanity. (See para. 6.1 onwards for a discussion of the nature of this defence.) A distinction must be made between the temporary impairment of the mental faculties produced by drink and drugs and the repeated taking of such substances which over a period of time produce an impairment of the mental processes which may persist though the individual concerned is sober. It is only the latter situation which may possibly give rise to a defence of insanity, though it has been self-induced.

The House of Lords considered this issue in *Attorney-General for Northern Ireland* v *Gallagher* [1963] AC 349. Their lordships determined that where an individual suffered from a mental condition (in the instant case psychopathy) which was not sufficiently grave or extensive to constitute insanity, e.g., because it merely weakened the will to control conduct, the taking of alcohol or drugs which brought such a quiescent mental condition into a full state of insanity could not constitute a defence within the M'Naghten rules. The reason for this is that the cause of the insanity in such cases is the voluntary taking of drugs or alcohol and not the quiescent mental condition.

6.3.7 Offences of specific/ulterior intent

In *DPP* v *Majewski* [1977] AC 443 the House of Lords determined that in cases of offences of specific/ulterior intent (see below) an accused who was a self-induced automaton or voluntarily intoxicated may be able to claim that because of these mental states he lacked the requisite *mens rea* for such an offence or claim the defence of automatism. The justification for this rule is that offences of specific/ulterior intent may not be committed recklessly (in whatever sense the latter term is used in the criminal law). The act of self-induced automatism or voluntary intoxication even when intentionally undertaken does not in itself amount to a criminal act though it may be considered as being reckless within the terms of an offence of basic intent. Nevertheless an individual who is intoxicated or who is an automaton (even when voluntarily induced) may lack the capacity to form an *intention* to carry out the conduct element within the *actus reus* of a crime or a more fundamental element with regard to the external elements of an offence in cases of automatism (see para. 1.2 and *R* v *Bailey* [1983] 2 All ER 503). The accused cannot in such circumstances be said to have satisfied the *mens rea* element within an offence which is one of specific/ulterior intent which can only be fully constituted by conduct which is intentional. In the words of Lord Salmon in *DPP* v *Majewski* [1977] AC 443 (at p. 481) referring to the fact that voluntary intoxication may well establish a defence to crimes of specific/ulterior intent:

> This does not mean that drunkenness, of itself, is ever a defence. It is merely some evidence which may throw a doubt upon whether the accused had formed the special intent which was an essential element of the crime with which he was charged.

His lordship, however, gave a clear proviso to this principle:

> Often this evidence [i.e., involuntary intoxication] is of no avail because obviously a drunken man may well be capable of forming and does form the relevant criminal intent: his drunkenness merely diminishes his powers of resisting the temptation to carry out this intent.

It was once the law that an accused needed to establish that he was totally incapable because of his voluntarily intoxication from forming the prescribed *mens rea* with regard to the *actus reus* of a crime of specific/ulterior intent. It was not sufficient merely to leave the issue of whether the accused's voluntary intoxication, e.g., deprived him in fact of the capacity to form such an intent. In view of the opinion expressed by Lord Salmon concerning s. 8 of the Criminal Justice Act 1967 in *Majewski*, it is clearly not a requirement of the law today. An accused need only lay a fit and proper issue to the jury that he was intoxicated (though voluntarily induced) and that as a consequence of his condition he was incapable of forming the prescribed *mens rea* for a crime of specific/ulterior intent. It is then for the jury to determine whether the fact of intoxication so deprived the accused of this crucial element necessary for criminal liability. Similar considerations will apply in cases of self-induced automatism (see *R* v *Bailey*).

6.3.8 The definition of specific intent

What are to be regarded as offences of specific intent within the context of the matters discussed above is not entirely clear. The issue of offences of specific intent has already been considered in chapter 2.

In *DPP* v *Majewski* [1977] AC 443 Lord Simon of Glaisdale, refining his views in *DPP* v *Morgan* [1976] AC 182 (see below) expressed the opinion that specific intent was constituted in offences where an accused's state of mind contemplated consequences beyond those defined in the *actus reus* (this intent is sometimes called an ulterior intent). An example of such an offence would be burglary with intent to steal under the Theft Act 1968, s. 9(1)(a) (see chapter 8), the intent to steal being a consequence contemplated beyond that defined in the *actus reus* which involves entry into a building or part thereof as a trespasser. This could not form the basis of any workable classification of specific intent offences for it is too narrow and does not encompass many of the offences that prior to *Majewski* were regarded as being offences of specific intent for the purposes of self-induced automatism or voluntary intoxication. This same criticism may be levelled at a definition which seeks to limit specific intent crimes to offences such as those in *R* v *Steane* [1947] KB 997 (see chapter 2) which are only satisfied by a 'direct intent', i.e., where it is the accused's object or aim to bring about the elements of the *actus reus* of an offence (per Lord Simon).

Even a definition of specific intent that provides for the requirement of oblique intention, i.e., an awareness that the consequences of one's conduct will be to bring about the *actus reus* of an offence, would not have included the crime of murder following the House of Lords decision in *Hyam* v *DPP* [1975] AC 65.

Nevertheless a majority of their lordships in *Majewski* recognised that an offence of specific intent was one which would encompass all the mental states considered, which now clearly includes murder (see *R* v *Moloney* [1985] 2 WLR 648) but excluding recklessness, be it of the *Cunningham* or *Caldwell* type. This seems the most acceptable definition. Examples of other crimes which have been classified as specific intent offences include an assault under s. 18 Offences against the Person Act 1861, (see chapter 7). Theft, robbery (see chapter 8) and criminal damage contrary to the Criminal Damage Act 1971, s. 1(2) dependent upon satisfaction of the ulterior intent (see para. 2.5) of endangering the life of another by such damage. All offences that may be committed recklessly are for these purposes crimes of basic intent, e.g., any form of criminal damage other than that noted above.

6.3.9 Dutch courage

Notwithstanding that an offence is one of specific/ulterior intent and that an accused may at the time of the commission of the *actus reus* of such an offence lack any capacity to form the prescribed *mens rea* he may nevertheless while in a state of voluntary intoxication or self-induced automatism be held criminally responsible for such a crime. This is where an accused forms a clear intention to execute such an offence, but then takes drink or drugs in order to give himself the nerve to carry it out. Such an individual must have formed such an intention before the taking of the intoxicants. The principle of Dutch courage rules out any defence for such an individual, notwithstanding his mental state at the time of the commission of the offence. In such cases his resolve to carry out the crime is through the medium of drink or drugs married with the *actus reus* when he brings it about (see Lord Denning in *Attorney-General for Northern Ireland* v *Gallagher* [1963] AC 349.)

6.3.10 Involuntary intoxication

Where an individual without his knowledge is subjected to drink or drugs, e.g., through having his drink 'spiked' by another as a practical joke, then the fact of his subsequent intoxication or automatism may afford him a defence to any crime be it of basic or specific/ulterior intent (see *DPP* v *Majewski* [1977] AC 443). Where intoxication has only resulted in a loss of self-restraint or control, such that the individual concerned satisfies the *mens rea* of the offence he has committed, then irrespective of whether the offence is one of specific/ulterior or basic intent, or whether the intoxication has been induced voluntarily or involuntarily, the accused has no defence. A drunken intent is nevertheless a sufficient intent for criminal purposes (*R* v *Davies* [1983] Crim LR 741). The law in considering criminal liability takes no cognisance of weakness of will or loss of self-control induced by intoxicants or narcotics, though this may have a bearing on sentence.

6.4 MINORS

6.4.1 Children below the age of 10

There is an irrebuttable presumption of law (see Murphy, *A Practical Approach to Evidence*) that a child below the age of 10 is incapable of committing a criminal offence (see Children and Young Persons Act 1933, s. 50 as amended). Though cast in the form of an evidential proposition, the fact that it is irrebuttable means that no evidence as to such a child's capacity to commit an offence can be adduced. It thus amounts in effect to a substantive rule of law. Such children are regarded by the law as being '*doli incapax*', i.e., incapable of crime.

6.4.2 Children between the ages of 10 and 14

Non-sexual offences Children between the ages of 10 and 14 are presumed to be incapable of committing an offence (i.e., *doli incapax*) but unlike children below the age of 10 this presumption may be rebutted by establishing the following matters:

(a) the commission of the *actus reus* with full *mens rea* and
(b) knowledge that the act was wrong.

The second element means either knowledge that it was legally wrong or morally wrong see *R* v *Corrie* (1918) 83 JP 136. An illustration of this point is provided by the case of *McC* v *Runeckles* [1984] Crim LR 499. The accused aged 13 had stabbed another child with a milk bottle. The Divisional Court of the

Defences

Queen's Bench Division upheld the findings of the magistrates' court that the presumption of *doli incapax* had been rebutted. The court had taken into account:

(a) The accused's coherent statement made under caution which matched that of the victim.
(b) The contents of the statement that showed the accused to have the normal mental capabilities of a child of her age (see *J.B.H. and J.H. (Minors)* v *O'Connell* [1981] Crim LR 632).
(c) Her conduct prior to the incident, consisting of taunts, threats and assaults upon the victim, and her conduct after the offence, i.e., running away.
(d) Running away from police officers and admitting she thought they were looking for her.

Such factors were sufficient to rebut the presumption of *doli incapax*. The evidence need only establish a minor is aware his or her conduct is seriously wrong. This would include establishing the child's knowledge that his or her conduct is morally wrong, which is but a species of what is seriously wrong. Other factors which may be taken into account in assessing a minor's knowledge that his or her conduct is seriously wrong are his or her family background and the fact of his or her previous convictions (see *B* v *R* (1958) 44 Cr App R 1).

6.4.3 Sexual offences

There is a special rule with regard to boys between the ages of 10 and 14, in respect of sexual offences. In the case of *R* v *Waite* [1892] 2 QB 600 it was accepted, endorsing the earlier authorities, that there was an irrebuttable presumption of law (see above) that a boy below the age of 14 was incapable of committing the offence of rape (or any offence which involved the act of sexual intercourse or the act of buggery).

However, it is uncertain whether a boy below the age of 14 can be convicted of an attempt to commit any offence which involves an act of sexual intercourse (see *R* v *Williams* [1893] 1 QB 320). In any event a boy between the ages of 10 and 14 may be convicted of any sexual offence which does not involve an act of sexual intercourse, e.g., indecent assault. Furthermore where a boy's conduct involves the infliction of physical harm or its threat he may be convicted of an appropriate offence of assault (see chapter 7). This irrebuttable presumption relating to sexual intercourse is only applicable where the boy is a principal offender (see chapter 4). There is no legal objection to holding a boy responsible as a secondary party to any offence which has in its *actus reus* the element of sexual intercourse.

6.4.4 Procedural matters

In cases of murder or indictable offences where the minor is charged jointly with an adult there must be a trial before a jury. All other cases of offences involving minors must be tried before magistrates normally in a specially constituted juvenile court (see Magistrates' Court Act 1980, s. 24(1)). The treatment of minors found guilty of such offences is a complex area of the law. A full discussion of the orders that a court may make in such circumstances is contained in Emmins, *A Practical Approach to Criminal Procedure*.

6.5 MISTAKE

6.5.1 Mistake and negating mens rea

The defences previously discussed share an underlying common thread. The accused lacks or is deemed to lack the capacity to bring about the *actus reus* of an offence with the prescribed *mens rea*; though the causes of that incapacity may differ in each instance. The rationale behind the defence now to be discussed is that though an accused has the capacity to commit an offence he lacks *mens rea* in the particular case. This absence of the prescribed mental state for a crime arises because the accused believes in certain facts which though not true he regards as being so, and the accused's mistaken belief thus negates the *mens rea* of the offence (see the discussion of *Morgan's* case below). The *mens rea* of a crime is usually constituted by intention, foreseeability, awareness, knowledge, wilful blindness or recklessness with regard to the consequences and circumstances of the *actus reus*. Where an individual's belief (though it is mistaken) is such that he cannot be said, e.g., to have intended to bring about the consequences of an *actus reus*, or he was unaware of the circumstances in which his conduct took place, he clearly and quite simply lacks *mens rea* with regard to that offence. The only issue to consider is whether such a belief needs to be not only honestly held but also based on reasonable grounds. This was the point of law raised in *DPP* v *Morgan* [1976] AC 182.

The accused invited three other defendants to his house and suggested they should have intercourse with his wife telling them that she was 'kinky' and any apparent resistance on her part would be a pretence. All three had intercourse with her despite her protests. They were charged with rape (see chapter 7), the accused with aiding and abetting (see chapter 4). The defence contended that the three defendants believed (though mistakenly) that the woman was consenting, and this negated the *mens rea* of the offence which requires that an accused be aware of or be reckless to the fact that the woman consents to the act of intercourse. It was contended by the prosecution that this mistaken belief needed to be honestly held and based on reasonable grounds. A majority of the House of Lords rejected the prosecution's contention and held that where an individual had unlawful intercourse with a woman without her consent (the *actus reus* of the offence) but he honestly believed that she was consenting he must be acquitted for the *mens rea* of the offence is negated. There is no need for the belief to be reasonable, in fact the jury must acquit an accused even if they are sure that there were no reasonable grounds for the belief, it need only be genuinely held.

In the opinion of Lord Fraser of Tullybelton (at p. 237) the jury were to consider the entirety of the evidence raised. If on the whole of the evidence the effect is that an accused believed or may have believed his victim was consenting, the prosecution has not discharged the onus of proving the offence. They have not established that the accused had the prescribed *mens rea*. An accused need only raise the issue of his belief, there is no need for the judge to be satisfied that

Defences

he has laid a fit and proper issue for the jury to consider (i.e., an evidential burden, see Murphy *A Practical Approach to Evidence*; contrast this with the defences noted above). This is because it amounts to no more than a denial that an accused has *mens rea* and amounts to a plea of not guilty. As a matter of practicality the accused must adduce some evidence of his belief for the issue to be considered by the jury.

Though it has been argued that the authority of *DPP* v *Morgan* is limited to rape (see *R* v *Phekoo* [1981] 3 All ER 84 and *R* v *Barrett* (1980) 72 Cr App R 212) it is certain following the Court of Appeal in *R* v *Kimber* [1983] 3 All ER 316 that *DPP* v *Morgan* endorsed a principle of general application. Thus in any offence which requires full *mens rea*, that element is negated by an honest but mistaken belief in facts which if true would negate the external elements of the offence in fact. This mistaken belief need not be based on reasonable grounds. However, as a matter of practical reality the reasonableness of a belief has a great bearing upon whether a jury may accept that it is honestly held (see now Sexual Offences Amendment Act 1976, s. 1(2)).

Since this defence negates the *mens rea* of an accused it may be argued that it can have no application when the *mens rea* of an offence can be satisfied by establishing *Caldwell*-type recklessness (see chapter 2). This is because it is argued this form of recklessness is 'objective' and is concerned not with an individual's actual mental state but that of the reasonable man. An individual's mistaken belief is therefore irrelevant.

Where the *mens rea* of an offence is satisfied by *Caldwell*-type recklessness, however, the presence of a mistaken belief may still operate to provide a defence. This is because in the case of *Caldwell*-type recklessness the issue is whether the risk is so gross and obvious to a reasonable man that either the inference must be that an accused has foreseen the risk, or his indifference and total lack of awareness of the risk in such circumstances is itself blameworthy. A man who has assessed a risk and has come to a mistaken belief that it does not exist is not reckless in the *Caldwell* sense, for he is neither indifferent to nor unaware of the risk and he does not foresee its materialisation.

6.5.2 Reasonableness in the defence of mistake

The law may demand that in certain instances an accused may not claim that a mistaken belief should provide him with a defence unless that belief be not only honestly held but also based upon reasonable grounds. The first such instance is where the offence may be committed negligently.

6.5.3 Crimes of negligence

Where an offence is capable of being committed negligently (see chapter 2) a mistaken belief in order to negate that factor must be honestly and reasonably held. This is because a mistaken belief which is not based upon reasonable grounds is itself negligent as falling below the standards of an ordinary reasonable man, and thus the required element of such an offence, i.e., negligence, is satisfied.

6.5.4 Defences of justification

Many offences which involve the application of personal violence, e.g., murder, and the statutory assaults within the Offences against the Person Act 1861 (see chapter 7) usually contain an element within their *actus reus* that an accused shall not act 'unlawfully'. For reasons considered in para. 1.5 it is suggested that this element of unlawfulness should not amount to a true constituent in the *actus reus* of the offence. (But see contra *R* v *Kimber* [1983] 3 All ER 316 and *R* v *Gladstone Williams* (1984) 74 Cr App R 276 below.) The element of unlawfulness in such cases is the express but negative reference to a species of generally applicable defences which, if established in a given case, justify an individual's conduct, constituting it lawful, notwithstanding that the accused has brought about all the external elements of the offence with the prescribed *mens rea*. Examples include self-defence and the reasonable application of force in the prevention of crime (see below). The law once determined that where an accused mistakenly believed that certain facts existed, which would if true constitute his conduct lawful (within the sense discussed above), that belief in order to provide a defence should not only be honestly held but also based on reasonable grounds. Such was the consequence of the Queen's Bench Divisional Court decision in *Albert* v *Lavin* [1981] 1 All ER 628. This decision determined that it was no defence to a charge of 'assault' (see chapter 7) that an accused honestly but mistakenly believed his conduct was justified as being in self-defence (i.e., a lawful 'assault') if there were no reasonable grounds for the belief. An accused needed to lay in evidence a fit and proper issue of his mistaken belief before it could be left to the jury. The prosecution could negate this defence only by contrary evidence which satisfied the jury beyond reasonable doubt that the mistaken belief was not honestly held. It does not seem too harsh as a matter of policy that an accused should not knowingly use violence against another unless he can justify his conduct by reference to its reasonableness (see *R* v *Dadson* (1850) 4 Cox CC 358, para. 1.6). In the situation of rape noted above an accused who is mistaken as to a woman's consent to sexual intercourse is not knowingly carrying on a violent act—his belief should not in such a case be determined by reference to whether it is reasonable.

Nevertheless the conceptual clarity between the two forms of mistaken belief noted above has been clouded by *R* v *Kimber* [1983] 3 All ER 316 (a case concerning the offence of indecent assault upon a woman). The Court of Appeal took the opportunity to express the opinion that the element of 'unlawfulness' in offences involving the application of violence (see para. 1.5) does form an element in the *actus reus* of a crime. This is contrary to the view expressed by the Divisional Court in *Albert* v *Lavin*. The consequence of this is that the principle in *DPP* v *Morgan* [1976] AC 182 is applicable to the element of unlawfulness when contained in the definition of offences of assault with all the attendant consequences. Thus an accused bears no evidential burden in establishing the fact that he believed he was acting lawfully, he need only raise the issue that he honestly believed that he was not acting unlawfully and thus lacked *mens rea* with regard to that element. The prosecution can only negate this defence by contrary evidence which satisfies the jury beyond reasonable doubt. In the case of *R* v *Gladstone Williams* (1984) 78 Cr App R 276, the principle in *Kimber* was directly applied to a mistaken belief which negated the 'unlawful' element in an offence of

Defences

an assault occasioning actual bodily harm. (See also *R* v *Robinson* [1984] 4 NIJB which determined that an honest belief by an accused who killed another thinking that his life was in danger may provide a defence to a murder charge. There was no requirement that the belief be based on reasonable grounds.) It would appear that the view expressed by the Divisional Court in *Albert* v *Lavin* is now of doubtful validity and the number of situations where a mistaken belief needs to be both honestly held and based on reasonable grounds reduced considerably.

Nevertheless questions remain. Does the law still recognise certain areas where a mistaken belief to constitute a defence must be both honestly held and based on reasonable grounds? It is submitted that it does. In the case of *R* v *Tolson* (1889) 23 QBD 168, the accused was charged with the offence of bigamy, contrary to s. 57 of The Offences against the Person Act 1861. The only mental element required on the part of the accused in this crime is the intention to go through a valid ceremony of marriage. The remaining elements of the *actus reus*, e.g., that the accused is still validly married to another, require no mental element. The offence can thus be said to be one of strict liability (see chapter 3). The section provides its own defences, one of which is that an accused believes that a former spouse is dead due to their absence for a period of at least seven years. In *R* v *Tolson* it was determined that an accused could claim the defence that she believed her former spouse was dead. The case determined, however, that the belief had to be both honestly held and based on reasonable grounds. This was because the belief did not relate to the *mens rea* of the offence (the intention to go through the ceremony of marriage). The accused had committed the *actus reus* of the crime with the prescribed *mens rea*. She was claiming a defence which amounted to a justification of her conduct and was external to the constituent elements of the offence. In such instances the accused also needed to establish her defence by adducing sufficient evidence to make it a fit and proper issue for the jury to consider.

Wherever the defence of mistaken belief raised by an accused is independent of the actual constituents of the crime it will, it is suggested, still be governed by the principles enunciated in *Tolson*. Where the mistaken belief bears upon an element in the offence and negates it (usually an element of the *mens rea*) then the principle endorsed in *DPP* v *Morgan* (and *Kimber* and *Gladstone Williams*) will be applicable. As a footnote to illustrate the differences between the two types of mistaken belief, if Mrs Tolson had claimed that she believed (though mistakenly) that her bigamous marriage ceremony had been a rehearsal or a practical joke, she would be denying that she intended to go through a valid ceremony of marriage. The mistaken belief, because it would relate to the *mens rea* of the offence, would be governed by the principles contained in *Morgan*; it would be in essence a plea of not guilty. Even where a mistaken belief to constitute a defence needs only to be honestly held, the practical reality is that the factor of reasonableness will play a crucial element in the jury's assessment of whether the mistaken belief is truly held. Thus the distinction between the various types of mistaken belief (at least with regard to this element) is more apparent than real.

6.5.5 Statutory defences

Statutes like the Criminal Damage Act 1971, s. 5 (see para. 1.10 and above) provide that an accused's belief (mistaken or not) may in certain cases provide a defence to a charge under that statute by providing an accused with a lawful excuse to destroy property. In this case the statute provides that the mistake need only be genuinely held. In contrast, by s. 1(2) of the Sexual Offences (Amendment) Act 1976 it is provided that a jury in considering whether an accused's mistaken belief as to the issue of the woman's consent (an element in the *mens rea* of the offence of rape) must take into account the presence or absence of reasonable grounds for that belief. These examples illustrate that in relation to any statutory offence, the evidential consequences which a mistaken belief will take and whether it needs to be based on reasonable grounds or not are generally a matter of interpretation of that Act and are not dependent upon the nature of the mistaken belief.

6.5.6 Conclusion

The mistaken belief, whatever form it may take, must relate either to the constituent elements of an offence or to a recognised substantive defence, e.g., the belief that the conduct was necessary as an act of self-defence (see below). If the mistaken belief is not pertinent to either type of situation it is legally irrelevant and cannot form the basis of a defence in any event. The mistaken belief must be as to fact. Generally a mistake of law is no defence (see *R* v *Esop* (1836) 7 C & P 456). However, in some cases, an accused's mistake of law, e.g., a belief that he is the owner of property, may provide him with a defence to a charge of theft (see chapter 8) or to a charge of criminal damage (see *R* v *Smith* [1974] QB 354), for in both instances the mistaken belief as to his legal rights deprives him of *mens rea*. Such a belief need only be honestly held and may relate to legal rights other than those in property.

6.6 THE LAWFUL APPLICATION OF FORCE

6.6.1 Self-defence and the prevention of crime

The common law recognised that a man may have a defence to his use of reasonable force (see para. 6.6.2) against another if it was in self-defence or in the defence of another or in the defence of property, (see para. 6.6.8).

By the Criminal Law Act 1967, s. 3(1), it is provided that an individual may use reasonable force in the prevention of crime, or in effecting, or assisting in, the lawful arrest of offenders or of persons unlawfully at large (see para. 6.6.7). To this extent an accused has a statutory defence to his use of reasonable force or violence. This provision overlaps considerably with the common law defences noted above, for an individual protecting himself with reasonable force from a vicious unprovoked assault (see chapter 7) is acting in self-defence and also preventing a crime. In the case of *R* v *Cousins* [1982] 2 All ER 115, the Court of Appeal accepted that the common law defence of self-defence (and presumably where appropriate the other common law defences) could be claimed

Defences 179

concurrently with the statutory defences contained in s. 3(1) in respect of the same incident. Nevertheless there are situations where only the common law defences may be available. Thus where an accused uses violence against another but the latter does not come within the terms of s. 3(1), because, e.g., he is not being lawfully arrested, or he is not committing a criminal offence because he himself has a defence (e.g., he is an automaton), the accused must rely on the common law defences to escape criminal responsibility for his conduct.

However, both the common law and statutory defences have common elements and these must now be considered.

6.6.2 The use of reasonable force

By the Criminal Law Act 1967, s. 3(1), it is provided that in helping to bring about any of the situations envisaged therein the use (or threat) of violence by an accused will be justified only if it is the use of reasonable force in all the circumstances (see para. 6.6.2).

Any common law rules relating to what constitutes reasonable force within any of the situations found in s. 3(1) have been abrogated by s. 3(2).

What is reasonable force will be dependent upon a number of factors including:

(a) The nature and degree of the force used.
(b) The gravity of the crime or evil to be prevented.
(c) Whether it was possible to prevent the crime or evil by other means (see *Allen* v *Metropolitan Police Commissioner* [1980] Crim LR 441).
(d) The relative strength of the parties concerned and the number of persons involved.
(e) An unwillingness to use violence (see *R* v *McInnes* [1971] 3 All ER 295 and *R* v *Bird* [1985] 1 WLR 816).

It is a matter of fact for a jury to decide taking into account the above factors whether an individual has in a given circumstance used reasonable and therefore lawful force within the terms of s. 3(1). The fact that the force used must be reasonable determines that these factors must be assessed on an objective standard. A jury must be satisfied that no reasonable man in possession of the facts known or believed by the accused would, taking into account all the circumstances of the case (see *Farrell* v *Secretary of State for Defence* [1980] 1 All ER 166) and in view of the possibility for reflection, consider the violence which the accused used or exposed his victim to justifiable. Nevertheless the law always concerned with human frailties has conceded that in assessing whether an accused has used reasonable force, the measure though based upon reasonableness and objectivity should not be the cool objective assessment of the reasonable man viewing the incident in isolation with a dispassionate air. In the case of *Palmer* v *R* [1971] AC 814 Lord Morris of Borth-y-Gest (at p. 832) in considering the defence of self-defence determined that a jury should take into account that:

> it will be recognised that a person defending himself cannot weigh to a nicety

the exact measure of his necessary defensive action. If a jury thought that in a moment of unexpected anguish a person attacked had only done what he honestly and instinctively thought was necessary that would be most potent evidence that only reasonable defensive action had been taken.
(See also *R v Shannon* (1980) Cr App R 192.)

Though the case of *Palmer v R* was concerned with the common law defence of self-defence it is suggested this principle is applicable to s. 3(1). A jury must, therefore, in making an objective assessment of whether an accused in the circumstances of a case used reasonable force, combine the unique situation and personal viewpont of that individual with the concept of the reasonable man and determine whether it was the use of reasonable force by *that accused* in those circumstances. The concept of reasonable force is thus tinged with an element of subjectivity and shows the uneasy marriage of the needs of policy with the need to do justice to the individual accused.

This statutory concept of reasonable force is based upon a modification of the original common law formulation. It is suggested that this definition is now applicable to the common law defences (see *Attorney-General for Northern Ireland's Reference (No. 1 of 1975)* [1977] AC 105.

6.6.3 Aspects of the common law defences

It has been suggested that the construction given to the concept of reasonable force by the Criminal Law Act 1967, s. 3(1), is now applicable to the common law defences, removing many technical restrictions to which they were previously subject. Thus many of the rules which determined as matters of law whether in a given instance the force used was reasonable and which attached to these defences have been reduced to factors which are to be considered in determining whether an accused's use of force was reasonable in the circumstances, some of which have been noted above.

Thus in *R v McInnes* [1971] 3 All ER 295 it was determined following *R v Julien* [1969] 2 All ER 856 that it was no longer a condition of the common law defence of self-defence that an accused must initially retreat from the scene of the incident. The unwillingness to use violence was merely a material factor in considering whether the ultimate use of violence was reasonable. (See *R v Bird* [1985] 1 WLR 816).

In *R v Hussey* (1924) 18 Cr App R 160 it was accepted that a man, either in self-defence or in the defence of his home, may kill another who would forcibly remove the former from his domain. Lord Hewart LCJ was of the opinion that a man in such circumstances was under no obligation to retreat from the trespasser. Though such a situation could not *per se* now amount to a defence in view of the development of the law since the time of *Hussey*, it must be accepted that the fact that a trespasser may be seriously interfering with an individual's right to enjoy his peaceful enjoyment of land is a most pertinent factor in permitting the use of considerable force, and where appropriate in determining whether that force is reasonable, both for the purposes of the common law defences and for the Criminal Law Act 1967, s. 3(1).

In *Attorney-General's Reference (No. 2 of 1983)* [1984] AC 456 it was accepted

Defences

that an individual may make an explosive substance, i.e., petrol bombs, for a 'lawful object' within the terms of s. 4(1) of the Explosive Substances Act 1883 and thus have a defence to a charge under that section of possessing an explosive substance. In the Court of Appeal's opinion the 'lawful object' could be self-defence. This decision recognises that an individual may take action to prevent an unlawful assault upon himself, his family or his home even when it is only apprehended. The law thus recognises that an individual may strike first against another in the use of violence, but that conduct may nevertheless constitute in the circumstances reasonable force. This factor must also be recognised as being relevant to the situation within s. 3(1).

6.6.4 Evidential matters

The common law defences and the Criminal Law Act 1967, s. 3(1), share a further underlying common factor. An accused, in adition to having to establish that his use of force was reasonable in the circumstances of the case, must lay sufficient evidence of this fact to make it a fit and proper issue for the judge to leave to the jury (see *R* v *Lobell* [1957] 1 QB 547). Upon the establishing of this evidential burden the prosecution must prove that the accused's conduct did not amount to reasonable force beyond reasonable doubt.

6.6.5 Effect of mistake

This issue of mistake has already been considered. The mistaken belief as to the right to use reasonable force need, it appears, be only honestly held (see para.6.5.4). Furthermore it has been held that a mistaken belief as to the right to use reasonable force which has been induced by drunkenness may nevertheless constitute a defence (see para. 6.3.5). It is difficult to accept that this principle can stand following *DPP* v *Majewski* [1977] AC 443, certainly in relation to cases of violence which amount to offences of basic intent (see para. 6.3.3).

6.6.6 Excessive force

Where an accused has used force that has been determined as being excessive and unreasonable neither the common law defences of self-defence, defence of others or of property, nor the Criminal Law Act 1967;, s. 3(1), are available to a defendant. In the case of *R* v *McInnes* [1971] 3 All ER 295, a case involving murder, the Court of Appeal, approving dicta in *Palmer* v *R* [1971] AC 814 (see para. 6.6.2), determined that where excessive force is used by an accused in alleged self-defence and death results, it does not necessarily follow that there must be a conviction for manslaughter and not murder. The court emphasised that where a plea of self-defence fails because of the use of excessive force it affords no protection at all to a defendant. In such instances the accused's criminal liability is to be determined by reference to his *mens rea* (see also *Attorney-General for Northern Ireland's Reference (No. 1 of 1975)* [1977] AC 105).

6.6.7 Criminal Law Act 1967, s. 3(1), and the common law defences

It only remains to consider the peculiar characteristics of these various defences. By virtue of the Criminal Law Act 1967, s. 3(1), reasonable force may be used to bring about or aid another to bring about any of the following situations:

(a) The prevention of crime. This means any offence known to the criminal law, and is not limited to serious crime, i.e., an arrestable offence (see Introduction). However, in cases of minor transgressions the amount of force which may be considered reasonable to prevent it may be slight indeed.

(b) Effecting or assisting in the lawful arrest of offenders or suspected offenders or persons unlawfully at large.

Thus a police officer or a citizen (the latter alone or at the request of a constable to assist him) may use reasonable force to bring about a lawful arrest. It matters not that the individual arrested has actually committed an offence, it is sufficient he is suspected of having done so. This element of s. 3(1) therefore provides an accused with a defence to his use of force if it is reasonable in the circumstances and is an element in the apprehension of suspected or actual criminals. It is not dependent upon the fact of self-defence.

6.6.8 Self-defence, defence of others and defence of property

An individual may use reasonable force in protecting his bodily integrity even though the aggressor is not guilty of any criminal offence (see para. 6.6.1). This principle is applicable to the defence of others. In *R* v *Rose* (1884) 15 Cox CC 540 it was accepted that reasonable force could be used to protect a relative, in the instant case a son protecting a mother. In *R* v *Duffy* [1967] 1 QB 63 it was determined that there was no requirement that an individual must be related either by blood or any other relationship with the person he seeks to protect. There is a general right to protect the weak from the conduct of the strong. Violence is justified and lawful if it is necessary to restore the peace by rescuing a person who is being attacked (see also the House of Lords decision in *Albert* v *Lavin* [1982] AC 546).

An individual may also use reasonable force in the protection of his home from trespassers (see *R* v *Hussey* (1924) 18 Cr App R 160) though frequently such a situation will have overtones of personal self-defence as well as the prevention of criminal offences.

6.7 DEFENCES BASED UPON PUBLIC POLICY

6.7.1 Duress

An individual who brings about the *actus reus* of an offence with the prescribed *mens rea* may have a defence if he can establish that he was not a willing party to that act. Such is the defence of duress.

In cases of duress an individual commits an offence because he is so overborne by the threats of another that though it cannot be said that he has ceased to be a

Defences

free agent, the law in deference to human frailty recognises he would not have committed the offence but for the operation of that threat upon his mind. The law does not in such cases hold such an individual criminally responsible. However, the defence of duress is only available in the following circumstances.

(a) An accused must be put under a threat of violence unless he commits an offence (see later). This threat may be express or implied, and must encompass the accused's death or serious bodily harm (see *R v Hudson and Taylor* [1971] 2 QB 202, discussed below).

This much is clear though there is authority that the threat need only carry the promise of violence or the loss of personal liberty see *R v Steane* [1947] KB 997 (see para. 2.6). This is almost certainly not the law since the House of Lords decision in *DPP for Northern Ireland v Lynch* [1975] AC 653. Their lordships were of the opinion that the seriousness of a threat for the purposes of the defence of duress should be commensurate with the gravity of the crime committed. This would appear to suggest that in less serious crimes the threat should be correspondingly proportionate. However, their lordships formulated this principle within the context of duress requiring a threat involving death or serious bodily harm. Even though duress is a defence of general application, it would be unwise to place any reliance upon *R v Steane* [1947] KB 997 given the emphasis on death or serious injury in *Lynch*. The law has not surprisingly rejected threats which do not involve any element of physical harm, e.g., threats to property (see *R v McGrowther* (1746) Fost 13 or to expose indiscretion (see *R v Singh* [1973] 1 All ER 122).

There is no English authority determining whether duress is available to an accused when the threat of death or serious bodily harm is made in respect of his family and/or friends. There is no reason in principle why threats of such a grave nature in respect of a man's wife or children or close relatives should not provide him with the defence of duress. Furthermore there appears no objection in extending such a principle to threats made in relation to an accused's friends or even strangers, at least with regard to less serious offences.

In *R v Graham* [1982] 1 All ER 801, the Court of Appeal determined that public policy required that an accused should in relation to threats to his bodily integrity have the self-control and steadfastness reasonably to be expected of the ordinary citizen in his situation. This meant that whether an accused could claim the defence of duress following his commission of a crime was dependent upon his establishing that *he* was impelled to act as he did because, having regard to what he reasonably believed, following what another had said or done, he had good cause to fear the other would kill him or inflict serious bodily harm if he did not act as he did. This is the subjective element concerned with the accused's actual mental state. However, the promotion of the policy noted above requires an additional objective element which must also be established before an accused can claim he has been the victim of duress. This element asks whether a sober person of reasonable firmness, sharing the defendant's characteristics, e.g., age or sex, would have responded to the threats as the accused actually did. This objective factor balances the rights of the individual to escape criminal responsibility for his actions when he is faced with an agonising choice between his death or serious injury and the injuries he may inflict upon other members of society as a result of his choice to preserve himself from harm. In such instances that choice must be regarded as a reasonable decision by that very society.

(c) The threat must still be an operative factor at the time of the commission of the offence see *R* v *Hudson and Taylor* [1971] 2 QB 202, (discussed below). If the threat has ceased to have any effect upon an accused's mind at the time of the commission of the offence, there can be no defence of duress. If an accused has an opportunity to avoid committing the crime (an avenue of escape) without incurring the threatened consequences the defence of duress will not be available to him (see *R* v *Gill* [1963] 2 All ER 688).

However this 'avenue of escape', e.g., by informing the police must, within the *Graham* test noted above, be a reasonable course of action for the accused to take. This is illustrated by *R* v *Hudson and Taylor* [1971] 2 QB 202. In this case the Court of Appeal accepted that in assessing whether an accused had a reasonable opportunity of rendering the threat ineffective by an 'avenue of escape', regard should be had to the accused's age, his circumstances and, perhaps crucially, the risks to him which may be involved in removing the threat. This would include the ease with which the threat could be executed and the availability and effectiveness of police protection.

(d) The threat, though it must be an immediate one, in the sense that it must be operating on the mind of the accused at the time of the commission of the offence, does not have to be capable of being carried out instantly. In the case of *R* v *Hudson and Taylor* the Court of Appeal accepted that a threat was no less compelling because it could not instantly be executed, if it could be carried out the very night on which the accused had refused to commit the offence. How remote the possibility of the execution of the threat must be before it ceases to operate on the mind of an accused is unclear. It is presumably a matter of fact, which must be taken into account (in accordance with the *Graham* test) in assessing whether an accused was subjected to duress.

6.7.2 Availability of the defence

The defence is available to all accused, except those who have voluntarily joined an organisation dedicated to violence or terrorism. Where such individuals are then compelled by other members of that organisation to commit acts of violence, terrorism or crimes which promote their nefarious aims the defence of duress is unavailable, see *R* v *Fitzpatrick* [1977] NILR 20 (and *R* v *Calderwood and Moore* [1983] 10 NIJB).

Subject to the above proviso the defence is available in relation to all crimes, including treason. This has been recognised since *Oldcastle's case* (1419) 1 Hale PC 50. The opinion expressed in *R* v *Steane* [1947] KB 997 to the contrary is against the balance of authority. It has been recognised that the defence is available to an accused charged with murder (see *DPP for Northern Ireland* v *Lynch* [1975] AC 653). However, their lordships in this case held by a majority that the defence of duress in cases of murder was available to secondary parties (see chapter 4). Whether the defence was available to a principal (see para. 4.1) was left unclear. In the case of *Abbott* v *R* [1977] AC 755 the Privy Council by a majority determined that the defence of duress should not be available to a principal to a murder. This decision has been criticised. It has been suggested it is

Defences

illogical, for an accused as a secondary party to an offence may have as great a criminal responsibility as a principal. It has also been pointed out that a man charged with attempted murder may have the defence of duress available to him but not if his victim subsequently dies. Nevertheless the ingenious mind is always capable of visualising extreme situations where the most sensible and practical rules of law may be illustrated as unworkable. It is suggested that the defence of duress must be subject to limitations. It does not seem unreasonable to draw the line at the principal to a murder (see also *R* v *Calderwood and Moore* [1983] 10 NIJB).

6.7.3 Evidential matters

It is for an accused to adduce sufficient evidence of the fact of duress to leave it a fit and proper issue for a jury to consider. It is then for the prosecution to negate any element of the defence beyond reasonable doubt.

6.7.4 Nature of the defence

It has been determined since *R* v *Bourne* (1952) 36 Cr App R 125 and affirmed in *R* v *Hudson and Taylor* [1971] 2 QB 202 and *DPP for Northern Ireland* v *Lynch* [1975] AC 653 that the defence of duress negates neither an element in the *mens rea* nor *actus reus* of an offence. It is a defence which excuses an accused who has committed a crime because the law as a matter of policy recognises the weakness of individuals to resist the threat of serious violence or death upon their person if they do not commit an offence.

6.8 COERCION

At common law there was a rebuttable presumption of law (see Murphy, *A Practical Approach to Evidence*) that a wife who committed an offence (subject to exceptions, principally treason or murder) in the presence of her husband had been subjected to coercion. This was a defence which the prosecution had to negate beyond reasonable doubt. This principle had been based upon the premise that the wife had no separate will of her own when confronted by her husband's presence. By s. 47 of the Criminal Justice Act 1925 this presumption was abolished. It is now for a wife to establish that in relation to any offence (except treason or murder to which coercion does not apply) she was coerced by her husband to commit it. Coercion is similar to duress but is in one aspect wider. It will involve threats of death or the infliction of serious bodily harm, but also it seems threats by a husband upon a wife to inflict physical harm or even to exert moral pressure will also suffice (see *R* v *Rickman* [1982] Crim LR 507). The defence is little used and its ambit is uncertain. It cannot be said when a wife will be regarded as being in the 'presence' of her husband, for the purposes of the defence. It seems unlikely it will ever be settled for the defence is for practical purposes a dead letter.

6.9 SUPERIOR ORDERS

Though the defence of superior orders is usually found in a military context (see *Keighley* v *Bell* (1866) 4 F & F 763) it is a possible defence of wider application (see however *Lewis* v *Dickson* [1976] RTR 431 which suggests the contrary).

Where a superior gives orders to a subordinate, e.g., employer and employee, which compels conduct on the latter's party which is unlawful, then the subordinate, if charged with a criminal offence, may be able to claim the fact that he has been ordered to perform the act provides him with a defence. Such a defence does not negate *mens rea* or the *actus reus* of an offence, it appears to exist on a principle of public policy. The accused, it appears from the authorities, must not be aware that the conduct ordered is manifestly unlawful and he must act in good faith (see *R* v *James* (1837) 3 C & P 131). It must be admitted that the authorities do not clearly and universally recognise the existence of this defence. Many authorities which appear to support the defence of superior orders can be justified on other grounds, e.g., that the accused was under a mistaken belief of fact that would provide him with a defence (see para. 6.5.4).

6.10 NECESSITY

The principle behind this possible defence is that an accused commits the *actus reus* of a crime with the prescribed *mens rea*, but has done so from his motive to avoid a greater evil. The law has recognised such a defence in relation to particular statutory offences or within a statutory context. For example the Road Traffic Regulation Act 1984, s. 87, provides that fire engines, ambulances etc. if being used for their usual or police purposes are exempted from speed limits, if such limits would be likely to hinder the use of the vehicle for the purpose for which it is being used. This is a statutory recognition of the defence of necessity (see also the Criminal Damage Act 1971, s. 5, para. 1.10, and the concept of lawful excuse, which justifies the destroying of property if it is to save other property from greater damage or to prevent injury to persons).

Whether there is a general common law defence of necessity is uncertain. Authorities such as *R* v *Vantandillo* (1815) 4 M & S 73 and *Johnson* v *Phillips* [1976] 1 WLR 65 appeared to recognise the existence of such a defence. In *Southwark London Borough Council* v *Williams* [1971] 2 All ER 175 the Court of Appeal expressed the opinion that there was a general defence of necessity in the criminal law. The defence in such a case would appear to be based upon the necessity to commit a crime because the alternative would be to permit the occurrence of a greater peril. In contrast in *Buckoke* v *Greater London Council* [1971] 2 All ER 254, the Court of Appeal Civil Division rejected any defence of necessity, with regard to failure to observe traffic signs or lights. The situation is unclear but it is suggested that there is no general defence of necessity and reference must be made to the express or implied intention of a statute as interpreted by case law or the law reports in common law crimes to determine whether a given offence has as one of its incidents a defence of necessity.

It would appear that there is one offence which can never accept a defence of necessity, the crime of murder (see *R* v *Dudley and Stephens* (1884) 14 QBD 273).

Nevertheless the recognition of human frailty should determine that the

Defences

presence of necessity may amount to a powerful mitigating factor, which should result in either the non-prosecution of an accused, or a nominal or light sentence or pardon following conviction.

6.11 THE SCENARIO

The scenario discloses several possible defences available to some of the parties. Consideration will first be given to Bruce.

Bruce   Bruce may be able to claim that if he was aiding Donald in his rape of Sarah (see Chapter 4), by driving him to the house knowing what would happen, he may nevertheless be able to claim a defence of duress.
   Bruce would have to establish that Donald's utterance 'that it would be worse for him' was a threat to inflict at least grievous bodily harm or even to kill him. He would have to show within the test propounded in *R v Graham* that he was the victim of duress. Furthermore there must be no reasonable avenue of escape, Bruce must only have the choice of aiding Donald or suffering at least severe injury at the hand of the latter. Donald's threat must have been operative upon Bruce's mind while he was driving to the scene of the crime.

Donald   His only defence to a charge of rape of Sarah (assuming he had survived Rex's attack) is that he honestly believed (though mistakenly) that Sarah was consenting to the act of intercourse. He is merely denying that he has the prescribed *mens rea* of the offence. Though he is voluntarily intoxicated the case of *R v Woods* determines this factor may not be considered in assessing whether Donald's belief in Sarah's consent is honestly held or based upon reasonable grounds (see Sexual Offences Amendment Act 1976, s. 1(2)).

Rex   Rex may claim that his murderous assault upon Donald was justified and lawful (assuming that Donald appeared to be about to assault Sarah either sexually or non sexually). One of his defences may be that he was under a mistaken belief that Donald was about to assault Sarah. The mistaken belief needs to be honestly held but not it appears based on reasonable grounds. Whether his mistaken belief may still be regarded as providing him with a defence to murder (a specific intent offence) where he is voluntarily intoxicated is certain, but where an accused is charged with a basic intent offence the situation is unclear.
   Rex's belief is as to the existence of facts which if true would constitute his assault upon Donald justifiable. If the mistake is honestly held the facts he believes exist will be deemed true. If Donald was actually in the course of assaulting Sarah, Rex would be using force in the prevention of a crime (see Criminal Law Act 1967, s. 3(1)) or acting in the defence of another, a common law defence.
   However, whether the fact of the assault by Donald upon Sarah is true or regarded as true because of Rex's belief, the latter's use of force must be reasonable in the circumstances. This will be determined by reference to matters such as: could the assault upon Sarah have been prevented by other means, e.g., by calling the police? Was it such a serious incident that it could only be stopped by the most grave action on Rex's part? Were the nature and degree of the force

used by Rex reasonable in view of the above matters and in comparing his size and strength with that of Donald?

Whether Rex was using reasonable force is to be considered by reference to an objective standard, taking into account the factors noted above; nevertheless this standard also takes into account Rex's personal situation.

Edward and John If Edward and John were in a state of self-induced automatism or involuntary intoxication, they may claim that such conditions may provide a defence to a charge of wounding with intent (Ron's slashed cheek) contrary to the Offences against the Person Act 1861, s. 18. This is because it is an offence of 'specific intent'. Such a crime requires an intention to bring about the external elements of the offence, and their drunkenness may deprive them of this ability. Such a defence may be used if it was relevant to their theft, and other offences of dishonesty, which are also offences of specific intent.

However, if Edward and John were charged with criminal damage in respect of the fire they started in Rex's house or of certain lesser assaults upon Rex (e.g., Offences against the Person Act 1861, ss. 20 and 47 (see chapter 7) then the fact of their intoxication will not provide them with defences. These offences are of basic intent and may be committed recklessly. Their intoxication actually supplies that element.

6.12 QUESTIONS

1. *Majewski* determines that the voluntary intoxication of an accused in offences of basic intent is tantamount to recklessness and satisfies the *mens rea* of such crimes. Does this principle conflict with the authority of *Gladstone Williams* that a mistaken but honest belief in the right to self-defence will provide a defence to an 'assault'-based crime (even of basic intent) though that mistaken belief is induced by voluntary intoxication?

2. *Gladstone Williams* determined that the element of 'unlawfulness' in offences involving the infliction of violence does form an element in the *actus reus* of such crimes. This element may therefore now be negated by an honest but mistaken belief in facts which would render an accused's conduct lawful if they existed in fact (such a belief need not now be based on reasonable grounds). If the belief relates to the right to act in self-defence the use of force must, however, itself be reasonable.

   (a) How is this latter factor affected by *Gladstone Williams*?

   (b) Is it logical that an accused's mistaken belief that he is acting in self-defence need not be based on reasonable grounds in conflict with the fact that the actual use of violence must be reasonable in the circumstances? If not, why not?

3. *Hardie* determined that the voluntary taking of sedatives may produce a state of mind which provides a defence to an accused even in cases of basic intent.

   (a) Can the law readily distinguish between 'safe' drugs like Valium which because of their soporific effect can provide such a defence from 'dangerous'

Defences

drugs like alcohol?
  (b) Is there any policy behind *Hardie*?
  (c) What category of persons may potentially escape criminal liability while their mind is affected by sedatives because of *Hardie*? Should such persons be excepted from the rule in *Majewski*?

7

Offences Against the Person

7.1 INTRODUCTION

In the scenario numerous acts of physical violence occur. Various persons are either injured, violated or killed. Sarah is assaulted and raped by Donald. Donald subsequently is assaulted and killed by Rex. Later, having escaped from Rex's house, Edward and John attack Ron, a taxi driver, and William, a passer-by joins in the attack which culminates in Ron breaking Edward's arm and Edward producing a knife unexpectedly, which he uses to slash Ron's face.

Leaving aside any possible defences which might be raised, all these physical injuries or threatening activities can be classified as offences against the person. This category includes any threatened or actual physical contact with the body of another human being. In a common-sense way the law assumes that we all have impliedly consented to ordinary, everyday bodily contacts which are part and parcel of living in a modern, congested society. Bumping into persons in crowded corridors and subways, being squashed up against someone in a crowded bus or train carriage, these and other commonplace contacts are not the concern of the law. There comes a point, however, at which contact becomes criminal and then the more severe, violent and deliberate the contact, the more serious the offence committed. For convenience of discussion such offences are divisible into the non-fatal and fatal categories.

The former of these generally involve injury but stop short of causing the victim's death. It can be further subdivided into two other distinct groups of non-fatal offences, those which are non-sexually motivated and those that obviously are sexually motivated. The first of these groups includes common law assault and battery and the various statutory offences such as assault occasioning actual bodily harm, malicious wounding, assault causing grievous bodily harm, administering poison and assault on a constable in the execution of his duty. The sexually motivated group of non-fatal offences against the person includes such offences as indecent assault, gross indecency, indecency with children and in particular rape.

The aim of this (and the next) chapter is to illustrate, through the study of selected substantive offences, the general principles of criminal law set out in particular in chapters 1 to 3. Obviously what is required by way of *mens rea* is significant in itself in relation to each offence in deciding whether or not an accused will be guilty but also it may decide whether or not certain defences are available to him, e.g., the defence of voluntary intoxication generally is available for crimes of specific intent only (see para. 6.3.7).

Offences Against the Person

7.2 NON-SEXUAL, NON-FATAL OFFENCES

This category consists of some common law offences (assault and battery) and some statutory crimes largely to be found in the Offences against the Person Act 1861. It is imperative at the outset to appreciate the nature of the two common law offences noted above because that will contribute to the understanding of the statutory offences of both the non-sexual and the sexual variety.

7.2.1 The common law offences: assault and battery

Confusion is not uncommon in relation to these two offences. It arises largely through the way in which the word 'assault' has come to be used. In its narrow technical, common law sense it means putting another individual in fear that unlawful physical contact is imminent. There is no actual contact only fear that it will occur. If and when there is an unlawful contact (ranging from however slight to however violent) with another person, that is a battery at common law. The word 'assault', however, has come to be used in everyday speech by ordinary people (not by lawyers) to include actual contact with another and secondly even in legal circles the word 'assault' is used (this time correctly) to include what is a battery when referring to the statutory offences, many of which are contained in the Offences against the Person Act 1861: such as aggravated 'assault' wounding and causing grievous bodily harm and 'assault' occasioning actual bodily harm. They use the word 'assault' rather than 'battery' in a way and in a context that clearly includes both. But in so far as the common law is concerned 'assault' and battery remain even today as two distinct offences and although the maximum prescribed penalty for both is the same it is usual for common law battery to attract a greater penalty than common law assault because it involves physical contact. Battery, however, is an uncommon offence today because the police would choose to charge a person with one of the statutory 'assault' offences instead. Likewise common law assault (i.e., putting someone in fear) also is not a common charge, and the penalty imposed is nominal if an accused is convicted, because no one actually is injured physically in such instances, and if they are, then the police generally would charge one of the statutory 'assault'-based offences. It is precisely because those offences are based on assault, however, that the nature of the two common law offences needs to be understood. Remember throughout, that apart from those instances where reference is being made to common law assault, the word 'assault' when used in relation to all the statutory offences is defined for that purpose to mean not just 'putting in fear' but actual contact or battery.

7.2.2 The elements of common law assault

Assume for the moment that when Donald and his three compatriots arrived at Rex's house they decided to test whether or not anyone was in the house by first ringing the doorbell. Assume Sarah came to the door and that Donald asked if her parents were at home and received a negative reply. Further assume that Donald had then said to Sarah in an abusive manner: 'You lying cow I will destroy your good looks with this.' at the same time producing a broken bottle which he pointed towards her. First, despite the fact that Donald had not touched Sarah at that point he has committed the *actus reus* of common law assault because it is sufficient for him to have caused Sarah to believe that unlawful, physical contact was imminent. In short, the *actus reus* of assault is the effect of Donald's actions or words on Sarah's mind. Without more, by putting her in fear of immediate injury he has satisfied the *actus reus* requirement. Secondly on the question of *mens rea*, the case law is clear (see *Fagan* v *Metropolitan Police Commissioner* [1969] 1 QB 439, *DPP* v *Morgan* [1976] AC 182 and in particular *R* v *Venna* [1975] 3 All ER 788). For Donald to produce that belief in Sarah's mind either intentionally or recklessly, will satisfy the *mens rea* requirement. Common law assault, therefore, is a crime of basic intent. Intention here means either direct intention as would be the case if Donald deliberately aimed to produce that belief in Sarah's mind, or oblique intention, such as where Donald was aware that that belief inevitably would be produced in Sarah's mind. It also encompasses recklessness, but how is that word to be defined in this instance?

R v *Venna* [1975] 3 All ER 788 held that proof of recklessness was sufficient to satisfy the *mens rea* elements of common law assault or battery or any statutory 'assault' offence except those which are crimes of specific intent. In that case youths were causing a disturbance late at night. After warnings a police officer arrested the accused who struggled so much that four officers were needed to restrain him yet he continued to kick and in the process injured the hand of one of the officers. The accused was convicted of 'assault' occasioning actual bodily harm (s. 47 of the Offences against the Person Act 1861) but the judge stated that the *mens rea* for that offence was the same as for common law assault or battery. The accused appealed on the basis that he had not intended to touch let alone injure the victim. His appeal was dismissed on the basis that the trial judge had correctly stated the law when he said that the jury could find the accused guilty if they found that he had lashed out with his feet, reckless as to who was there, not caring one iota as to whether he kicked somebody. This sort of recklessness is what was earlier described as *Cunningham*-(1957)-type, conscious risk-taking. Does it now include the new *Caldwell*-(1981)-type recklessness, i.e., failure to think about an obvious risk? Given that *R* v *Seymour* [1983] 2 AC 493 (see para. 2.7.12) declared *Caldwell*-type recklessness to be of general application then the initial reaction is to answer that question affirmatively. A persuasive argument to the contrary, however, is made by Professors Smith and Hogan in their textbook entitled *Criminal Law* 5th ed., 1983, see pp. 52–3 and 354) to the effect that *R* v *Venna* [1975] 3 All ER 788, decided before *Metropolitan Police Commissioner* v *Caldwell* [1982] AC 341, was referring to *Cunningham*-type recklessness and that remains so today for offences defined in terms of 'maliciousness' as opposed to 'intention and recklessness' which is the terminology used in more modern statutes (see *W (a minor)* v *Dolbey* [1983] Crim LR 681). The reason being that although common law assault and battery are not statutory offences they are akin to the assault-based offences defined in the Offences against the Person Act 1861 which, because they contain the word 'maliciously' arguably are said to require proof of intention or *Cunningham*-(1957) *and only Cunningham*-(1957)-type recklessness. Given that proof of *Caldwell* recklessness will not suffice, obviously proof that Donald negligently caused Sarah to apprehend immediate, unlawful, physical

Offences Against the Person

contact equally would not suffice although it may be sufficient to found a civil action in tort.

7.2.3 Problematic aspects of assault and battery

Battery as stated earlier is simply any unlawful contact with another. That this is a separate offence from common law assault can be illustrated in the scenario. While Edward and John were arguing and fighting with Ron, the taxi driver, William, who was a passer-by, recognised Ron as someone with whom he had a 'score to settle'. If William came up behind Ron and put his arms about Ron or hit him, pushed him or pulled him, that would be battery. The fact that Ron did not expect an attack from behind and did not see William approach (i.e., the fact that there was no common law assault) is irrelevant. William is liable for battery at least. Likewise earlier in the scenario when Rex struck the unconscious body of Donald those blows were batteries even though Donald was unaware of them. (Subsequent events allow for much more serious charges to be brought against Rex.) Whether or not harm results, the striking, punching, pushing or pulling, even of another person's clothing is sufficient to constitute the *actus reus* of the offence. Furthermore there seems to be no reason why that *actus reus* may not be committed indirectly. For example, having arrived at Rex's house and having rung the doorbell to test whether anyone is in the house, if Sarah opened the door and Donald kicked the door knowing it would 'fly open' and as a consequence strike Sarah, that would be a battery. Likewise, if Sarah had opened the door wide and Donald had bent down and pulled the rug from under her feet sending her crashing to the ground, that too would be battery although he had not laid a finger on her directly.

Secondly, can words (whispered, spoken or shouted) ever constitute common law assault? In attempting to answer that question two points clearly can be made. In the scenario, assume Donald rang the doorbell at Rex's house, that Sarah opened the door and that Donald said to her: 'If you do not let us in now we will beat you up *next week* when you go on your usual visit to your grandmother's house!' That threat to attack Sarah sometime in the future will not be a common law assault because assault requires that Sarah be made to fear that the use of violence is immediate or imminent. Further, when Sarah answered the doorbell, assume Donald had waved his fist and said to her: 'But for the fact that a policeman is standing on the other side of the road watching us, I would punch you in the teeth!' In that situation, if a policeman was in fact evident to Sarah as well as Donald, then again there would be no assault. Both are aware from the fact, together with the words used by Donald, that he had no intention to make Sarah believe she was about to be struck and equally in those circumstances she could not have formed the belief that she was about to be struck by him. In other words what otherwise would have been a common law assault (i.e., the intentional or reckless waving of the fist at Sarah putting her in fear of violence) is prevented from being an assault because of the qualifying words pertaining to the presence of the policeman. Words alone can prevent certain threatening conduct or actions from constituting assault. In theory there is no good reason why words alone should not constitute assault if they cause the hearer to believe that unlawful, physical contact was imminent. One old case,

Mead's and Belt's case (1823) 1 Lew CC 184, stated that a threatening act, and not words only, was necessary to constitute assault although there are more modern decisions (such as *R* v *Wilson* [1955] 1 All ER 744) which support the view that words alone will be sufficient. Assume that when Sarah opened the front door Donald said to her (without making any gesture whatsoever): 'Don't scream or I will break your jaw!' That must be an assault if it puts Sarah in fear of immediate harm. This can be tested against the yardstick of the question: what if there was a power strike and it was pitch dark when Sarah opened the door so that she only heard Donald's words but could not see him, let alone any gestures made by him? The answer must be that if on hearing the words alone she is put in fear of immediate harm then an assault has been committed. That last scene from the scenario raised another issue. Surely Donald's threat is conditional and similar to the earlier scene when the presence of a policeman nearby had caused Donald to state that otherwise he would have struck Sarah? These two situations are not, however, the same. In the scene involving the policeman his presence or absence is an extraneous factor over which neither Sarah nor Donald had any control and both knew of his presence and consequently that since no blow would be struck there would be no common assault. The other situation ('Don't scream or I will break your jaw') also involves a conditional threat but here the impending violence does not depend on an external factor over which there is no control, but on internal factors, i.e., Sarah's willingness or ability not to scream out in those circumstances. Her fear that she will be struck if she does scream must amount to an assault.

Does it matter that Donald is incapable of carrying out any of the threats that he might have made to Sarah? (Assume for instance that Donald suffers from some disease that permits him to form a fist and raise it in another's direction but prevents him from doing anything more than that.) The answer must be that if in the circumstances he has induced Sarah to believe that he will strike her then it is immaterial whether or not he could strike her. This is analogous to the case of *R* v *St George* (1840) 9 C & P 483 where it was held to be an assault for one person to present and point an unloaded gun at another person.

Finally the case of *Fagan* v *Metropolitan Police Commissioner* [1969] 1 QB 439 (see chapter 2) makes it clear that both common law assault and in particular battery may be committed by omission. Generally deliberate or reckless conduct is necessary but in that instance the accused had neither of those states of mind, with regard to his conduct initially, his driving of his car on to the policeman's foot was accidental. However, his omission to remove the car (or his deliberate decision not to remove it) once he realised it was on the officer's foot was held to be sufficient *mens rea* which the court combined with the continuing *actus reus* to make the accused liable.

7.2.4 Special defences to assault and battery offences

In relation to common law assault and battery and to those statutory assault offences which are based on and incorporate the two common law offences the general defences are applicable (see chapter 6) but in addition there are three special defences available in some instances. These are:

(a) inevitable accident,
(b) consent,
(c) lawful and reasonable chastisement of a child by its parent or schoolmaster.

7.2.5 Inevitable acccident

From what has been said about the *mens rea* of assault and battery it should be clear that the purely accidental instances of physical contact which occur in daily life are not criminal 'assaults'. Likewise, subject to what was said about *Fagan's* case in para. 7.2.3, negligent contact with another is not an offence. Also given the nature of modern city life, conduct which involves a reasonable amount of intentional or reckless contact with others, such as the pushing that occurs in crowded bars or on public transport or in queues, must not be criminal. We all can be said to have impliedly consented to a certain amount of physical contact, deliberate, careless or unavoidable.

7.2.6 Consent

Consent to physical contact (ranging from the slightest touch to sexual intercourse) will be a defence to battery and any 'assault'-based statutory offence except certain sexual 'assaults'. Consent, however, must be freely given; it will not be a defence if it was obtained by force or threats of force. Also in some instances if the consent was induced by fraud then that consent will be vitiated. This generally arises in relation to sexual assaults such as rape although it may have wider application. In such instances fraud negates consent only if it is 'as to the nature of the act itself, or as to the identity of the person who does the act' (see *R* v *Clarence* (1888) 22 QBD 23 at p. 44).

Fraud as to the nature of the act is best illustrated in the above case. There the accused's wife understood the nature of sexual intercourse and she knew that the man with whom she was engaging in the act of intercourse was her husband. The fact that he had not told her he had a transmissible disease may have been fraudulent but as far as the law is concerned it was irrelevant to the wife's consent. She understood the nature of the physical contact and who was in contact with her, therefore the court held she could not subsequently withdraws her consent because she did not appreciate all the risk involved in that contact. Whether or not the husband wilfully concealed the risk is irrelevant to whether or not she actually gave consent.

Fraud as to the identity of the person who does the act will only negate the defence of consent in rare instances because it requires the accused successfully to impersonate someone actually known to the person (the victim) who was duped into consenting. The obvious example is where the accused impersonates the spouse or another person with whom the person giving consent is on terms of intimate physical relationship. The fraud (i.e., the impersonation) will negate the victim's consent to physical contact. These two rules and *Clarence's* case show that the purpose of the law in this area is to prevent physical assaults and not to punish morally reprehensible conduct which is not within the traditional interpretation of what constitutes assault or battery. The law of 'assault' both at common law and in its wider statutory context is not in existence to punish injury to pride, thoughts or feelings; its aim is to protect our bodies. For this reason there is another limitation imposed by law on the general view that consent is always a defence to a charge of assault. Consent cannot excuse physical contact which is unlawful in itself such as assault in the course of either a prize-fight or a duel (see *R v Coney* (1882) 8 QBD 534) or assault which is likely to occasion bodily harm (see *R v Donovan* (1934) 25 Cr App R 1). The law, however, allows some special justification such as consent to injury during the pursuit of lawful games, conducted according to the rules and under proper safeguards (see *R v Billinghurst* [1978] Crim LR 553) which held that the consent of players to contact and injury during a rugby match could not be a defence to a charge of fracturing another player's jaws by a punch thrown in an 'off-the-ball situation'. In other words a person's consent to an act likely to result in his death or in serious injury to him is no defence. No person can consent to the infliction upon himself of a degree or kind of harm which is in itself unlawful. In the light of this the legality of boxing is not entirely free from doubt (but see below).

In *R v Donovan* (1934) 25 Cr App R 1 the accused had induced a 17-year-old girl to go with him to a garage where he severely beat her with a cane 'in circumstances of indecency'. One of the offences of which he was convicted was common law assault to which charge he had raised the defence of consent based on the fact that he had told her over the telephone what he intended to do and that therefore her presence, together with her conduct throughout, made it obvious that she consented to everything. The court stated that consent could be no defence:

> If an act is unlawful in the sense of being in itself a criminal act, it is plain that it cannot be rendered lawful because the person to whose detriment it is done consents to it ... As a general rule, although it is a rule to which there are well-established exceptions, it is an unlawful act to beat another person with such a degree of violence that the infliction of bodily harm is a probable consequence, and when such an act is proved, consent is immaterial.

Bodily harm was stated to be any harm or injury calculated to interfere with health or comfort and which need not be permanent but which must be more than merely transient and trifling. The exceptions cited in that case were lawful sports and 'horseplay' neither of which have as their aim the infliction of bodily harm. The reasonable chastisement of a child, although at first sight similar, is not an example of an exception to the general rule as stated in *Donovan* that consent cannot be given to the infliction on oneself of a serious degree of bodily harm because the right exists in common law to chastise reasonably irrespective of the child's consent. But a clear exception would be the case of consent to a surgical operation.

Denning LJ said, *obiter* and in dissent, in *Bravery v Bravery* [1954] 3 All ER 59 (a family law case in which a woman sued for divorce on the ground of cruelty but failed because of her consent to her husband's having undergone a sterilisation operation) that from a criminal law view an ordinary surgical operation which is done for the sake of a man's health with his consent is perfectly lawful because there is just cause for it. 'If, however, there is no just cause or excuse for an operation, it is unlawful even though the man consents to it.' (It would follow that even if the man does not consent, provided the operation is necessary it would be lawful.) Denning LJ went on to give examples where an operation consented to and even performed by oneself would be unlawful, such as maiming oneself or another in order to avoid work or military service or so as to be better able to beg or obtain social benefits. His lordship included in this category (a) an operation for abortion unless it was necessary to prevent serious injury to the health of the mother (subsequently the Abortion Act 1967 has rendered lawful an abortion operation carried out in compliance with that Act); (b) plastic surgery that is purely cosmetic and/or done to avoid detection for criminal purposes and (c) sterilisation operations unless performed to prevent serious injury to health or prevent the transmission of hereditary diseases. However:

> Take a case where a sterilisation operation is done so as to enable a man to have the pleasure of sexual intercourse without shouldering the responsibilities attaching to it. The operation then is plainly injurious to the public interest. It is degrading to the man himself. It is injurious to his wife and to any woman whom he may marry, to say nothing of the way it opens to licentiousness; and, unlike contraceptives, it allows no room for a change of mind on either side. It is illegal, even though the man consents.

The distinction made in *Donovan* between unlawful harm and lawful sport is unsatisfactory. The motive to injure cannot be a distinguishing feature because boxing is a lawful sport and yet only the most unrealistic of people would maintain that in professional boxing at least, there is no motive to injure the opponent. The same point can be made in relation to other combative sports. Likewise the whole purpose of horseplay more often than not, is to provide amusement and pleasure from the sight of someone else being injured. The motive to injure, therefore, does not satisfactorily distinguish caning or flagellation to satsify some perverse sexual gratification from manly sports and idle horseplay. The true reason for distinguishing between acceptable or lawful, and unacceptable or unlawful consent must be public policy. This may mean that if social mores have changed since 1934 then *Donovan's* case might well be decided differently today or similar situations not even prosecuted, provided the injuries inflicted were not gross and likewise Lord Denning's views in *Bravery* v *Bravery* concerning consent to 'unnecessary' surgery may no longer be, and definitely in light of the Abortion Act 1976 (see below para. 7.6.11) are not, the law on some of the issues discussed, but as the law stands there is no logic to it and it is safe to assume that only if the infliction of bodily harm is for a socially beneficial or other approved purpose will it be considered lawful.

This view is borne out by the decision in *Attorney-General's Reference (No. 6 of 1980)* [1981] QB 715 where the accused and a youth had a fist fight in a public street. The youth suffered a bleeding nose and bruises. The accused was charged with assault and found not guilty by the jury on a direction that if the victim had agreed to fight and the force used by the accused was reasonable then the latter should not be guilty. The Attorney-General referred the question whether consent could be a defence to a charge of assault arising out of a fight to the Court of Appeal under s. 36 of the Criminal Justice Act 1972. The court held that the definition of 'assault', as in its wide sense including battery, was 'the actual intended use of ... force to another person without his consent ... or any other lawful excuse'. Ordinarily consent was a defence but the discussions in *Coney* (1882) and *Donovan* (1934) showed there was an exception when the public interest required it. The issue in such cases is at what point the public interest required the court to say that the victim's consent was immaterial. On the facts before it the court held that it was not in the public interest for people to try to cause, or to cause, each other actual bodily harm for no good reason and it was irrelevant whether or not the act occurred in private or in public. It was an 'assault' if actual bodily harm was intended or caused. The court stated that properly conducted sports, lawful chastisement, reasonable surgical interference and dangerous exhibitions were unaffected by this decision and still legal. Again no guidance as to the criteria for social utility was provided. This means the law is left in an uncertain state with the judge, *ad hoc*, as the arbiter of the public interest. Most fights, however, minor tussles aside, are now unlawful regardless of consent.

7.2.7 Reasonable chastisement

Reasonable physical chastisement of a child by a parent or schoolmaster is permissible: *Cleary* v *Booth* [1893] 1 QB 465. Where this defence is raised the issue for the jury is whether the accused used such force upon the child that it went beyond anything that could properly be regarded as reasonable and moderate chastisement. The prosecution must prove that the accused did more than the law allowed but it is open to the jury to consider the state of mind of the accused when administering the punishment (see *R* v *Smith (David George)* (1985) 82 LS Gaz 198). Likewise in *R* v *Taylor, The Times*, 28 December 1983, the Court of Appeal stated that although a schoolmaster currently has the right to chastise his pupils, he must do this in a reasonable and controlled way. The throwing of missiles (e.g., wood-backed blackboard dusters) at pupils was held to be neither reasonable nor controlled and if a pupil is injured then the master will have no defence to a charge of assault occasioning actual bodily harm or a more serious charge depending on the injury and his state of mind. If the parent or schoolmaster did not know or ought not reasonably to have been expected to know, that death or grievous bodily harm was a likely result, then that person will not be liable even if the death of the child results, provided the chastisement is not unlawful (in the sense of being unreasonable). If, on the other hand, it was unreasonable, and death resulted, that would warrant a charge of manslaughter (*R* v *Hopley* (1869) 2 F & F 202). In the recent case *R* v *Smith (David George)* (1985) 82 LS Gaz 198, the Court of Appeal held that where the accused is charged with assault and raises the defence of lawful chastisement, the case for the jury is whether the prosecution has satisfied them that the accused used force which went beyond anything that could properly be regarded as reasonable and moderate chastisement. The prosecution must satisfy the jury that the accused did more than the law allows and the jury may consider, in reaching a verdict, i.e., what was the state of mind of the accused when administering the punishment. Irrespective of the defence the prosecution must prove either intent to injure or recklessness whether or not injury is caused to the child. If the injury is caused by

Offences Against the Person

accident or mishap the accused will not be liable.

The rulings of the European Court of Human Rights are binding on signatories to the treaty known as the European Convention on Human Rights and Britain has agreed to be bound and to comply with that Convention. In a recent judgment in the case of *Campbell and Cosans* v *United Kingdom* (1982) 4 EHRR 293, the European Court had to consider whether the British government was in breach of its obligations for permitting schools to administer corporal punishment. The parents of a child objected to the use of corporal punishment as a disciplinary measure at their child's school. They complained that its use violated Article 3 of the Convention ('No one shall be subject to torture or to inhuman or degrading treatment or punishment'), and Article 2 of Protocol No. 1 ('No person shall be denied the right to education . . . [In respect of education] the State shall respect the rights of parents to ensure such education . . . in conformity with their own religious and philosophical convictions.'). The European Court held that there was no violation of Article 3. There was no evidence that the schoolchildren underwent suffering of the level . . . in the notion of 'torture' or 'inhuman treatment' nor were they degraded — that required their humiliation or debasement in their own eyes or the eyes of others of a minimum level of severity which was not established on the facts in that case. In relation to Article 2 of Protocol No. 1, however, the court said that the expression 'philosophical convictions' denoted convictions worthy of respect in a democratic society and compatible with human dignity. The court considered that the applicants' views on corporal punishment related to 'a weighty and substantial aspect of human life and behaviour and satisfied those criteria'. The court further declared that the duty of the British government to respect parental convictions in this sphere cannot be overridden by the alleged necessity to strike a balance between conflicting views nor is the government's policy to move gradually towards the abolition of corporal punishment in itself sufficient to comply with this duty. The upshot would seem to be that currently the common law permits reasonable physical chastisement by the parent or schoolmaster but in the latter instance those who object to corporal punishment will have an action under the European Convention of Human Rights against the British government until corporal punishment in schools is abolished.

7.3 STATUTORY ASSAULTS CATEGORISED

Parliament has by statute created various permutations of the common law offences of assault and battery to recognise and differentiate for purposes of punishment varying degrees of aggravation associated with what otherwise would have been common law assault or battery. These permutations are contained largely in the Offences against the Person Act 1861 and they can be divided into three categories each involving aggravation. First, assaults with particular intentions (crimes of specific intent), e.g., unlawfully and maliciously to do any of the following:

    (a)   To wound or cause grievous bodily harm *with intent* to do some grievous bodily harm (s. 18).
    (b)   To attempt to choke etc., or to use chloroform etc., *with intent* to enable

himself (i.e., the accused) or any other person to commit an indictable offence (ss. 21 and 22).

(c) To administer poison *with intent* to injure, aggrieve or annoy (s. 24).

(d) To cause gunpowder to explode, or to send any person any explosive substance or to throw corrosive fluid on a person *with intent* to do grievous bodily harm (s. 29).

(e) To place or throw in, into, upon, against or near any building, shop etc, any explosive with intent to do any bodily injury (s. 30).

(f) To set or place any spring gun, mantraps calculated to destroy human life or inflict grievous bodily harm *with the intent* to inflict death or grievous bodily harm (s. 31).

(g) To place wood, stones etc. on railway lines or to take up rails etc, or to alter any points etc. or turn, hide or remove any signals etc. *with intent* to endanger the safety of travellers (s. 32).

(h) To throw stones etc. on to trains *with intent* to injure or endanger the safety of any person on the train (s. 33).

(i) To assault with intent to resist or prevent lawful apprehension or detainer of oneself or any other person (s. 38).

(j) To assault with intent to obstruct or deter another from, or to compel him to, buy or sell any grain (s. 39).

(k) To raise force to hinder or prevent seamen working or to use any violence to such persons *with intent* to hinder or prevent them from working (s. 40).

(l) To administer drugs or use an instrument *with intent* to procure an abortion (s. 58).

(m) To procure drugs etc. to cause abortion *with intent* to cause an abortion (s. 59).

(n) To knowingly have or to make any explosive etc. *with intent* to commit any serious offence (s. 64).

Secondly, assaults with particular results (crimes of basic intention). The three most important in this category are:

(a) Inflicting any grievous bodily harm with or without any weapon or instrument (s. 20).

(b) Administering poison etc. so as to endanger life or inflict grievous bodily harm (s. 23).

(c) Assault occasioning actual bodily harm (s. 47).

Others include: not providing apprentices or servants with food etc. or doing bodily harm whereby life is endangered or health permanently injured (s. 26); exposing children whereby life is endangered (s. 27); causing bodily injury by gunpowder (s. 28); doing or omitting to do anything so as to endanger train passengers (s. 34); injuring persons through the furious driving of any carriage or vehicle (s. 35). In addition abortion, robbery and kidnapping are all aggravated 'assaults'.

Thirdly, assaults on particular persons such as:

(a) To obstruct or assault a clergyman or other minister on the way to or in

Offences Against the Person

the discharge of his duties in a place of worship or a burial ground (s. 36).
 (b) To assault a magistrate, officer or authorised person performing his duty to preserve any wreck or proceeds of a wreck (s. 37).
 (c) To assault any female or boy under 14 years (s. 43).
 (d) To assault any constable or any person assisting him in the execution of his duty (Police Act 1964, s. 51).

All of these crimes are offences of basic intent except for the offence contained in s. 40 concerning assaults on seamen, which, in relation to that aspect at least, is a crime of specific intent.

7.3.1 Statutory assaults generally

The three most important of the above categories of statutory offences because they occur with monotonous regularity in daily life and because they illustrate the principles involved are: wounding with intent to cause grievous bodily harm (Offences against the Person Act 1861, s. 18) unlawful wounding (s. 20) and occasioning actual bodily harm (s. 47). Of these s. 18 is the most serious offence and carries with it the prospect of a greater penalty on conviction. For that offence the maximum penalty imposable is life imprisonment. For s.20 the maximum penalty is 5 years' imprisonment. The maximum penalty on indictment for a s. 47 offence is not specified. It is generally something less than for a s. 20 offence but more than the penalty on indictment for a common law assault which is specified by s. 47 as being at the court's discretion but with a maximum of one year's imprisonment. One significant feature of this branch of the law is that statutory 'assaults' are in effect common law batteries with or without an attendant common law assault and with varying circumstances of aggravation added. The more serious the consequence or harm resulting from the 'assault' in each of the circumstances specified by statute, the more serious the offence for purposes of the penalty or punishment for those who are convicted. Also a consequence of this notion that statutory or aggravated 'assaults' are merely common law batteries with something aggravating added is that a jury may find an accused person guilty of a lesser statutory 'assault' offence than the one with which he is charged and it is always open on an indictment for an aggravated 'assault' for the jury to return a verdict of common law assault and/or battery if they are not satisfied that the circumstances of aggravation have been proved.
 In the scenario, Edward, having been badly hurt in the fight with Ron, the taxi driver, draws a knife and slashes Ron's cheek. Edward could be charged with the most serious statutory or aggravated 'assault' (s. 18). It would be open to the jury at his trial to return a verdict (apart from guilty of that charge or not guilty) or guilty of a lesser statutory 'assault' offence such as s. 20 (unlawful wounding) or even to find him guilty of common law assault and/or battery.

7.3.2 Mens rea of statutory assaults

Both s. 18 and s. 20 of the Offences against the Person Act 1861 open with the words: 'Whosoever shall unlawfully and maliciously'. It is to the meaning of these words which we now turn and to the distinction between these two offences which illustrates the distinction between *all* the offences listed in the first category on the one hand and all those in the second category and most of those in the third category on the other. It is in effect the distinction between crimes of specific and crimes of basic intention and that classification dictates what must be proved by way of *mens rea* in order to obtain a conviction. The *mens rea* requirement in crimes of specific intent can only be satisfied by proof of intention (direct or oblique) whereas in crimes of basic intent proof either of intention or of recklessness will suffice. Both s. 18 and s. 20 require that the accused 'unlawfully and maliciously' injure another person, in addition to that the s. 18 offence requires that the accused be proved to have *intended* to cause a specified injury, namely grievous bodily harm. Whereas for both offences proof of intention or recklessness will satisfy the *mens rea* aspect relating to the injury caused to the victim, *only* proof of intention will satisfy the additional requirement for the s. 18 offence that the accused intended to cause the victim grievous bodily harm.

The distinction is well put by Diplock LJ (as he then was) in *R v Mowatt* [1968] 1 QB 421 when he said that:

> under s. 18, the real issues of fact . . . are: (1) are [the jury] satisfied that the accused did the act? (2) if so, are they satisfied that the act caused a wound or other serious physical injury? (3) . . . [D]o they think that the accused may have done the act in self-defence? (4) If the answer to (1) and (2) is 'yes' and to (3) . . . is 'no', are [the jury] satisfied that when he did the act he intended to cause a wound or other really serious physical injury? If (3) . . . is answered 'no' and (1) and (2) are answered 'yes', the lesser offence under s. 20 is made out; and if (4) is also answered 'yes' the graver offence under s. 18 is made out.

The inclusion in that section of the words 'with intent' and indeed the inclusion of those words in all the offences included in the first category above, means that only proof of direct or possibly oblique intention (see chapter 2) will satisfy the special *mens rea* requirement imported by those two words into those sections.

For s. 20 and all the other statutory assaults whose wording does not include those two special indicators, the *mens rea* element may be satisfied by proof of intention or recklessness. What does recklessness mean in this context? Does it include *Caldwell*-type recklessness? The best answer at the present time must be that it does *not* include *Caldwell* (failure to consider an obvious risk) type recklessness. The reason for this is that the leading case concerning recklessness prior to *Caldwell* was *R v Cunningham* [1957] 2 QB 396 (see also para. 7.2.2) which determined that recklessness required actual foresight of the risk and that case specifically dealt with one of the statutory assaults within the Offences against the Person Act 1861 (namely s. 23, unlawfully and maliciously administering or causing to be administered or taken, any poison or other noxious thing so as to endanger life or inflict grievous bodily harm). Although it relates to administering substances it is otherwise similar to s. 20.

7.3.3 Actus reus of statutory assaults

The *actus reus* of both s. 18 and s. 20 of the Offences against the Person Act 1861

Offences Against the Person

requires that the accused be proved to have 'wounded' or, in the case of s. 18, 'caused grievous bodily harm' and in the case of s. 20 'inflicted grievous bodily harm' to the victim. In the case of the s. 47 offence (the least serious of these three aggravated assaults) the accused must have 'occasioned actual bodily harm'.

These various words and phrases have received judicial attention over the years so that their meaning is more certain. First, the classic statement of what does *not* amount to a wound is contained in *R* v *Wood* (1830) 1 Mood CC 278 where the issue was whether the breaking of another's collar-bone was a wound. It was held that bruises, burns and possibly even scratches are not necessarily wounds. The victim's skin in effect must be breached or broken. This idea that there must be a break in the continuity of the whole skin of the victim is confirmed in *C (a minor)* v *Eisenhower* (1984) 78 Cr App R 48. There the accused fired an airgun and the pellet hit the victim in the eye but only caused damage to the internal blood vessels in the eye and no actual break in the skin or the surface of the eye, consequently it was held not to amount to a wound. But in relation to either a s. 18 or s. 20 offence the prosecution does not have to charge wounding, it may charge the accused with causing or inflicting grievous bodily harm. The accused may be liable on that basis even though he has not wounded the victim. He would only be liable for the more serious s. 18 offence if it could be shown that he *intended* to cause the victim grievous bodily harm.

For purposes of both s. 18 and s. 20, 'grievous bodily harm' means any 'really serious bodily harm' according to Viscount Kilmuir LC in *DPP* v *Smith* [1961] AC 290. He said:

> I can find no warrant for giving the words 'grievous bodily harm' a meaning other than that which the words convey in their ordinary and natural meaning. 'Bodily harm' needs no explanation, and 'grievous' means no more and no less than 'really serious'.

However, in the recent case, *R* v *Saunders (Ian), The Times*, 8 February 1985, the Court of Appeal held that there is no difference between 'serious injury' and 'really serious injury' and that any judge directing a jury on the meaning of 'grievous bodily harm' need not use the latter phrase. In relation to s. 47 (occasioning actual bodily harm) the words 'bodily harm' have been interpreted in *R* v *Miller* [1954] 2 QB 282 as a hurt or injury calculated to interfere with a person's health or comfort, including causing a hysterical or nervous condition.

In the recent case of *R* v *Dawson (Nolan and Walmsley), The Times* 23 March 1985, the three accused had attempted to rob a petrol station attendant late at night. They had approached the cash cubicle wearing masks and brandishing a pickaxe handle and a 'replica gun' and they banged on the counter demanding money but fled when they realised that the elderly attendant had activated an alarm. Shortly after they fled the attendant suffered a heart attack and died. The accused were charged with and convicted of manslaughter although they pleaded guilty to attempted robbery. The Court of Appeal quashed their manslaughter conviction on the basis that it was unsafe in light of two aspects of the judge's direction to the jury one of which was that putting a person in terror so that he may suffer emotional or physical disturbance which is detrimental is harm. On this point the Court of Appeal held that an unlawful act might constitute 'harm' in the context of manslaughter if it so shocked the victim as to cause him physical injury; emotional disturbances, however, which had been produced by terror did not amount to such 'harm'. There has to be injury or harm to the person through the operation of shock emanating from terror or fright. (For the other issue in this case see the discussion of involuntary manslaughter in para. 7.6.8).

Over the years the words 'cause' in relation to 'grievous bodily harm' in s. 18 and the word 'occasion' in relation to 'actual bodily harm' in s. 47 have given rise to little difficulty in interpretation but the word 'inflict' in the *actus reus* of s. 20 has required some clarification. In *R* v *Clarence* (1888) 22 QBD 23 it was said that 'inflict' necessitates an injurious assault of some sort (i.e., an 'assault' in its wide sense). Later cases have established that the injury need not be brought about directly by the accused. For example, assume in the scenario that Donald, Bruce, Edward and John went to Rex's house, not to steal from it, but simply to play a practical joke or possibly just to frighten the inhabitants. Assume they effect their purpose by first blocking or barring the external doors, then wafting smoke through an open window and shouting 'Fire'. Assume that Sarah was frightened on seeing the smoke and panicked when the doors would not open so that she ran upstairs and jumped from a window injuring herself, would the four practical jokers or tormentors be criminally liable for her injury? The answer dates from two old cases. In *R* v *Halliday* (1889) 61 LT 701 Lord Coleridge said:

> if a man creates in another's mind an immediate sense of danger which causes that person to try to escape and in so doing he injures himself, the person who creates such a state of mind is responsible for the injuries.

In the slightly earlier case of *R* v *Martin* (1881) 8 QBD 54 a practical joker who had produced panic and injury in a crowded theatre by turning out the lights, barring the exits and shouting 'Fire' had been held liable for a s. 20 offence. Likewise in relation to s. 47 as shown in *R* v *Roberts* (1971) 56 Cr App R 95 where the accused's unwanted sexual molestations while driving in a car caused the female passenger to jump from the moving vehicle resulted in his being liable for the injuries indirectly caused by his conduct. The civil law's tortious doctrine of, or any doctrine similar to, contributory negligence arising from the conduct of the victim has no part to play in assessing criminal liability in this or similar situations (see rape, para. 7.5).

The possible liability arising from 'assault' can be illustrated by the scenario. Rex fires his gun at Edward and John who are fleeing from his house. Assume the gun is a shotgun and that pellets do in fact hit both of them, of what offence will Rex be liable? First he can only be liable under s. 18 if it can be proved that the pellets drew blood and that he intended to cause grievous bodily harm. If Rex claimed that he knew they were too far away to be hurt and if we assume they were hit by pellets but not hurt then s. 18 cannot apply. Secondly *R* v *Martin* (1881) 8 QBD 54, discussed above, shows that even though Rex had no personal malice towards Edward and John, the fact that he did an unlawful act calculated to injure would be sufficient to make him liable under s. 20 provided it can be shown that, on the facts known to him at the time, he actually foresaw that a particular kind of harm might be done to the victims (see *W* v *Dolbey* [1983] Crim LR 681) and provided that Edward and John were in fact injured. If the pellets

Offences Against the Person

have neither broken their skin nor caused serious injury, s. 20 *cannot* apply. If the pellets hurt or interfered with the comfort of Edward or John (e.g., if their backsides were bruised so that it was painful to sit down) or so frightened them as to make them ill then s. 47 would apply. Failing that Rex would be liable at common law for battery and common law assault (in the latter instance if Edward and John saw that he was about to shoot at them and were put in fear of being hit). If the fear caused was such that either had a heart attack, and died, Rex may be liable for manslaughter (see *R v Dawson (Nolan and Walmsley), The Times,* 23 March 1985, see above and para. 7.6.9). It is well recognised that while it is not open to a jury to find an accused guilty of a more serious 'assault' than that with which he is charged, it is perfectly proper for the jury to convict of a lesser 'assault' even though it is not charged (see *R v Taylor* (1869) LR 1 CCR 194). This is confirmed by two recent cases. In *R v Carpenter* (1983) 76 Cr App R 320 the Court of Appeal held that in relation to s. 20 the word 'inflict' necessary connoted an assault and consequently when considering a s. 20 offence the jury are entitled to return an alternative verdict of guilty of occasioning actual bodily harm under s. 47. The House of Lords held likewise in *Commissioner of Police of the Metropolis* v *Wilson*; *R* v *Jenkins* [1984] AC 242 stating that the greater charge impliedly included allegations of the lesser.

7.4 SEXUAL/INDECENT ASSAULTS

Two things seem to come out of the case decisions in this area of the law. First, an assault is committed for purposes of indecent assault only if the accused does something to another or through his conduct causes that other person to fear that something will be done. Put another way, in this particular branch of the 'assault'-based offences, words alone would appear to be insufficient to make a person liable.

DPP v *Rogers* [1953] 2 All ER 644 states that the mere invitation to touch cannot be an assault on the invitee. There a father put his arm about his 11-year-old daughter's shoulders and invited her to go upstairs and touch his person in an indecent way. There was no force or compulsion beyond his request. Consequently he was not convicted of indecent assault. There may have been an indecent suggestion but there was no assault, indecent or otherwise. There was no conduct or gesture that could be construed as a threat. Had he pushed or pulled the child after a show of reluctance on her part that would have amounted to an 'assault' and further it would be an indecent assault if accompanied by an act of indecency. The effect of cases like this was for Parliament to introduce to our law the Indecency with Children Act 1960 which makes it an offence to commit an act of gross indecency with or towards a child under 14 years, *or to incite* a child under 14 to such an act with him or with another person. The law is still not happy in this area. For example in *R v Sutton* [1977] 3 All ER 476, the accused was the coach of a junior football team. He took three of the small boys home and photographed them there partially clothed as well as in the nude. He hoped to sell the negatives to a Scandinavian pornographic magazine. Throughout he remained fully clothed and only touched the boys decorously to arrange various poses. The boys consented to this and there was never any hostile or threatening conduct on the accused's part. The court held that there was no 'assault'. Clearly had his conduct been indecent in itself the consent of the boys would have been no defence. Section 15(2) of the Sexual Offences Act 1956 states that a boy under 16 years of age cannot give any consent which would prevent an act being an 'assault' for the purposes of the offence of indecent assault. But see now the statutory offence provided by s. 1 of the Protection of Children Act 1978 which makes it an offence to take, distribute, possess for show or distribution, or advertise for show or distribution, indecent photographs of a child under the age of 16.

In *R v Mason* (1968) 53 Cr App R 12, a middle-aged, married women had a propensity for virile youths, indeed she was regularly visited by six boys aged 14 or 15 years and at her, and sometimes their, suggestion, all had willingly engaged in acts of sexual intercourse. The court was of no doubt that a woman (as in this case) could be charged with indecent assault but it went on to say that neither the intercourse nor the acts leading to it were 'assaults' by the woman on the boys in that instance because the boys consented and as intercourse and associated caresses are not harmful so as to be criminal in themselves (see *R v Donovan* (1934) 25 Cr App R, discussed in para. 7.2.6, but see s. 15(2) of the Sexual Offences Act 1956) there could be no 'assault'. Even if there was an 'assault' it would only amount to an indecent assault if there was clearly indecency in the contact made or, in the view of the court in that case, there was some compulsion, threat, gesture, duress or show of reluctance. None of these features was present in this case.

Secondly, and interconnected with the first point is the notion of hostile intention to be found in a line of cases, starting with *Coward v Baddeley* (1859) 28 LJ Ex 260. In that instance the accused had persistently touched a woman who had told him repeatedly to go away. The court confused two issues. The fact that the accused's activities caused no injury and were simply an annoyance caused the court to classify it as part of the ordinary contacts of everyday life and therefore not battery. Whereas his activities should have been declared to constitute a battery irrespective of any injury or the size of the appropriate penalty. To rationalise the wrong decision (i.e., that the accused had not committed battery) the court declared that there was no evidence of hostility on his part. This erroneous notion was taken up in subsequent cases such as *Fairclough v Whipp* [1951] 2 All ER 834 and *DPP v Rogers* [1953] 2 All ER 644. This notion of so-called hostile intention is superflous. In assault and battery the *mens rea* element is satisfied by proof that the accused either intentionally or recklessly caused another to apprehend unlawful contact or by proof that he intentionally or recklessly touched some other person. Hostility is immaterial, if anything it is motive but motive must not be confused with *mens rea* (see para. 2.6). The same must be true of an indecent motive. An 'assault' cannot be converted into an indecent assault simply by the indecent motive of the person who commits the 'assault'. There arguably must be some indecent act and that it should be performed to or on the person of the victim. For example, assume Donald dragged Sarah from the doorstep of her father's house saying that he intended to have sexual intercourse with her and repeated that statement together with other lewd comments while he manhandled her to a secluded alleyway nearby and released her only when a passer-by came to her aid. Assume that for some reason Donald was not charged with attempted rape, could he have

Offences Against the Person

been charged with indecent assault? There was clearly battery or some sort of 'assault' but there was no indecent act other than the lewd and salacious words which preceded and accompanied the unlawful physical contact and force. Arguably those words in the circumstances should make the assault an indecent assault whereas indecent motive unknown to the victim probably would not. What if the indecent motive is manifested by an indecent act on the part of the accused in the presence of the person who is assaulted but that person is unaware that an indecent act is taking place? Such would be the situation where a schoolmaster does some indecent act to or with himself while caning a student in such a way that the student does not see the indecent act take place. If such a situation is held to be simply an assault and not an indecent assault, would the same be true if the person assaulted was blind or asleep or too young to understand that some indecent act was occurring at the same time as the assault?

In a recent Crown Court case, *R v Pratt* [1984] Crim LR 41 it was held that in order to prove indecent assault it was necessary to prove a common assault, circumstances of indecency and an indecent intention. There the accused had forced two boys to undress almost completely, revealing their private parts. His defence that his only motive was to search for cannabis which he thought the boys had taken from him was successful.

7.4.1 Practical aspects of indecent assaults

It is a fact of life that unlawful sexual intercourse is generally preceded by or accompanied by acts which would be indecent if performed in public or without consent. It is a nice question of procedure (see Emmins, *A Practical Approach to Criminal Procedure*) whether or not indecent assault as a separate offence is subsumed by the greater offences of a completed rape or an attempted rape or an offence of intercourse with a girl under 16 (see ss. 5 and 6 of the Sexual Offences Act 1956). If this is not the case the accused may be put in jeopardy of several convictions for what is in essence one offence. It is logical in such situations that the jury be directed to consider whether the alleged acts of indecency and the intercourse were so connected as to amount to one transaction and then to consider as a matter of practicality whether or not 'it' was consented to.

Can a man be convicted of indecent assault upon his wife? By analogy with the current situation relating to rape (see para. 7.5.3) the answer must be *no* unless his wife is legally separated from him. Unlike rape, indecent assault could be committed by either spouse on the other partner but in terms of reality and practicality it should not be unlawful for either spouse to say things, make gestures or perform acts which outside of marriage might well be regarded as indecent. They may be part and parcel of an approach leading to lawful sexual intercourse in marriage. Although on grounds of policy a husband is generally not liable for rape and neither spouse for indecent assault that is not to say that either spouse has *carte blanche* and that the law in any way condones violence or force in marriage. The whole gamut of assault and battery based statutory offences among others can be brought to bear on a violent spouse whether or not the violence occurs in a sexual context (see para. 7.5.3).

In *R v Caswell* [1984] Crim LR 111 it was held in the Crown Court that the law implied a wife's consent to intercourse and this meant that a lesser sexual act could not be indecent or repugnant to her or alternatively that acts preliminary to or during intercourse could not be regarded as indecent assaults. Where the accused allegedly forced his estranged wife into a public lavatory and forced her to remove her underwear and apply her lips to part of his anatomy, those acts were capable of being common assaults going beyond the lawful persuasion open to a husband whose wife was unwilling to have intercourse.

7.4.2 Other sexual assaults

The laws based on assault and battery aim to protect individuals in society from the unwarranted physical contact of others. In relation to the sexual offences dealt with so far the emphasis has been on the protection of females but males also are protected by the law of indecent assault (s. 15 of the Sexual Offences Act 1956 states 'It is an offence for a person to make an indecent assault on a man [or boy]'. In addition s. 13 of that Act makes it an offence for a man to commit an act of gross indecency with another man, whether in public or private, or to be a party to the commission by a man of such an act with another man, or to procure the commission by a man of such an act with another man. Also s. 16 states it is an offence to assault another person (i.e., it is not confined to males) with intent to commit the unnatural offence of buggery. But s. 13 and s. 16 no longer apply to certain males in certain circumstances who perform those acts. The Sexual Offences Act 1967, s. 1, states that homosexual acts (buggery or gross indecency with another man) in private shall not be an offence provided the parties consent and each have attained 21 years of age.

The issue of consent is of particular relevance to indecent assault as it is to rape. The relevance of any consent given in any instances of sex offences depends on the age of the person assaulted.

7.5 RAPE: ACTUS REUS

The Sexual Offences Act 1956, s. 1(1), states it is an offence for a man to rape a women. Rape is further defined in the Sexual Offences (Amendment) Act 1976, s. 1(1), to the effect that a man commits rape if he has unlawful sexual intercourse with a woman who at the time of the intercourse does not consent to it *and* at that time he knows that she does not consent to the intercourse *or* he is reckless as to whether she consent to it. There are various aspects of this definition that warrant further discussion.

First what is sexual intercourse in the eye of the law? A definition is provided in s. 44 of the 1956 Act. It states: 'Where ... it is necessary to prove sexual intercourse (whether natural or unnatural), it shall not be necessary to prove the completion of the intercourse by the emission of seed, but the intercourse shall be deemed complete upon proof of penetration only'. This means that in so far as the law is concerned the *slightest degree of penetration* by the male sexual organ of the female sexual organ will be sufficient to constitute intercourse without anything more occurring. In the recent Privy Council decision in *Kaitamaki* v *R* [1985] AC 147 her Majesty was advised that in so far as the New Zealand Crimes Act is concerned it is rape if a man continues intercourse once a woman has withdrawn her consent to intercourse after penetration by him has occurred. The

Offences Against the Person

Judicial Committee states that while intercourse is deemed complete on penetration that is a minimum requirement to prove intercourse, that the word complete in that context simply means that intercourse has 'come into existence', it does not mean that it has come to an end. The Committee took the realistic view that sexual intercourse continues until the male withdraws and that being so, if at any point until the male does withdraw, the female indicates that she is no longer consenting then it will be rape for the male wilfully or recklessly to refuse to withdraw. Although Privy Council decisions are not binding in English law they are persuasive and there is no reason why the same view should not be taken in this country. While it may be galling to the male ego and taxing to his self-discipline to have consent withdrawn during intercourse there is no reason why he should not be liable for failing to comply with the female's wishes.

Secondly, the act of sexual intercourse will be *'unlawful'* if it occurs outside of marriage. It is not appreciated by many people today that each and every act of sexual intercourse between persons who are not married to each other is unlawful in this sense. That is not to say that in itself such an act is criminal or illegal. The significance of the distinction between lawful and unlawful intercourse becomes evident in the light of the fourth point.

Thirdly, the act of unlawful non-consensual, sexual intercourse must be performed on *a woman*, a female, to constitute rape. A male cannot be raped in terms of the legal definition of that offence. Such an occurrence, however, would constitute either of the unnatural offences provided for by s. 12 (it is an offence for a person to commit buggery with another person or with an animal) or s. 13 (it is an offence for a man to commit an act of gross indecency with another man) or s. 15 (an indecent assault on a man), subject, of course, to the Sexual Offences Act 1967 (see para. 7.4.2) which allows for homosexual practices in private between consenting males over 21 years of age.

Fourth, sexual intercourse (i.e., the least penetration by the male sexual organ of the female sexual organ) which is outside of marriage (i.e., unlawful) is the serious offence of rape if accompanied by the prescribed *mens rea* and if it occurs *without the consent* of the female whose sexual organ is being penetrated by the male. If, however, the act of intercourse is lawful (i.e., between a couple who are married to each other) then it cannot constitute rape even if the wife does not consent to intercourse on that (or any) occasion.

In all instances of sexual intercourse outside marriage consent on the part of the female is a vital issue. If she has consented then the male has a complete defence to a charge of rape. It is the duty of the prosecution at a rape trial to prove that the female did not consent (*R* v *Harling* [1938] 1 All ER 307). Further, the prosecution must prove that the accused knew she was not consenting or was reckless as to whether she consented or (in the light of the recent decision in *Kaitamaki* v *R* [1985] AC 147) continued the act of sexual intercourse after having been made aware of the fact that the female had withdrawn her consent.

In *R* v *Olugboja* [1982] QB 320 the meaning of the word 'consent' in the Sexual Offences (Amendment) Act 1976, s. 1(1), was in issue. The accused had maintained that the 1976 definition was declaratory of the common law and that at common law rape was unlawful sexual intercourse by force, fear or fraud which negated the victim's consent. Consequently, it was argued, the only threat that vitiates consent is that of violence to the victim or, by analogy to duress, to some close or near relative. Blackmail, moral or economic leverage or other sorts of threats short of death or violence such as in this particular case where the threat was that the girl would not be taken home if she did not consent, would not be sufficient. The court held that the 1976 Act makes no mention of force, fear or fraud. The essence of the offence is a lack of consent. The issue is whether or not the woman consented. Consent can range from desire down to grudging acquiescence but clearly the jury needs to be made aware of the difference between actual consent and submission. Just as there is a scale for consent so too non-consent can range from vigorous, vociferous resistance to mere numbed submissiveness. Furthermore the fact that the rape victim was hitch-hiking or walking alone at night, or was drunk or was wearing a short skirt, is immaterial to whether or not she was raped. That turns solely on whether or not her vagina was penetrated by a male organ without her consent. Contributory negligence or any such doctrine has no part to play in assessing criminal liability.

In the scenario if Sarah did not consent to intercourse with Donald, it is immaterial whether he used force, fear or fraud to have his way, although obviously from an evidential point of view her lack of consent is more easily proved if one or more of those features was present. On the other hand if Sarah did 'consent' because of force, fear or fraud then as has been shown earlier (see para. 7.2.6) her so-called 'consent' is vitiated and will provide the accused with no defence.

The fact that consent is a special defence available for battery and assault based offences has been discussed above (see para.7.2.6) as were the instances when consent is negated (see para. 7.2.6). The same holds true for the offence of rape and in fact s. 1(2) of the Sexual Offences Act 1956 states that it is rape to induce a woman to have sexual intercourse by impersonating her husband. That is another way of stating that consent given in error as a result of a mistake as to the identity induced by the fraud of the accused is not real consent.

Also the other rule that her consent is ineffective where a woman is deceived as to the nature of the act being performed, because of the fraud of the accused, is well illustrated by rape cases. So if a doctor induces a young lady to consent to intercourse having erroneously led her to believe he was performing a 'medical treatment' or cure, then he has committed rape: *R v Flattery* (1877) 2 QBD 410. Likewise in *R v Williams* [1923] 1 KB 340 the accused who was a church choirmaster was found guilty of rape where he had induced a naive woman to consent to intercourse on the understanding that it was an exercise that would improve her breathing and therefore her singing. But the limit of this rule that negates consent is shown by the Australian case *Papadimitropoulos v R* (1957) 98 CLR 249. There the woman, who did not understand English, thought she had been married and therefore engaged in a perfectly moral act when she had intercourse with the man who she thought was her lawful wedded spouse. In fact she was not married; he had deceived her into thinking that what was a rehearsal was an actual wedding. The court said that the deception could not negate her consent to intercourse: '[O]nce the consent is comprehending and actual the inducing causes cannot destroy its reality and leave the man guilty of rape'.

Assume that Donald talks his way into Rex's house and then talks Sarah into freely having sexual intercourse with him. If he induces her to consent by stating

Offences Against the Person

that he is a very wealthy man and that he will marry her and shower her with riches then because she is not deceived as to who he is or as to the nature of the act her consent will preclude Donald being liable for rape even if everything he says about wealth and marriage is a lie. But it is important to note that if, having commenced the act of intercourse, Donald blurts out that everything he has said has been a lie, then Sarah at that point may withdraw the consent previously given and if that happens and it is made clear to Donald, then he will become liable for rape if he does not desist from what he is doing and withdraw immediately from the act of intercourse (see *Kaitamaki* v *R* [1985] AC 147, discussed above).

7.5.1 Mens rea of rape

In short the *mens rea* of rape as embodied in the Sexual Offences (Amendment) Act 1976 is an intention to have sexual intercourse with a woman either knowing that she does not consent or being reckless as to whether she consents. This embodies the House of Lords decision in *DDP* v *Morgan* [1976] AC 182. The accused invited three fellow airmen to his house and suggested that they should all have intercourse with his wife. The other three did not know the accused's wife and did not take him seriously at first, but were induced by his fabrications about his wife's sexual aberrations involving sham resistance. The men dragged her from her bed and despite her struggling and screaming throughout they held her down and each had intercourse with her. The three were convicted of rape and appealed claiming a misdirection. The trial judge had said that the prosecution must prove intent to have unlawful sexual intercourse without her consent and he went on to say that if they honestly believed she was consenting then they would not be guilty, *but* their belief must be a resonable belief. He said:

> It is not enough for [the accused] to rely upon a belief, even though he honestly held it, if it was completely fanciful; contrary to every indication which could be given which would carry some weight with a reasonable man.

The Court of Appeal held that on proof of absence of consent from the circumstances, the accused is presumed to appreciate their significance and an evidential burden is then cast on him to show that he honestly and reasonably believed that she consented. The appeal therefore was dismissed but a point of law of general public importance was permitted to be put to the House of Lords. The issue was whether in rape an accused can properly be convicted notwithstanding that he in fact believed that the woman consented if such belief was not based on reasonable grounds? The House of Lords answer was in the negative and therefore favourable to the accused on the point of law, but this decision did not affect the accused's conviction because the court decided (as it is empowered to do under s. 2(1) of the Criminal Appeal Act 1968) that no miscarriage of justice had or conceivably could have occurred on the facts.

The House of Lords decision on the point of law caused considerable public disquiet and ultimately led to Parliament's inclusion in the Sexual Offences (Amendment) Act 1976 of s. 1(2) which declares:

that if at a trial for a rape offence the jury has to consider whether a man believed that a woman was consenting to sexual intercourse, the presence or absence of reasonable grounds for such a belief is a matter to which the jury is to have regard, in conjunction with any other relevant matters, in considering whether he so believed.

This injunction simply is a counterbalance to the stark decision of the House of Lords. It invites the jury to apply common sense and (as with s. 8 of the Criminal Justice Act — see para. 7.6.2) it entitles the jury to deduce what the accused knew or foresaw from what they believe an ordinary, reasonable man would have known or foreseen in the circumstances. It is a matter for them.

7.5.2 Reckless rape

Rape is a crime of basic intent. Proof of recklessness will satisfy the *mens rea* requirement but what does recklessness mean in this context? Clearly it encompasses *Cunningham* (1957) (conscious risk-taking) type recklessness and until recently there was uncertainty whether or not *Caldwell* (failure to consider an obvious risk) type recklessness would apply. This notion of recklessness is inappropriate to the offence of rape in any instance where the accused pleads that he believed the woman consented. That belief predicates that the accused gave the matter some thought and therefore at first sight it would seem that such a person is precisely the accused that Lord Diplock had in mind in *Metropolitan Police Commissioner* v *Caldwell* [1982] AC 341 (see para. 2.7.4) when he provided the 'escape hatch' that a person could avoid liability if he thought about the matter but wrongly concluded that there was no risk. That, however, is not the case because, according to another passage in his judgment, if the risk would have been obvious to a reasonable man then it should have been obvious to the accused (unless he is abnormal) and is attributed to him, but in relation to rape it remained an issue whether or not an 'obvious risk' meant a risk obvious to the defendant who thought about it or obvious to an ordinary, reasonable man who thought about it. *Caldwell's* case suggested the former, *R* v *Lawrence* [1982] AC 510 suggested the latter. *Elliott* v *C* [1983] 1 WLR 939 interpreted *Caldwell* and *Lawrence* as creating an objective rule or criteria in attributing liability for recklessness and *R* v *Seymour* [1983] 2 AC 493 (see para. 2.7.12) endorsed that interpretation as a rule of general application. In the interim, however, the Court of Appeal in a rape case, *R* v *Mohammed Bashir* (1983) 77 Cr App R 59, had ruled that the trial judge had misdirected the jury with regard to 'recklessness' by introducing the concept of the reasonable man. The proper test as to whether the accused charged with rape acted recklessly was *not* whether the reasonable man would have acted in the same way but whether the actual accused acted recklessly. This reiteration of the traditional subjective approach of ascertaining the actual state of mind of the accused lost some of its assertiveness because the Court of Appeal in so doing expressed the misconception that *Caldwell* and *Lawrence* removed the 'objective' or 'reasonable man' test from the law of recklessness. The subjective approach, however, has been confirmed in so far as reckless rape is concerned by the Court of Appeal in *R* v *Satnam and Kewal* (1984) 78 Cr App R 149. The court quashed the convictions for rape on the basis that the jury were given no direction to the effect that a genuine though mistaken belief that the girl was consenting offered a defence to a charge of reckless rape and then the court went on to state that in effect 'ordinary observers' or 'reasonable men' had no part to play in a direction as to reckless rape. The judge should base his direction as to the definition of rape upon s. 1 of the Sexual Offences (Amendment) Act 1976 and upon *DPP* v *Morgan* [1976] AC 182 *without* regard to *Caldwell* or *Lawrence* which, the court said, were concerned with recklessness in a different context and under a different statute. While this view of the law may be desirable, it is not to say that it is legally correct because the Court of Appeal makes no mention of the House of Lords decision in *R* v *Seymour* where the view was clearly expressed by a majority of the Law Lords that the rule expressed in *Caldwell* and *Lawrence* is of general application.

Given that rape is confirmed as an exception, the position today as stated by the Court of Appeal in *R* v *Satnam and Kewal* (1984) 78 Cr App R 149 is that the trial judge should:

> in dealing with the state of mind of the defendant, first of all direct the jury that before they could convict of rape the Crown had to prove either that the defendant knew the woman did not want to have sexual intercourse, or was reckless as to whether she wanted to or not. If they were sure he knew she did not want to they should find him guilty of rape knowing there to be no consent. If they were not sure about that, then they should find him not guilty of such rape and should go on to consider reckless rape. If they thought he might genuinely have believed that she did want to, even though he was mistaken in his belief, they would find him not guilty. In considering whether his belief was genuine, they should take into account all the relevant circumstances (which could at that point be summarised) and ask themselves whether, in the light of those circumstances, he had reasonable grounds for such a belief. If, after considering those circumstances, they were sure he had no genuine belief that she wanted to, they would find him guilty. If they came to the conclusion that he could not care less whether she wanted to or not, but pressed on regardless, then he would have been reckless and could not have believed that she wanted to, and they would find him guilty of reckless rape.

The latter proposition being based on the dictum of Lawton LJ in *R* v *Kimber* (1983) 77 Cr App R 225 which was considered to provide a practical definition of recklessness in sexual offences generally. There, on a charge of indecent assault the accused had said 'I was not really interested in [the victim's] feelings at all'. The Court of Appeal concluded that:

> [A] reasonable jury would inevitably have decided that he had no honest belief that [the victim] was consenting. His own evidence showed that his attitude to her was one of indifference to her feelings and wishes. This state of mind is aptly described in the colloquial expression, 'couldn't care less'. In law this is recklessness.

This has been reiterated by the Court of Appeal in *R* v *Breckenridge* (1984) 79 Cr App R 244 where it was confirmed that in order to convict in a 'reckless rape' case the jury must be directed to convict only if they find the accused could not care less whether or not the complainant (victim) was consenting. (See now para. 2.7.9 for a summation of the ways in which 'recklessness' currently is defined in relation to various offences and the recent case *R* v *R (SM)* (1984) 79 Cr App R 334.)

7.5.3 Rape of a wife

As the law stands a husband cannot rape his wife: *R* v *Clarke* (1949) 33 Cr App R 216. That he cannot be liable as a principal offender is based on the idea that consent to marriage is also consent to sexual intercourse which cannot be revoked while the marriage subsists: 1 Hall PC 629. This seems to be an unsatisfactory basis for the law today. Family law, which regulates matrimonial relations among other things, recognises situations when the wife (or either spouse for that matter) may withdraw consent to intercourse and in doing so affect the legal position of both the spouses. Policy directs that it is only proper for the wife to make clear the permanence of her withdrawal of consent by some legal act of separation. Currently the law recognises that her assent is revoked if a judicial separation has occurred; if there is in existence an agreement to separate especially if it contains a non-molestation clause; if a matrimonial order including a non-cohabitation clause or a formal non-cohabitation agreement has come into existence and also where a decree nisi has been pronounced leading ultimately to a decree absolute of divorce. In all those situations the criminal law of rape will apply to the 'husband' because he has either consented to give up his matrimonial rights or given his 'wife' grounds to end the marriage. It should be noted, however, that in *R* v *Miller* [1954] 2 QB 282 it was stated that there was no recognised revocation of consent to intercourse by the wife merely by the presentation of a petition for divorce. This is anomalous but still seems to be the law today.

While it is true that, those exceptions aside, a husband cannot rape his wife that does not give a husband *carte blanche*, it gives him no right to use violence to have his way. No matter what his motive he, like everyone else, is subject to the law of assault: common assault, battery, actual bodily harm, wounding and grievous bodily harm (such as false imprisonment, kidnapping etc.) in relation to the way in which he treats his wife. Furthermore it should be remembered that the husband is only exempt as a principal from rape; it has long been the law that he may be guilty as a secondary part to the rape of his wife: *R* v *Lord Audley* (1613) 3 St Tr 402, 1 Hall PC 629. Also it appears from the unsatisfactory decision in *R* v *Cogan* and *R* v *Leak* [1975] 2 All ER 1059 that a husband may be guilty as a secondary party even though the principal is found innocent of the offence (see para. 4.5.6).

7.5.4 Procedure and evidence

As to the procedure and evidence peculiar to a rape trial see Murphy, *A Practical Approach to Evidence*, and Emmins, *A Practical Approach to Criminal Procedure*. It should be noted, however, that the Sexual Offences (Amendment) Act 1976, s. 2(1) restricts the questions or evidence that may be put without the leave of the

Offences Against the Person

judge to a complainant about her sexual experience with any person other than the person accused of raping her. In *R v Viola* [1982] Crim LR 515 the Court of Appeal stated that if the trial judge considers a question in this category relevant, then he has to be satisfied that to refuse to allow it or a series of related questions would be unfair to the accused in that if allowed it might reasonably lead the jury to take a different view of his evidence than if it were not allowed, (see *R v Mills (Leroy)* (1979) 68 Cr App R 327. The judge must decide whether or not such questions or evidence is simply an attack on the character of, and therefore an attempt to undermine the credibility of, the woman or whether those questions were relevant to the issue of consent. The decision often is a difficult one; for example, sometimes such questions may not be seeking to imply that the woman in question is likely to tell lies but to show that she is likely to have consented to sexual intercourse as in *R v Bashir and Manzur* [1969] 3 All ER 692 where the accused sought by such questions to show that the woman was a prostitute and therefore more likely to have consented.

Secondly, s. 4(1) of the 1976 Act protectively restricts the publication of matters likely to enable the victim (complainant) in a rape case to be identified by the public. Overall the substantive and procedural laws relating to rape are an attempt to provide a fair balance in a very difficult area of law. It is an attempt to recognise that the physically more powerful male generally has the ability to overcome the female's resistance and at the same time to take into account the fact that an allegation of rape is easily made sometimes as a result of a change of heart after intercourse for reasons ranging from guilt and remorse to pique and spite. The two statutory provisions mentioned above show the law attempting to protect females from unwarranted aspersions as to their character and to protect their privacy after the harrowing ordeal that rape and its aftermath all too often entail.

7.6 HOMICIDE

From a practical point of view for the student of criminal law homicide, which is simply the killing by one human being of another human being, attracts far more attention that its occurrence in daily life deserves. Homicide, causing the death of another, is not necessarily a crime. For legal purposes homicides are divided into two categories: those which are lawful and those which are not. The former category includes: (a) killing an enemy soldier in battle; (b) formal execution by sentence of a court (this could still apply, e.g., for treason during time of war and piracy on the high seas); (c) killing in self-defence (including the defence of others and those instances covered by s.3(1) of the Criminal Law Act 1967, see para. 6.6.1); and (d) causing death by misadventure (blameless accidents and the like). In these relatively rare instances of lawful or justified homicide there is no offence committed even though death is caused deliberately or intentionally. There is deemed to be no *actus reus* or offence because the law says that killing in each of those instances is not unlawful. The category of unlawful homicides which are each criminal offences includes: (a) murder, (b) manslaughter, (c) child destruction, (d) infanticide, (e) statutory offences such as causing death by the reckless driving of a motor vehicle contrary to s. 1 of the Road Traffic Act 1972. Manslaughter, as will be seen later (para. 7.6.3), is divisible into two categories each of which can be established in a number of different ways.

From the point of view of publicity, lucky will be the common lawyer who has the limelight of a manslaughter let alone a murder trial at some stage in his career. From society's point of view, however, killing another person is morally, ethically and socially abhorrent. To do it deliberately is considered the most antisocial and one of the most serious crimes, if not the most serious crime in our law. Fortunately from the point of view of personal security offences involving death are relatively rare, but despite that they are significant in that the modern notions of *mens rea* in the law were largely developed in connection with those offences.

Originally, back in the ancient annals of our legal history, to have caused the death of another was sufficient to warrant liability and punishment. In modern terminology the causing of another's death in those days was an offence of strict liability, an absolute offence, an offence for which no excuse would be entertained. Today the fact that death has been caused no longer carries automatic liability with it, the emphasis has shifted from the fact of death to the *mens rea* or state of mind of the person responsible for it. This means that a jury (or a majority at best) must be convinced beyond reasonable doubt that the accused not only voluntarily caused the victim's death but also that he did so with one of the guilty states of mind specified by the law. Earlier in Chapter 2 all this was summed up (a) in the concept *'actus reus non facit nisi mens sit rea'* and (b) in the knowledge that what amounts to *mens rea* varies from offence to offence. These points have been illustrated already by the discussion in this chapter of non-fatal offences against the person and are further illustrated by the law of homicide and in particular by the offence of murder.

7.6.1 Actus reus of unlawful homicides

This generic category is divided into a number of offences in each of which the central core of the *actus reus* is the same, i.e., voluntarily causing the death of another human being by an act or omission (see para. 1.8 and para. 7.3.3 for a general review of the authorities upon the fact of causation). Generally, however, that is only one aspect of the *actus reus* which, depending on the crime in question may have other conditions or circumstances which equally have to be proved and which vary from crime to crime. The different categories of unlawful homicide, however, are explainable not so much by technical variation in *actus reus* but by reference to variations in the *mens rea* that is to be proved in each instance. Manslaughter, child destruction and infanticide were all developed as a means of ameliorating the law of murder at a time when the penalty for that offence was itself death so as to give recognition to the fact that not all killing is deliberate or in certain circumstances, even if deliberate, as blameworthy as other killings. For example *deliberately* killing a person who is dying slowly in great agony and who begs the accused to put him out of his misery may be seen as less abhorrent than the drunken driver's *reckless* or *negligent* killing of his passenger or a pedestrian.

In relation to unlawful homicides, unless a statute specifies to the contrary, the prosecution must prove that the accused unlawfully caused the death of another human being who was within the Queen's peace (i.e., the jurisdiction) and that

Offences Against the Person

the victim died within a year and a day of the last death-causing act of the accused.

Dealing with each of these requirements in turn, first the difference between lawful and unlawful homicide has been discussed above. The important instances of justified killing are where it results from the use of reasonable force in the circumstances used in the prevention of crime or in effecting or assisting in the lawful arrest of offenders or suspected offenders or of persons unlawfully at large: Criminal Law Act 1967, s. 3(1), which probably includes self-defence and defence of others at common law (see para. 6.6.1). Also a killing is lawful where death results from misadventure, for example, from a pure accident such as the doing of some lawful act without negligence.

Secondly the requirement that there be the death of a human being is not as straightforward as it first appears. The law is imprecise as to when an individual becomes, and when he ceases to be, a human being. At common law the unborn child was not considered a human being and therefore was not protected by the law that punished unlawful homicides. The child had to be completely expelled from its mother's body to obtain that status and the protection that goes with it: see *R* v *Reeves* (1839) 9 C & P 25. This position partly explains the creation by Parliament of the offence of child destruction in the Infant Life (Preservation) Act 1929 which punishes the wilful destruction of the life of a child capable of being born alive (i.e., a child alive in its mother's womb for more than twenty-eight weeks: s. 1(2)).

At the opposite end of life's spectrum similar issues of uncertainty arise as to an individual's status in the eye of the law. Currently the law is not certain as to when an individual might be considered dead and therefore no longer a human being. The law and the politicians have abrogated that difficult decision to the medical profession: see *R* v *Malcherek* [1981] 2 All ER 422.

Thirdly the killing must be within 'the Queen's peace'. This has two aspects to it:

(a) If 'the Queen' is at war the killing of her enemies in battle is lawful: *R* v *Page* [1954] 1 QB 170 but even in wartime the killing of the enemy in certain circumstances, such as the shooting of prisoners and other breaches of the Geneva Convention may constitute a war crime in so far as international law is concerned.

(b) Those words 'within the Queen's Peace' can also mean that (wartime aside) the crime must occur within the jurisdiction of the English courts. That means that it must have been committed by someone (irrespective of his nationality) within England or Wales or their territorial waters or on a British ship or aircraft. But Parliament has provided that certain crimes are triable in English courts no matter where they are committed provided the accused is a British citizen in terms of the British Nationality Act 1981. Murder and manslaughter, by s. 9 of the Offences against the Person Act 1861, are made offences of this sort.

Fourthly, the victim's death must occur within a year and a day of the last injury caused or inflicted by the accused: *R* v *Dyson* [1908] 2 KB 454. This time-limit is purely arbitrary and is not based on medical science or deduced logic. If the person injured by the accused lived for more than the specified time then it is to be assumed that his subsequent death is attributable to some other cause even though medical science today has advanced to the point where the cause of death might be pin-pointed with a degree of accuracy and certainty unavailable in 1908. The rule remains part of our law today for outmoded reasons of precedent and policy. Does it serve any useful purpose? If the cause of death can be attributed with accuracy to the accused thirteen months, or even years after an injury caused by him, why should he escape punishment on the technicality of an arbitrary time-limit? It is anomalous that the doctor who injects his wealthy, diabetic wife with insulin in such a way as to cause her immediate death would be liable for murder and the doctor who injected her in such a way as to produce her death 13 months later would not and the doctor whose injection sent the wife into an irreversible coma which lasts for five years could not be liable for murder but could be liable for attempted murder among other offences.

7.6.2 Murder

Murder has the *actus reus* of unlawful homicide as defined in the preceding paragraphs. In addition to proving the four aspects of the *actus reus* the prosecution must prove that the accused had a specified state of mind when he killed or caused the injury that resulted subsequently in the victim's death. This has been discussed already in considerable detail in the chapter on *mens rea* (see paras 2.6.1 and 2.6.2).

In English law murder is not defined by statute. At common law it was traditionally defined as unlawful homicide (the *actus reus*) with malice aforethought (the *mens rea*). Those two words 'malice aforethought' have a special meaning in the context of criminal law but what the meaning is has varied from time to time. The modern law is contained in five significant cases: *R* v *Vickers* [1957] 2 QB 664; *DPP* v *Smith* [1961] AC 290; *Hyam* v *DPP* [1975] AC 55; *R* v *Cunningham* [1982] AC 566 and *R* v *Moloney* [1985] 2 WLR 648.

Initially if the accused was found to have caused the death of another person he was strictly liable no matter what the explanation and whether or not the death was deliberately caused. Until the Homicide Act 1957 the doctrine of constructive murder deemed a person guilty of murder if he happened to cause a death during the commission of another intended crime, such as rape or robbery. If the prosecution proved that the accused intended to commit the crime that he was engaged in when he caused the death of another then he was held liable for murder; he was said to have the malice aforethought of murder. Likewise if he caused the death of an officer of justice while intentionally resisting arrest or affecting or assisting an escape or rescue from legal custody. In both those instances the prospect of death occurring may never have entered the accused's head and certainly not been intended by him.

The Homicide Act 1957 purported in s. 1 to abolish these notions of 'constructive malice' which attributed an intention to kill in situations where death was neither desired nor foreseen. However in that same year the Court of Appeal in *R* v *Vickers* [1957] 2 QB 664 held that an accused who had caused death while intending to cause grievous bodily harm was guilty of murder. That decision meant that despite the Homicide Act the courts still recognised and

Offences Against the Person

retained a vestige of the notion of constructive malice. After all the intention to cause grievous bodily harm is the necessary mental state for the specific crime provided by s. 18 of the Offences against the Person Act 1861, namely causing grievous bodily harm with intent. The person who intends to cause such harm may not in every instance have thought that, or foreseen that, death might result, let alone intended it to happen. The correctness, however, of the decision in *Vickers* was confirmed by the majority of the House of Lords in *Hyam* v *DPP* [1975] AC 55 and the doubts raised by Lord Diplock dissenting in that case on this point have been laid to rest finally by the House of Lords in *R* v *Cunningham* [1982] AC 566 and reaffirmed by that court in the leading case on the *mens rea* of murder, *R* v *Moloney* [1985] 2 WLR 648.

Before looking in more detail at what was the leading authority (*Hyam's* case) and what is today the leading authority on the *mens rea* of murder (Moloney's case), it should be noted first that four years after the Homicide Act and *Vicker's* case there was another attempt to revive the doctrine of constructive malice but this time on a much broader basis than *Vicker's* case allowed.

The notorious decision of the House of Lords in *DPP* v *Smith* [1961] AC 290 appeared to resurrect the full doctrine of constructive malice aforethought (i.e., implying intention or foresight to the accused) because it expounded an objective test (rather than a subjective one) as to the state of mind of the accused at the time he caused the victim's death. In that case the accused was driving away a car full of stolen goods. A policeman ordered him to stop and when it appeared he would not, the policeman threw himself on to the bonnet of the car in an attempt to make the accused stop. On the contrary the accused drove on in an erratic way calculated to shake the policeman off the car. This eventually happened with the result that the policeman was run over by an oncoming vehicle and later died from the injuries which he had received. The accused was convicted at first instance of murder and that verdict (despite having been altered by the Court of Appeal to manslaughter) was confirmed by the House of Lords.

In effect the House of Lords was saying that a person could be convicted of murder if he intentionally did an unlawful act and was aware of the circumstances, if that act in those circumstances would have led a reasonable man to decide that death or grievous bodily harm (in accordance with *Vicker's* case) would result.

In other words if it was proved that the accused (Smith) knew the policeman was clinging to the car and that he (Smith) had intentionally tried to shake the policeman from the vehicle by his mode of driving that would be sufficient for criminal liability if a reasonable person would have concluded that such conduct was likely to cause death or grievous bodily harm. If that was the law it would not be necessary to prove that the actual accused intended or foresaw death or grievous bodily harm as certain or even as a remote possibility.

As has been pointed out already the acceptance into our law of the doctrine '*actus non facit reum nisi mens sit rea*' was a recognition of advances in notions of civilisation, civil liberties, justice and freedom in that a man is to be liable for a serious, imprisonable offence, if and only if he has a guilty mind. In a society such as ours it is the accused's state of mind that should dictate his liability and not the state of mind of some hypothetical, reasonable bystander.

In response to the general public antipathy shown for the regressive and dangerous nature of the House of Lords decision, Parliament passed into law s. 8 of the Criminal Justice Act 1967. Whether or not it overrules the bad decision in *Smith's* case is uncertain. The section states that:

A court or jury, in determining whether a person has committed an offence:

(a) shall not be bound in law to infer that he intended or foresaw a result of his actions by reason only of its being a natural and probable consequence of those actions; but

(b) shall decide whether he did intend or foresee that result by reference to all the evidence, drawing such inferences from the evidence as appear proper in the circumstances.

Clearly the section does not prevent a jury deciding on its own initiative that the accused intended death because death was the natural and probable consequence of his actions *but* it does preclude the jury being mandatorily directed to reach such a conclusion by the trial judge. In *R* v *Wallet* [1968] 2 QB 367 the Court of Appeal allowed an appeal against a conviction for murder and substituted a verdict of manslaughter because the trial judge had suggested the 'ordinary' and 'reasonable' man test of foresight. The Court of Appeal considered that this was contrary to s. 8 which required the jury to apply a subjective test and seek to find what in fact the particular accused intended or foresaw.

Whatever the effect of s. 8 on *Smith's* case it was thought a definitive classification of the states of mind sufficient to amount to the malice aforethought (i.e., the *mens rea*) of murder was contained in *Hyam* v *DPP* [1975] AC 55. Arguably proof of any of the four states of mind described in that case, and *only* any of those four (together with proof of an appropriate *actus reus*) would produce a conviction for murder.

The jury, it was thought, was to be satisfied that the accused had one of the following states of mind:

(a) intention to kill;
(b) an intention to cause grievous bodily harm;
(c) foresight that death was a (highly) probable consequence of his conduct;
(d) foresight that grievous bodily harm was a (highly) probable consequence of his conduct.

Even though the degree of culpability varied between the first and the last of these instances, proof of any of them, it was thought, would constitute the necessary malice aforethought of murder. In other words malice aforethought or the *mens rea* of murder was thought to be proof of either an intention to kill or to cause grievous bodily harm *or* foresight that either death or grievous bodily harm was a (highly) probable consequence of one's actions.

Clearly under such a view and if that was the substantive law then murder was not similar to s. 18 of the Offences against the Person Act 1861 which requires proof specifically of intention to produce the forbidden consequence (in that instance, grievous bodily harm). *Hyam* appeared to say that proof of other less

Offences Against the Person

blameworthy states of mind than intention to kill would suffice for murder as a matter of law. Consequently this offence was strictly speaking, following *Hyam*, *not* a crime of specific intent. However, for certain purposes it was treated as a crime of specific intent (for example, in relation to the defence of intoxication, see para. 6.3.8). Following *Hyam* it appeared that although the prosecution *did not need to rely on proving intention to kill or an intention to cause grievous bodily harm* (because foresight of either was then thought to suffice), if it did so rely, it would prove such intention then and still can do so today by proving in either of the former cases direct or oblique intention (see para. 2.5 and for what constitutes grievous bodily harm see para. 7.3.3).

On the issue of foresight of death or grievous bodily harm, *Hyam's* case raised some problems. The trial judge had said that the accused's foresight of either of these consequences had to be highly probable at least. But in the House of Lords each of the majority judges had a different opinion as to what the degree of culpable foresight should be. One said (agreeing with the trial judge) that foresight of those consequences must be highly probable. A second said it need be probable and a third said that the test was whether 'the accused intended to expose the victim to a serious risk of death or grievous bodily harm'. The test propounded by each judge varied considerably in degree. The third test of foresight was much more easy for the prosecution to satisfy to obtain a conviction than if it had to prove the accused foresaw that death or grievous bodily harm was a highly probable consequence of his conduct. Recently in *R v Moloney, The Times*, 22 December 1983, the Court of Appeal appeared to endorse the third formulation noted in *Hyam's* case that the prosecution must prove that the accused foresaw a serious risk of either consequence. All of these problems and uncertainties in theory have now been resolved by the House of Lords judgment in *Moloney's* case. Now it can be stated with certainty that if the prosecution proves foresight even of a high probability then it is not entitled to a conviction unless the facts are such that it is appropriate for the judge to leave to the jury for their consideration the foresight of the accused as evidence from which intention might properly be inferred in the circumstances.

Although since *Moloney* it should be of historical signficance only, the fourth category in *Hyam*, i.e., foresight of grievous bodily harm, was *not* confined to foresight of injuries likely to cause death, consequently the risk was that if it was proved that an accused foresaw that he would cause grievous bodily harm he would be guilty of murder if the victim died within a year and a day of the infliction of the injuries. This was despite the fact that he had not foreseen, and indeed that even a reasonable man would not have foreseen, that death was highly probable or even a probable risk. The great width of this purported category of malice aforethought is obvious and it is precisely because of that and because in the past the courts have shied away from saying that proof of a reckless state of mind is sufficient to constitute malice aforethought that it appeared both innovative and dangerous. That fourth category in *Hyam* was in reality a recognition of recklessness as malice aforethought under the guise of foresight. In effect foresight of grievous bodily harm could have been misused to make liable for murder the man who consciously took the risk that death might result and therefore was a reckless man in the *Cunningham* (1957) sense *or* in the *Caldwell* (1981) sense if he failed even to consider the risk that death might result if that risk was obvious to a reasonable man. The danger of too wide a category is that it may ultimately have reintroduced the objective notions of liability in *DPP v Smith* [1961] AC 290 which are objectionable to many in a society such as ours, and this was clearly appreciated recently by their lordships in unanimously agreeing with the judgment of Lord Bridge of Harwich in *Moloney* that foresight of consequence is *not* as a matter of substantive law sufficient to satisfy the *mens rea* of murder. That offence was reaffirmed as a true specific intent offence requiring proof of intention alone to cause either death or grievous bodily harm (from which death results).

7.6.3 Categories of manslaughter

Manslaughter is principally unlawful homicide without malice aforethought as defined by *R* v *Moloney* [1985] 2 WLR 648. Manslaughter is divisible into two categories: voluntary and involuntary manslaughter. The former category can be further subdivided into (a) provocation, (b) diminished responsibility and (c) suicide pacts.

The latter category, involuntary manslaughter, also can be subdivided into (a) manslaughter based on negligence (sometimes referred to as killing by gross negligence) or reckless and (b) manslaughter based on an unlawful act (sometimes referred to as constructive manslaughter).

7.6.4 Voluntary manslaughter

The law may permit an accused who otherwise has all the qualifications or attributes to be convicted of murder to be found guilty of manslaughter if any one of the three excuses or mitigating factors is present, either provocation or diminished responsibility or a suicide pact.

In short each of these events or occurrences may reduce murder to manslaughter. None of them, if accepted by the jury, will provide a complete defence resulting in the accused's acquittal.

7.6.5 Provocation

The Homicide Act 1957, s. 3, states:

> Where on a charge of murder there is evidence on which the jury can find that the person charged was provoked (whether by things done or by things said or by both together) to lose his self-control, the question whether the provocation was enough to make a reasonable man do as he did shall be left to be determined by the jury; and in determining that question the jury shall take into account everything both done and said according to the effect which, in their opinion, it would have on a reasonable man.

The reason why provocation is recognised as part of our substantive law in relation only to murder lies in the fact that where the commission of offences other than murder is involved a court can take the provocation of the accused into account in passing sentence upon him whereas murder carries a fixed penalty of life imprisonment. Without a specific rule that provocation may reduce murder to manslaughter it could not play any part in ameliorating the outcome for a person convicted or likely to be convicted of murder.

Today, if a person accused of murder was provoked by his victim into so losing his self-control that he killed, he should be guilty of manslaughter. The wording of the Homicide Act, s. 3, is explained to some extent by some knowledge of the previous law. Prior to that Act the common law had required that provocation could only arise from the acts of the victim (by implication, words alone were insufficient to provoke) and those acts had to be such that they would have caused a reasonable man to lose his self-control. Also the old common law had required that the killing must have occurred in the heat of the moment, that there had to be a reasonable correlation between the provocation and the retaliation and also that it was a question of law for the judge whether or not there was sufficient provocation on the facts of the case. Clearly, s. 3 has affected those old common law rules though retaining the objective, reasonable man test. Parliament attempted to state a rule based on a generally accepted standard of conduct which would be applicable to everyone disregarding individual idiosyncracies of temperament or mentality that might make an individual easily provoked. It is this area of peculiar susceptibility to provocation, mental abnormality, subnormal intelligence and excitable dispositions that, in relation to the reasonable man test, has been the main issue in this area of law since the passing of the Homicide Act 1957. The policy behind the retention of the objective test was to foster in society notions of self-control and restraint, but should the only issue for the law be whether or not the accused lost his self-control? Given that a person convicted of manslaughter is still liable to a term of imprisonment up to a maximum of life imprisonment should it make any difference whether or not he was hot-tempered and more easily or even unreasonably provoked? Is there any logic or reason in that person being guilty of murder whereas a man who lost his self-control 'reasonably' should be guilty of manslaughter. Both could be found guilty of the lesser homicide and justice between them regulated by the difference in the sentence imposed on each.

Currently the law continues to apply a reasonable man test. In the past the reasonable man was not excitable (see *R* v *Lesbini* [1914] 3 KB 1116), or drunk (see *R* v *McCarthy* [1954] 2 QB 105) or impotent (see *Bedder* v *DPP* [1954] 2 All ER 801). In the latter case the House of Lords had held that the test of provocation was not the effect on a reasonable impotent man (in that instance the accused killed a prostitute who had jeered at his inability to have sexual intercourse and this insulted him in a particularly painful way) but on a reasonable man.

Presumably the view was taken that a reasonable man, because he would not be impotent, would not have got himself into such a predicament. Partly in response to this case the Homicide Act 1957,, s. 3 (quoted above), makes it clear that today the issue of provocation is one of fact for the jury in light of all the circumstances and this is so even though the judge is of the opinion that no reasonable jury could find that there was sufficient provocation to cause a loss of self-control: *R* v *Gilbert* (1977) 66 Cr App R 237. Clearly the judge cannot now withdraw the defence from the jury on the ground that no reasonable man in the circumstance would have been provoked because that question 'shall be left to be determined by the jury'. Although the judge cannot dictate whether or not a reasonable man would have lost self-control he can advise the jury as to the attributes of the reasonable man. In the leading case since s. 3 became law, *DPP* v *Camplin* [1978] AC 705, a boy aged 15 years had been forced by a man to submit to the offence of buggery and later, when his violator laughed at him, the boy struck the man with a heavy frying-pan and killed him. Despite a plea of provocation the boy was convicted of murder. The trial judge had said that only if a man of full age and maturity would have been provoked into striking the deceased would the defence apply. The House of Lords held on appeal that s. 3 had overruled *Bedder's* case and now allowed the particular characteristics of the accused to be taken into account. Today, according to Lord Diplock, a judge should explain to the jury that the reasonable man:

> is a person having the power of self-control to be expected of an ordinary person of the sex and age of the accused, but in other respects sharing such of the accused's characteristics as they think would affect the gravity of the provocation to him; and that the question is not merely whether such a person would in like circumstances be provoked to lose his self-control but also whether he would react to the provocation as the accused did.

The effect of *Camplin* would seem to be that today the jury must first clothe themselves in the accused's characteristics and attributes, normal or abnormal, and then assess the effect of the provocation on such a person. The difficulty for the jury in such an exercise and the mental gymnastics they may have to perform are obvious and well illustrated by *R* v *Raven* [1982] Crim LR 51. There the accused, who was charged with murder, was found to have a physical age of 22 years but a mental age approximately that of a nine year old and in addition he had been a squatter for some time. The reasonable man in such an instance is someone who has lived the same type of life as the accused for 22 years but who has his mental retardation. Furthermore the *Camplin* test means that the reasonable man might be a criminal, e.g., as burglar or a blackmailer (see *Edwards* v *R* [1973] AC 648 where a blackmailer claimed to be provoked into stabbing the victim).

Finally in relation to provocation the old common law rules that the killing must be in the heat of the moment, that there must be a reasonable correlation between provocation and retaliation and that provocation must move from the deceased all remain, but are affected by s. 3 to the extent that they are no longer rules but remain as matters of great evidential significance, in that no jury is likely to believe that the accused was provoked unless these factors are satisfied, (see *R* v *Brown* [1972] 2 QB 229; *R* v *Twine* [1967] Crim LR 710 and *R* v *Davies* [1975] QB 691).

7.6.6 Diminished responsibility

The Homicide Act 1957, s. 2 states:

> (1) Where a person kills or is a party to the killing of another, he shall not be convicted of murder if he was suffering from such abnormality of mind

(whether arising from a condition of arrested or retarded development of mind or any inherent causes or induced by disease or injury) as substantially impaired his mental responsibility for his acts and omissions in doing or being a party to the killing.

(2) On a charge of murder, it shall be for the defence to prove that the person charged is by virtue of this section not liable to be convicted of murder.

(3) A person who but for this section would be liable, whether as principal or as accessory, to be convicted of murder shall be liable instead to be convicted of manslaughter.

(4) The fact that one party to a killing is by virtue of this section not liable to be convicted of murder shall not affect the question whether the killing amounted to murder in the case of any other party to it.

Diminished responsibility is a defence only to murder. Equally the prosecution may choose to charge an accused with manslaughter on the basis of diminished responsibility rather than charging that person with murder. Where it is raised as a defence the accused (as with insanity, of which diminished responsibility is a version) must prove on a balance of probabilities that he was suffering from mental abnormality in which case he will be found not guilty of murder but guilty of manslaughter unless the prosecution (who may consider the accused a danger to society) is able to prove beyond reasonable doubt that he is in fact insane. Failing that, the judge on a verdict of manslaughter has a wide discretion as to what to do with the accused whose plea of diminished responsibility is successful. The same states of mind generally will constitute insanity (see para. 6.1) and diminished responsibility, consequently the plea of diminished responsibility has eclipsed insanity as a defence because the sentencing prospects are more varied and less daunting. To plead diminished responsibility successfully the accused must suffer from an abnormality or disease of the mind (unlike insanity, however, whether or not he appreciates what he is doing and appreciates that it is wrong, are immaterial). That state of mind must be shown to have been caused by arrested or retarded development, some inherent cause or injury or by disease. Finally that abnormality must be shown to have substantially impaired his mental responsibility for his acts and omissions in killing or being a party to the killing. What is 'substantial' is an issue for the jury to decide in such cases but according to *R v Lloyd* [1967] 1 QB 175 while the impairment need not be total it must be more than trivial in nature. The clearest formulation of the attributes of diminished responsibility are contained in the judgment of Lord Parker in *R v Byrne* [1960] 2 QB 396 at 403 where he said:

Abnormality of mind, which has to be contrasted with the time-honoured expression in the M'Naughten Rules defect of reason, means a state of mind so different from that of ordinary human beings that the reasonable man would term it abnormal. It appears to us to be wide enough to cover the mind's activities in all its aspects, not only the perception of physical acts and matters, and the ability to form a rational judgment as to whether an act is right or wrong, but also the ability to exercise will power to control physical acts in accordance with that rational judgment. The expression 'mental responsibility for his acts' points to a consideration of the extent to which the accused's mind is answerable for his physical acts which must include a consideration of the extent of his ability to exercise will power to control his physical acts.

In the recent case of *R v Gittens* [1984] QB 698 the Court of Appeal suggested that the effect of alcohol or drugs on the accused should be ignored by the jury in deciding what they think the substantial cause of the accused's behaviour might be, since as a general rule abnormality of mind induced by those substances is not due to inherent causes and therefore not within s. 2(1) of the Homicide Act 1957. That is not to say that prolonged misuse of drink or drugs as in the case of alcoholism may not amount to an inherent cause of mental abnormality. Such instances aside the jury should disregard the effect of drink or drugs and look to see if there are other truly inherent causes present which substantially impaired the accused's mental responsibility. Furthermore the test of diminished responsibility is *not* whether 'a person can be described in popular language as partially insane or on the borderline of insanity'. Evidence of some degree of abnormality less than that could justify a verdict of manslaughter: *R v Seers* (1984) 79 Cr App R 261 where the accused who suffered from a serious depressive illness was granted the benefit of the defence even though he could not be said to be partially insane or on the borderline of insanity.

7.6.7 Suicide pact

The Homicide Act 1957, s. 4, states:

(1) It shall be manslaughter, and shall not be murder, for a person acting in pursuance of a suicide pact between him and another to kill the other or be a party to the other being killed by a third person.

(2) Where it is shown that a person charged with the murder of another killed the other or was a party to his being killed, it shall be for the defence to prove that the person charged was acting in pursuance of a suicide pact between him and the other.

(3) For the purposes of this section 'suicide pact' means a common agreement between two or more persons having for its object the death of all of them, whether or not each is to take his own life, but nothing done by a person who enters into a suicide pact shall be treated as done by him in pursuance of the pact unless it is done while he has the settled intention of dying in pursuance of the pact.

Where the accused has deliberately killed another person he would normally be guilty of murder but he may be found guilty of manslaughter if he can prove on a balance of probabilities that the killing was pursuant to an agreement whereby he was to have killed both the victim and then himself. His intention also to die at the time of the killing is all-important. If there was a suicide pact and the deceased killed himself then the other party or parties would be guilty of the offence of aiding, abetting, counselling or procuring the suicide of another under s. 2 of the Suicide Act 1961 which is punishable by up to 14 years' imprisonment.

Offences Against the Person

7.6.8 Involuntary manslaughter

In these instances (killing by gross negligence, killing by a reckless act and killing by an unlawful act) the accused has unjustifiably killed another (i.e., caused an unlawful homicide) but without sufficient *mens rea* (malice aforethought) to be convicted of murder.

Killing by gross negligence has already been discussed in detail in chapter 2 including Lord Hewart's words in *R v Bateman* (1925) 19 Cr App R 8. Basically negligence is a failure to exercise that degree of care which a reasonable man would have exercised in the circumstances. It can also be doing things which in the circumstances a reasonable man would not have done, or failing to foresee the consequences of one's actions which a reasonable man would have foreseen. Manslaughter by gross negligence necessitates the prosecution proving that in the circumstances a reasonable man would have foreseen that if he acted or failed to act in the way the accused acted or failed to act somebody would almost certainly be killed. Clearly the foresight for gross negligence must be of a high probability at least.

Manslaughter arising from an omission or failure to act has been discussed in chapter 1. There must be in effect a failure to perform a duty (which may arise in a number of ways) which, provided the death which resulted was not intended so as to amount to the malice aforethought of murder, will lead to a manslaughter charge.

7.6.9 Killing recklessly

An accused may also commit the offence of involuntary manslaughter where he is reckless as to the harm he may by his conduct or omission have inflicted upon another. Thus where the death or the causing of grievous bodily harm upon another is foreseen by an accused not as a high probability (for that may lead a jury, properly directed, to the inescapable conclusion or inference that he intended to kill or cause grievous bodily harm, i.e., that he had the *mens rea* of murder, see *R v Moloney* [1985] 2 WLR 648) but as a consequence of some lesser degree of probability he can be said to be reckless. This conscious risk-taking is *Cunningham*-(1957)-type recklessness and it can be said that this constitutes manslaughter. This would also appear to be the case where the risk of death or grievous bodily harm as a consequence of an accused's conduct would be obvious to a reasonable man, i.e., *Caldwell* type recklessness see *R v Seymour* [1983] 2 AC 493).

Where by either form of recklessness the consequence of an accused's conduct that would or could be foreseen was a degree of harm less than grievous bodily harm upon a victim, e.g., actual bodily harm, then the death of the victim could only amount to manslaughter (see *R v Pike* [1961] Crim LR 547). All the above situations would still amount to manslaughter where the accused recklessly omitted to act, see *R v Stone and Dobinson* [1977] QB 354.

7.6.10 Manslaughter by unlawful act

This category of involuntary manslaughter, sometimes called constructive manslaughter is the most significant and the most difficult. The doctrine of constructive murder held a man liable for murder if the death of an individual followed the commission of a violent crime or any 'felony' (see Introduction), such as rape or robbery, likewise the parallel doctrine of constructive manslaughter developed at common law to deem an accused liable for manslaughter if death was caused in the course of performing any unlawful act even if such acts were civil wrongs (i.e., torts) which did not also amount to criminal offences, e.g., if the accused accidentally caused the death of another person while trespassing on that person's land. Today the position would seem to be that a person can be charged with unlawful act or constructive manslaughter if the act causing death amounted to a criminal offence (this will generally be the case because of the width of the common law offences of assault and battery) and provided it was likely to cause some harm. In *R v Larkin* [1943] 1 All ER 217, where the accused waved a razor about intending to frighten his mistress's lover, and then inadvertently slipped and in consequence cut the throat of their mistress, the Court of Criminal Appeal said:

> Where the act which a person is engaged in performing is unlawful, then, if at the same time it is a dangerous act, that is, an act which is likely to injure another person, and quite inadvertently he causes the death of that other person by that act, then he is guilty of manslaughter.

The producing of a razor or knife or gun in order to frighten is to use such an object for an unlawful purpose. That in itself amounts to a common law assault. If accidental death is then caused the requirements for a manslaughter conviction are satisfied, see *R v Hall* (1961) 45 Cr App R 366 (see, however, the discussion of *R v Dawson (Nolan and Walmsley), The Times*, 23 March 1985, below), likewise if a person is accidentally killed while fleeing from the accused who put him in fear, see *R v Mackie* (1973) 57 Cr App R 453. In one of the leading authorities on unlawful act manslaughter, *R v Church* (1965) 49 Cr App R 206, Edmund-Davies J said:

> the unlawful act must be such as all sober and reasonable people would inevitably recognise must subject the other person to, at least, the risk of some harm resulting therefrom, albeit not serious harm.

It is clear from this and from *Larkin's* case that it is unnecessary for the accused to know that the act is dangerous or unlawful or to show that he foresaw any possibility of harm to the deceased. It is sufficient if sober and reasonable people would have recognised or foreseen the danger. This does not mean that the test for unlawful act manslaughter is purely objective. This offence is a crime of basic intent and this means that at least the accused must be proved to have intent (direct or oblique) to do the acts which constituted the unlawful act or be shown to have been reckless (in either sense explained in chapter 2) as to whether or not the unlawful act occurred. Provided that much is proved then whether or not he foresaw the consequential harm or injury is irrelevant. This is confirmed in *DPP v Newbury and Jones* [1977] AC 500 where youths pushed stones off a railway bridge on to a passing train killing the guard. Those accused were convicted of manslaughter and the House of Lords held on appeal that an accused can be properly so convicted even if he did not foresee that his act might cause harm to another. However, in *R v Dalby* [1982] 1 All ER 916 the new notions were introduced that the unlawful act must be directed at the victim and likely to cause immediate injury, but the law as stated in *Newbury's* case seems to have been unaffected (at least that should be so in most cases) as shown by the subsequent decisions in *R v Pagett* (1983) 76 Cr App R 279 and *R v Mitchell* [1983] QB 741. In *Pagett* the issue was whether the accused could be convicted of manslaughter when the victim's death resulted from the intervening act of a third person, in this instance a policeman who had fired a gun at the accused who was holding the victim hostage and the victim was killed. Either the accused's assault on the victim in putting her in the line of fire or the unlawfulness of his shooting at the policeman which caused the policeman to fire back would satisfy the requirement of an unlawful act. No mention was made of the need in the latter instance for that act to be directed at the victim. Likewise in *Mitchell's* case where the accused pushed in a queue causing an old woman to fall and break her leg (an injury from which she subsequently died) and the accused on appeal (relying on *Dalby*) claimed that his unlawful act was not directed at the victim. The court rejected the argument and held that the doctrine of transferred malice (see *R v Latimer* (1886) 17 QBD 359 in chapter 2) applied to unlawful act manslaughter and that the identity of the victim was irrelevant. While the unlawful act it seems need not be aimed at the victim and while the identity of the victim would appear to be irrelevant, the unlawful act must be one which all sober and reasonable people would realise was likely to cause some, albeit not serious, harm. The recent Court of Appeal decision in *R v Dawson (Nolan and Walmsley), The Times*, 23 March 1985 (the facts of which are outlined in para. 7.3.3), held that the requisite harm sufficient to constitute the *actus reus* of manslaughter would be caused if the unlawful act (attempted robbery wearing masks and brandishing weapons in that instance) so shocked the victim as to cause him physical injury (in that instance a heart attack from which he died). The victim had for two years prior to the incident and his death, suffered from a severe heart disease and had had heart attacks for which he was receiving treatment. The court also held that the trial judge's direction that the jury should consider whether 'all reasonable people who knew the facts that you know would realise that the (appellant's) acts inevitably created the risk of some harm to (the victim)' might have given an erroneous impression as to the knowledge that could be ascribed to the 'sober and reasonable man'. Their lordships' view in the Court of Appeal was that the 'sober and reasonable man'. had the same knowledge as the men attempting to rob and no more. Since it had never been suggested in that case that the three accused knew that the victim of their attempted robbery had a bad heart their conviction for manslaughter should be quashed as unsafe and unsatisfactory. (From this it would appear that the 'eggshell skull' principle of civil law has no application to this branch of criminal law so that the accused's liability can turn not on being deemed to take the victim as one finds him 'but on the accused's actual knowledge of the likely effect of his unlawful act on that victim in the particular circumstances'.)

7.6.11 Other homicide offences

There are three other significant statutory offences involving unlawful killing. These are dealt within the Infanticide Act 1938 (infanticide), the Infant Life (Preservation) Act 1929 (child destruction) and the Road Traffic Act 1972 (causing death by reckless driving).

Infanticide can only apply to a mother who has killed a child who has been born but not attained the age of 12 months. It may be charged as an offence or raised as a defence to a charge of murder. In either instance (if found guilty or if the defence is accepted) a mother who killed her child under the age of 12 months will be punished as if she had been convicted of manslaughter. It is a recognition that the balance of a mother's mind may be disturbed by reason of either not having fully recovered from the effect of the childbirth or of lactation consequent on the birth of the child. The mother must adduce evidence that the balance of her mind was so disturbed but the burden of disproving it is on the prosecution: *R v Soanes* [1958] 1 All ER 289.

Child destruction under s. 1 of the 1929 Act can be charged where any person, with intent to destroy the life of a child capable of being born alive, by any wilful act causes it to die before it has an existence independent of its mother. It states that if the woman has been pregnant for more than 28 weeks then the child is prima facie capable of being born alive. However, s. 1 of the 1929 Act contains the proviso that if the death of the child was caused in good faith for the purpose only of preserving the life of the mother (these phrases were interpreted in *R v Bourne* [1939] 1 KB 687 to mean preserving the mother's physical or mental health) then no offence is committed. Likewise no offence would be committed if the child capable of being born alive was destroyed in compliance with the rules laid down for the termination of pregnancy under the Abortion Act 1967. Strict compliance with that Act will also provide the woman and those responsible for the termination with a defence to a charge under s. 58 of the Offences against the Person Act 1861 of administering drugs or using instruments with intent to procure an abortion, or under s. 59 of that Act of procuring or supplying drugs or instruments to cause an abortion, the former of which is otherwise punishable with a maximum of life imprisonment.

The Road Traffic Act 1972, s. 1, states: 'A person who causes the death of another person by the driving of a motor vehicle on a road recklessly . . . shall be guilty of an offence'. That offence is punishable on indictment by imprisonment for up to five years and/or a fine.

8

Offences Against Property

8.1 INTRODUCTION

This chapter will consider some of the ways in which an individual may incur criminal liability by interfering in the rights of others to enjoy their property and possessions. The most common instance of such criminal interference is when an individual commits the offence of theft.

8.1.1 The crime of theft

This offence is fully outlined in s. 1(1) of the Theft Act 1968 which provides that: 'A person is guilty of theft if he dishonestly appropriates property belonging to another with the intention of permanently depriving the other of it'.

The external elements or *actus reus* of the offence are that an individual:

(a) appropriates
(b) property
(c) which belongs to another.

The *mens rea* which is peculiar to the offence is that the appropriation of property which belongs to another be:

(a) dishonest and
(b) with the intention of permanently depriving the true owner of that property.

8.1.2 The subject matter of theft

The principal subject-matter of the offence of theft is property which belongs to another. These two concepts of property and belonging to another will be considered separately.

8.1.3 Property

The offence of theft is concerned with the criminal interference in rights of property, it is this factor that is principally responsible for much of the crime's complexity. The law of property which has defined the different rights and interests a man may have in his possessions and even what kinds of tangible objects he may possess is fraught with difficult and subtle rules. It is this complex body of civil law which is the foundation-stone of the offence of theft (see *R* v *Walker* [1984] Crim LR 112). The Theft Act 1968, however, provides a partial definition of the kinds of property that can form the subject-matter of an offence of theft. By s. 4(1) of the Act property is defined as including:

(a) money
(b) real property, i.e., generally rights and interests in land
(c) personal property, i.e., generally, rights in property other than land
(d) things in action, e.g., cheques or debts owed to an individual
(e) intangible property, e.g., ownership of a patent.

This definition is qualified, however, both by case law and by s. 4 itself.

8.1.4 Case law

In the case of *Handyside* (undated) 2 East PC 652 it was determined that a body-snatcher could not be convicted of stealing a corpse, since there is no property in a cadaver. This may be qualified, it seems, in cases where a corpse has been subject to work upon it to render it in whole or in part of some inherent or intrinsic value to an individual, e.g., a medical student's skeleton or some medical specimen. In the case of *R* v *Welsh* [1974] RTR 478 it was accepted that body fluids could be the subject of the charge of theft, in this case the accused's own urine samples which he had supplied to the police for the purpose of analysis and quantification of alcohol in his bloodstream.

The law has also determined that an individual who entered another's premises and used the telephone there to make a call could not be convicted of theft of the electricity that had been used (*Lowe* v *Blease* (1975) 119 SJ 695). By s. 13 of the Theft Act 1968 it is an offence to abstract or use electricity dishonestly. This section is necessary because electricity cannot be regarded as property for the purposes of the Theft Act, not even within the term intangible property (see s. 4(1) and above).

Finally in the case of *Oxford* v *Moss* [1976] Crim LR 119 it was decided that confidential information which presumably includes such things as trade secrets could not be regarded as property within the terms of s. 4(1) of the Theft Act 1968. The accused, a university student, could not therefore be convicted of theft of the information contained on the proof of an examination paper which he had dishonestly obtained (see also *R* v *Downes* (1983) 77 Cr App R 260 and *R* v *Storrow and Poole* [1983] Crim LR 332).

8.1.5 Theft Act 1968, s. 4(2)

The comprehensive definition of property contained within the Theft Act 1968, s. 4(1), is, however, further restricted by s. 4(2), which provides that 'A person cannot steal land, or things forming part of land and severed from it by him or by his directions'. This excepts land from the kinds of property that may form the subject-matter of the offence of theft. If Rex, following a dispute with his next-door neighbour Alf, had during the middle of the night moved the boundary fence between their properties and annexed several square metres of land, he could not be convicted of theft. Though this appears a lacuna in the law the problem is more apparent than real. Land is a unique form of property; it lasts forever and is incapable of being moved. An individual such as Rex cannot flee from the scene of his conduct, neither can he avoid the consequences of his action. It was thought that the civil remedies for the recovery of land available to individuals in Alf's situation provided sufficient protection to landowners' interests without the need to criminalise any physical seizure of such property.

However, s. 4(2) then provides that notwithstanding the fact that land is not generally capable of being stolen, there are exceptional situations where an individual's appropriation of land may amount to an offence within s. 1(1) of the Theft Act 1968. The first such situation is that contained in s. (4)(2a).

Persons in positions of trust (s. 4(2)(a))   The Theft Act 1968, s. 4(2)(a), applies to an individual who holds land:

(a)   as a trustee, i.e., he holds it for the benefit of another (see later) or
(b)   as a personal representative, i.e., holding the land for the purpose of transferring it from the estate of a deceased person to another entitled by law or by the will of the deceased to that property, or
(c)   as a person authorised to sell land by power of attorney, i.e., an authorisation to an individual empowering him to sell land owned by another and on the latter's behalf and in accordance with his instructions, or
(d)   as a liquidator of a company, i.e., an individual appointed to dispose of a company's assets including its land on the winding up of that company.

Where any individual holds land not for his own benefit but on any of the bases noted above he may commit the offence of theft with regard to such land. This is dependent, however, upon his appropriation of that land (see later) and by his dealing with it in breach of the confidence reposed in him, e.g., while trustee he sells the land or grants a lease or tenancy to another and does not account for the proceeds of sale or rent to the beneficiaries of the trust (the persons entitled to enjoy the benefits of ownership of the land) (see later).

Persons not in possession of land (s. 4(2)(b))   The law deems that land is not limited to the physical earth, but also includes anything growing from it, either naturally or by cultivation, or anything which is attached or affixed to the land permanently. It is therefore not possible *per se* to steal trees, plants, grasses, buildings, stone walls etc. for those things are regarded as forming part of the land itself (see Theft Act 1968, s. 4(2)). Section 4(2)(b) provides, however, that if an individual who is not in possession of land enters upon it and severs or causes to be severed anything forming part of that land (or finds objects that are already severed) then such objects may become the subject-matter of theft.

If Edward and John had on entering Rex's property:

(a)   dug up any of the topsoil in the garden
(b)   uprooted any trees or shrubs
(c)   broken any stones from his garden wall

(d) removed any guttering from the house.

they would have severed or caused to be severed things forming part of the land. If they had then appropriated any of these things and satisfied the other requirements of s. 1(1) of the Theft Act 1968 they could be convicted of stealing such objects. Though s. 4(2)(b) provides that things that have already been severed from the land may form the subject-matter of an offence of theft, it was always the position at common law that anything that had been severed from land was, from that point in time, personal property and was therefore capable of being stolen in any event. This remains the case irrespective of the operation of s. 4(2)(b).

Tenants (s. 4(2)(c))   A person occupying land:

(a) as a statutory tenant under the Rent Acts or
(b) under a weekly, monthly, quarterly or yearly tenancy or
(c) under a lease for a term of years, e.g., three years,

may not generally be guilty of theft of that land or any part thereof. He may, e.g., dig up topsoil, and remove trees and dispose of them, without incurring criminal responsibility under the Theft Act 1968. However, s. 4(2)(c) provides that if a tenant appropriates (see later) the whole or part of any fixture or structure let to be used with the land, he may commit the offence of theft. Fixtures are things attached to the land or to a building (i.e., a structure) which are intended to be permanent and to be an improvement to the land. Thus if a tenant removed a fireplace or wash-basin (fixtures) or tiles from the roof of the house (part of the structure) he could be convicted of stealing such objects.

It is not necessary for a tenant to sever or cause to be severed any fixtures or part of a structure, it is sufficient to incur liability under s. 4(2)(c) if he appropriates them, and this may be done by selling or purporting to sell a fixture or part of a structure to a third party (see later).

8.2 WILD FOLIAGE

It is provided by the Theft Act 1968, s. 4(3), that:

(a) mushrooms (or any fungi)
(b) flowers
(c) fruit
(d) foliage from a plant (including any shrub or tree),

if they are growing wild, cannot generally be the subject-matter of a theft. However, if an individual not in possession of land enters upon it and picks any such flora, fungi etc. (as noted above) for reward or for the purposes of sale or any other commercial purposes, he may in such circumstances steal such products of the soil. If Edward and John had picked some blackberries growing wild at the end of Rex's garden they could only steal the fruit (assuming all the elements of the offence are present) within s. 1(1) of the Theft Act 1968 if they

Offences Against Property

intended, e.g., to sell the berries on their own account (a sale) or to sell them to a fruit shop (a commercial purpose). It must be remembered that s. 4(3) is limited to things growing wild. Fruit taken from a cultivated plant, tree or shrub, etc. may be stolen (see s. 4(2)(b) above).

8.3 WILD ANIMALS

Though wild animals are to be regarded as property they may not be stolen unless the following conditions are satisfied:

(a) They are tame animals or
(b) They are ordinarily kept in captivity.

Thus dogs, cats and other household pets may by virtue of s. 4(4) be stolen as may animals which though normally wild have been domesticated in a particular case. Animals in zoos are examples of creatures that are ordinarily kept in captivity and may therefore be stolen.

Wild animals not tamed or ordinarily kept in captivity may only become property capable of being stolen within s.4(4) where, as regards the potential thief, they have been 'reduced into possession' (i.e., killed or captured) by someone other than the potential thief. Reducing into possession may also include cases where the killing or capturing of the animal by an individual (other than the potential thief) is carried out on behalf of a third party. The reduction into possession may have been completed or be in the course of completion. However, the person reducing or having reduced the animal into his possession must not have abandoned the right to possession in such an animal or have lost it.

Wild animals 'reduced into possession' become the property of the landowner where the killing or capture took place or was finally completed. Where the owner of land has granted sporting rights to an individual, it is the latter who becomes the owner of any wild animals reduced into possession upon that land. The same rights of property as have been discussed above also exist in relation to the carcass of a wild animal. The consequence of this narrow recognition of rights of property in wild animals not ordinarily held in captivity is that a poacher cannot steal such creatures. Where an individual enters upon another's land, and reduces into possession a wild animal not ordinarily kept in captivity he interferes with the landowner's rights of property in that creature which arise when it is killed or captured. Such conduct may constitute an offence of poaching. In fact there are numerous offences created by a number of statutes, principally dating from the 19th century, which govern 'poaching' offences relating to various kinds of animal, e.g., fish, game, deer. Any conduct which comes within the mischief of any of these offences is not theft, however. Where a poacher on another's land is responsible for reducing or is in the course of reducing a wild creature into possession that animal is not property within the terms of s. 4(4). Wild creatures can only be stolen by an individual when they have been reduced or are in the course of being reduced into possession by or on behalf of another, i.e., wild animals cannot be stolen by the person who actually reduces them into possession or is in the course of doing so, though he may commit an offence of poaching. An individual may, however, steal wild animals that have been reduced or are in the course of being reduced into possession by a poacher, for then the requirements of s. 4(4) are satisfied. For reasons that will be considered later such a wild animal would be stolen not only from the landowner but also from the poacher.

8.4 PROPERTY THAT MAY BE STOLEN

8.4.1 Property belonging to another

It is not an offence to appropriate property which has been abandoned and is owned by no one, nor can an individual generally steal his own possessions (see later for exceptions to this principle). This is because the crime of theft requires that the property which is appropriated by an individual should belong to another. The Theft Act 1968, s. 5, defines the circumstances when the law will consider property as belonging to an individual, and thus capable of being stolen from him.

By s. 5(1): 'Property shall be regarded as belonging to any person having possession or control of it, or having in it any proprietary right or interest (not being an equitable interest arising only from an agreement to transfer or grant an interest)'.

The various rights in property which have been recognised in s. 5(1) for the purposes of theft will now be considered in turn.

8.4.2 Proprietary right or interest

This may mean (a) full ownership in an object or (b) rights in property which fall short of total dominion over a possession.

In the scenario Rex and his wife will have full ownership in the camera, jewellery, and candlesticks which were taken by Edward and John. They are the persons having (within the meaning of s. 5(1)) a proprietary right or interest in those objects and as such these possessions are capable of being stolen from them.

However, ownership in an object consists of a number of rights which may include the right to enjoy the use of that possession, to sell, hire or lease it to another, or even to destroy it. An individual may still have a proprietary right or interest in property within the terms of s. 5(1), though he does not enjoy full rights of ownership in a possession. A man may be a trustee of property, that is, he may hold that property for the benefit of another (the beneficiary). Neither party in the case of a trust enjoys all the benefits of ownership in the property concerned. The trustee has the legal rights of ownership, i.e., to sell, dispose or exchange that property, though these rights are usually restricted or controlled both by the law and by the terms of the trust determined in the trust instrument (i.e., the legal document which created it). The kernel of a trust consists, however, of the rights which are possessed by the beneficiary, principally the right to enjoy the use, or fruits of that property, such rights being known as equitable rights or interests. Generally when a person has full ownership of a possession he enjoys both the legal and equitable interests in it. In the case of trustee and beneficiary the law regards both as having a proprietary right or interest in the trust property

Offences Against Property

for the purposes of s. 5(1) though neither has full ownership. One form of equitable interest which is expressly excluded from the definition of proprietary right or interest is 'an equitable interest arising only from an agreement to transfer or grant an interest'. This principally refers to the situation where there has been a formal exchange of written contracts between a vendor and purchaser for the sale of land. In such cases the purchaser of that property is regarded as having an equitable interest in it until he gains full ownership by a conveyance or transfer under seal, signed by the vendor. Because of the exclusion of this equitable interest from the ambit of s. 5(1), the vendor may, notwithstanding the existence of a contract of sale of land to a purchaser, transfer or convey that land to a third party without incurring criminal responsibility. It is thought that the civil remedies available to a purchaser to seek damages or even to recover the land itself from a third party who agreed to purchase it from the original vendor are sufficient protection of the purchaser's equitable interests in the land without the need for a criminal sanction.

Other examples of proprietary rights or interests in property within s. 5(1) are a lien, i.e., a right to retain another's possession until payment has been made for work executed upon it. In *R v Turner (No. 2)* [1971] 2 All ER 441 (see below) the property concerned was the accused's car upon which a garage had executed repairs. To that extent the garage had a right to retain that car against third parties and the owner until payment for those repairs had been made. Unfortunately the judge at first instance had removed the issue of the existence of a lien from the jury's consideration. Nevertheless it is suggested that a lien is a proprietary right or interest within the terms of s. 5(1).

Where an employee makes a profit from the misuse of his employer's property which has been entrusted to him for the purpose of carrying out his contract of employment, the employer is regarded by the law as having a proprietary right or interest in those profits. In the scenario if Ron was employed as a taxi-driver and he had used his employer's taxi-cab on his own private ventures to earn extra cash, the law regards that cash as belonging to the employer. It has been determined that this principle is not applicable to money received by an employee as a bribe, see *Powell* v *MacRae* [1977] Crim LR 571. The rationale of the general precept is that the employee is regarded by the law as a trustee of the profits which he has made by his misuse of his employer's property (known as a constructive trust). The employer as the beneficiary of this constructive trust has a proprietary right or interest in those profits within the meaning of s. 5(1).

Since the law recognises various forms of proprietary rights or interests in property it follows that those rights or interests may be vested in more than one person. Theft of property in such circumstances is theft from all those persons (see later).

8.4.3 Possession and control

Property also belongs to an individual within the terms of the Theft Act 1968 s. 5(1), when he possesses or controls that property, irrespective of whether he also has a proprietary right or interest in it, though generally an individual who has full ownership in a piece of property also has possession and control of it. Possession and control of goods may be separated from full ownership and be vested in different persons. An example where ownership and possession are separated is the situation known to the law as bailment.

In bailment an individual entrusts his property to another. (The owner of the property being known as the bailor, the person in receipt the bailee.) The bailment may be either for the purposes of safe-keeping of the possession or of effecting a repair, or so that the bailee may enjoy the use of that possession for a limited time or purpose. In cases of bailment the property must generally be ultimately redelivered to the bailor or to a third party in accordance with the bailor's instructions.

A person also becomes a bailee when he hires goods or purchases them under a hire-purchase agreement. In this situation he remains the bailee of those goods until all the hire-purchase instalments and option to purchase fee have been paid, when he then becomes the full owner. The bailor until the payments have been completed retains his proprietary right or interest in the property within the terms of s. 5(1), though the bailee has possession of the goods within the meaning of the subsection.

In all cases of bailment, though the bailee does not have a proprietary right or interest in the bailed property, the fact that he has possession of such property determines that it may be stolen from him. In the case of *R* v *Turner (No. 2)* [1971] 2 All ER 441 it was recognised a bailee had possession of bailed goods. This was a case of a bailment at will, which could be determined instantly at the behest of the bailor. This right of possession exists not only against third parties but also against the owner of the property itself (see later) though doubt has been cast upon this latter point in *R* v *Meredith* [1973] Crim LR 253 (see later).

Possession as an independent right in property can be illustrated by the following situations. A person who owns property or a person who does not have full ownership in an article (e.g., a bailee) may possess goods:

(a) over which he exercises actual physical dominion, e.g., clothes or jewellery worn on the person, or

(b) over which an individual has a right to exercise physical dominion.

Thus goods which are kept at a person's home are possessed by him. An individual does not lose possession of articles merely because he is not at home. A man does not cease to possess his motor car when he leaves it in a car-park. A further example is a shopkeeper who possesses his stock.

Possession of goods is not dependent upon knowledge of their existence. An individual may possess articles which are on his land though he is ignorant of their prescence. In *Hibbert* v *McKiernan* [1948] 2 KB 142 it was determined that a golf club retained possession of golf balls left on its course by its members. However, this was because there was no one who had a greater right to possession. The original owners of the balls having lost them and abandoned their right of possession in them. This illustrates that possession is a relative concept and may be claimed by several persons in respect of the same piece of property. The law in accordance with a complex and somewhat conflicting body of case law has determined in given circumstances which of one or more claimants may have the greater right to possession.

Hibbert v *McKiernan* (see above) shows that an individual may lose his right of

Offences Against Property

possession in an article by abandoning it. Thus if an article is lost and the owner no longer seeks it (this is important as the mere loss of an article does not result in an individual losing his right of possession) or if it is thrown away by him and he becomes indifferent to its fate, then possession (and any greater rights enjoyed in that property) will be lost. The final right in property to consider is the concept of control.

8.4.4 Control

This means bare physical control. A shopper examining wares in a supermarket has control of such articles which are in his hand or in a wire basket provided by the shop. The shopkeeper retains possession and full ownership in the goods. Physical control exercised by an individual with regard to a piece of property may thus exist without any additional rights in property. This is so especially in cases where it is uncertain who if anyone enjoys a greater right in a possession (see *R v Woodman* [1974] QB 754).

8.4.5 Summary

All the above rights which an individual may enjoy with regard to property may be vested in a single person. However, they may also exist independently and be enjoyed by more than one person. It appears logical that a man with a lesser right in an article, e.g., control, can steal such a piece of property from an individual who has possession or a proprietary right or interest in it. In the case of *R v Turner (No. 2)* [1971] 2 All ER 441 it was determined that a person enjoying any right in property could be the victim of a theft even where the person interfering with that right enjoyed *a greater* interest in that property. In this case the accused had handed over his car to a garage proprietor to effect certain repairs. Though promising to pay for the repairs he returned with a spare set of keys and drove away his vehicle without making a payment after the completion of the work required. On appeal against conviction for theft of the car it was contended by the accused that the issue of a lien (see above) having been withdrawn from the jury by the judge at first instance, the garage proprietor had no proprietary right or interest in the car. Removing the car could not therefore amount to theft from the garage owner.

It was accepted that the garage owner was only a bailee at will (see para. 8.4.3). The accused maintained that this was not a sufficient interest in the property to permit the garage owner to enjoy either possession or control of the car. This was rejected by the court. Lord Parker CJ was of the opinion that the words 'possession or control' within the Theft Act 1968, s. 5(1), should not be qualified. The garage owner had certainly enjoyed control of the motor car and the removal of the car by the accused was an interference in that right of control. As a bailee the garage owner also enjoyed a right of possession. It was irrelevant that the accused had a greater proprietary interest in the vehicle. It does not seem unreasonable to expect even the owner of an article to recover possession or control of it from another in accordance with the law or the terms of the agreement by which the owner originally parted with his goods.

A case sometimes said to conflict with *R v Turner* is that of *R v Meredith* [1973]

Crim LR 253. Here the accused took his vehicle from a police station yard after it had been impounded by them. Before removal he should have paid a fine. The court considered that the police had no right or interest in the vehicle which justified their retention of it. On this basis it was accepted the accused could not steal the car from the police. Though this appears to conflict with *R* v *Turner* it is suggested that the latter authority is to be preferred. The acquittal of the accused in *R* v *Meredith* can be justified more readily on the grounds that he was not dishonest. On this basis he lacked a crucial element in the *mens rea* of the offence (see later). In *R* v *Turner* the accused had throughout acted dishonestly and it is suggested this is the relevant distinguishing factor between the two authorities which justify their differing conclusions as to guilt in apparently identical situations.

The Theft Act 1968 also makes provision for special circumstances relating to property where it is thought that s. 5(1) might not be applicable. It is these provisions that must now be considered.

8.5 SPECIAL FORMS OF PROPRIETARY RIGHT

8.5.1 Theft Act 1968, s. 5(2)

Certain trusts, such as charitable trusts, have no named beneficiaries. On this basis the beneficial interest in such trusts does not belong to anyone within the terms of the Theft Act 1968, s. 5(1). Section 5(2) therefore provides that:

> Where property is subject to a trust, the persons to whom it belongs shall be regarded as including any person having a right to enforce the trust, and an intention to defeat the trust shall be regarded accordingly as an intention to deprive of the property any person having that right.

It is determined by law that the Attorney-General is the person having the right to compel the trustees to perform their duties under a charitable trust (or other special trusts where there are no specific beneficiaries). By virtue of s. 5(2) the Attorney-General is deemed to be a person to whom the beneficial interest in the trust belongs. Appropriation of the trust property by a trustee or a third party in cases such as charitable trusts would therefore be theft from the Attorney-General

8.5.2 Theft Act 1968, s. 5(3)

This subsection provides:

> Where a person receives property from or on account of another, and is under an obligation to the other to retain and deal with that property or its proceeds in a particular way, the property or proceeds shall be regarded (as against him) as belonging to the other.

Though this subsection also covers situations of bailment or trusts its principal function is to cover cases which though analogous to such situations may not

Offences Against Property

clearly be within the terms of s. 5(1).

The subsection covers cases where an individual receives property (usually money) from or on account of another and is legally obliged to retain and deal with that property in a particular way. In such cases the person handing over the property still retains an interest in it because by virtue of s. 5(3) the property is regarded as still belonging to him for the purposes of the offence of theft.

Take the situation where an individual as a customer hands over money to another in accordance with an agreement that the latter will obtain or provide some services or goods to the value of that money. Whether that money will be regarded as belonging to the customer (within the terms of s. 5(3)) in the event of its appropriation by the person receiving it without providing the required goods or services is dependent upon the existence of a legal obligation imposed upon the recipient to use *that* actual money to obtain or provide the services or goods demanded. The usual inference when money is handed to another in pursuance of a contract for goods or services is that property in that money passes to the recipient. There is only a contractual obligation ultimately to provide the services or goods. The recipient may, therefore, use the money as he sees fit, for he has become the owner of it. The situation is different, however, where because of the nature of the agreement between the parties or because of the status of the recipient the latter is under a legal obligation to retain *that* money and to use *that* money to obtain or provide the services or goods. Thus in *R* v *Hall* [1973] 1QB 126, the accused carried on a business as a travel agent and received money as deposits and payments for trips to the USA. The accused's business failed, he did not provide the air trips nor did he refund any of the money he had received. The accused claimed the deposits and payments had become his property on receipt and he had lawfully used these sums in the conduct of his business, he could not therefore be guilty of theft of the deposits and payments merely because his firm had sunk into bankruptcy and the money had been dissipated. He was convicted at first instance. He appealed on the ground, *inter alia*, that as the deposits and payments belonged to him he was under no obligation under s. 5(3) to retain or deal with those monies in a particular way, i.e., to provide the air trips. This was accepted by the appellate court. Though the customers would normally expect the eventual receipt of air tickets and other relevant documents for their intended journeys and this placed the accused under a contractual obligation to supply these, there was no evidence that the customers expected him to retain and deal with their deposits or payments for that particular purpose. There was no undertaking by the accused to deal with those monies in that way. The monies therefore did not belong to the customers under s. 5(3). The accused had not committed theft with regard to those deposits or payments.

The situation would be different if the monies had been paid over on the express or implied understanding that *that* money would be used to purchase the air tickets and relevant documents (see *Davidge* v *Bunnett* [1984] Crim LR 297). Consider, for example, the case of a builder who had agreed to build an extension upon Rex's home and Rex had paid him a sum of money with which to purchase building materials. If Rex had made it known that that sum of money *must* be used to purchase the building materials to be used upon his home, then if that money was used to support the builder's business or to purchase materials for another customer this would be theft of that money by him because of s. 5(3) (assuming the other elements of the offence were present).

An example of an implied understanding to deal with money in a particular way would be the handing over of a sum of money by a client to his solicitor to complete the purchase of a house on his behalf. The solicitor is by virtue of his professional status obliged to place his client's money in a separate client account, and not to use that money for any purpose other than the particular house purchase.

8.5.3 Proceeds

The Theft Act 1968, s. 5(3), is also applicable to the proceeds of any property handed over to a recipient. Thus if the builder had used the money given to him by Rex to purchase the required building materials, but had then used the materials in carrying out building work for another customer, that would be a misuse of the *proceeds* of that property (i.e., the money) which would be deemed to belong to Rex by virtue of s. 5(3). Whether a recipient of such property is under a legal obligation to retain and deal with that property in accordance with the terms of s. 5(3) is a matter of law for the judge. However, the establishing of the primary facts which give rise to such an obligation is a matter of fact (see *R* v *Mainwaring* (1982) 74 Cr App R 99).

8.6 THEFT ACT 1968, S. 5(4)

This subsection provides that:

> Where a person gets property by another's mistake, and is under an obligation to make restoration (in whole or in part) of the property or its proceeds or of the value thereof, then to the extent of that obligation the property or proceeds shall be regarded (as against him) as belonging to the person entitled to restoration, and an intention not to make restoration shall be regarded accordingly as an intention to deprive that person of the property or proceeds.

It is not always necessary for the owner to rely upon this subsection in certain cases where his property is transferred by him to another under a mistake. In the law of contract there are a number of confusing authorities which nevertheless seem to determine that certain mistakes which induce the transfer of property by the owner to another will not result in ownership in such a possession passing to the recipient. These situations include cases where the person parting with the property is under a mistaken apprehension as to the identity of the recipient (see *Cundy* v *Lindsay* (1878) 3 App Cas 459). In such cases the owner would not have parted with ownership of the property concerned had he been aware of the recipient's true identity. This must be contrasted with a situation where the mistake is only as to the attributes of the recipient (e.g., his creditworthiness), such a mistake will not prevent ownership in the property passing (see *King's Norton Metal Co. Ltd* v *Edridge, Merrett & Co Ltd* (1897) 14 TLR 98.

Other cases of transfer of goods under a mistake where property will not pass to the recipient will involve situations where there is a mistake as to the nature of the goods. This does not refer to their quality, e.g., the transfer of a painting

Offences Against Property

which is believed to be worthless but is later found to be a masterpiece. An example of a mistake as to nature would include the receipt of valuable gold bullion by a purchaser of scrap metal when it was intended by the vendor to sell only lead or iron scrap. It has been held that a mistake as to quantity or value may also negate the transfer of ownership in property. For example, if an individual in the dark of a taxi-cab handed over two £20 notes believing them to be £1 notes in tendering payment of the fare then property in those notes would not pass to the driver.

In such cases of mistake as noted above property in goods does not pass. The person handing over the goods retains a proprietary right or interest in them by virtue of s. 5(1) and they may therefore still be stolen from him by virtue of this subsection. Reliance on s. 5(4) is unnecessary. An individual will also retain a proprietary right or interest in goods where he intends to part only with possession or control of them but not ultimate ownership. Thus if an individual is induced to part with possession or control of goods under the mistaken belief that he is merely lending them to the recipient, but the latter intends to appropriate them permanently, the owner retains ultimate ownership and a proprietary right or interest in them within the meaning of s. 5(1).

Section 5(4) is applicable where goods are transferred under a mistake, and the nature of that mistake is such that ownership of those goods is transferred as well as possession and control. This is illustrated by the case of *Moynes* v *Cooper* [1956] 1 QB 439. The accused was paid his wages by a wages clerk who had by a mistake overpaid the accused by some £6. The accused discovered that he had been overpaid when he opened his wage packet at home later that same day. It was determined by the appellate court that property as to all the money contained in the wage packet passed to the accused. (It would have been different had the accused known of the overpayment at the time he received his wage packet or he had induced the overpayment by a fraudulent misrepresentation as to the actual amount due to him — see later.) The purpose of s. 5(4) was to determine that in cases such as *Moynes* v *Cooper* property so transferred would still be regarded for the purposes of the offence of theft as belonging to the person who had originally transferred the property. Though the recipient of property in cases like *Moynes* v *Cooper* has become their owner the law regards him as being unjustly enriched. The law of restitution determines that in such circumstances the recipient of such goods is to the extent of his enrichment under a legal obligation to return those goods or their proceeds to the original owner. Any goods or their proceeds subject to such a legal obligation are now deemed by virtue of s. 5(4) to belong to the original owner for the purposes of the offence of theft. In the case of *Attorney-General's Reference (No. 1 of 1983)* [1985] QB 182 the accused's bank account was mistakenly credited with a sum of money in respect of overtime which she had not worked. The accused knew nothing of this erroneous overpayment, though on discovering this fact, she did nothing to rectify the error. Neither did her employers. It was held by the Court of Appeal that this overpayment was property capable of being stolen. Since the accused had clearly received the money by another's mistake she was under an obligation to restore it to the true owner (her employer). The overpayment, by virtue of s. 5(4), belonged to her employers from the time the accused realised it was in her bank account. If she had then appropriated it (see later) with the dishonest intention permanently to deprive her employer of the money (which could be demonstrated by a resolve not to make a repayment) she would be guilty of theft. If without realising that she had been overpaid the accused had spent the money she could not be so convicted. This is because at the moment of appropriation she could not be said to be acting dishonestly. If the accused had purchased some goods with the money, however, these *proceeds* could be the subject-matter of an offence of theft (see s. 5(4)), a dishonest resolution not to return these proceeds to the true owner being sufficient. In one instance a resolution not to make repayment of such an overpayment cannot amount to a theft notwithstanding s. 5(4). This is where the money has been spent by an individual (without realising that there has been a bank error) on intangible or consumable commodities. In such a case there is no property or proceeds which can then be said to belong to another. However, the civil obligation to make restitution may still exist.

There must be a legal obligation to make restitution, a moral obligation is insufficient to invoke s. 5(4). This can be seen from the case of *R* v *Gilks* [1972] 3 All ER 280. The accused was mistakenly paid out by the manager of a betting-shop in respect of a horse backed by him. The horse had not been placed but the manager paid the accused as if it had been. It was determined by the appellate court that the payment had been made under a wager. The law does not recognise any legal rights arising from a wagering contract and the money paid to the accused was irrecoverable by any legal process. There was thus no legal obligation imposed upon the accused to return the money. Section 5(4) was therefore inapplicable.

Curiously, however, the court relied upon the old case of *R* v *Middleton* (1873) LR 2 CCR 38 to determine that on the facts of the case ownership in the money paid over by the betting-shop manager to the accused had not passed. It still belonged to the bookmakers under s. 5(1).

It is difficult to justify the application of *R* v *Middleton* to the case of R v *Gilks*. The former case involved payment of money under a mistake of identity of the recipient and would seem to be inappropriate to the facts of *R* v *Gilks*. If the case of *R* v *Middleton* is generally held applicable to cases such as *R* v *Gilks* it should also apply to similar cases where s. 5(4) could be utilised, rendering the subsection largely otiose.

8.7 SUBSEQUENT APPLICATION OF S. 5(1) IN SPECIAL CASES OF FRAUD

In cases where the owner of goods is persuaded to part with them under a contract of sale which has been induced by fraud, he may on discovering that fraud avoid the contract by notifying the recipient of the goods (or where that person cannot be ascertained by informing the police of his wish to avoid the contract). From that moment the ownership of those goods returns to the original owner and for the purposes of theft again belongs to him within the terms of the Theft Act 1968, s. 5(1). There is no need in such instances to make reference to s. 5(4).

Offences Against Property

8.8 THE CONDUCT ELEMENT IN THE ACTUS REUS OF THEFT

8.8.1 Appropriation

All the circumstances of the external elements of theft have now been considered. The *actus reus* requires that property belonging to another is appropriated. This latter factor must now be considered.

Appropriation is 'the assumption of the rights of an owner' (see Theft Act 1968, s. 3(1). These rights have already been considered (see above). It is not necessary that an individual assumes all the rights of an owner, an assumption of any of the rights of ownership will amount to appropriation.

The leading case upon the meaning of appropriation is the recent House of Lords decision of *Anderton* v *Burnside* [1984] AC 320. Their lordship's were of the opinion that appropriation per Lord Roskill (at p. 332): 'involves not an act expressly or impliedly authorised by the owner but an act by way of adverse interference with or usurpation of those rights' (i.e., the rights of ownership). Lord Roskill expanded further upon this definition (at p. 333):

> It is the doing of one or more acts which individually or collectively amount to such adverse interference with or usurpation of the owner's rights which constitute appropriation under s. 3(1) and I do not think it matters where there is more than one such act in which order the successive acts take place, or whether there is any interval of time between them.

His lordship gave examples (at p. 333) of cases of appropriation, e.g., a shopper in a store putting goods into a receptacle be it supermarket trolley or the individual's own shopping bag.

Appropriation requires:

(a) Conduct on the part of the potential thief which usurps or interferes in another's rights of ownership, possession or control in goods. There is no need that it be a clearly demonstrable overt act, i.e., objectively established to be adverse to the proprietary interests of a third party or the owner, (see Lord Roskill at p. 334).

(b) The conduct to amount to appropriation requires a mental resolve on the part of the potential thief to usurp the rights of the person or persons with a proprietary right or lesser interest in the goods. This does not form, however, an element in the *mens rea* of the offence (see para. 1.2).

(c) Conduct by an individual to amount to appropriation must be outside the authority express or implied which has been given by the owner (and/or by individuals with a proprietary right or other interest in the property) to deal with his goods. This is illustrated by the case of a shopkeeper. The shopkeeper impliedly authorises persons to enter his premises and to examine his goods. A shopper is also authorised to place them in a receptacle provided for that purpose prior to purchasing them. However, it is suggested, on the same principle as the concept of trespass in burglary (see later) and by the tenor of the judgment of Lord Roskill in *Anderton* v *Burnside*, that though an individual may appear to be acting within the scope of an implied authority to deal with goods, a mental resolve on the part of the potential thief to assume the rights of ownership in them may well constitute his conduct an appropriation. For in such situations the individual concerned is acting outside the authority given to him by the owner to deal with his possession. Returning to the scenario it is suggested that as soon as Edward or John physically seize, e.g., the camera (which for the purposes of this example belongs to Sarah) with the resolve to assume rights of ownership in that article, their conduct must be outside the authority given to them by Sarah to deal with her possession and this amounts to appropriation.

On this basis it is suggested that it is unnecessary for an individual intending to steal goods from a supermarket to do something demonstrably, objectively and overtly outside that which he is authorised to do, e.g., put the goods in his own shopping bag or inside a pocket of his jacket.

It has been suggested that this interpretation of what constitutes appropriation is too wide and is not justified by the speech of Lord Roskill in *Anderton* v *Burnside*. The basis of this view is principally his lordship's approval of the decisions of *Eddy* v *Niman* (1981) 73 Cr App R 237 and *R* v *Skipp* [1975] Crim LR 114 and *R* v *Meech* [1974] QB 549. These cases suggested that a resolution by a potential thief to appropriate property together with their physical seizure (and therefore exercise of possession or control) could not without more amount to acting outside the owner's authority to deal with such goods. The above decisions suggest that a thief must be seen to have overtly and demonstrably exceeded the authority given to him by an owner to handle or deal with his goods, by reference to his conduct. This means, e.g., that a thief must be seen to put articles in his own bag when in a supermarket or pass by the check-out without paying. A resolution to steal such goods and their placing in the supermarket trolley would not on this basis be an act outside the authority given by the supermarket to deal with its goods. However, the approval of these decisions is, it is suggested, qualified by his lordship's speech. His lordship was of the view that (at p. 333): a trail through a forest of decisions, many briefly and indeed inadequately reported, will tend to confuse rather than to enlighten'.

His lordship, in approving the cases of *R* v *Meech* and *R* v *Skipp* and contrasting them with the apparently conflicting decision of *R* v *McPherson* [1973] Crim LR 191 was 'far from convinced that there is any inconsistency between them and other cases, . . . once it is appreciated that facts will vary infinitely' (at pp. 333–4). His lordship also approved *Eddy* v *Niman* as being 'correctly decided on its somewhat unusual facts' (at p. 334). Though his lordship rejected the opinion in that case that appropriation required the thief to perform some 'overt act' with regard to another's goods.

The approval of these decisions is consistent therefore with the view suggested in this book as to when an express or implied authority given by an owner to deal with his goods may be exceeded by another. In *Lawrence* v *Metropolitan Police Commissioner* [1972] AC 626 Viscount Dilhorne was of the opinion that theft did not require that an appropriation be 'without the consent of the owner'. This was approved by Lord Roskill in *Anderton* v *Burnside*. Though it is unclear as to what is meant by this term, it is inconceivable that it means that the consent of the owner of goods is always irrelevant to the offence of theft. (It would be strange to regard an individual as a thief when he appropriated property with the full

Offences Against Property

knowledge and consent of the owner.) However, the fact that the lack of consent of the owner, with regard to another's appropriation of his property, is not generally a relevant element in the offence of theft emphasises, it is suggested, that the law is not principally concerned with the mind of the owner of the goods in such cases. The reliance upon the fact that appropriation of goods requires that they are dealt with outside the express or implied authority given by an owner to deal with his goods is, it is suggested, laying greater emphasis both upon the conduct and mental state of the potential thief.

It is suggested that an insistence that it be established that an individual's conduct has overtly and demonstrably exceeded the express or implied authority of the owner to deal with his goods, before appropriation can be deemed to take place is to confuse evidential matters with the needs of the substantive law. In practical terms it may be prudent to await such an outward sign to ensure a conviction, but this should not prevent the establishing of appropriation with regard to an individual's conduct, where though he appears to be acting within the scope or authority given to him to deal with another's goods, he has a mental resolve to treat them as his own and he has combined this with physical seizure of the goods. The physical seizure and thus taking of possession or at least control of those goods is, because of the mental resolve of the appropriator, the first but crucial step in the ultimate exercise of ownership by him, usurping the rights in those goods enjoyed by the true owner. Such conduct, it is suggested, must be outside the express or implied authority given by the true owner to another to deal with his property.

8.8.2 Examples of appropriation

Though physical seizure is the most common form of appropriation a thief may appropriate goods without obtaining possession or control. Thus if Edward and John on entering Rex's house telephoned a local pawnshop dealer, Brian, purporting to be the owner of the jewellery and candlesticks in Rex's home and offering to sell them, this would amount to an appropriation, see *R* v *Pitham and Hehl* (1976) 65 Cr App R 45.

8.8.3 Theft Act 1968, s. 3

A person may appropriate property though he is in possession or control of it (see paras 8.4.3 and 8.4.4). The Theft Act 1968, s. 3(1) provides for the special circumstance where an individual has come by property (whether innocently or not) without stealing it and he later assumes the right of ownership in those goods, in such circumstances that later assumption of ownership will amount to an appropriation. If an individual finds a piece of jewellery in the street he will have come by that property innocently and will be in possession and control of it. If he later finds the identity of the true owner but resolves to keep the article he will by virtue of s. 3(1) be appropriating it.

A further example of obtaining goods and subsequently appropriating them within the terms of s. 3(1) is obtaining possession of a motor vehicle under a hire-purchase agreeement. If before all the instalments have been paid the individual concerned sold or purported to sell the vehicle to a third party this would amount to appropriation, see *R v Hircock* (1978) 67 Cr App R 278.

However, s. 3(2) provides a defence to a charge of theft where an individual retains possession and control and maintains a right of ownership in goods which he knows to be stolen. For example, if property or a right or interest in property is purported to be sold by a thief or handler to an individual who acts in good faith and who gives value then any later assumption of the right in that property the purchaser believed he was obtaining cannot amount to theft, notwithstanding the defect in title to the goods. This is to protect the person who in good faith (neither knowing nor suspecting goods to be stolen) purchases them. In such cases retaining or disposing of such goods as against the original owner is not theft.

Theft is a continuing offence. A stolen object, notwithstanding its constant use by a thief, is the subject only of a single act of theft, see *R v Devall* [1984] Crim LR 428.

8.9 MENS REA

A potential thief must amongst other things act dishonestly when he appropriates property belonging to another (i.e., he must have the intention to act fraudulently). The Theft Act 1968 provides a partial guidance as to what may be regarded as a dishonest intent.

By virtue of s. 2 it is provided that an individual's appropriation of another's property is *not* to be regarded as dishonest in the following situations:

(a) Where he believes he has a right in law to deprive the other of that property either for himself or for a third party.

This belief of a right in law to appropriate property need not be reasonable (though that is a factor as to whether it is believed by a jury) and is not negated by the use of force in taking the property, see *R v Robinson* [1977] Crim LR 173. It must be a belief as to a legal right and not a moral one. Thus it would not be a dishonest appropriation if the bailee of goods upon hire-purchase sold them to a third party believing in law that he was entitled to do so.

(b) Where an individual appropriates another's property believing the latter would have consented to the appropriation if he had known of the circumstances.

This is self-evident. 'Friends' will frequently 'borrow' one another's possessions. Student communal life is full of situations where food and other consumables are utilised or used by one occupant of a student house when such items are owned by another occupant. It is usual in such cases that consent to such appropriations though not given is assumed. In such cases appropriation is not dishonest.

(c) Where (except in cases where the property has come to an individual as trustee or personal representative) he appropriates property in the belief that the person to whom the property belongs cannot be discovered by taking reasonable steps.

Thus an individual may retain goods which he has found and which have been lost by another without the taint of dishonesty until the owner or a person entitled to or a greater right to possession or control is ascertained. Until the occurrence of such events an honest belief on the part of the appropriator that the owner (or a person with a greater right or interest in the property) is undiscoverable by the exercise of reasonable diligence will ensure that an appropriation will not be regarded as dishonest. Thus the nature of the goods found, where they were found, their value and their characteristics are highly relevant factors. A lost but worthless mass-produced trinket would not require the same steps to ascertain the owner as compared to a valuable and personally engraved diamond brooch. Ironically the standards of honesty of the finder are also relevant: the higher his own standards the more it may be expected of him to take steps to ascertain the owner of lost goods. Once the owner has been ascertained any later assumption of the rights of the owner by the finder will amount to an appropriation by virtue of s. 3(1) (see above).

Section 2(2) provides that a person's appropriation of property may still be dishonest notwithstanding a willingness to pay for those goods. It is only the owner of goods who can decide to sell them.

The provisions as to dishonesty in s. 2(1) are matters of law for the judge to decide. Nevertheless there is a body of case law which has determined as a matter of fact (i.e., for the jury to determine) where an individual's conduct may be regarded as dishonest. In *R* v *Feely* [1973] 1 QB 530, the accused, an employee, contrary to his employer's instructions, 'borrowed' from the till, but put in an IOU as to the amount borrowed. At first instance the judge had directed the jury that as a matter of law the accused's conduct was dishonest. This was held by the Court of Appeal to be a misdirection. In their lordships' opinion dishonesty within the offence of theft referred to an individual's state of mind. The ascertaining of that state of mind was a matter of fact for the jury. The word dishonesty should not be defined by the judge since it was a word in common usage.

This test was affirmed and expanded in the case of *R* v *Ghosh* [1982] QB 1053. The Court of Appeal endorsed the opinion expressed in *Feely* that the element of dishonesty in the offence of theft referred not to an individual's conduct but to his state of mind. This state of mind was to be determined subjectively. However, the jury were not to consider whether the accused was dishonest by reference to his moral standards unless they corresponded with the standards of ordinary reasonable men. If the accused had a different moral code from that of the norm the accused's dishonesty could nevertheless be established if the jury were satisfied that the accused must have realised that he was dishonest by reference to the standards of honest and reasonable men — in this latter circumstance he would then be acting dishonestly. This would deal with the 'Robin Hood' syndrome, i.e., the man who knew his actions were dishonest by the standards of society, but who regarded his conduct as right by reference to his own moral code.

8.10 INTENTION PERMANENTLY TO DEPRIVE

At the time of appropriation of property an individual must intend permanently to deprive the owner of it. An intention merely to borrow is insufficient to constitute his conduct criminal. It is usually clear from the nature of the property, the act of appropriation and subsequent conduct of an appropriator whether there is an intention permanently to deprive. Consuming a valuable bottle of vintage port or spending money which belongs to another evinces an intention permanently to deprive another of that property as well as bringing about that situation in fact. The borrowing of a book is clearly insufficient. Whether an individual has an intention permanently to deprive another of goods he has appropriated is a matter of fact (*R v Lloyd and others* [1985] 3 WLR 30). In cases where the property appropriated has a limited utility or life, e.g., a hired article, e.g., scaffolding for house painting, the use of that scaffolding by a 'borrower' may be for a such a time (e.g., beyond the hire period) as to exhaust the value of such a piece or property to the hirer (who has possession or control of the property). It would be difficult to come to any conclusion other than that the 'borrower' intended to deprive the hirer of his limited right of property permanently.

The Theft Act 1968, s. 6, provides that in certain circumstances an individual will be regarded as having an intention permanently to deprive an owner of goods though he may not in reality have that intention.

By s. 6(1) a person appropriating property belonging to another without meaning the other permanently to lose the thing will nevertheless be regarded as having such an intent where:

(a) he intends to treat the thing as his own to dispose of regardless of the other's rights, or
(b) he borrows or lends the property for a period and in circumstances rendering it equivalent to an outright taking.

An example of the first situation would be if an appropriator of another's property pledged it or abandoned it after using it, being indifferent as to whether it is recovered by the owner. However, in the case of abandoning property consideration would have to be given to the nature of the goods and the surrounding circumstances. Thus to abandon an umbrella belonging to another on an omnibus may be within s. 6(1), leaving another's motor car in a busy street would not (since it would almost certainly be recovered).

An example of the second situation would be an individual's borrowing of a season ticket be it for travel, theatre or sporting activity and using it until it is expired and valueless to the owner. Whether a 'borrowing' of such a ticket to the extent that it is not entirely exhausted would constitute an intent to deprive an owner permanently of his property within the terms of s. 6(1) is unclear, if so the extent to which its value must be reduced before s. 6(1) applies would be a matter of fact and degree.

If an individual lawfully in possession of another's goods, then lent them to another in such circumstances that the property may not be returned to him, or returned only after the value of the property to the original owner is extinguished or substantially reduced, may also constitute conduct which could lead to the inference that there was an intent permanently to deprive the true owner of those goods.

By s. 6(2) if an individual has possession or control (whether lawful or not) of property belonging to another, and he parts with that property under a condition as to its return which he may not be able to perform and this is done for the

Offences Against Property

individual's own purposes without the owner's authority, this will be regarded as treating the property as his own to dispose of regardless of the owner's rights. On this basis such an individual would be regarded as having an intent permanently to deprive the owner of those goods. Section 6(2) would be satisfied if a repairer of jewellery holding a necklace for a client pledged it to a third party to secure a loan for his own purposes. He risks its non-return by failure to repay the loan. Section 6 of the Act is not exhaustive as a definition of what consitutes an intention permanently to deprive and it is always open to a jury to infer that an individual intends to deprive the owner of his property permanently from conduct and circumstances outside the ambit of s. 6.

8.11 CONDITIONAL INTENT

An individual intending to appropriate a particular piece of property and permanently to deprive the owner of it conditional upon that property being found upon examination by him to be valuable does not commit the offence of theft. This is unobjectionable. An individual who lacks a clear intent to appropriate and/or permanently to deprive an owner of property lacks not merely *mens rea*, but because of the nature of appropriation (see para. 1.2) an element in the *actus reus* of the offence of theft. See *R* v *Easom* [1971] 2 QB 315 and *R* v *Husseyn* (1978) 67 Cr App R 131.

These authorities with greater objection perhaps also determined that an individual in such cases may not be charged with attempted theft (see chapter 5). These authorities seemed to ignore the realities of thefts and the *modus operandi* of thieves, and resulted in serious difficulties in securing convictions in cases where the thief had not clearly completed the act of theft.

The effects of these authorities have been considerably circumscribed in the case of attempted theft by *Attorney-General's References (Nos. 1 and 2 of 1979)* [1980] QB 180 and *R* v *Bayley and Easterbrook* [1980] Crim LR 503. The principle of 'conditional' intent as first enunciated in *Easom* is still applicable and available as a defence in all cases of theft or attempted theft where a thief intends to steal one *particular* or specific object or objects (dependent of course, e.g., upon the goods being sufficiently valuable). However, where an individual is charged with attempted theft of any object or objects within a specified class of possessions, e.g., within a handbag, trunk, room or house, then a conviction for attempted theft may be sustained (see *Attorney-General's References (Nos. 1 and 2 of 1979)*). This is so even where it can only be established that an accused had a *general* conditional intent to steal anything which he might find valuable. This development of the law has removed many of the problems caused by *Easom* and its progeny. Many thieves undertake the stealing of possessions on the basis of opportunity and usually have a 'conditional' intent to steal *anything* they may find useful. *Attorney-General's References (Nos. 1 and 2 of 1979)* recognises the frequency of this situation and has for the sake of practical convenience extinguished 'conditional' intent in such cases as a defence where the thief has not yet completed the act, or has abandoned his nefarious activities as being of little or no advantage to him.

The application of conditional intent as a defence to cases of attempted theft will now be rare in view of the requirement that it should relate to the theft of a *particular* object or objects. It will be a very infrequent occurrence where a thief resolves to steal particular possessions with only a conditional intent to appropriate or permanently to deprive the true owner.

8.12 BURGLARY

Burglary is an example of an offence which may be committed in a number of ways. In its various forms it comprises its own unique elements with the commission of or intent to commit a number of offences which are in their own right separate substantive offences.

8.12.1 Burglary under Theft Act 1968, s. 9(1)(a)

The form of burglary which shall be considered first is that contained in s. 9(1)(a) of the Theft Act 1968. This may be committed in a number of ways. An individual must enter a building or part thereof as a trespasser with an *intent*:

(a) to steal anything in the building or in any part thereof, or
(b) to inflict grievous bodily harm upon any person in the building or any part thereof, or
(c) to rape any woman in the building or part thereof, or
(d) to do any unlawful damage to the building or part thereof or to anything contained therein.

The *actus reus* of this form of burglary comprises the following elements. These elements are, however, common to all forms of burglary contained in s. 9.

8.12.2 Circumstances

The conduct required of an individual is the entering of a building or part thereof. Before consideration is given to this element of the offence the circumstance that entry must be made into a building or part of a building as a trespasser will be examined.

8.12.3 Building or part of a building

This concept is partially defined by s. 9(3) of the Theft Act 1968. It includes any 'inhabited vehicle or vessel, and shall apply to any such vehicle or vessel at times when the person having a habitation in it is not there as well as at times when he is'.

This subsection provides that physical structures such as houseboats and caravans are within the protective sphere of the offence of burglary, dependent upon their being occupied. Vehicles or vessels which are occupied intermittently, e.g., during summer vacations will it seems only be a building within the requirements of s. 9 during those periods of habitation.

What is a building, however, is left to general interpretation. Any permanent structure will amount to a building, be it a dwelling-house, factory, shop, warehouse etc. It would appear that even a temporary or prefabricated structure

Offences Against Property

can be a building within the terms of s. 9, if it is on a permanent site and is used as a building see *B and S* v *Leathley* [1979] Crim LR 314

8.12.4 Part of a building

The reference in s. 9 of the Theft Act 1968 to 'part of a building' recognises that a single structure may be divided into parts. Examples abound. A block of flats, a multi-storey office block which houses different businesses. A less obvious example includes different rooms or partitions in a house. The importance of this lies in the fact that when Donald and his friends were invited into Rex's home by Sarah, that invitation may only extend to part of the house (the significance of this will be examined in the section below). A building may be divided into parts though there are no physical partitions. A shop, be it supermarket or corner shop, may have areas which are divided into those where the public may go and those where they may not. This separation may be indicated by no more than a sign excluding customers from part of the shop, or a counter, or markings upon the floor (see *R* v *Walkington* [1979] 2 All ER 716). An individual who enters a building or part of a building where he has no right to enter is a trespasser and this circumstance of the *actus reus* of the offence must now be examined.

8.12.5 'As a trespasser'

Not only must an individual enter a building or part thereof but to constitute a possible offence of burglary he must at the time of entry be a trespasser. A trespass is a civil law concept which is nevertheless an element in the *actus reus* of the offence of burglary. It involves entry into a building or part thereof without a right in law to do so, or without the permission or authority of the owner of such premises and/or the occupier (i.e., the person in physical possession).

The police under a search warrant or officials of certain nationalised industries, e.g., from British Gas or an electricity board, may by virtue of statutory authority enter a building or part thereof without the permission of the owner and/or occupier. Entry must be in accordance with the authority given by the terms of the statute or warrant, otherwise the entry, if without the permission of the owner or occupier, will be a trespass.

The permission of the owner and/or occupier of a building or part thereof to enter his premises may be express or implied. Sarah as an occupier (though not the owner) has given express permission for Donald and his friends to enter Rex's house. Though that permission may be withdrawn and from that moment all concerned rendered trespassers, this does not make them burglars. This is because a person must *enter* the building *or* a part thereof as a trespasser — an individual who becomes a trespasser after entry is not within the terms of s. 9, see *R* v *Collins* [1973] QB 100.

Permission to enter a building or part thereof may be implied. Thus a shopkeeper gives implied permission for all to enter his premises to examine his wares and to purchase them. However, permission to enter the shop, be it express or implied, will not be applicable to individuals who enter the premises with the secret intention to commit any unlawful act, for in such cases the individual is regarded by the law as entering the premises in excess of that permission and is thus a trespasser, see *R v Jones and Smith* [1976] 3 All ER 54. A shop is nearly always divided into parts, those where the public may go and those where they may not, e.g., behind a shop counter where the tills are kept. (See *R v Walkington* [1979] 2 All ER 716). An entry by a member of the public into such a prohibited area is usually without the permission of the shop owner and thus a trespass. The significance of the fact that entry may be effected with regard to part of a building is that a person may enter premises without being a trespasser, but later, forming a criminal intent, he may negate the initial express or implied permission to enter. He may then subsequently enter a part of that building without the necessary authority or permission and thus become a trespasser for the purposes of an offence of burglary with regard to that part but not as to the building as a whole.

Thus in the scenario Donald and his friends have express permission to enter Rex's home (given by Sarah). If they enter with the intention to steal, cause criminal damage, rape Sarah etc. they have entered the building in excess of the permission given to them. They are trespassers from their entry and if they have the prescribed *mens rea* (see below) they are burglars within the terms of s. 9(1)(a).

If permission to enter a building is given by the owner and/or occupier to an individual under a misapprehension of fact as to the latter's identity or status (and would not have been given if the true state of affairs had been known) then, whether or not such a misapprehension has been induced by fraud or by the conduct of that individual, he is a trespasser, for the purposes of the offence of burglary, see *R v Collins* [1973] QB 100. The final factor in the *actus reus* of burglary to be considered is the fact of entry into a building.

8.12.6 Entry of a building or part thereof

In the case of *R v Collins* [1973] QB 100 it was determined that an individual must make 'an effective and substantial entry' into a building. This remains an ambiguous concept. Under the old law (pre Theft Act 1968) the former offence of burglary required only the intrusion of part of the body into a building for entry to be completed. This included the use of any mechanical device or instrument, but only where such a device or instrument was used to commit an offence, and not merely to facilitate entry. Thus, if a jemmy was used to break open a window or door and was inserted into a building, this did not consititute entry for the purposes of burglary. If an instrument, e.g., a hook was used to pull out a carpet from a home this would be an entry and a burglary. Thus the pre Theft Act 1968 law was artificial but unambiguous. The new formulation in *R v Collins* that the entry be 'effective and substantial' lacks clarity and remains just as artificial as the old formulation. It would appear that the use of an instrument to gain entry to a building or part of a building would not be regarded as an entry under the *Collins* formulation. It would also appear that the mere intrusion of an instrument over a threshold in order to commit an offence or a part of the body of an individual, e.g., fingers, hand, leg etc. would not be a 'substantial or effective entry'. It would seem, however, that an individual can make a substantial and effective entry into a building without the whole of his body having crossed the threshold (see *R v Brown, The Times*, 31 January 1985). The *Collins* formulation of what constitutes an entry into a building is, however, a matter of fact (see

Offences Against Property   255

Murphy, *A Practical Approach to Evidence*) for the jury to decide. There is little to be gained therefore from further considering this element of the *actus reus* of burglary.

8.12.7 The mens rea of burglary: Circumstance: The fact of trespass

It was determined in *R v Collins* [1973] QB 100 that it was not sufficient that an individual entered a building or part thereof as a trespasser. An accused must know or be reckless as to that fact. Thus if an occupier invited another on to his premises and the latter was aware that the invitation was meant for another (or he foresaw that it may be for another but nevertheless took up the invitation) then the individual concerned would be entering those premises knowing himself to be a trespasser or being reckless as to this fact. At the time of *Collins* it was subjective *Cunningham*-style recklessness to which the court was referring (see chapter 2). Following the House of Lords decision in *R v Seymour* [1983] 2 AC 493 it may well be that *Caldwell*-style recklessness (see chapter 2) will also apply.

8.12.8 With intent to commit an offence

For an offence of burglary to be committed under the Theft Act 1968, s. 9(1)(a), an accused must enter a building or part thereof with intent to commit one or more of the offences noted above (see para. 8.12.1 and s. 9(2)). It would appear that only a direct intent to commit one or more of these offences will suffice (see chapter 2). The issue of 'conditional' intent (see para. 8.11) as applied to the offence of theft was also raised as regards this form of burglary. In the case of *R v Walkington* [1979] 2 All ER 716 the Court of Appeal considered the application of 'conditional' intent as a defence to a charge of burglary under s. 9(1)(a) which involved an intent to steal. A burglar will usually enter a building with intent to steal anything which he may find or which he considers of value. This is a general intent but not a conditional intent within the terms of the *R v Easom* [1971] 2 QB 315 and *R v Husseyn* (1978) 67 Cr App R 131 (see para. 8.11) which has now been interpreted as constituting a defence only where there is an intent to steal a *specific* object which is clearly in the mind of the potential thief and which will only be stolen e.g., if it is subsequently believed to be of value (see para 8.11). This will rarely be the mental state of a burglar, who intends to steal and thus *R v Husseyn* is not generally applicable to such cases of burglary. The case of *R v Greenhoff* [1979] Crim LR 108 which purported to apply *R v Husseyn* to cases of burglary which involved an intent to steal was overruled in *R v Walkington*. (See also *Attorney-General's References (Nos. 1 and 2 of 1979)* [1980] QB 180.) It is difficult to conceive of situations where conditional intent could possibly be applicable to the intentional elements in the other forms of burglary within s. 9(1)(a).

8.12.9 Burglary under Theft Act 1968, s. 9(1)(b)

The second form of burglary within the Theft Act 1968 has the following common elements with s. 9(1)(a).

8.12.10 As to the actus reus

The individual must:

(a) enter (see para. 8.12.6)
(b) a building or part of a building (see para. 8.12.3)
(c) as a trespasser (see para. 8.12.5).

8.12.11 As to the mens rea

The individual must know or be reckless as to the fact that he is a trespasser (see para. 8.12.7)

However, there is no requirement that an individual enters a building or part thereof as a trespasser with an *intent* to commit an offence. The form of burglary contained in s. 9(1)(b) is only satisfied when an individual *having entered* the building or part thereof as a trespasser actually commits one of the following offences:

(a) The offence of theft or attempted theft (see above) from the building or part thereof (see *R* v *Gregory* (1983) 77 Cr App R 41).

(b) The infliction or attempted infliction of grievous bodily harm upon a person (see chapter 7) within the building or part thereof.

The realisation of or reckless indifference to the fact that he is a trespasser must occur before he commits or attempts any of the above offences.

8.12.12 Comparison of s. 9(1)(a) and (b)

A comparison of the differences between the two forms of burglary can be made by considering the activities of Donald and his friends at Rex's home. If, when Donald was invited in by Sarah he intended to rape her he would be entering the property as a trespasser and at the point of making a 'substantial and effective entry' into the house he would be a burglar within s. 9(1)(a). If Bruce, Edward and John, not intending to commit any of the offences within s. 9(1)(a), had nevertheless entered Rex's home as trespassers (because the invitation to enter had not been extended to them) then they could not commit the offence of burglary as prescribed in s. 9(1)(a). However, having *entered* as trespassers if Edward and John then steal the camera, jewellery and candlesticks they may commit the offence of burglary within the terms of s. 9(1)(b). This is dependent, however, upon them, e.g., realising or consciously taking the risk or possibly failing to appreciate that they are trespassers when that circumstance was an obvious possibility (i.e., being reckless to the fact) that they entered the premises as trespassers. This realisation or reckless indifference as to their status must occur before they steal the articles.

There may of course be a considerable overlap between s. 9(1)(a) and s. 9(1)(b). A given situation may give rise to liability under both sections. If Edward and John entered Rex's house in the scenario intending to steal they would on entry (dependent upon them having the prescribed *mens rea*) commit an offence of

Offences Against Property 257

burglary under s. 9(1)(a). Their subsequent theft of the camera, etc. would result in liability under s.9(1)(b). It appears to be usual to charge an individual under s. 9(1)(b) in such cases, see *R* v *Taylor* [1979] Crim LR 649. However, if the facts of a case disclose that criminal liability can only be incurred under one subsection, e.g., under s. 9(1)(a), a charge under the other subsection, i.e., under s. 9(1)(b), will be ineffectual, see *R* v *Hollis* [1971] Crim LR 525.

8.12.13 Aggravated burglary (Theft Act 1968, s. 10)

This offence involves committing either form of burglary under s. 9, but with the aggravating factor that at the time of the commission of such a crime the burglar has with him any firearm (including an imitation) or any weapon of offence or any explosive (see s. 10).

The terms 'firearm' (see s. 10(1)(a)) and 'explosive' (s. 10(1)(c)) need no explanation. However, the term 'weapon of offence' is defined by s. 10(a)(b) and means 'any article made or adapted for use for causing injury to or incapacitating a person, or intended by the person having it with him for such use'.

This definition will include any article which has been made for offence, e.g., a sheath-knife, or adapted for such use, e.g., a piece of lead piping, or used with that intention, e.g., a household article taken up in a moment of panic. Whatever the nature, the weapon must be able to injure or incapacitate (e.g., restrain) an individual. It appears that the burglar must have the weapon in his physical possession so that it may be immediately available for use. He must be aware of its existence before he can be regarded as having such a weapon of offence 'with him' in accordance with s. 10(1) (see *R* v *Russell, The Times*, 4 January 1985).

The weapon of offence must be 'with' a burglar at the time when he commits the offence of burglary otherwise there is no offence under s. 10. This means in the case of burglary under s. 9(1)(a) when he makes a 'substantial and effective' entry into a building or part thereof with the prescribed intent. In the case of burglary under s. 9(1)(b) the weapon must be with the burglar at the time he steals, inflicts grievous bodily harm upon a person or attempts either of these offences.

8.13 DISHONESTY OFFENCES OTHER THAN THEFT

8.13.1 Deception

Theft is not the only way in which an individual may dishonestly obtain property which belongs to another. There are a number of offences in which an individual may obtain property by deceiving the owner to part with possession, control or ownership of his goods. One such offence is that contained in s. 15(1) of the Theft Act 1968. By virtue of that subsection an individual who 'by any deception dishonestly obtains property belonging to another, with the intention of permanently depriving the other of it' commits an offence.

This offence has many common elements with theft.

8.13.2 As to the actus reus

The subject-matter of an offence under s. 15(1) consists of:

(a) *Property.* This has a similar meaning to property within the offence of theft. However, by s. 34(1) of the Theft Act 1968 only s. 4(1) is applicable to offences committed under s. 15(1) (see para. 8.1.3). This means that all property may be the subject-matter of an offence under s. 15 including land.

(b) *Belonging to another.* By s. 34(1) of the Theft Act 1968 only s. 5(1) applies to an offence committed under s. 15(1). Thus only where an individual is deceived into parting with possession, control or with a proprietary right or other interest in a possession within the provisions of that subsection can he be the victim of an offence of deception. (See paras 8.4.1 to 8.4.5 for a full discussion of this provision.)

8.13.3 As to the mens rea

(a) *Dishonesty.* Though the provisions of s. 2 (see para. 8.9) are generally inapplicable to an offence committed under s. 15(1) the test of dishonesty created by the common law is applicable (see *R* v *Greenstein* [1975] 1 All ER 1) (para. 8.9). Thus a direction to a jury in terms of an accused's claim of right as provided by s. 2(1)(a) negating dishonesty in an offence of deception adds nothing to a general direction given in terms now required by *R* v *Ghosh* [1982] QB 1053 and is to be discouraged (see *R* v *Woolven* (1983) 77 Cr App R 231).

(b) *Intention permanently to deprive.* This has the same meaning and application to s. 15(1) as in cases of theft (see para. 8.10). Section 6 is also applicable to offences committed under s. 15(1) but is suitably adapted to the offence of obtaining by deception by virtue of s. 15(3). Reference must now be made to the elements of the offence of obtaining by deception which are its unique and essential characteristics.

8.13.4 The actus reus of the offence

Deception An individual must deceive another and by such a deception obtain that individual's property. A deception is defined by the Theft Act 1968, s. 15(4), as: 'any deception (whether deliberate or reckless) by words or conduct as to fact or as to law, including a deception as to the present intentions of the person using the deception or any other person'. The essential requirement of a deception is that a person is deceived (see *DPP* v *Ray* [1974] AC 370 endorsing the view originally expressed by Buckley J in *Re London & Globe Finance Corporation Ltd* [1903] 1 Ch 728, and para. 8.13.7). Deception may take several forms.

Deception by conduct An example of conduct which amounts to a deception is dressing as an individual of a particular status, e.g., a student. In *R* v *Barnard* (1837) 7 C & P 784 the accused entered an Oxford shop wearing a student's cap and gown to which he was not entitled, and on the strength of this conduct obtained goods on credit from the shopkeeper. The shopkeeper provided such credit facilities to Oxford students but not to his general customers.

Offences Against Property

An individual's conduct may give rise to an implied representation which amounts to a deception. Thus where a thief offers to sell goods to a third party, he impliedly represents by the act of offering to sell the goods that he is the owner of them and that he has the right in law to sell them, but a thief or handler cannot possibly have such rights. In the case of *Metropolitan Police Commissioner* v *Charles* [1977] AC 177 it was accepted that a person who draws a cheque upon his account (though his funds are inadequate to meet it) impliedly represents that it will be met on presentment in the ordinary course of events and if accepted by the payee it is in the belief it will be met, see Viscount Dilhorne in *Metropolitan Police Commissioner* v *Charles* at p. 186 and *R* v *Gilmartin* [1983] 1 All ER 829. Thus drawing a cheque knowing that in the ordinary course of business it will not be honoured due to inadequate funds is in itself a deception. The situation is different, however, where a cheque card is used. Where a cheque is drawn and backed by a cheque card the bank is legally obliged to honour the cheque if the conditions as to the card's use are complied with. A cheque backed by a cheque card will be honoured irrespective of whether the bank has withdrawn its authority for the drawer to use the card or where he has exceeded his authority to use it. The drawer of a cheque backed by a cheque card does not represent to the payee that he has adequate funds in his account or that the cheque will be met in the ordinary course of business on presentment, since the correct use of the cheque card guarantees the bank will honour the commitment in any event. However, the use of a cheque card when drawing a cheque is a representation by the drawer to the payee that he has the actual authority of his bank to enter on its behalf into a contract between the bank and the payee (the terms of which are contained on the card) to the effect that the bank will honour the cheque on presentment in any event. Where a bank has withdrawn its authority from a customer to use a cheque card, or the latter has exceeded that authority, the subsequent drawing of a cheque using a cheque card by the drawer will amount to a deception as to the bank's willingness to enter into such a contract with the payee. In such cases the bank no longer authorises its customer to represent that it is bound contractually with the payee of cheques drawn on the customer's account to honour the latter's cheques. This principle has been held to apply to the use of credit cards, see *R* v *Lambie* [1982] AC 449. An individual may deceive another by words alone. Thus a telephone call or a letter may in themselves constitute a deception. However, frequently a deception takes the form of words and conduct.

8.13.5 Deception by omission

Generally an individual is under no duty to correct a misconception in another's mind which he has not been responsible for bringing about, though he may benefit from that misconception. As a general rule an individual may not deceive by omission, i.e., by failing to correct a misconception in another's mind. However, the situation may well be different where an individual has been responsible for inducing another to believe that a certain state of affairs exists, and that state of affairs subsequently alters and the individual is aware of this change of situation. In the case of *DPP* v *Ray* [1974] AC 370 the accused obtained a meal in a restaurant. After eating the main course he resolved not to pay for the meal, and ran from the restaurant without doing so. The House of Lords determined that the accused's conduct from his entering the restaurant to his consuming the meal was to be regarded as one transaction. During the continuaton of this transaction the accused represented by his initial conduct that he was an honest customer who had an intention to pay for the meal. His change of mind and resolution not to pay and his *omission* to correct what had now become a misrepresentation as to his intentions amounted to a deception.

8.13.6 Deception of fact, law and intention

It has been seen how an individual may by his words and/or conduct deceive another. Consideration must be given as to what form a deception may take. A deception may be as to the existence of facts which do not exist, examples of such a deception can be seen in the cheque card case of *Metropolitan Police Commissioner* v *Charles* [1977] AC 177 (relating to the bank's willingness to enter into a contractual relationship with a third party). An individual cannot deceive another if he merely expresses an opinion; though if he alleges an opinion which is based upon facts which he knows to be untrue, this would amount to a deception.

A person may deceive another as to the law, though frequently this will also involve a deception in part as to facts upon which the legal misrepresentation is based. An individual may deceive another as to his intentions (see Theft Act 1968, s. 15(4)). Thus if a man, as in the case of *DPP* v *Ray* [1974] AC 370, had entered a restaurant never intending to pay for a meal he is about to consume, his conduct amounts to a deception, relating to his intentions, for he never intends to pay for the meal though his conduct suggests otherwise.

The essence of the offence under s. 15(1) is that an individual is induced to part with either possession, control or ownership of his goods (see s. 5(1) and above) to another. The latter obtains the goods not by an act of theft, i.e., appropriation, but by his conduct, which deceives or tricks the true owner into parting with his property. Such deceptions will include, e.g., representations as to a person's identity or creditworthiness to induce a void or fraudulent contract of sale, or drawing a worthless cheque in payment for goods received.

8.13.7 An individual must be deceived

A deception must deceive another. In the case of *Re London & Globe Finance Corporation Ltd* [1903] 1 Ch 728 Buckley J was of the opinion that: 'To deceive is . . . to induce a man to believe that a thing is true which is false'. In so far as this dictum suggests that an individual must positively believe that a deception is true, it would not appear to represent the law today. In *Metropolitan Police Commissioner* v *Charles* [1977] AC 177 their lordships seemed to require only the following matters to be established before it could be said that an individual has been deceived for the purposes of an offence under s. 15(1).

(a) That the individual concerned was not aware of the truth.
(b) That he had acted in reliance upon the deception.
(c) That he would not have acted in such a way had he known the truth.

Offences Against Property

This is clearly illustrated in the case of *Metropolitan Police Commissioner* v *Charles*. The individual concerned who had accepted cheques drawn by the accused backed by a cheque card was deceived because:

(a) he was not aware that the bank had withdrawn their authority from the accused to use the card and cheques,
(b) he accepted the cheques in reliance upon the accused's conduct and
(c) he would not have accepted the cheques in return for supplying gambling chips had he known the truth.

8.13.8 The deception must be the cause of the obtaining of the property

If an individual is not deceived by a misrepresentation made by another but nevertheless the latter obtains property from that individual there is no full offence committed under s. 15(1) though there may well be an attempted offence of obtaining by deception (see *R* v *Hensler* (1870) 22 LT 691 and para. 1.8). Neither will a full offence within s. 15(1) be committed if the deception did not influence an individual's conduct in parting with his property and was not a causal link in the deceiver obtaining the former's property see *R* v *Laverty* [1970] 3 All ER 432. In this case the accused obtained money from the sale of a stolen car. It was not established that the purchaser of the car who had parted with the money had been induced to do so by the accused's deception relating to the vehicle's false number-plates. Since there had been no reliance upon this deception by the purchaser and it had not influenced his conduct, it could not be said that the accused had obtained the purchase price as a result of his deception. The situation would have been different if it had been argued that the accused's act of selling the vehicle amounted to an implied representation that he had a right to sell the car as the true owner (see above) and it could have been established that the purchaser had relied upon this representation. In the case of *R* v *Collis-Smith* [1971] Crim LR 716 the accused obtained petrol by representing to the garage attendant that he was authorised to draw petrol for his private motor car on the account of his employer. He made this representation (which was false) only after he had obtained the petrol. Since the misrepresentation had not operated on the mind of the garage attendant at the time when the petrol was obtained there had been no deception within the terms of s. 15(1) for it had not been a cause of the property being obtained.

It is not necessary that property is obtained from the person deceived. In the case of *Metropolitan Police Commissioner* v *Charles* [1977] AC 177 the accused was charged under s. 16(1) of the Theft Act 1968, an offence which involves an accused obtaining a pecuniary advantage by deception (see later). Though the person deceived was the payee who received cheques in return for supplying gambling chips, he suffered no loss because the cheques were honoured by the bank. The bank, however, was obliged, in essence because of the accused's deception, to extend his overdraft (though unwillingly) — this was the pecuniary advantage obtained by the accused which is the subject-matter of an offence under s. 16. The victim of this offence, the bank had not been deceived, however.

The subject-matter of an offence under s. 15(1) is the obtaining of property belonging to another (see para. 8.13.2). An individual obtains the property in goods following a deception where he obtains ownership, possession or control of them (see s. 15(2)). By s. 15(2) 'obtaining' property includes obtaining for a third party or enabling another to obtain or to retain property. Thus if an individual induces another to transfer his rights of ownership, possession or control in property to a third party an offence under s. 15(1) is committed. A case of enabling another to retain property would include the situation where an individual by a deception induces the true owner of goods not to seek the rightful return of his property which is in the possession of a third party.

8.13.9 Mens rea

The *mens rea* of an offence under the Theft Act 1968, s. 15(1), involves that the property be obtained:

(a) Dishonestly (see para. 8.13.3).
(b) With the intention permanently to deprive the owner of those goods (see para. 8.13.3).
(c) By a deception. This deception may be made deliberately, i.e., intending to deceive (with either a direct or oblique intent, see chapter 2), though it may also be made recklessly. This has always meant subjective *Cunningham*-style recklessness (see chapter 2), i.e., making a representation of fact, law or intention, by words or conduct knowing there is a risk that it may be untrue but nevertheless making it, see *R* v *Staines* (1974) 60 Cr App R 160.

It would appear that notwithstanding the House of Lords decision in *R* v *Seymour* [1983] 2 AC 493 as to the general application of *Caldwell*-type recklessness (see chapter 2) to statutory offences, it is not applicable to s. 15(1). This would appear to be based upon the requirement that an individual's conduct be dishonest. An individual who makes a representation which he does not appreciate is a deception, but its nature is such that it would have been gross and obvious to a reasonable man that it was a deception, cannot be said to be dishonest within the context of s. 15(1). Dishonesty suggests that the individual is aware of, or foresees the consequences and circumstances of his actions, and is incompatible with an objective assessment of an individual's conduct.

8.13.10 The relationship between theft and obtaining property by deception

An individual's conduct with regard to a piece of property may amount both to an offence of theft and of obtaining property by deception. A person who by a deception obtains possession or control of goods, but not ownership of them, e.g., by representing that he wishes only to borrow the article concerned from the owner clearly obtains such property by deception contrary to s. 15(1). However, since the owner retains a proprietary right or interest in those goods, i.e., ownership within the terms of s. 5(1), a subsequent appropriation of that property (see para. 8.8.1) by the deceiver concerned will also amount to an offence of theft by him.

This overlap may result in the offences being committed simultaneously. In the case of *Lawrence* v *Metropolitan Police Commissioner* [1972] AC 626 the accused was a taxi-driver. One of his customers, a foreign gentleman, was unsure of the fare and proffered an open wallet bulging with banknotes. The accused took more money than he was entitled to by physically seizing it and taking it from the customer's wallet which remained in the latter's hand. It was determined that the accused could be convicted of obtaining property by deception *and* theft. The act of seizing the bank notes was conduct on the part of the accused which amounted to a representation that he had a right to that particular sum. This was a deception and on the strength of that deception he had obtained the property in that money. On the facts of the case the accused had also stolen the money. The accused had appropriated the bank notes (see para. 8.8.1) without his customer's authority to do so and at the precise moment in time of the appropriation when the accused took hold of the money the customer still had possession and control of it, for he held the wallet in his hand (see paras 8.4.3 and 8.4.4) —it was capable, therefore, of being stolen from him.

It has been mooted that *Lawrence* has a wider authority, that it determined that all cases of obtaining property by deception will also amount to theft at the moment that the property is appropriated. This, it is suggested, is going too far. The House of Lords determined that the offence of theft did not require that the appropriation of property should 'be without the consent of the owner'. Furthermore it determined that the offences of theft and obtaining by deception were not mutually exclusive and that in certain cases a course of conduct could amount to an offence of theft and of obtaining by deception. However, there were instances where only one of the offences could be charged.

It has been suggested that *Lawrence*, in so far as it suggests that the appropriation of the customer's money took place when the accused seized it, conflicts with the authorities of *R v Skipp* [1975] Crim LR 114, *R v Meech* [1974] QB 549 and *Anderton v Burnside* [1984] AC 320 (see para. 8.8.1). These authorities, it has been argued, determine that an appropriation of property can only take place when a potential thief does some act with regard to another's possessions which is clearly established as being outside the express or implied authority given by the owner to deal with his goods by reference to the thief's conduct (see para. 8.8.1). The authorities can be reconciled, however. First it could be said their lordships took the view in *Lawrence* that on the facts of the case the implied authority given by the customer to the accused to deal with his money had been exceeded. A second ground of reconcilation is that the authorities do not conflict with the view of *Lawrence* suggested above that in all the above cases the express or implied authority of the owner to deal with his goods either was or was not exceeded dependent upon the facts of each case but that an express or implied authority given by an owner to deal with his goods may be exceeded by an act of physical seizure of those goods together with a mental resolve on the part of the potential thief to deal with that property as his own. In such cases it cannot be said that the owner would have so authorised such conduct (see para. 8.8.1). It is certain that the customer in *Lawrence* would not have authorised the accused to take the money from his wallet, if he had known the accused's intentions.

8.13.11 Property transferred under a mistake

It has been seen (para. 8.6) that property transferred to a party under certain types of mistake will result in the recipient of those goods obtaining only possession or control of them and not ownership. In such cases if the individual concerned has obtained the property by deception, he can if he subsequently appropriates it also commit the offence of theft, for the true owner still has a proprietary right or interest in the goods by virtue of the Theft Act 1968, s. 5(1). Though the other subsections of s. 5 are inapplicable to cases of obtaining property by deception (see para. 8.13.2) they are applicable to all cases of theft. The consequence of this is that in a case like *Moynes* v *Cooper* [1956] 1 QB 439 (for facts see para. 8.6), if the accused had represented to the wages clerk that he was entitled to the overpayment he would have obtained that money by deception. If later he had spent it he would have appropriated it. By virtue of s. 5(4), in so far as he is under a legal obligation to make restitution of that overpayment, it would be regarded as belonging to his employer for the purposes of the offence of theft (see para. 8.6). His spending the money could in such cases therefore amount to theft. Only where a mistake (be it by virtue of the common law or s. 5(4)) negates the transfer of all or some of the rights and interests in a possession will there be a possible overlap between theft and obtaining by deception. Where by a deception an individual obtains ownership, possession and control of property, though he commits an offence under s. 15(1) there cannot generally (but see *Lawrence* v *Metropolitan Police Commissioner* [1972] AC 626) be an offence of theft, because the property does not belong to another within the provisions of s. 5(1) at the time of appropriation. An example would include a contract of sale induced by a fraudulent deception (which had not been avoided at the time of the act of appropriation, see para. 8.7). Where an individual obtains property belonging to another without any deception, e.g., by physically seizing it, he can, of course, only commit the offence of theft.

8.13.12 Other offences involving deception

There are other offences where deception forms an important element in the formulation of the *actus reus*. These offences differ from s. 15 of the Theft Act 1968 principally in their subject-matter, i.e., what may be obtained as a consequence of the deception.

By s. 16(1) of the Theft Act 1968 it is an offence if an individual by a deception obtains a pecuniary advantage. This may include borrowing by way of overdraft, taking out an insurance policy or annuity contract (or obtaining an improvement of the terms on which he is allowed to do so), see s. 16(2)(b).

One example of this type of offence can be seen in *Metropolitan Police Commissioner* v *Charles* [1977] AC 177. The accused had by writing cheques backed with a cheque card forced his bank to honour them. He had thus in effect obtained an overdraft from the bank by this method though his bank had revoked their authority for him to use the card or cheques. This overdraft had arisen because the accused had 'deceived' a third party into accepting those cheques backed with his cheque card in return for gaming chips.

An offence under s. 16(1) may also be committed where by a deception an

Offences Against Property   265

individual obtains an opportunity to earn remuneration or greater remuneration in an office or employment, or to win money by betting s. 16(2)(c).

Thus if an individual falsely represented that he was a university graduate and on this basis secured a post as a graduate trainee manager in a company he would commit an offence within s. 16(1).

8.13.13 The Theft Act 1978

There was an additional way in which an offence under s. 16(1) of the Theft Act 1968 could be committed, the terms of which were laid down by s. 16(2)(a). Section 16(2)(a) was repealed and replaced by a new set of offences now contained in the Theft Act 1978.

By s. 1 of the Theft Act 1978 it is an offence to obtain services by deception. In the scenario Edward and John obtain a taxi ride from Ron. If they do not intend to pay for the ride they may commit an offence under this section.

By s. 2 of the Theft Act 1978 there are created three separate offences in which an individual by any deception:

(a) dishonestly secures the remission of the whole or part of any existing liability to make payment, whether his own liability or another's; or

(b) with intent to make permanent default in whole or in part on any existing liability to make a payment, or with intent to let another do so, dishonestly induces the creditor or any person claiming payment on behalf of the creditor to wait for payment (whether or not the due date for payment is deferred) or to forgo payment; or

(c) dishonestly obtains any exemption from or abatement of liability to make a payment.

These complicated offences cover the multifarious and devious ways in which debtors may seek by deception to escape their liabilities for their debts, or the debts of others either in whole or in part or with regard to instalments that may become payable in respect of a debt. This includes not only full evasion but improperly obtained extensions of credit with a view to eventual evasion.

To take a rather prosaic example, a student assures his landlord that a supplement to his grant which will enable him to pay his arrears will soon be coming from his invalid recently widowed mother following the settlement of family affairs. However, both his parents are fit and well and there will be no cheque forthcoming from them. This despicable reliance upon sympathy results in the landlord forgoing payment of the rent arrears. If the student intends to abandon the premises and avoid payment to the landlord of his dues permanently he commits an offence within s. 2(b).

The Theft Act 1978, s. 3 This offence does not require that the accused deceives another. However, as a matter of practical reality a deception by an individual may be a prerequisite to the commission of the offence. By s. 3(1) a person who, knowing that payment on the spot for any goods supplied or service done is required or expected from him, dishonestly makes off without having paid as required or expected and with intent to avoid payment of the amount due is guilty of an offence.

In the scenario Edward and John take a ride in Ron's taxi, if they then dishonestly make off without paying the fare they will commit an offence within s. 3(1). In the scenario they entered the taxi not intending to pay for the ride. This is a deception and would constitute a possible offence within s. 1(1) of the Theft Act 1978, i.e., obtaining services by deception. This illustrates that the offences within the Theft Act 1978 and s. 16(1) of the Theft Act 1968 may overlap, and that a course of conduct by an individual may constitute simultaneously an offence under any of these statutory provisions.

8.14 HANDLING

8.14.1 The rationale of handling

It is an offence for a person to 'handle' stolen goods. By s. 22(1) of the Theft Act 1968 a person handles "stolen" goods if:

> (otherwise than in the course of the stealing) knowing or believing them to be stolen goods he dishonestly receives the goods, or dishonestly undertakes or assists in their retention, removal, disposal or realisation by or for the benefit of another person, or if he arranges to do so.

Since the Act determines that the 'handling' must be 'otherwise' than in the course of stealing it is not possible for a thief during the course of his appropriation of property to be a handler, though a handler may be a thief (see *R v Sainthouse* [1980] Crim LR 506). Though the Court of Appeal has determined that the prosecution does not have to prove that a handler is not the original thief or that the handling is 'otherwise' than in the course of stealing (see *R v Cash*, [1985] 2 WLR 735). The jury may make that inference merely on consideration of the entirety of the evidence adduced at the trial, though that inference must be made if an individual is to be convicted of handling stolen goods. If after stealing the goods the original thief abandons the property and then either repossesses, finds or purchases them from a third party he may then commit an offence under the section.

An offence under s. 22(1) may be committed in a multiplicity of ways. This concise but complex section was intended to combat theft or offences under s. 15 of the Theft Act 1968 by making it unprofitable and difficult for thieves and deceivers to dispose of the fruits of their criminal activities. This policy could only be promoted if a wide range of activities carried out by individuals which so aided thieves and deceivers were subsumed under a general offence of handling which concentrated upon the consequences and effects of a 'handler's' conduct and not the particular forms it may take.

8.14.2 The actus reus of handling

The *actus reus* of handling can be established in a multitude of ways. However, one element of the *actus reus* common to all kinds of handling is that the goods

Offences Against Property

are stolen (a circumstance) (see later). The various form of conduct which can amount to handling can now be considered.

8.14.3 Receiving

A person commits the *actus reus* of receiving stolen goods when he takes physical possession or control (see paras 8.4.3 and 8.4.4) of them either personally or through an agent or employee authorised to take receipt of them. In the latter case those parties also commit the *actus reus* of receiving. Receiving is illustrated in the scenario when Edward and John arrive at Edith's home. If Edith took possession of the stolen articles from Edward and John or permitted them to remain in her home she would have committed the *actus reus* of receiving. If Edward and John while in Edith's home retained entire possession and/or control of the articles concerned then Edith could not receive the goods within the meaning of s. 22(1) of the Theft Act 1968. Edith would remain a receiver, however, if she took control or possession of the stolen goods though for a 'limited time' or purpose. It is irrelevant whether or not she gained financially from her actions.

8.14.4 Arranging to receive

Dependent upon the fact that goods have been stolen it is an offence under s. 22(1) of the Theft Act 1968 for an individual to arrange to receive stolen goods. That is, the thief and prospective handler agree that the latter will receive them. Thus Edith would be guilty of this form of handling if, following their escape from Rex's home, Edward and John had telephoned her and all three had agreed that she should take possession of the stolen articles. If the telephone conversation had been cut short before Edith had communicated her agreement to receive the stolen goods then such conduct would probably amount to an attempt to arrange to receive and therefore an offence of attempted handling (see chapter 5).

8.14.5 Retention, removal, disposal, realisation

The forms of handling discussed so far above are simple to understand from a reading of s. 22(1) of the Theft Act 1968. However, the rest of s. 22(1) creates a multiplicity of ways in which a person may handle stolen goods, namely, retention, removal, realisation or disposal, the *actus reus* of each will be discussed later. It is important first to appreciate the interpretative nightmares that this latter part of the subsection has created for the judiciary. In the case of *R v Sloggett* (1971) 55 Cr App R 532 the Court of Appeal Criminal Division favoured a literal interpretation of the subsection. In the words of Roskill J (as he then was, at p. 537, emphasis added):

> It seems clear that the adverb 'dishonestly' governs both the verb 'undertakes' *and* the words 'assists in' *and* that the following four nouns, namely 'retention', 'removal', 'disposal' and 'realisation', are in their turn all governed by the crucial words 'by *or* for the benefit of another person'.

In his lordship's opinion the four forms of activity noted above, namely, 'retention', 'removal', 'disposal' and 'realisation' of stolen goods (see below), could be undertaken by an individual personally or he could assist in any one of those forms of activity which were being carried out by another. This created eight forms of handling. In addition either the personal undertaking of any of these activities or the assisting in any of the four forms of handling being carried out by another could in each instance be either by another or for the benefit of another. This literal interpretation produces 16 different ways of committing these forms of handling (32 if the element of arranging is taken into consideration) some of which seem either impossible or difficult to visualise. Such a case is the permutation of 'undertaking the retention of stolen goods *by* another'. It requires a considerable mental astuteness to conceive of cases where an individual personally undertakes the retention of stolen goods which is nevertheless carried out *by* another. It would seem either the individual concerned undertakes the retention himself or another retains them. In the latter case the individual could only assist the other in such an activity. This confused situation was resolved by the Houe of Lords in the case of *R v Bloxham* [1983] 1 AC 109. To make this complicated issue more clear it is intended to consider the facts of *Bloxham* is some detail.

In January 1977 the accused had agreed to buy a car from one C for £1,300. The car was stolen property, but the accused was not aware of this. He paid some £500 on account, agreeing to pay the balance upon receipt of the registration documents. These were never produced and the accused began to suspect that the vehicle was stolen. The accused continued to use the vehicle until excise duty upon it came due for payment. To cut his losses and avoid further possession of a stolen vehicle the accused sold it to a third party for £200 on the understanding that the registration documents were not available.

The accused was charged with undertaking the disposal or realisation of the vehicle for the benefit of another, i.e., the purchaser of the vehicle. On a plain, literal interpretation of s. 22(1) the accused's conduct was clearly within the ambit of the section. He was convicted at first instance and this conviction was affirmed by the Court of Appeal which endorsed the literal interpretation of the subsection, as propounded in *Slogget*.

The House of Lords accepted a different view as to the interpretation of s. 22(1). Their lordships expressed concern at the consequences that followed a strictly literal approach to the subsection. The section should be examined in context and in its entirety. On this basis only certain combinations of words could realistically be envisaged in producing a limited number of forms of handling.

The section recognises four separate activities which may comprise handling, namely:

(a) Retention of stolen goods. This is constituted by an individual 'keeping possession of, not losing or continuing to have stolen goods' (see *R v Pitchley* (1972) 57 Cr App R 30). However, retaining stolen goods purchased in good faith after discovering their true nature will not constitute the *actus reus* of handling, see *Bloom v Crowther, The Times,* 15 May 1984.

(b) Removal of stolen goods. This is self-evident: it means, e.g., taking them

Offences Against Property

from one place to another.

(c) *Disposal of stolen goods.* This will include changing their form, e.g., breaking up a stolen motor car with a blowtorch, or throwing or giving them away or destroying them entirely.

(d) *Realisation of stolen goods.* This means the sale of such goods to a third party or their exchange for other articles.

In the opinion of Lord Bridge of Harwich in *Bloxham* there were two principal ways in which these four forms of handling could be carried out by an individual.

(a) *Undertaking for the benefit of another.* In Lord Bridge's view an individual could personally undertake any of the above activities but *only* where it was solely 'for the benefit of another person'. This means where an individual either alone or jointly with another undertakes either the retention, removal, disposal or realisation of stolen goods there can be no *actus reus* of handling within s. 22(1) unless those activities are 'for the benefit of another person'. The only form of activity within s. 22(1) which can be carried out by an individual on his own behalf and for his own benefit is receiving or arranging to receive (see above). Thus Bloxham, though he had undertaken the realisation of stolen goods, had not done so *for another's* benefit. It had not been established that the realisation of the car had been for the original thief's benefit (Bloxham had not been an agent for the thief and had not sold the car on his instructions). The purchaser had benefited only by receiving the car through his purchase of it and not from the realisation of the car *per se*. (Though the purchaser may benefit if he subsequently sold the car.) Thus Bloxham had not committed the *actus reus* of handling.

(b) *Assisting in the retention, removal, disposal or realisation of stolen goods by another person.* Where another, e.g., the original thief or another handler undertakes the retention, removal, disposal or realisation of stolen goods an individual may commit the *actus reus* of handling by assisting that other in their undertaking of any of the above activities. According to *R* v *Bloxham* the fact of assistance to another is the crucial factor in this form of handling. In such cases the assistance rendered by an individual may also be for that other's benefit. Though this latter element is not the governing factor in the formulation of this kind of handling, it is the fact that an individual assists in any of those forms of activity which are carried out *by* another which is its distinguishing mark. In the scenario, if Edith a well-known 'fence', helped Edward and John to dispose of or realise the camera, jewellery and candlesticks, e.g., by selling these articles, or dumping them, she would be assisting the two friends in their realisation or disposal of the stolen goods. If Edith when she drove Edward and John to the hospital had allowed them to take the stolen articles in the car and to hide them in an abandoned warehouse she would be assisting them in removing the stolen goods. The nature of assisting was considered in the case of *R* v *Kanwar* [1982] 2 All ER 528. The accused had been charged with handling stolen goods by assisting in their retention *by* and for the benefit of another. Her husband had brought home articles; the accused knew them to be stolen. When the police had searched the house she told them there were no stolen goods on the premises, and in answer to questions regarding specific items in the house, she lied to the police telling them she had bought them. These facts are similar to those diclosed in the scenario with regard to Edith. The Court of Appeal Criminal Division in *Kanwar* determined that the *actus reus* of assisting in the retention of stolen goods could be constituted by positive physical action, but also by verbal representations. There is no need for the assistance to be successful in its aim. Thus Edith in the scenario could be charged with handling stolen goods (i.e., the camera, jewellery and candlesticks) by assisting in their retention by another (i.e., Edward and John). The crucial factor as determined in *Kanwar* is that the conduct of an individual like Edith had as its purpose that another is enabled to retain stolen goods. The authority of *R* v *Kanwar* is almost certainly applicable to the other forms of handling, i.e., removal, realisation or disposal.

Arranging to undertake or to assist in the retention, removal, disposal or realisation of stolen goods by or for the benefit of another Arranging to undertake, for the benefit of another *or* arranging to assist in the retention, removal, disposal or realisation of stolen goods by another will also comprise additional ways in which the conduct element of the *actus reus* of handling stolen goods within s. 22(1) may be constituted. Arranging in this sense bears the same meaning as in arranging to receive (see above) and needs no further discussion.

To sum up there are, according to *R* v *Bloxham* [1983] 1 AC 109, 18 different ways of committing the *actus reus* of handling, receiving or arranging to receive stolen goods, and 16 additional forms which are constituted by various ways in which an individual may undertake or assist (or arrange to do either of these things) in the retention, removal, realisation or disposal of stolen goods. The unwieldy literal interpretation of *R* v *Sloggett* (1971) 55 Cr App R 532 is no longer good law.

8.14.6 Handling by omission

In one instance it appears that the conduct element of the *actus reus* of handling may be brought about by an omission to act (see chapter 1, para. 1.3 onwards). This is where the handling takes the form of assisting in the retention of stolen goods by and for the benefit of another person. For example, if an individual permits the original thief or another handler to bring stolen goods on to his premises. Then if, knowing them to be stolen, he takes no steps to have them removed, and when questioned by the police as to their nature he refuses to say anything about them, he may, though this is an omission to act, be regarded as having assisted another in retaining such goods. This seems to be the consequence of the decisions of *R* v *Pitchley* (1972) 57 Cr App R 30 and *R* v *Brown* [1970] 1 QB 105.

8.14.7 Procedural elements

Lord Bridge of Harwich in *R* v *Bloxham* [1983] 1 AC 109 suggested that s. 22(1) created two distinct offences of handling (the circumstances in each of the offences (see para. 8.14.8) and the required *mens rea* (see para. 8.14.9) being in both situations identical). The two offences of handling were to be distinguished on the basis of their conduct elements. The first form of handling, in his

Offences Against Property

lordship's opinion, was that constituted by receiving goods (or arranging to do so); and the second the various ways in which an individual may undertake or assist in the retention, removal, disposal or realisation of stolen goods (or arrange to do any of these things). The importance of this view lies in its consequences for criminal procedure. If there are two distinct offences within s. 22(1) then a charge must specify which one an accused has committed. An attempt to charge an individual with both forms of offence for a single incident of possible handling must be bad for duplicity (see Emmins, *A Practical Approach to Criminal Procedure*). Notwithstanding the opinion of his lordship as to the nature of s. 22(1) it appears that the balance of authority (see, e.g., *R v Nicklin* [1977] 2 All ER 444) favours that the subsection creates but one offence of handling which can be committed in a multitude of ways. Thus where an individual receives stolen goods or undertakes or assists in their retention etc. (or arranges to do any of these things) he commits the conduct element of the *actus reus* of handling stolen goods within s. 22(1). This removes the issue of duplicity from this criminal offence.

8.14.8 Circumstances of the offence

Whatever form the conduct element of the *actus reus* of handling takes the goods must be stolen at the time of the handling or at the time when the arrangement to handle the goods is made. Though it appears to have been determined that where an individual believes he is handling stolen goods which are not in fact stolen, he may not be convicted of attempted handling (see *Anderton v Ryan* [1985] 2 WLR 969 and para. 5.6.11). The circumstances of the offence are that the goods are stolen. These elements will now be examined.

Goods This includes money and every other description of property. However, land (except things severed from the land) is not included in the definition (see s. 34(2)(b) Theft Act 1968).

Stolen This means goods which have been obtained by an individual as a result of theft (see above), obtaining by deception (see above) or by blackmail. This is the consequence of s. 24(4) of the Theft Act 1968. Even goods which have been stolen abroad (as understood in the sense considered above) are stolen goods for the purposes of handling if by the law of that country the goods would be regarded as stolen (see s. 24(1)). If goods cease to be stolen before they are the subject of an act of handling there can be no full offence committed within the terms of s. 22(1) nor an offence of attempted handling (see above). Goods cease to be stolen in either of the following two circumstances:

(a) If they have been restored to the person from whom they were stolen *or* to other lawful possession or custody (see s. 24(3)). (The problem with regard to this requirement is what is meant by 'other lawful possession or custody'. It appears to apply where stolen goods have been reduced into the possession of individuals such as police officers. Whether goods are reduced into an individual's possession is dependent upon a mental resolve on the part of that person to obtain possession of such goods in addition to the physical act which brings about that state of affairs (see *Attorney-General's Reference (No 1 of 1974)* [1974] QB 744).)

(b) If the person from whom they have been stolen and any other person claiming through him have otherwise ceased, as regards those goods, to have any right of restitution in respect of the theft (see s. 24(3)). This means, e.g., where an individual has parted with goods under a voidable contract of sale which he has been induced to make because of a deception; if knowing of the deception he nevertheless affirms the contract he loses the right of restitution with regard to those goods. From that time the goods cease to be stolen and cannot form the subject-matter of a full offence of handling. The original owner must therefore still retain a proprietary right or interest in the goods concerned (see *R v Cording* [1983] Crim LR 175).

It is not only the original products of a theft, deception or blackmail which are stolen goods for the purposes of s. 22(1) but also any direct or indirect proceeds of dealings with those goods.

By s. 24(2) of the Theft Act 1968, stolen goods include not only the original stolen goods or parts of them (whether or not in their original state) but also (s. 24(2)(a)):

[A]ny other goods which directly or indirectly represent or have at any time represented the stolen goods in the hands of the thief as being the proceeds of any disposal or realisation of the whole or part of the goods stolen or of goods so representing the stolen goods.

There is a similar provision which covers stolen goods or their proceeds which are in the possession of a handler, see s. 24(2)(b).

The consequences of s. 24(2)(a) and (b) are that stolen goods or any part thereof (in whatever form) in the hands of the thief or any handlers remain stolen goods. Any goods or cash given to a thief or a handler by an individual in exchange for those stolen goods or any part thereof also become stolen goods. This means that for the purpose of s. 22(1) such goods are capable of being the subject-matter of a separate offence of handling. Such goods are deemed stolen for the purposes of s. 22(1) because they directly represent in whole or in part the original stolen goods — they are the proceeds of their realisation or disposal. Such goods or cash which have been exchanged for the original stolen goods may themselves be further exchanged for cash and/or goods, and these latter goods also become stolen goods within the terms of s. 22(1) with all the attendant consequences. This is because they indirectly represent the original stolen goods and are in whole or in part the proceeds of the realisation or disposal of the original stolen goods. For s. 24(2)(a) and (b) to apply to goods or cash which are so exchanged for stolen goods or their proceeds the individual effecting the exchange with a thief or handler must himself be a handler, i.e., he must be aware he is receiving stolen goods, or their direct or indirect proceeds, either in whole or in part. Where an individual receives any goods which are stolen or are deemed stolen by virtue of either s. 24(2)(a) or (b) without knowing or believing them to be the direct or indirect proceeds of actual stolen goods they remain stolen goods. If, however, still unaware of their tainted nature he sells or exchanges them for further goods such cash or articles received would not be deemed stolen within

Offences Against Property

the terms of s. 24(2)(b) (which applies to handlers). This is because, lacking *mens rea* (see below), he is not a handler within s. 22(1). The goods or cash he has received do not directly or indirectly represent the proceeds (either in whole or in part) of the realisation or disposal of the original stolen goods.

8.14.9 Mens rea

A handler, no matter what form of activity he undertakes within s. 22(1), must have *mens rea* with regard to his conduct. This comprises two principal elements, apart from his intention to undertake the handling. An individual must:

(a) *Act dishonestly.* This would appear to have the same meaning as the common law formulation of dishonesty in theft and reference is made to para. 8.9 and the cases cited there.

(b) *Know or believe the goods to be stolen.* An individual must know or believe the goods he is handling are stolen. Knowedge is not to be assessed on an objective basis, i.e., whether a reasonable man would or should have appreciated that goods were stolen, but on a subjective basis. It must be established that the accused himself knew the goods to be stolen, see *Atwal* v *Massey* [1971] 3 All ER 881. It is the second and alternative mental state that has caused consternation amongst the judiciary.

Belief It is better that a judge should not direct a jury as to the meaning of 'belief', and to leave that tribunal with the task of discerning its nature. This practice has received judicial approval in the case of *R* v *Reader* (1977) 66 Cr App R 33. If a judge chooses to define the term to a jury he must not equate it with either 'wilful blindness', i.e., shutting one's eyes to the fact of the obvious or the suspicious (see *R* v *Griffiths* (1974) 60 Cr App R 14 and *R* v *Moys* [1984] Crim LR 495) or to the fact that an individual believes or suspects that goods are probably stolen (see *R* v *Reader*). Neither is it sufficient to equate belief with mere suspicion as to whether goods are stolen, see *R* v *Ismail* [1977] Crim LR 557 and *R* v *Grainge* [1984] Crim LR 493. Belief seems only to be satisfied by 'a positive belief that the goods are stolen', see *R* v *Reader*. This appears to equate belief with knowledge. It would seem therefore that the use of the term 'or believing them to be stolen' within s. 22(1) is redundant. In the case of *R* v *Hall The Times*, 14 March 1985 the Court of Appeal laid down a formulation as to what constitutes knowing or believing for the purposes of the offence of handling. The Court considered knowing required first hand knowledge. Believing was constituted even in cases where 'The belief was something short of knowledge. It might be said to be the state of mind of a person who said to himself "I cannot say I know for certain that those goods are stolen, but there can be no other reasonable conclusion in the light of all the circumstances I have heard and seen".'

The Court affirmed that mere suspicion was insufficient. This decision would appear to add nothing to the requirement of positive belief laid down in *R* v *Reader*. However, the test does appear to have tones of objectivity from which a jury may make an evidential inference as to an accused's state of mind. This conforms to a general judicial trend (see *R* v *Moloney* [1985] 2 WLR 648 and *R* v *Ghosh* [1982] QB 1053.

Though objectivity has no place as a matter of law in the establishing of either knowledge or belief that goods are stolen, as a matter of practical reality and fact, where it would be obvious to a reasonable man that goods are stolen it may be an irresistible inference for a jury to make that an individual knew or believed goods he was handling were stolen. Furthermore the fact of suspicion, wilful blindness and probability may also lead to that inference (see *R* v *Moys* [1984] Crim LR 494).

As in all crimes the *actus reus* and *mens rea* must coincide. A person may initially receive stolen goods innocently. If later he discovers their nature and dishonestly undertakes or assists in any form of handling (other than receiving or arranging to do so) he may then commit the offence of handling. This is easier to establish in cases such as retaining stolen goods as this is usually a continuing offence, and the prescribed *mens rea* need exist only during part of the continuance of the *actus reus*.

8.14.10 Theft Act 1968, s. 27(3)

Where an accused is charged with handling stolen goods and evidence has been adduced at his trial of this fact, s. 27(3) permits the establishing of the accused's *knowledge or belief* of the fact the goods were stolen by reference to his previous conduct. The prosecution to establish such knowledge or belief may adduce:

(a) evidence that in the last 12 months the accused had in his possession or undertook or assisted in handling stolen goods or

(b) (on giving written notice to the accused) evidence of the accused's convictions within the last five years of offences of theft or handling.

This does not preclude the prosecution, however, from establishing the accused's dishonesty in the instant case.

At common law it is permissible to draw an inference that an individual is handling stolen goods, e.g., by assisting in their disposal, and has the prescribed *mens rea* by the fact that he has been found in recent possession of stolen goods (see *R* v *Ball* [1983] 1 WLR 80).

Appendix

This brief concluding chapter has three objects. First it will reiterate the influences alluded to in the Introduction which affect the alteration and application of criminal law in the courts.

Secondly it will sum up the scenario and reiterate that the principles contained in chapters 1-6 can be applied to provide an understanding of the nature and scope of any offence not dealt with in this book of which the reader subsequently becomes aware.

Thirdly it will pose several general questions pertaining to events that occurred in the scenario set out at the beginning of chapters 1, 3 and 4.

UNDERLYING INFLUENCES

Students of the English or common law system will know that the system is adversarial not inquisitorial and generally it does not permit the judiciary to consider and rule on points (or give interpretations of the meanings of statutes) which are not in issue on the facts of the case brought before the court (in civil law by a party and in criminal law generally by or on behalf of the State) or arising on an appeal. The courts cannot take the initiative and clarify criminal law principles *ad hoc*. They must wait until the obscure or difficult points come before them. Even then the court's ruling will be authoritative only on the particular point in issue. As a consequence frequently the courts consider an issue relating to criminal liability in one case without reference to the effect such a decision may have on other parts of the criminal law because that effect is not in issue. The recent developments with regard to the defence of mistaken belief (see chapter 6) provide a good example. On the one hand a court has determined that an accused commits no offence if, under a mistaken belief that he is acting in self-defence, he uses force or acts of violence, and it has recently become the law that his mistaken belief need be only honestly held and not based in addition upon reasonable grounds. On the other hand, however, it remains the law that the actual use of force in real cases of self-defence needs to be reasonable in the circumstances of the case. Such an anomaly with regard to the presence or absence of the element of reasonableness within two closely related areas of law is not a deliberate creation of the judiciary. It is rather the result of the accident of circumstance which raised the issue of mistaken belief without reference to other areas of the criminal law. For example, the new reformulation of the principle of mistaken belief, may possibly be in conflict with other criminal law rules as shown above because they may still require the element of reasonableness. Because the judiciary cannot consider and rule on points which are not in issue on the facts of the case before the court such areas of potential conflict between rules and principles of criminal law may only be resolved where an individual case raises such issues simultaneously or where the point in conflict is raised specifically in a subsequent case or on appeal. Considerable time may pass before any of these events occur. Meanwhile academics may be critical and pressure may grow amongst the public for Parliament to change or clarify the law by legislation.

The courts, however, sometimes voluntarily undertake the creation of principles of criminal law which produce complex rules and uncertainty in their attempts to expand or contract existing criminal liability. For example, in chapters 2 and 7 it is shown that once the belief was that where an accused intended his conduct to produce certain consequences (such as the death or serious injury of another) or he foresaw as a matter of high probability the occurrence of those consequences he could, if his conduct caused the death of another, be convicted of murder. As shown in chapters 2 and 7 it has now been determined that foresight of consequences is neither an alternative nor an equivalent of intention. Murder and certain other offences (known as offences of specific or ulterior intent, see chapter 2) now can only be committed where an accused intends to bring about the consequences of an offence. Nevertheless, the judiciary tell us that foresight of such consequences may still lead to an irresistible inference that those very consequences were in fact intended by an accused. A jury *may*, therefore, come to the conclusion as a matter of evidence or fact that if an accused foresaw certain consequences resulting from his actions, he intended to bring them about but a jury is no longer *compelled* because of a rule of law to come to that conclusion.

Sometimes the judiciary create or change law which remains part of the realm of common law (i.e., those areas of our law not legislated but traditionally derived from court decisions) by an express pronouncement or reformulation of a rule of substantive law. A good example is shown in chapter 5 in the cases concerning conspiracy to corrupt public morals and conspiracy to outrage public decency. Although academics may debate the point it would appear that the judiciary in those instances clearly created new criminal offences. Sometimes, however, the judiciary alter the law by more arcane methods. In the example noted above relating to murder and specific intent offences the courts had classified an element of the offence as a rule of substantive law which permitted but one conclusion (see *Hyam's* case in relation to murder) and later reclassified that element as a matter of adjectival law, in other words as a matter of evidence or fact which is a matter for a jury to determine from its own conclusions (see *Moloney's* case in chapters 2 and 7). Whether or not this particular change will have any practical effect upon the law or is of interest to academics only is at present uncertain. Nevertheless such a development illustrates the subtle ways in which the judiciary may work a reformulation of the criminal law. It should become clear from a reading of chapters 2 and 7 that if the judiciary expand or contract the definition of intention (by saying that foresight is or is not included) or the definition of recklessness (by saying that failure to consider a risk either is or is not included), or if they impose an objective test as opposed to a subjective test for *mens rea* (see the discussion of recklessness), they are contracting or expanding the net within which persons may be made liable for particular offences. Likewise if the judiciary declare an offence to be one of strict liability as opposed to one requiring proof of *mens rea* (see chapter 3) they are widening the net and increasing the possibility of persons being found guilty of that particular offence. The reasons why the judges seek to change our criminal law in such a covert way are partly social and partly political. Today the constitutional position of the judiciary is such that they must avoid being seen overtly to create new offences or to widen the ambit of existing criminal liability. This function is now, in theory at least, the responsibility of Parliament but in reality what should be clear is that the judges always have played a part either directly in developing the common law or by the process of interpreting the will of Parliament in pronouncing on the meaning of statutes. What affects the judges' views, amongst other things, may well be what they perceive, rightly or wrongly, to be socially desirable or what they consider a danger to society, its culture, its ethos, its Judaeo-Christian morals and its liberal-democratic tradition. There is no doubt that the judges play a very significant role in our society. Two things should be evident, first that at various stages in the criminal process (prosecution, adjudication and sentence) there are few guidelines or rules and much discretion left in the first instance to the prosecutors and in the latter instances to the judiciary. Their beliefs and attitudes about criminals and crime, about public policy (which is a guise for public opinion or more often public acceptability) become very important. If their views are too idiosyncratic or flexible they may not attain proportionality by way of punishment and equality of treatment or justice between offenders and may create uncertainty in society because there would be no predictability. On the other hand if their views are too stereotyped or ultra-conservative or radical they may detract from the second constitutional function of the judge which is to protect our traditional freedom and liberties.

Apart from learning the current rules of substantive criminal law and the principles that underlie these rules, a student must be aware of the factors and policies which mould the criminal law causing the creation of and constant reshaping of criminal offences. An appreciation of the nature of and reasons for the criminal law being as it is, together with the judicially contrived mechanisms for its reformulation should provide a better understanding of the subject as a whole. A realisation of the influences and policies behind the judicial or parliamentary mind, which in a constantly changing society are themselves necessarily unstable, gives an understanding of the impetus for change in the criminal law and an explanation of its fluidity. The motivation of individuals and pressure groups (including the prosecutors, the magistracy and the judiciary) seeking to change or to prevent change in the law can range from vested interest to genuine belief (sometimes valid) that it is in the best interests of society as a whole, essential for the protection of individuals or a class, or unwarrantedly detrimental to freedom. This book sets out the general rules of criminal law and the principles to be applied in the analysis of any offence not specifically dealt with in its chapters but it is also concerned to make students aware of the complex issues underlying those rules.

THE SCENARIO

The scenario, though exaggerated in its detail, was constructed to show the practical application of the legal principles raised in the chapters to a set of factual situations. By now the reader will know that one or other of the characters in the scenario has committed one or more of the substantive offences or related inchoate offences or been a party to one of the following offences: theft, being drunk in charge of a motor vehicle, failing to display a road tax disc, possession of proscribed drugs, assault, rape, criminal damage, possible burglary, aggravated assault, possible murder or at least manslaughter, firearms offences, and handling by receiving and assisting in the retention of stolen goods. For some of the characters in the scenario defences are mentioned or are evident, especially intoxication, duress and provocation.

In everyday life the reader will witness, hear about or possibly be the victim of offences which are not dealt with specifically in the scenario or the chapters of this book. This is not surprising since a book of this size cannot deal with every serious offence let alone the literally thousands of statutory offences that exist today. Serious offences not dealt with include kidnapping and taking of a child under 16, administering poison, incest, possessing firearms and offensive weapons, offences relating to prostitution, indecent exposure, robbery, blackmail, abstracting electricity, possessing articles for housebreaking, forgery, counterfeiting, arson, bigamy, publishing obscene material, blasphemy, perjury, contempt, refusal to aid a police constable, impeding the apprehension or prosecution of arrestable offenders, making false declarations, false imprisonment, public order offences such as unlawful assembly, riot, affray, incitement to racial hatred, breach of the peace, public nuisance, obstruction of the highway, entering with violence and adverse occupation of premises, criminal eviction and harassment, piracy and hijacking, treason, sedition, spying, wrongful communication of information, belonging to a proscribed (terrorist) organisation and criminal libel. In addition there are of course the vast number of more minor, regulatory, health and safety, hygiene, fiscal and transport offences contained in numerous statutes. Whatever the offence an application of the principles contained in chapters 1-3 will provide an understanding of its nature and scope, of what must be proved for a conviction and the likelihood of liability; while a knowledge of chapters 4 and 5 will indicate possible wider ramifications and chapter 6 the possible defences available.

QUESTIONS RELATING TO THE SCENARIO

1. What offences have each of the characters (including Donald — assuming he lived to be prosecuted) individually committed in the scenario? Which of these offences are offences of basic intent? Which are specific or ulterior intent offences? Which are strict liability or absolute offences?

2. What, if any, defences do you consider to be available to each of the characters in the scenario for each of the offences which each has appeared to have committed?

3. Is the fact that Bruce is aware of his friends' criminal conduct on prior occasions of any significance with regard to:

Appendix

   (a)   Donald's rape of Sarah?
   (b)   Edward and John's theft of jewellery, etc?
   (c)   Edward and John's criminal damage of the window and the burning down of Rex's house?

4.   Does the fact of possible duress in relation to Bruce give any indication of his *mens rea*?

5.   If Bruce was aware of Donald's plan to have intercourse with Sarah irrespective of consent would this make him a party to the rape? If so, could Bruce avoid liability before the commission of the offence:

   (a)   By getting drunk?
   (b)   By telling Donald on the doorstep of Rex's house that he no longer wished to aid or connive at this conduct?
   (c)   By telephoning the police in a drunken state of remorse while Donald was in the act of raping Sarah?

6.   What if Bruce knew nothing of Donald's intention to rape Sarah but Bruce enters a room while Donald is raping Sarah, would Bruce be liable for any offence if he simply stood by and watched?

7.   Would the fact that Alf is a close friend of the family and godfather of Sarah provide him with any defence if having heard Sarah's screams and observed her rape it was he who killed, or was a party to, the killing of Donald?

8.   In the scenario at the beginning of chapter 3, Bruce is evasive when questioned by the police in relation to the roadworthiness of his vehicle, the excise licence for it and the drugs in the glove compartment. Does Bruce's conduct amount to wilful obstruction of a constable?

9.   What offence could Edward and John commit with regard to the taxi ride in the scenario at the beginning of chapter 4 if:

   (a)   They enter the taxi without intending to pay?
   (b)   They resolve not to pay while in the taxi?
   (c)   They resolve not to pay at the moment they should tender the fare?
   (d)   When they arrive at their destination they divert the taxi-driver's attention and run off while he is looking the other way?
   (e)   They assault Ron, the taxi-driver, with the idea of avoiding payment?

10.   Would John's liability with regard to the slashing of Ron's cheek be different if:

   (a)   He was unaware that Edward had a knife?
   (b)   He was aware, or had reason to suspect, that Edward had a knife but did not believe it would ever be used?

(c) He knew of the presence of the knife and suspected Edward might use it only to threaten as he had on a past occasion?

11. If Ron was an expert in martial arts and he fractured Edward's arm in order to prevent Edward's escape without paying the fare, would that constitute reasonable force in the prevention of an offence within s. 3(1) of the Criminal Law Act 1967?

At what point, if any, in the scenario would Ron's breaking of Edward's arm no longer constitute reasonable force at common law or within s. 3(1) of the Criminal Law Act 1967?

12. In the scenario to chapter 1 would Marian's omission to summon medical assistance for the badly injured Donald fix her with criminal liability for his eventual death?

Can the principle of *R* v *Miller* [1983] 2 AC 161 (see chapter 1) ever apply to secondary parties?

Index

Abandoning possession 238-9, 250
Abetting 102-3
   vicarious liability and 123
Absence in *actus reus* 24-5
Absolute prohibition offences *see* Strict liability offences
Accessories
   after the fact 118
   before the fact 117-18
Actus reus 11-32
   absence 24-5
   burglary 256
   causation 26-7
   circumstances 22-3, 24, 25
   coincidence of *mens rea* and 60-3
   commission by principal offender 110-12
   consequences 26
   conspiracy 149-50, 153-5
   deception 258-9
   duty to act 16-20
   handling 266-7
   incitement 155
   individual action in 26
   omissions 15-16
   positive acts 14-15
   proof of 66
   rape 208-11
   state of affairs 20-2
   statutory assault 202-5
   theft 245-8
   unlawful homicide 216-18
Agent, liability of 123
Aggravated burglary 257
Aiding 100-2
Appeals 7
Appropriation 15, 22, 70, 245-8
Arrestable offences 6
Arson 19, 52
Assault and battery 191-5
   common law 191-3
   problematic aspects 193-4
   special defences 194-5
Assisting offenders 116
Attempts
   circumstances and 141-2

Attempts—*continued*
   common law 134-7
   impossible 142-7
   law of 133-4
   mens rea of 137-40
   negligent 141
   reckless 140
   uncompleted crimes 132-3
   vicarious liability 123
Automatism 14
   insane 159-64
   non-insane 164-5
   self-induced 46, 165-8, 188
Avenue of escape 184, 187

Bailment 238, 239
Basic intent 38-41, 45
   offences 166-8
   recklessness 51-2
Battery *see* Assault and battery
Belief 273-4
Beyond reasonable doubt 66
Blasphemous libel 73-4
Borrowing 248, 249-50
Boxing 196, 197
Buildings in burglary 252-5
Burden of proof 64-6
Burglary 39, 127, 252-7
   aggravated 257
   buildings in 252-3
   entry 252-5
   intent 255
   mens rea 255
   Theft Acts 252, 255-7
   trespass 253-4

Caldwell recklessness 52, 108, 142, 175, 192, 212, 227
   avoiding 57
   limiting 58
   scope of 58-9
Cannabis cultivation 90
Causation 26-9, 46, 48
Chastisement *see* Reasonable chastisement
Cheque cards deception 259, 260, 264
Child destruction 230

Index

Children
 conspiracy with 153–4
 defences 172–4
 prosecution of 7–8
Circumstance 23, 24
 actus reus 22–3
 attempts and 141–2
 mens rea as to 59–60, 107–10
Civil liberties 149
Civil rights 82
Coercion defence 185
Common law
 attempt at 134–7, 144–5
 conspiracy 149–50
 defences 180–2
 exceptions to *Majewski* 168–9
 strict liability offences 73–4
 vicarious liability at 120
Company liability 118–20, 154
Complicity *see* Secondary participation
Conditional intent 251–2, 255
Conduct
 crimes 22
 deception by 258–9
 duty to act arising from 18–20
Conscious risk-taking 49, 50, 192, 212, 227
 see also Recklessness
Consent
 sexual 210
 to contact 195–8
Consequences
 in *actus reus* 26
 mens rea as to 106–7
Conspiracy 147–55
 actus reus 149–50, 153–5
 common law definition 149–50
 mens rea 151–3
 rationale of 147–9
 to defraud 150
 to do impossible 155
Constructive malice 219
Constructive manslaughter 227–9
Constructive murder 218
Constructive trust 237
Contempt of court 73
Contract 16–17
Control of property 239
Corporal punishment *see* Reasonable chastisement
Corporate liability 154
 identification doctrine 119–20
 rationale of 118
 statutory construction 118–19
Counselling 103
Credit cards deception 259
Criminal acts, definition 3–5
Criminal damage 30–1, 70
Criminal libel 73, 120
Culpability 51

Decency conspiracies 150–1
Deception 257–66
 actus reus 258–9
 by conduct 258–9
 by omission 259–60
 obtaining property by 261–3
 of fact, law and intention 260
Defect of reason 160–1, 169
Defences 25, 46, 159–89
 alcohol and drugs 165–72
 assault and battery 194–5
 coercion 185
 insanity 65, 66, 159–64
 involuntary conduct 164
 justification 25, 176–7, 187
 lawful application of force 178–82
 legal impossibility 145–7
 mistaken 174–8, 187
 mitigation 91–4
 necessity 186–7
 no negligence 92
 non-insane automatism 164–5
 of others 182
 of property 182
 provocation 112, 222–4
 public policy 182–5
 self-defence 23, 178–9, 182
 superior orders 186
 vicarious liability 123
Defraud, conspiracy to 150
Delegation 122–3
Demonstrations 149
Diminished responsibility 161, 162, 163, 224–6
Direct intention 41, 45, 49
'Directing mind' 119–20
Disease of the mind 160–1
Dishonesty other than theft 257–74
Disposal of stolen property 267–70
Double jeopardy 8
Drugs
 non-dangerous 169
 unlawful possession 85–8
Duress defence 182–4, 185, 187
Dutch courage 171–2
Duty to act
 by conduct 18–20
 by contract 16–17
 by office 18
 by relationship 17–18
 by statute 16

Eggshell skull principle 229
Employee liability 123
Entry in burglary 252, 253–5
Equitable interest in property 237
Equivocality test 136
European Convention on Human Rights 199

Index

European Court of Human Rights 199
Evidence 8-9
Evidential burden 94, 131
   insanity defence 65, 66
   non-insane automatism 164-5
Excessive force 181
Extensive construction 121-2
External element of offence *see Actus reus*
Extradition 8

Factual element of offence *see Actus reus*
Felony 5
   participants in 117-18
Foresight
   and intention in murder 45-8
   and recklessness in murder 49-50
   of consequences 43, 46-7, 49-50
   of high probability 42-3, 45
   test of 221
Fraud 244
   as to identity 195-6
   as to nature of act 195
   conspiracy to defraud 150

General arrest powers 6
Grave social danger 82-90
Grievous bodily harm 203
Gross negligence
   manslaughter by 34, 37, 38, 58
   recklessness and 54-5
Guilty but insane 162

Handling
   actus reus 266-7
   by omission 270-3
   circumstances of offence 271
   mens rea 273-4
   procedure 270-1
   rationale 266
   receiving 267-70
Harmful consequences 52, 53, 54
Heat of the moment 224
Homicide 215-30
   actus reus of unlawful 216-18
   manslaughter 222-9
   murder 218-22

Identification doctrine 119-20
Immunity from prosecution 7
Impersonation 195
Impossibility
   attempts *see* Impossible attempts
   conspiracy to do 155
   inciting the 156-7
   legal 145-7
   test 137
Impossible attempts 142-7
   at common law 144-5
   legal impossibility 145-7

Inactive party 104-6
Inchoate offences 125-58
   acts of preparation 129-32
   attempts 132-47
   conspiracy 147-55
   inchoate 157-8
   incitement 155-7
   participation and 158
   penalty for 158
   secondary participation 116-17
Incitement 155-7
   actus reus of 155
   inciting the impossible 156-7
   mens rea of 156
Indecent assault 205-8
Indictable offences 6-7
Inevitable accident 195
Infanticide 230
Innocent agent 98-100
Insane automatism defence 159-64
Insanity defence 159-64
   burden of proof 65, 66
   evidence and procedure 162
   pretrial 163
   verdict of insanity 162-3
   voluntary intoxication and 169
Intention 38-48
   burglary with 235
   murder 42-5
   murder, foresight and 45-8
Intention permanently to deprive 249-52
   conditional intent 251-2
Internal element of offence *see Mens rea*
Intoxication
   involuntary 172, 188
   voluntary 46, 165-72, 187
Involuntary conduct defence 164
Involuntary intoxication 172, 188
Involuntary manslaughter 227
Irresistable impulse 161, 164
Issue estoppel 8

Judicial process 2
Jurisdiction 8
Justification defence 25, 176-7, 187

Killing
   by gross negligence 227
   recklessly 227
'Knowingly' 74-6

LSD 85
Land, theft of 232-4
Lawful application of force 178-82
   excessive force 181
   reasonable force 179-81
   self-defence and prevention of crime 178-9

Lawrence's case 52-3
Legal impossibility 145-7
Liability *see* Corporate *and* Vicarious liability
Libel
 blasphemous 73-4
 criminal 73, 120
Lien on property 237, 239
Limitation period 7
Locus paenitentiae 136-7

Mujewski rule 167, 168-9, 170, 171
Malice
 aforethought 47, 218, 220
 constructive 219
 transferred 63-4, 229
'Maliciously' 192, 201
Manslaughter
 constructive 227-9
 diminished responsibility 224-6
 gross negligence 34, 58
 involuntary 227
 killing recklessly 227
 mens rea 45-6, 58
 provocation 222-4
 recklessness 54
 suicide pact 226
 unlawful act 227-9
 voluntary 222
Mens rea 13, 14, 33-70
 attempt 137-40
 basic and specific intent 38-41
 burglary 255, 256
 circumstances 59-60, 107-10
 coincidence of *actus reus* and 60-3
 consequences 106-7
 conspiracy 151-3
 deception 262
 dishonesty 258
 evil mind 34-5
 handling 273-4
 imported 74-7
 incitement 156
 mistake and negating 174-5
 negligence 36-8
 proof 64-8
 rape 211-12
 recklessness 48-59
 secondary party 106-10
 states of mind 35-6
 statutory assaults 201-2
 theft 248-9
 transferred malice 63-4
Mental defect and recklessness 56-7
Mental element of offence *see Mens rea*
Mentally disordered person 154
Minors *see* Children
'Mischievous disposition' 153
Misdemeanour 5

Mistaken defence 187
 justification 176-7
 negating *mens rea* 174-5
 reasonable force 181
 reasonableness 175
 statutory 178
Mistaken transfer of property 242-4, 264
Mitigation 91-4
Morality, enforcement of 4
 see also Public morals conspiracy
Motive 47
 see also Intention
Murder 14, 15, 23, 26, 29-30, 218-22
 foresight and intention 45-8
 foresight and recklessness 49-50
 intention in 42-5
 mens rea 45, 46, 47, 62, 69

Necessity defence 186-7
Negligence 36-8
 defence in crimes of 165-6
 mistaken defence 175
 negligent attempts 141
'No negligence' defence 92
Non-arrestable offences 6
Non-dangerous drugs 169
Non-insane automatism 164-5
Non-interference to prevent crime 105
Non-sexual, non-fatal offences
 assault and battery 191-5
 consent to contact 195-8
 inevitable accident 195
 reasonable chastisement 198-9
 statutory assaults 199-205
Not guilty by reason of insanity 162

Oblique intention 42, 43, 45, 49, 139
Obstructing a police officer 76-7
Obtaining property by deception 261-3
Offences against property 231-74
 burglary 252-7
 deception 257-66
 handling 266-74
 theft 231-52
Offences against the person 190-227
 homicide 215-30
 non-sexual, non-fatal 191-9
 sexual/indecent assaults 205-15
 rape 208-15
 statutory assaults 199-205
Officials, duty to act 18
Omission 19
 actus reus 15-16
 deception by 259
 handling by 270

Participation in criminal offences 97-124
 actus reus, principal offender 110-12
 assisting offenders 116

Index

Participation in criminal offence—*continued*
  corporate liability 118-20
  felony 117-18
  inactive presence 104-6
  inchoate offences and 158
  liability for unforeseen circumstances 114
  mens rea, secondary party 106-10
  principal participation 97-8
    innocent agent and 98-100
    repentance 115
  secondary participation 100-4
    convicted on different offence 112-14
  vicarious liability 120-4
  victims as secondary parties 115-16
Pecuniary advantage 261
Permission to enter 253-4
Picketing 149
Positive acts in *actus reus* 14-15
Possession 237-8
  controlled drugs 85-8
  firearms 84
Preliminary offences *see* Inchoate offences
Preparation, acts of 129-32
Prevention of crime defence 178-9
Principal participation 97-8
  actus reus 110-12
  innocent agent and 98-100
  liability for unforeseen 114
Proceeds of property 242
Procuring 103-4
Proof 64-8
  burden of 64-6
  of *actus reus* 66
  of incitement 155
  of *mens rea* 66-8
  standard or level of 66
Property 231-4
  proprietary rights 236-7, 240-2
  that may be stolen 236-40
  transferred under mistake 242-4, 264
Proprietary rights or interests 236-7
Prosecution, limits on 7-8
Provocation defence 112, 222-4
Proximity test 135-6
Public morals conspiracy 150-1
Public nuisance 73, 81-2, 120
Public policy defence 28-9, 44, 166
  availability 184-5
  duress 182-4
  evidence 185

Quasi criminal offences 78-81, 89

Rape 14, 15, 22, 23, 29
  actus reus 208-11
  mens rea 68-9, 211-12
  of wife 214
  procedure and evidence 214-15
  reckless 57, 58, 212-14

Realisation of stolen property 267-70
Reasonable chastisement 196, 198-9
Reasonable force defence 179-81
  evidence of 181
Reasonable man test 223
Reasonableness in mistaken defence 175
Receiving 267-70
Reckless attempts 140
Reckless driving 52-3, 98, 230
Reckless killing *see* Killing recklessly
Recklessness 48-59
  Caldwell's 52, 57-9, 108, 142, 175, 192, 212, 227
  conscious risk-taking 49, 50, 192, 212, 227
  gross negligence and 54-5
  Lawrence's case 52-3
  mental defect and 56-7
  murder, foresight and 39-50
  new definitions 50-2, 54
  social utility and 55-6
  see also Foresight of consequences
Reduction into possession 235-6
Regulatory offences 78-81
Relationship duty to act 17-18
Removal of stolen property 267-70
Repentance 115, 136
Restitution 243-4
Result crime 22, 26
Retention of stolen goods 267-70
  assisting 269-70
Risk of harmful consequences 52, 53, 54
  see also Recklessness
'Robin Hood' syndrome 249

Secondary participation
  abetting 102-3
  aiding 100-2
  counselling 103
  inchoate offences and 116-17
  procuring 103-4
  strict liability offences 110
Secondary parties
  conviction on different offence 112-14
  inactive presence of 104-6
  liability for unforeseen 114
  mens rea of 106-10
  victims as 115-16
Self defence 23, 178-9, 182
Self-induced automatism 46, 165-8, 188
  basic intent offences 166-8
  crimes of negligence 165-6
  statutory offences 168
Sexual/indecent assaults 205-15
  by children 173
  indecent assaults 207-8
  rape 208-15
Single-transaction argument 62

Social danger
  grave 82–90
  test 137
Social utility 55–6
Sources of criminal law 3
Specific intention 38–41, 45, 46, 139
  alcohol, drugs and 170–1
Sport 196–7
Standard or level of proof 66
State of affairs in *actus reus* 20–2
State of mind 34–6
Statutory amendment 9–10
Statutory assaults 199–205
  actus reus of 202–5
  mens rea of 201–2
Stolen goods, definition 271–3
Strict liability
  justification for 94–5
  presumption against imposition of 88–90
Strict liability offences 71–96
  at common law 73–4
  enforcement of 90–1
  grave social danger 82–8
  mitigation of 91–4
  nature of 71–3
  public nuisance 81–2
  quasi criminal or regulatory 78–81
  secondary participation 110
  statutory offences 74–8
Suicide pact 226
Summary offences 6–7
Superior orders defence 186

Temporary impairment of mental faculties 169
Theft 14, 15, 22, 30, 40, 231–52
  Acts 232–4, 240–4
  mens rea 69–70, 248
  obtaining by deception and 262–3

Theft—*continued*
  property 231–4, 136–40
  wild animals 235–6
  wild foliage 234–5
Transferred malice 63–4, 229
Trespass 253–4, 255, 256
Trustee of property 236–7
'Type of offence' 109–10

Ulterior intention 39, 45, 170–1
Unauthorised action 114
Uncompleted crimes *see* Attempts
Unconscious dramatic piracy 82
Unforeseen consequences
  liability for 114
Unjustly enriched 243

Vicarious liability 120–4
  abetting or attempting offences 123
  common law 120
  defences 123
  delegation 122–3
  employee or agent 123
  statutory 121–2
Victims as secondary parties 115–16
Voluntary intoxication 46, 165–72, 187
  basic intent offences 166–8
  crimes of negligence 165–6
  insanity 169
  statutory offences 168
Voluntary manslaughter 222

Wild animals theft 235–6
Wild foliage theft 234–5
Wilful blindness 107
'Wilfully' 77
Wolfenden Committee Report 1957 5